Swept Up Lives?

RGS-IBG Book Series

Published

Domesticating Neo-Liberalism: Spaces of Economic Practice and Social Reproduction in Post-Socialist Cities
Alison Stenning, Adrian Smith, Alena Rochovská and Dariusz Świątek

Swept Up Lives? Re-envisioning the Homeless City
Paul Cloke, Jon May and Sarah Johnsen

Aerial Life: Spaces, Mobilities, Affects
Peter Adey

Millionaire Migrants: Trans-Pacific Life Lines
David Ley

State, Science and the Skies: Governmentalities of the British Atmosphere
Mark Whitehead

Complex Locations: Women's geographical work in the UK 1850–1970
Avril Maddrell

Value Chain Struggles: Institutions and Governance in the Plantation Districts of South India
Jeff Neilson and Bill Pritchard

Queer Visibilities: Space, Identity and Interaction in Cape Town
Andrew Tucker

Arsenic Pollution: A Global Synthesis
Peter Ravenscroft, Hugh Brammer and Keith Richards

Resistance, Space and Political Identities: The Making of Counter-Global Networks
David Featherstone

Mental Health and Social Space: Towards Inclusionary Geographies?
Hester Parr

Climate and Society in Colonial Mexico: A Study in Vulnerability
Georgina H. Endfield

Geochemical Sediments and Landscapes
Edited by David J. Nash and Sue J. McLaren

Driving Spaces: A Cultural-Historical Geography of England's M1 Motorway
Peter Merriman

Badlands of the Republic: Space, Politics and Urban Policy
Mustafa Dikeç

Geomorphology of Upland Peat: Erosion, Form and Landscape Change
Martin Evans and Jeff Warburton

Spaces of Colonialism: Delhi's Urban Governmentalities
Stephen Legg

People/States/Territories
Rhys Jones

Publics and the City
Kurt Iveson

After the Three Italies: Wealth, Inequality and Industrial Change
Mick Dunford and Lidia Greco

Putting Workfare in Place
Peter Sunley, Ron Martin and Corinne Nativel

Domicile and Diaspora
Alison Blunt

Geographies and Moralities
Edited by Roger Lee and David M. Smith

Military Geographies
Rachel Woodward

A New Deal for Transport?
Edited by Iain Docherty and Jon Shaw

Geographies of British Modernity
Edited by David Gilbert, David Matless and Brian Short

Lost Geographies of Power
John Allen

Globalizing South China
Carolyn L. Cartier

Geomorphological Processes and Landscape Change: Britain in the Last 1000 Years
Edited by David L. Higgitt and E. Mark Lee

Forthcoming

Globalizing Responsibility: The Political Rationalities of Ethical Consumption
Clive Barnett, Paul Cloke, Nick Clarke & Alice Malpass

Spatial Politics: Essays for Doreen Massey
Edited by David Featherstone and Joe Painter

The Improvised State: Sovereignty, Performance and Agency in Dayton Bosnia
Alex Jeffrey

In the Nature of Landscape: Cultural Geography on the Norfolk Broads
David Matless

Learning the City: Translocal Assemblages and Urban Politics
Colin McFarlane

Fashioning Globalization: New Zealand Design, Working Women and the 'New Economy'
Maureen Molloy and Wendy Larner

Swept Up Lives?

Re-envisioning the Homeless City

Paul Cloke, Jon May
and Sarah Johnsen

WILEY-BLACKWELL

A John Wiley & Sons, Ltd., Publication

Blackwell Publishing was acquired by John Wiley & Sons in February 2007. Blackwell's publishing program has been merged with Wiley's global Scientific, Technical, and Medical business to form Wiley-Blackwell.

Registered Office
John Wiley & Sons Ltd, The Atrium, Southern Gate, Chichester, West Sussex, PO19 8SQ, United Kingdom

Editorial Offices
350 Main Street, Malden, MA 02148-5020, USA
9600 Garsington Road, Oxford, OX4 2DQ, UK
The Atrium, Southern Gate, Chichester, West Sussex, PO19 8SQ, UK

For details of our global editorial offices, for customer services, and for information about how to apply for permission to reuse the copyright material in this book please see our website at www.wiley.com/wiley-blackwell.

The right of Paul Cloke, Jon May and Sarah Johnsen to be identified as the author of this work has been asserted in accordance with the UK Copyright, Designs and Patents Act 1988.

Library of Congress Cataloging-in-Publication Data

Cloke, Paul J.
  Swept up lives? : re-envisioning the homeless city / Paul Cloke, Jon May and Sarah Johnsen.
    p. cm. – (RGS-IBG book series)
  Includes bibliographical references and index.
    ISBN 978-1-4051-5386-7 (hbk. : alk. paper) – ISBN 978-1-4051-5387-4 (pbk. : alk. paper)
1. Homelessness. 2. Homeless persons–Social conditions. 3. Urban policy. I. May, Jon. II. Johnsen, Sarah. III. Title.
  HV4493.C56 2010
  362.5–dc22
                                          2009052086
A catalogue record for this book is available from the British Library.

Set in 10/12pt Plantin by SPi Publisher Services, Pondicherry, India

1   2010

Contents

Figures and Tables

Series Editors' Preface

The RGS-IBG Book Series only publishes work of the highest international standing. Its emphasis is on distinctive new developments in human and physical geography, although it is also open to contributions from cognate disciplines whose interests overlap with those of geographers. The Series places strong emphasis on theoretically informed and empirically strong texts. Reflecting the vibrant and diverse theoretical and empirical agendas that characterize the contemporary discipline, contributions are expected to inform, challenge and stimulate the reader. Overall, the RGS-IBG Book Series seeks to promote scholarly publications that leave an intellectual mark and change the way readers think about particular issues, methods or theories.

For details on how to submit a proposal please visit:
www.rgsbookseries.com

Kevin Ward
University of Manchester, UK

Joanna Bullard
Loughborough University, UK

RGS-IBG Book Series Editors

Acknowledgements

The research on which this book is based was funded by the Economic and Social Research Council (ESRC Award R000238996 Homeless Places: the uneven geographies of emergency provision for single homeless people). We are very grateful for the support.

Some of the material presented in this book has appeared elsewhere in different forms and we would like to thank the editors and referees of the following journals for their advice and guidance: *Antipode; Area; Environment and Planning A; Gender, Place and Culture; Geoforum; Health and Place; Journal of Rural Studies; Policy and Politics; Social and Cultural Geography; Society and Space*. Numerous friends and colleagues have also listened to various presentations, or read drafts, of the material used here. They are too numerous to mention all by name, but we would especially like to thank Chris Philo at the University of Glasgow, Mark Goodwin at the University of Exeter, Justin Beaumont at the University of Groningen and Miles Ogborn and Isabel Dyck at Queen Mary University of London. Due to Paul's back injury and subsequent surgery, it has taken much longer than we anticipated to get the final manuscript of this book to press and we would especially like to thank the Human Geography Editor of the RGS-IBG Book Series, Kevin Ward, for his patience and support.

On a more personal note, Paul would once again like to acknowledge the utterly wonderful and irreplaceable context of love and support provided by Viv, Liz and Will. Without you, all this would be empty and meaningless. He would also like to thank Mary and Jim, Helen and Mike, Rachel and Rob and Clare and Stu for their special friendship both in Bristol and in deepest Devon.

Jon would like to thank Chris and Lorna, whose unwavering support to both him and the family over the years means more than he can say; Di and Rog, whose example continues to inspire and who have themselves started to volunteer at a local day centre (good on you!); the New Zealand Whanau

(Pete and Louise, Joe, Neil and Nick) who were there for Jon and the family at such an important time in their lives and in the life of this book; and of course and most of all, Vicki, Max and Mo, whose life and love put all this kind of thing into perspective.

Sarah would like to extend thanks to her family and friends for their ongoing support (and willingness to forgive her for her lengthy, and neglectful, absences when doing fieldwork!), and to her colleagues at the Centre for Housing Policy for so generously sharing their expertise and encouragement.

Finally, none of this would have been possible without the hundreds of people (service users, managers, staff and volunteers) with whom we talked, shared photographs or just hung out, and who shared their experiences of homelessness and of homeless places with us. We hope that the following captures something at least of what you wanted to say.

Abbreviations

ASBO	Anti-Social Behaviour Order
B&B	Bed and Breakfast (hotel)
CLG	(Department of) Communities and Local Government
COS	Charity Organisation Society
DCLG	Department of Communities and Local Government
DETR	Department of Environment, Transport and Regions
DOE	Department of Environment
E&V	Entrenched and Vulnerable
FBO	Faith-Based Organization
HAP	Homelessness Action Programme
HMO	House in Multiple Occupation
LHS	Local Homelessness Strategy
LSCRCP	London Soup and Clothing Run Co-Ordination Project
NASS	National Asylum Support Service
ODPM	Office of the Deputy Prime Minister
RSI	Rough Sleepers Initiative
RSU	Rough Sleepers Unit

Chapter One

Introduction: Re-envisioning the Homeless City

Introduction

the 'extermination' scenario is never far from the surface of the homeless experience ... Constrained to exist in public spaces, the homeless are constant targets of regulation, criminalization, expulsion, and erasure.

(Randall Amster, *Patterns of Exclusion*, 2003: 214)

'Now, do you want your food? 'Cos it's cooked with love.' Because it's cooked with love, that's what she said. ... It's like – how can I put it ... it's genuine. Do you understand? ... They care ... I mean, they don't get paid, they volunteer to do it ... [and] they do cook their food with love.

(Andy, 38, homeless service user speaking
of the volunteers at St Barnabas Day Centre, Wimpster)

'Love' is not a word one comes across very often in writings on homelessness. In academic accounts at least, the talk is more usually of 'exclusion', 'banishment', 'annihilation' (Mitchell, 1997: 311) or 'extermination' (Amster, 2003: 214; Mitchell, 2003: 81). Indeed, thanks mainly to the writings of Mike Davis, Neil Smith, Don Mitchell and a handful of other scholars working mostly in a North American context (see, for example, Davis, 1990, 1999; Smith, 1992, 1996a, b, 1998, 2001; Sorkin, 1992; Matieu, 1993; Dangshat, 1997; Mitchell, 1997, 2001, 2003, 2005; Metraux, 1999; Arapoglau, 2004; Coleman, 2004; Herbert & Brown, 2006; Blomley & Klodawsky, 2007a, b, c), critical narratives of homelessness have become increasingly dystopic in recent years, inextricably tangled up in ideas about neoliberal politics and the geographies of social control. In a spectacular triumph of structure over agency, and of the general over the specific, it would appear that homeless people everywhere are being swept up and out of the prime spaces of the city, victims both of a seemingly insatiable appetite for high-value commodification of urban landscapes and imagery, and of a recidivist re-imagination of the norms of citizenship rights and welfare, criminality and social justice.

Such accounts are framed by a very particular reading of the geographies of homelessness – based around the streets – and a very particular logic, of social control. In this book we pose some significant questions about this characterization of the 'homeless city', seeking to extend our readings of both the geographies and politics of urban homelessness. To be clear, we do not deny that the past ten to fifteen years have seen the emergence of an increasingly punitive approach to the 'management' of urban homelessness. Evidence of such an approach – including new by-laws that restrict homeless people's access to prime, public space, business improvement districts, Controlled Drinking Zones, or Anti-Social Behaviour Orders (ASBOs) – is all around us, whether we look in Britain, Germany, Greece, the United States, Canada or New Zealand (Mitchell, 1998a, b; Collins & Blomley, 2003; Laurenson & Collins, 2007; Doherty et al., 2008; Johnsen & Fitzpatrick, 2010). But we do want to issue a caution lest this approach becomes the only frame through which discussions of urban homelessness can proceed. As a small number of academics are beginning to recognize (Johnsen et al., 2005a; Laurenson and Collins, 2006; DeVerteuil et al., 2009; Johnsen & Fitzpatrick, 2010) and people like Andy (quoted above) have long known, there are other spaces (of the soup kitchen, day centre or hostel) and other logics (of compassion and care) we must take account of when mapping the 'homeless city'.

Rather than the streets, the current book is therefore mostly focused upon these other spaces. But we identify such spaces as an example of wider currents in the contemporary city, currents that speak less of containment and control than of compassion and care and – more particularly – of a growing rapprochement between secular and religious approaches to urban politics and welfare (see also Beaumont, 2008; Beaumont & Dias, 2008; Wills et al., 2009a). In contrast to the assumed divide between public secularism and private religion, these broadly 'postsecular' service spaces – of the night shelter, hostel, day centre and soup run – represent spaces of praxis in which secular and faith motivation collude in new forms of ethical citizenship that run counter to, and sometimes actively resist, more familiar models of social control. In this way, we argue for a more complex understanding of the ways in which homelessness is governed, paving the way for a characterization of homelessness that pays more attention to the agency of homeless people themselves, to the complexity of homeless geographies, and to the construction and peopling of those spaces of homelessness in which homeless people experience a range of relationships that include compassion and care – even love – as well as regulation, containment and control.

In this chapter we set out the wider context of these arguments with a brief summary and critique of recent writings on urban homelessness framed by variations of the 'revanchism' thesis, before moving on, in chapter 2, to set out an alternative framework through which recent developments in the 'homeless city' can be explored. The chapter also introduces the project from which the material we make use of was drawn, and provides a brief overview of the structure of the book.

Homelessness and Revanchism

The framing of homelessness within an apparently 'punitive turn' in urban policy and politics (DeVerteuil et al., 2009) has been sparked by a series of attempts by scholars in North America to use homelessness as *the* exemplar of how urban policy from the late twentieth century onwards has willfully marginalized the visible poor. Drawing inspiration from economic and political geographies of global as well as urban change, attention has been directed to the increasingly bipolar nature of the contemporary city, within which islands of extreme wealth, power and influence are interspersed with places characterized by deprivation, exclusion and a lack of self-determination. These landscapes of power (Zukin 1991) are being exacerbated by the uneven distribution of benefits from globalization – with those able to benefit from the new technologies and mobilities of a globalizing age capitalizing on their enhanced power to overcome space to their own advantage; and those who are disempowered by the unevenness of globalized economies tending instead to become socially and spatially incarcerated (Graham & Marvin, 2001). Geopolitical reorganization is giving obvious spatial manifestation to this bipolar distribution of power. As Swyngedouw and Kaika (2003: 6) explain:

> The powerful … are now able to insulate themselves in hermetically sealed enclaves, where gated communities and sophisticated modes of surveillance are the order of the day … in the closely surveilled spaces of leisure and mass consumption malls and in their suburban housing estates. Concurrently, the rich and powerful can decant and steer the poor into clearly demarcated zones in the city, where implicit and explicit forms of social and bodily control keep them in place.

The picture here, then, is of a 'militarization' (Davis, 1990) of urban space in which the physical form and shape of the city reflects the uneven and polarizing power relations of the age – space is being reordered to suit the desires of the powerful, who are increasingly able to use politico-legal and cultural means to 'decant' the poor out of prime urban zones required for the furtherance of urban redevelopment.

This increasingly orthodox and sweeping picture of urban change does of course beg a number of important questions. Who are the powerful elites who are doing the 'steering', and the marginalized downtrodden who are being 'steered'? What spaces are being 'decanted' from and into, and does this spatiality differ from city to city? What powers are being used to give precise spatial expression to political bipolarity? To what extent are such processes the unthinking outcome of processes of 'progress', or the result of the malignant and malevolent purposefulness of actors, organizations and systems geared to achieve power and wealth whatever the cost? Where in this picture is the resistance to such processes, either from the marginalized themselves or from within wider society?

Some of these questions have been taken up in formative accounts of geographical bipolarization and – more specifically – the changing geographies of homelessness, in particular in US cities. Beginning in Los Angeles, for example, in *Cities of Quartz* (1990), Mike Davis painted a picture of 'Fortress LA', demonstrating how a fear of crime and disorder became mapped onto the otherness of marginalized people such as the homeless – a process aided and abetted by tightly controlled media representations of social and spatial geographies of fear in the city. As a result, the built environment of Los Angeles became represented as a 'carceral city', with a cartography of fortified residential enclaves and marginal no-go spaces, and heavily policed and culturally purified shopping malls and public spaces. According to Davis, homeless people in early 1990s Los Angeles were increasingly disciplined by policies of exclusion and containment, and he charts the measures used to expel and exclude homeless people from areas in and adjacent to Downtown – including more vigorous policing, and the deployment of defensive city architectures (such as sprinkler systems used to repel rough sleepers and panhandlers as well as to nourish vegetation). As a result, Los Angeles' homeless were apparently either increasingly hemmed into a shrinking skid row, or reduced to an existence of 'urban Bedouins' (Davis, 1990: 236) – wandering fugitives fleeing from official policing and culturally sadistic repression.

Not coincidentally, perhaps, the welfare services so vital to homeless and other poor people gained very little attention in these overarching narratives of urban bipolarization. Where they did appear, service-providers tended to be characterized either as the unwitting handmaidens of a punitive state, or as groups of people principally interested in 'moral selving' (Allahyari, 2000) – responding to charitable impulses that are self-serving and identity-building rather than constitutive of any progressive response to the plight of homeless people. Thus, groundbreaking studies of the service-dependent ghetto (Dear & Wolch, 1987, 1994; Rowe & Wolch, 1990), for example, many of them also conducted in Los Angeles, demonstrated the regulatory force by which the marginal spaces of the city (the 'stem', or 'skid row') were brought into being and became filled with homeless people, and how the location of these services tended in turn to shape the wider geographies of the homeless city itself (Wolch et al., 1993; see also Takahashi, 1996), as homeless people's day-to-day routines develop around the service nodes that provide a source of the material and, to a lesser extent, emotional sustenance and support necessary to make the adjustment from 'housed' to 'homeless' (Rowe & Wolch, 1990).

The more general picture provided by such studies, then, was of an era of 'malign neglect' (Wolch & Dear, 1993), an era in which homeless people came to be increasingly ghettoized into designated marginal spaces even as their mobility within and through prime city spaces became ever more restricted. Such narratives began to change somewhat with Smith's tour de force *The New Urban Frontier*, published in 1996. Based on his reading of developments in New York, Smith sought to connect up evidence of the increasingly punitive interventions taken against homeless people in New York City with gentrification – drawing the two together through the concept of the *revanchist* city. If the Los Angeles narrative was one of containment, Smith's emphasis on revanche (revenge) invoked a vengeful reassertion of power over, and overt criminalization of, marginalized groups in the city. Gentrification, he argued, increasingly requires a bold public defence of its progress based on a 'frontier' sensibility by which hostile neighbourhoods can be regenerated, cleansed and re-imagined according to middle-class values. Such a defence inherently involves a policy regime that both reclaims and defends prime city spaces from the devaluing presence of marginalized people, especially homeless people. Indeed, as MacLeod (2002) argues, gentrification requires the inculcation of 'acceptable' patterns of behaviour commensurate with the requirements of free-flowing commerce and the political and cultural aesthetics of new urban lifestyles, such that 'the new urban glamour zones conceal a brutalizing demarcation of winners and losers, included and excluded' (p. 604).

Smith's vision of a 'revanchist city' thus goes somewhat beyond the bipolar differentiation of wealth and poverty outlined above. Instead it insists that the winners are becoming increasingly vicious in the defence of their privilege:

> The benign neglect of the 'other half' … has been superseded by a more active viciousness that attempts to criminalise a whole range of 'behaviour', individually defined, and to blame the failure of post-1968 urban policy on the population it was supposed to assist. (Smith, 1996a: 227)

Smith's intervention has shaped much of the subsequent interest in urban homelessness. The practices and techniques of regulating homeless people he drew attention to have become objects of fascination, whether the (apparently) overpowering coalitions of local businesses, developers and city governments that have led the fight against homeless people (rather than homelessness); the new technologies of surveillance used to detect, measure, punish and prevent the incursion of 'unacceptable' behaviours of homelessness in prime spaces of the city; or the media campaigns that have sought to manage public opinion and to defend the commercial necessity and ethical legitimacy of attempts to clear homeless people from the streets (see, for example, Matieu, 1993; Dangshat, 1997; Coleman, 2004).

Strangely, with some notable exceptions (Takahashi, 1996; Mitchell, 1997), there has been rather less emphasis on what exactly it is about homeless people that inspires such overt antipathy, especially given that as a social group they exert little social power and pose little direct economic, political or physical threat to the dominant culture. Indeed, as Amster (2003: 196) suggests, 'The threat is more one of perception than reality, more of a societal pre-emptive strike against an as-yet-unborn threat that originates from within the dominant culture itself, but finds concrete expression in some abject, powerless element of society.' If Amster is right, then perhaps this unborn threat is in fact lodged in the potential for more politically progressive and ethically motivated responses to the injustices and exclusions faced by homeless people. Yet such responses receive very little airtime in the revanchist thesis, presumably on the grounds that they can (apparently) easily be mapped on to the idea that any kind of charitable response merely reinforces the structural status quo, and are therefore inevitably incorporated into ideologies of revanchism.

This failure to consider other responses to the problems of homelessness notwithstanding, Smith's portrayal of the 'revanchist city' helped to establish a narrative of urban homelessness that quickly assumed the power of conventional wisdom. Within this narrative, homeless people were understood as being caught in a pincer movement that was leading to the effective collapse of spaces of homelessness in the city: subject to both a proliferating range of local state measures and zero-tolerance policing techniques designed to clear them from prime city spaces on the one hand, and pushed back into 'skid row' districts that were themselves increasingly falling victim to urban 'regeneration' and gentrification on the other hand.

For Don Mitchell (1997, 2001) this dual attack represents nothing less than an attempt to annihilate the spaces of homelessness in the city, and thus in fact to annihilate homeless people themselves – who cannot exist if there is no space for them to exist in. Accordingly, for Mitchell (1997), urban revanchism is understood to have resulted in the emergence of the *postjustice* city, in which urban poverty has become criminalized, and questions of social justice and redistribution usurped by questions of how best to simply make homeless people disappear from view.

Mitchell's concept of the postjustice city expands on the logic of revanchism outlined by Smith in a number of ways (see DeVerteuil et al., 2009). First, the earlier emphasis on gentrification is widened to recognize broader attempts by city managers to provide appropriate local conditions for the attraction of international capital. Urban political regimes preoccupied by the need to present an appropriately positive image of the city for global investors and tourists have introduced a raft of anti-homeless ordinances in order to cleanse prime public spaces by banishing homeless people to the unseen margins of the city. This is not simply a vengeful claiming of the urban prize by successful elites, but part of the creation of 'sustainable' conditions for global success. Second, Mitchell provides a much wider portfolio of examples than does Smith, to show how many US cities – even those with previously liberal local administrations – have adopted similar systems of policing and regulating homeless people. As a result, he is able to develop a more generalized and potent critique of the ways in which the annihilation of homeless space is leading to a changing conception of urban citizenship more generally – in ways that see the exclusion of homeless people constructed not only as necessary but as just and good. Put simply, the rights of homeless people, he argues, simply do not register in the same ways as the rights of shoppers or middle-class residents, denying homeless people the citizenship that would give them sovereignty over their own actions. Third, Mitchell (2003) begins to address the role that local service providers play in the logic of the postjustice city – arguing, in a manner reminiscent of earlier work on Los Angeles, that initiatives like the Matrix outreach programme in San Francisco (designed to entice people off the streets and find them places in shelters provided by local voluntary organizations) need be understood as doing little more than legitimating – if not indeed actively complicit in – attempts by city authorities, business and the police to sweep homeless people from the streets.

Questioning the Revanchist Orthodoxy

Recent reviews reveal the influence that Smith's idea of urban revanchism, and Mitchell's concept of the postjustice city, have had in shaping understandings of the geographies of urban homelessness (see, for example, DeVerteuil et al., 2009). Like DeVerteuil et al. and others (see, for example, Laurenson & Collins, 2006, 2007; Johnsen & Fitzpatrick, 2010), however, we are concerned that the current orthodoxy may lead to what will at best be an incomplete and at worst an inaccurate portrayal of homelessness in the city. There are three main components to this concern.

First, while the revanchist model emphasizes the regulatory control of the spaces in which homeless people dwell and move, it often remains silent about attempts by homeless people to negotiate, or resist, such regulation. As Lees (1998) argues, the street is a complex space that tells a variety of stories, and one crucial narrative must surely be that of how homeless people themselves exercise autonomy within the wider constraints of social and cultural regulation. For example, Ruddick (1990, 1996) has drawn attention to a vision of homeless people as *social subjects* who both create themselves, and are created, in and through the evolving spaces and politics of the city – and contrasts the apparent victimization and annihilation of homeless people with their tenacity and ability to cope with the change going on around them. She points, in particular, to the capacity of homeless people to deploy a range of place-making devices that enhance the processes and practices of coping, with these tactics – to use de Certeau's (1984) terms – enabling them to overrule the predispositions and assigned meanings of space, and to transform the environment for unintended purposes. There are two important logics at work here. Most obviously, for Ruddick homeless people cannot and should not be regarded as political or cultural dupes, understood only as compliant or survivalist within the punitive socio-spatial order. Instead, within limits, they exercise choices and draw on enabling knowledges as well as on individual or collective creativity and capability. They form complex social networks, sometimes involving peer group cooperation, and there is evidence that the potential cohesion of shared territory, identity and defence can be a strongly positive experience (see also Rowe & Wolch, 1990; Wagner, 1993; Winchester & Costello, 1995; Duneier, 1999). Moreover, the continuing presence of homeless people in cities characterized by the regulatory and disciplinary codes of urban revanchism cannot adequately be understood simply in terms of socially constructed stigmata of deviancy and criminality. Instead, there is also a sense that the presence of homeless people among the power, wealth and leisure-orientation of prime urban spaces can undercut the very ideology of the revanchist/post-industrial/postjustice city itself (Mair, 1986).

Understood in these terms, recognizing the tactical agency of homeless people thus transcends the notion of mere survival, in the expression both of alternative social networks and of alternative political ideologies in the city. Indeed, we have argued elsewhere (Cloke et al., 2008) that overemphasis on the punitive geographies of the city cloaks a whole series of alternative cartographies of urban homelessness. Such cartographies need to embrace the ways in which homeless people journey not only to meet basic survival needs but also to earn money or to seek restful pauses in their daily practices, sometimes gathering communally, sometimes seeking solitude (see Cooper, 2001). Furthermore, such routines of movement and pause are intimately associated not only with the wider geographies of service provision and the continuum of prime and marginal space, but also with a practical knowledge of the micro-architectures of the city (Crang, 2000). They allow for the possibility of counter-inscription – of tracing over the formal understandings of city space and registering alternative signs and markers. They also point to the affective worlds of homeless people, as they co-constitute places of care, generosity, hope, charity, fun and anger both in the better-known spaces of homelessness and in those spaces that homeless people bring into being as 'homeless places' through practices of reinscription. These *human* geographies of homelessness need to be put to work alongside more regulationist understandings to offer a more complex understanding of homelessness and the city.

The second area of concern relates to the danger that a revanchist model might somehow be thought of as universally applicable. In fact, the available evidence suggests that both homelessness and recent responses to homelessness, and wider trends in urbanization and urban politics, take different forms in different countries. For example, as May (2009) has shown, both the scale and characteristics of the homeless population differs considerably in different national contexts; Swanson's (2007) research on the regulation of begging in Quito, Ecuador, argues for a particular 'twist' on revanchism characterized by an overt racial element to regulatory practices; MacLeod's (2002) study of the effects of gentrification in Glasgow notes a *selective* appropriation of a (US) revanchist political repertoire; and Slater's (2004) analysis in the Canadian context concludes that gentrification is neither revanchist or emancipatory, but that its outcomes remain highly dependent on contextual factors.

In fact, in the British context there is ample evidence of transatlantic policy transfer in the homelessness field. Thus, just as the nineteenth century saw the export of anti-vagrancy legislation from Britain to the United States (Cresswell, 2001), for example, so the late twentieth/early twenty-first centuries saw the importation into Britain from the USA of a number of technologies and techniques designed to 'manage' a problematic 'street culture' – the primary subjects of which, even if not always the originally intended targets, have been street homeless people. Such technologies include, but are not restricted to, variations of zero-tolerance policing, making begging a 'recordable offence', the 'designing out' of certain street activities, the introduction of 'diverted giving schemes', and the introduction of Designated Public Places Orders (to restrict the consumption of alcohol in public places) and of Anti-Social Behaviour Orders (Johnsen & Fitzpatrick, 2007, 2010).

Yet crucially, even if central and local government approaches to homelessness have undoubtedly become more targeted around issues of enforcement, containment and control in Britain in recent years, as we argue in chapter 2 these measures have been accompanied by programmes that are much less easily characterized as 'revanchist' – most notably, perhaps, the British government's *Rough Sleepers Initiative* and *Homelessness Action Programme*, which were designed to provide additional financial support to the voluntary sector agencies offering care and accommodation to street homeless people (May et al., 2005). In other words, and belying any universal approach to the management of homelessness, at the national level there is considerable variation both in problems of homelessness and in the responses those problems engender (see also Marr, 1997; Alcock & Craig, 2001; Huber & Stephens, 2001; von Mahs, 2005; Fitzpatrick & Stephens, 2007).

Similarly, at the local level it has been recognized that the imposition of anti-homeless measures is far more prevalent in some cities (notably, those with a heavy reliance upon the financial and creative industries, tourism and the convention trade) than in others (May, 2009). As we show in chapters 7 and 8, both the form and extent of welfare provision for homeless people also differ from place to place, with widespread variations in the servicing activities of local government, the availability of finance for third sector service activity, the local cultural signification of homelessness and the historic presence of caring institutions as part of the local urban scene.

Indeed, and forming the basis of our third concern about the revanchist framework, such a framework signally fails to capture the obvious importance of welfare services for homeless people. In some ways, of course, an infrastructure of poor-quality and sometimes unprofessional shelters and hostels, usually in the marginal spaces of the city, seems to be entirely compatible with overarching theses of control and containment. These services are the necessary containers into which homeless people can be swept up, thus preventing their unwanted presence in the prime areas of the city. They provide outlets for the expression of liberal or sentimentalist ideology, presenting opportunities for volunteers to feel good about themselves while upholding the underlying political structures of bipolarization. They even open out potential opportunities for the religious to proselytize to a captive audience. In these and other respects, they seem to reflect a close-knitted incorporation of third sector resources into the revanchist logic, thereby becoming objects of critique as part of that logic.

This account sounds like a caricature, and it is. Any reasonable exploration of the motivation, ethical codes and performative traits of the professionals and volunteers involved in providing services to homeless people is likely to uncover alternative ideas to those suggested by vicious revanchism. We do not seek here to present a romanticized version of these service environments, many of which lack adequate standards of security and comfort. Neither do we ignore the possibilities that serving homeless people provides for helping to build self-interested or self-absorbed charitable identities and subjectivities. But we do argue that it is a very considerable, and inaccurate, reductive leap to assume that providing welfare services for homeless people can only be understood in these terms. Instead, we recognize these service spaces as demonstrative of deep-seated and powerful forces of charity and care (Link et al., 1995; May, 2009) in which there is a genuine ethical expression of going-beyond-the-self, of caring about and caring for the victims of neoliberal excess.

In fact, we would argue that rather than within a revanchist framework, any analysis of current responses to homelessness is better conducted within the frame of neoliberalization, and in particular the shift from roll-back to roll-out neoliberalism (Peck & Tickell, 2002) unfolding in recent years (for an elaboration of this argument see chapter 2, and May et al., 2005). At one level such a suggestion is hardly surprising – not least, since Smith (1998: 10) himself has characterized revanchism as the 'the ugly cultural politics of neoliberal globalisation'. More specifically, however, we would argue that scholars of homelessness need to pay far more attention to the recent reworking of social welfare (Fyfe, 2005; Milligan & Conradson, 2006), including welfare provision for homeless people (May et al., 2005; Buckingham, 2009), along neoliberal lines and the effects of this reworking on homeless people and services.

In contrast to work proceeding under the revanchist or postjustice banner, the need here is therefore to trace the interconnections between the more punitive technologies of containment and control that are the subject of the more familiar accounts of the homeless city, neoliberal governmentality, and the processes by which welfare organizations and individuals (homeless people, members of the housed public, welfare professionals and service agency volunteers alike) become 'incorporated' in changing constructions of citizenship and subjectivity. In the British case, attention needs to be turned to the recent hollowing out of the welfare state, and the subsequent rolling out of neoliberal ideas and practices that contextualize the development of policies, partnerships and practices designed to deal with issues of homelessness.

In tracing changing responses to homelessness in Britain over recent years, however, we also argue that conventional understandings of neoliberal governance need to accommodate two crucial dissonances: first, the good intentions of government, which are not necessarily swallowed up entirely by the demands of neoliberal governing; and, second, the potential for resistance to neoliberal governance by organizations and individuals wishing to serve and care for homeless people. In the latter case, rather than assuming that such organizations and individuals will necessarily be incorporated into quasi-governmental resignation to the ideologies of neoliberalism, we question whether they represent a potential nexus for resistance to such ideologies – either practising alternative values from inside the system of governance, or fashioning spaces of resilient care in opposition to the joined-up orthodoxies of such governance (see also Larner & Craig, 2005; Carey et al., 2009).

Indeed, rather than automatically understanding homeless services as implicated in revanchism, we might begin to understand them as sites of potential resistance to revanchism. Sparke (2008) urges us to explore resistance in terms of the messy middle grounds where there is a mediation of control and opposition, structure and agency, incorporation and alternativeness. The provision of welfare services for homeless people represents one such messy middle ground: romanticized, yet often in practice deeply unromantic; easily dismissed as merely upholding the status quo, yet powered by an urge to do something about the injustice of that status quo; a cog in the revanchist engine, yet engineered and operated by people for whom revenge is the last thing on their mind. Katz (2004) has usefully differentiated between ideas of resistance, reworking and resilience as different parts of a multifaceted vocabulary of opposition to the impacts of globalization. Here, she incorporates respectively an oppositional consciousness that achieves emancipatory objectives (resistance), an impact on the organization of power relations if not their polarized distribution (reworking), and an enabling of survival in circumstances that do not allow changes to the causes that dictate survival (resilience). This nuanced exposition of what it is to 'resist' helps us to look at participation in providing services for homeless people in a progressive light. Rather than a simple incorporated involvement in neoliberal state practices fuelled by punitive revanchist ideologies, participation may involve a more complex attempt to engage in an oppositional politics of resilience and even reworking in the face of these ideologies.

We seek here to explore the confluence of these various ideas in practice, charting the changing politics of homelessness within a neoliberal phase of governance in Britain. We trace potential interconnections between techniques and governmentalities of neoliberalism and the punitive regulation of homeless people, especially in terms of spatial processes of control, containment and 'sweeping up'. At the same time, however, we are interested in assessing the ways in which specific geographical or political factors have emerged both nationally and locally in Britain to shape responses to homelessness, and the particular ideological, motivational or contextual factors that have shaped these particularities. As the state has embraced partnership with third sector agencies in the pursuance of its policies, we interrogate the possibilities for these partners to act as more than merely incorporated neogovernmental stooges, engaging in forms of care and charity that could be interpreted in terms of resistance rather than revanchism. It is also important to understand the role played by third sector service providers that – whether by choice or different forms of incompatibility – operate outside the boundaries of partnership with government, and may even be pursing goals that are contrary to the ideology and techniques of the current neoliberal regime. And, in so doing, we also want to leave space in our conceptual framework for questions of agency: the agency of homeless people – charting the way in which their actions shape the contours of the homeless city – but also of the professionals and volunteers who provide accommodation and care to homeless people in a fully peopled (welfare) state.

The Homeless Places Project

The material presented in this book is drawn from a research project that ran from June 2001 to March 2004. Funded by the Economic and Social Research Council, the Homeless Places Project examined the provision and governance of emergency services (night shelters, 'direct access' hostels, day centres and soup runs) for single homeless people in Britain.* Driven by a

---

* In discussions of homelessness in England distinctions are necessarily drawn between the 'statutory' and 'non-statutory' homeless, a distinction first made in relation to the 1977 Housing (Homeless Persons) Act and upheld in all subsequent revisions to the Act. The former refers to

desire to explore the geographical specificity of responses to homelessness, the project first constructed a map of national provision (with postal surveys of some 212 night shelters and hostels, 164 day centres and 63 soup runs across England, Wales and Scotland) before focusing upon the provision and use of such services in seven contrasting towns and cities in England, here referred to as: Benington, a large city in the south-west of England; Castlebridge, a small market town in southern England; Crossfield, an agricultural centre and market town in central England; Sandstown, a declining seaside resort in northern England; Steeltown, a large, manufacturing city in north-east England; Wimpster, a cathedral city in the west of England; and Winton, a small town in the far south-west of England. Precisely because, as outlined above, discussions of homelessness and of the 'homeless city' have tended to be shaped by developments in a small number of larger cities (most notably, perhaps, New York, Los Angeles, San Francisco and, to a lesser extent, London) a decision was made to explore experiences of homelessness beyond the metropolitan core, with research conducted in a number of smaller towns and rural areas. While appearing to stretch the concept of the 'homeless city' somewhat, as we demonstrate in chapters 7 and 8, much of what we often consider to be 'urban homelessness' has its roots in rural areas – as homeless people travel to the city from places further afield; or indeed, leave the city for the countryside. In this sense, urban and rural homelessness are connected by a range of movements – both geographical (the movements of homeless people themselves) and conceptual (as rural homelessness often only becomes rendered visible, and thus categorized as 'homelessness', when homeless people begin to congregate in urban centres) (see Cloke et al., 2002). At the same time, because we were concerned with the governance of homelessness, we also felt it important to explore not only the 'home spaces' (Peck & Tickell, 2002) but also the 'extremities' of neoliberal welfare restructuring – so as to gain a keener understanding of the ways in which such restructuring unfolds, often very unevenly, across different types of social space. Thus, case study research was conducted in towns and cities of different sizes across England – ranging

---

those to whom the local state has a statutory duty of care, namely the provision of accommodation: people with dependants or those otherwise found in 'priority need' (by virtue of age or ill-health, for example), who have not made themselves 'intentionally' homeless and who are legally entitled to public welfare provision. In contrast, the non-statutory homeless have no such right to either emergency or more permanent accommodation and are mainly dependent upon non-statutory organizations for emergency shelter. Because historically the majority (though by no means all) of the non-statutory homeless population have been single, it has become commonplace to refer to this group as single homeless people (Pleace et al., 1997). Those sleeping rough on the streets or living in night shelters and 'direct access' hostels (i.e. people experiencing some form of 'street homelessness' and whose experiences are examined here) are almost always part of the single homeless population. 'Direct access' hostels refer to those hostels that accept people directly from the streets without the need for a referral by another agency.

from a city of some 380,000 people to a small, market town of a little over three thousand – chosen so as to capture places of both relatively 'high' and relatively 'low' service provision (as revealed by the national survey of service providers).

The postal surveys sought to establish a basic picture of the nature and extent of emergency provision for homeless people – providing information on the kinds of organizations engaged in welfare services for homeless people, the nature of the services they provided, funding arrangements, staffing procedures and so on – together with an indication of the ethical motivations, or 'mission', of these organizations (see chapter 2). Work in each of the case studies then proceeded through a combination of participant observation (outlined below) and semi-structured interviews. Semi-structured interviews were conducted with 131 representatives of these services – including project managers (39), paid staff (29), volunteers (26) and a range of key informants (local authority housing officials, city centre management operatives, street outreach teams, police officers, volunteer bureau workers etc.) (37) – together with some 90 homeless people. Interviews with homeless respondents were supplemented by a further 160 or so less formal conversations with service users emerging out of the period of participant observation, and a further 17 semi-structured interviews conducted in support of the auto-photography work (see below).

Project manager interviews focused primarily on the history, ethos, structure and position of each project within the local service network. Interviews with *paid and volunteer staff* considered motivations for working in the sector, career paths and histories of volunteering, satisfactions and challenges, and views on the level and form of service provision in their area. *Service user* interviews were frequently more free-flowing but typically examined individuals' homeless life histories, mobility paths, experience of services within and outside the local area, and broader experience of an area's 'homeless scene'. Finally, interviews with *key informants* revolved around what we have termed the 'archaeology' of service provision in their area (including an account of services that had closed), the composition of the single homeless population, local geographies of rough sleeping, begging and street drinking, and local initiatives aimed at combating homelessness. Interviews were conducted in hostels and day centres and on the streets, as well as in the homes of volunteers and the workplaces of key informants. Most were conducted privately, though group interviews were held when interviewees expressed such a preference, or where private interview facilities were unavailable. Interviews ranged in length from 20 minutes to three hours. Where permission was given, interviews were tape recorded, transcribed verbatim and coded according to analytical themes.

One of the authors (Sarah) also engaged in an extensive period of overt participant observation in 18 night shelters, day centres and soup runs throughout the fieldwork period – sometimes working as a volunteer, sometimes simply 'hanging out' with service users. Though time consuming, such work proved vital in establishing relationships of trust with service users, who can otherwise be wary of talking with 'outsiders', in facilitating interviews with people with chaotic lifestyles, and in order to observe the dynamics shaping different service environments. Notes relating to the informal discussions with staff and services users, and on the dynamics of these spaces, emerging through the participant observation process were used to triangulate other forms of data.

Finally, 17 of our homeless respondents in two different case study areas (urban and rural) agreed to participate in an auto-photography exercise using disposable cameras to produce a record of their experiences of homelessness. Participants were given a set of prints to keep, and interviewed about their choice of images. Though also time-consuming, and difficult to arrange, the photo diaries provided very significant insight into homeless people's negotiation of spaces that would have been inappropriate or unsafe for members of the research team to access – for example, squats – and new understandings of apparently already 'known' spaces of homelessness such as day centres and hostels (for further discussion of this part of the project see Johnsen et al., 2008).

A selection of these images is included in chapters 3, 5 and 6. Their inclusion has less to do with simply 'illustrating' the various spaces of homelessness explored herein, than with providing a further mode of expression through which the people we talked with might 'witness' their experiences of homelessness in ways that are less constrained by the presuppositions and prejudices that to some extent always shape the conduct of research interviews and the selection and presentation of material from such interviews. Indeed, and as we hope will become clear, while some of the images selected for inclusion obviously reinforce the arguments being made at different points of the book, elsewhere they provide what might be termed a 'counter-narrative': providing readers with quite different 'views' of the spaces of homelessness described by other respondents and thus – we hope – drawing attention to the always multiple and contested nature of those spaces and of our, and our respondents', understandings of them.

Working from the information provided by service agencies in the national survey of provision, the characteristics of service users broadly matched the wider demographics of street homeless people in Britain (outside of the main metropolitan areas) (see Briheim-Crockall et al., 2008). That is, while the age of respondents varied from people as young as 19 to people in their late fifties, the majority of respondents were aged between 25 and 45 years of age, and all but one identified themselves as White British. Within this apparently otherwise relatively homogeneous group, however, people recounted widely varying histories of homelessness, ranging from those who had only recently gone on to the streets to those with a long history of rough sleeping and hostel use, and those whose homeless histories are better described as 'episodic' (May, 2000a). Not surprisingly, perhaps, these different groups tended to describe quite different experiences of life on the streets and of homeless service spaces, with these differences cross cut in complex ways by other positionalities; for example, a person's position in each of the main subgroups (variously labelled 'pissheads', 'smackheads' and 'straightheads' in street nomenclature) within the homeless population identified by our respondents, each of which tend to make use of different parts of the city, and – where possible – different service spaces (see chapters 3 to 6).

More obviously, perhaps, in line with the wider demographics of Britain's street homeless population, male respondents outnumbered female respondents by almost four to one (with 71 male respondents and 19 women). The homeless men and women we talked with also tended to articulate quite different cartographies of homelessness: in their movements around the city and the geographies of rough sleeping, for example (see chapter 3); in the likelihood of either group turning to key homeless services such as soup runs, day centres, and hostels; and in their experience of these service spaces (chapters 4 to 6).

While sensitive to such differences, we are also wary of overdetermining them. Though homelessness is quite clearly a gendered experience (Smith, 1999), there is a need to avoid an essentialist reading of the difference that gender makes. For example, it has been suggested that street homelessness is largely a male preserve (Higate, 2000a, b), with homeless women tending either to avoid the streets altogether (by remaining in (abusive) domestic relationships, for example) or to retreat into the shadows of the street homeless 'scene' (Wardhaugh, 1999). As we have argued elsewhere (May et al., 2007), it is in fact possible to trace a wide variety of experiences of homelessness among street homeless women: ranging from those who attempt to distance themselves from the broader street homeless population and 'street scene' for fear of the violence that often permeates that scene (sleeping rough in suburban rather than central city locations, or in hard to find spaces within the central city, for example, and rarely making use of emergency services); to those who are highly visible and obviously 'marked' as 'homeless' (sleeping rough in mixed sex groups in the central city, or assuming a key role in local street drinking 'schools', for example). Rather than essentialize, or treat the gendering of homelessness as a separate phenomenon, we have instead attempted to weave a sensitivity to the difference that gender makes to people's experiences of homelessness (and the experiences of the volunteers and paid staff who work in homeless services) throughout the main substantive chapters of the book. In so doing, we recount the sometimes quite different experiences of the streets and of homeless services articulated by homeless men and women, drawing attention to the difference that a person's gender seems to make to those experiences, without overdetermining them.

Of course, a project that puts homeless people – and the paid staff and volunteers providing homeless services – firmly at its centre raises a number of complex ethical issues. Again, we have already discussed these at some length elsewhere (Cloke et al., 2000a, 2003a; Johnsen et al., 2008; Johnsen, 2010) and do not have the space here to revisit these arguments in any great detail. But three such issues are worth reiterating. First, we would argue that the need to more fully (and critically) engage with the details of homelessness policy and provision is as much an ethical as a conceptual imperative. This was no more evident than when one of our homeless interviewees responded to our rather abstract explanation of the purposes of our research (couched in terms of its contribution to academic debates around urban homelessness) with: 'What the fuck's the point of that?!' (Cloke et al., 2003a). The desire to critically engage with, and contribute to, questions of social policy as well as academic debate, and to produce research that might have some real and positive value to the subjects of that research, is hardly unique. While there is a long history of 'action research' in the social sciences, the past few years have also seen a growing (if more narrowly focused) debate concerning geography's 'relevance' (Johnsen, 2010). It is, however, both surprising and – for us – a cause of real concern that these debates would seem to have had little impact on the nature of the research into the geographies of homelessness. As we have already suggested, too much of this research continues to proceed at a relatively high level of abstraction, with only a narrow engagement with the concrete changes shaping homeless people's lives (notably, those concerning changes to the regulation of public space, rather than welfare service provision) and with little or no discussion, via a field-based methodology, with the subjects of that research – namely, homeless people themselves.

Second, the kinds of ethnographic methods deployed here raise a number of issues around research design and supervision. Most obviously, perhaps, working in homeless service spaces faces the researcher with (some of) the dangers and distress that permeate such environments (see, for example, the account of St James' night shelter in chapter 6). That is, it confronts the researcher with issues with which homeless people, and homeless service providers, must deal on a day-to-day basis. Some such dangers can be avoided through careful research design, and the use of particular methodological techniques. As we noted above, one reason to turn to auto-photography was that is granted the research team access to spaces – such as squats – that we felt it would have been unsafe (and, with respect of people's privacy, inappropriate) to enter. When working in day centres and night shelters, we adopted the strategies employed by the volunteers and paid staff in those services to minimize the threats they sometimes face: going to and from a night shelter in the company of others, sitting near the door in interview rooms or undertaking interviews with service users within plain sight of (other) staff wherever possible, for example. The emotional strain that working with vulnerable people can produce – when one can find oneself listening to tales of great suffering – is hardly restricted to those working with street homeless people. But it is certainly difficult to 'design out' – indeed it would in many ways be counterproductive to do so, if only because such stories are sometimes a vital part of the issues under examination. For our own part, the emotional work involved in such research necessitated a careful and consistent process of research supervision, in which the main field researcher (Sarah) had the opportunity to regularly 'debrief' with another member of the research team. When working as a volunteer in such services, Sarah also participated in staff handover and incident debriefing meetings.

Third, and again we would argue that this is (or should be) an aim of any ethnographic work, it is vital that the subjects of such research are presented 'in the round'; as fully fleshed subjects in their own right, with all the messy and (sometimes) uncomfortable understandings, attitudes and practices that real people often articulate. Here, for example, we hope we have presented the volunteers who staff Britain's homeless services as neither paragons of virtue nor patronizing do-gooders, but 'ordinary' people engaged in transforming an ordinary ethics of care into an 'extraordinary' sense of ethical commitment to the other; and people who, even in the midst of such acts of kindness, sometimes articulate views of those they are serving which are anything but progressive. Likewise, we hope we have avoided the all too common tendency in some recent writings on homelessness to present homeless people as passive victims of forces beyond their control and/or as the standard bearers of resistance to a revanchist politics; that is, as convenient ciphers around which to build a wider critique of gentrification, public space law and so on (DeVerteuil et al., 2009). Such moves, it seems to us, strip homeless people not only of their agency, but also of their humanity. The hope, then, is that we have neither romanticized nor stimagtized homeless people, but given proper voice to the complex and often contradictory emotions, experiences, understandings and actions that homeless people too, and homeless people's lives, articulate.

At a more mundane level, it is also important to give some indication of the basic ethical protocols followed in this research. For example, information sheets were sent to all organizations involved in the research. While the principles behind interview protocol were consistent, the actual procedure for conducting interviews with homeless service users were adapted to accord with the wishes of individual respondents and project managers. Permission to publish photographs and (anonymized) information derived from interview transcripts was obtained from all participants, and all names (of individuals, service organizations and places) have been changed.

Finally, it is important to recognize the timing of the research reported here. Given the long lead times of academic publishing, it is of course always difficult for academic research to be as timely as its authors might like – especially in a field such as this, which is prone to what Peck (2001a) has referred to as a 'speeding up' of policy development and transfer. Nonetheless, and as we acknowledged earlier, this book has had an unusually long gestation period. Much of the primary research on which the book draws was conducted in 2001–2, a period in which the government's Homelessness Action Programme (HAP) was drawing to a close and local authorities and voluntary sector service providers alike were gearing up for the introduction of a new system of funding for supported accommodation services (Supporting People) and beginning to formulate the then soon to be introduced Local Homelessness Strategies (LHSs) – in which local authorities in England were, for the first time, required to set out their plans to meet the needs of single homeless people within their jurisdiction. With the phasing out of the central government funded HAP, and the introduction of LHSs, the governance of homelessness in Britain thus underwent (yet) further reorganization – as local authorities began to play a more direct role in determining the nature of any response to homelessness in their local areas; albeit within the limits set out by central government guidelines and funding streams (on the rescaling of homeless governance see May et al. 2005). Further reorganization has happened since, with the emergence, from 2005, of regional homelessness and supporting people strategies and with the launch, in 2008, of the Communities and Local Government's *No One Left Out* initiative (CLG, 2008a). Pledging to provide £200 million to its partners in the voluntary sector and local government, the initiative seeks to pick up where the Homelessness Action Programme left off – reducing levels of rough sleeping in England (to zero in some cases) by 2012, through a familiar toolkit of voluntary sector/local and central government 'partnerships' working according to a set of action plans and targets set by the centre.

However, in the current context at least, perhaps the most important aspect of the *No One Left Out* initiative is that it demonstrates how little has actually changed with regard to the core characteristics of British single homelessness policy over the past decade or so (though see chapter 2). Or, to put it more accurately, the key elements of the system of governance put in place by New Labour in an attempt to 'manage' the problem of single homelessness a little over a decade ago – deploying the resources of (selected) voluntary sector organizations to meet centrally determined targets on the reduction of rough sleeping, with central government funding streamed via local authorities who are themselves tightly constrained by central government 'codes of guidance' – have remained remarkably consistent since they were first introduced by the then Rough Sleepers Unit and rolled out in the government's Homelessness Action Programme (1999–2002). In this sense, while the names of some of the programmes and relevant government departments may have changed since we embarked upon this research, we believe that the arguments made here remain a pertinent reading of British single homelessness policy – because we have focused upon the deeper lying (slower moving and still persistent) logic of those policies rather than only their surface manifestation. Indeed, the research may provide a particularly valuable reading of this broader system of governance precisely because of the time at which it was conducted – a time when this system was new, and thus those responsible for enacting it (local and central government officials, voluntary sector organizations and homeless people) were highly reflective about its roots, current characteristics and likely future.

The Structure of the Book

In the remainder of this book we present detailed accounts of the conceptual and material spaces of homelessness that form the basis of our re-envisioning of the homeless city. Chapter 2 charts two conceptual landscapes from which this re-envisioning emerges. First, we take an interest in different facets of *neoliberalism* that are important to a fuller understanding of recent responses to homelessness: the mundane and everyday *techniques* by which neoliberalism constitutes itself in different spaces and social networks; the creation of different kinds of acting subjects, and in particular *homeless subjectivities*, regulated and enabled under neoliberalism; and the changing *processes* and *practices* of actually existing neoliberalism that serve to reconstruct the technologies and subjectivities of welfare provision and social exclusion. Second, we explore the possibilities inherent in the concept of *postsecularism* – exploring the idea that recent years have seen a reshaping of the supposedly binary relationships between secular publics and private religions and suggesting that the provision of services for homeless people represents one such arena in which a rapproachment of secular and faith-based ethical motivations is forging new forms of collaborative ethical praxis, and new geographies of compassion and care, in the city.

In chapter 3, we focus on homeless people's own accounts of the homeless city to demonstrate the importance of emotion and affect in the lives of homeless people and to trace the deposits of such emotions and affects on and in the homeless city. By drawing attention to the creative deployment of managing impressions, the performance of particular discursive roles and the pre-discursive and emotional aspects of homeless people's lives, we aim to restore to homeless people not only a stronger sense of agency but also a crucial sense of humanity so often missing in accounts of urban homelessness.

In chapters 4, 5 and 6 we turn our attention to the various service spaces in which homeless people spend so much of their time, presenting a detailed reading of Britain's soup runs (chapter 4), day centres (chapter 5) and night shelters and hostels (chapter 6). Methodologically the chapters are structured around the accounts of both service users and providers – giving voice to the homeless people that make use of such services but also to the staff and volunteers providing them. Conceptually, we trace the complex dynamics of these spaces, the ethical frames that underpin and are brought into being therein, and homeless people's experiences of them.

In chapters 7 and 8 the focus shifts from an examination of these homeless spaces to an examination of contrasting 'homeless places', charting the geographical unevenness of contemporary homeless service provision. Drawing on our research in Benington and Steeltown, chapter 7 suggests a raft of historical, political and organizational reasons why different patterns of service provision emerge in different cities and the interconnections between service *provision* and service *consumption*. We argue that such unevenness leads to culturally significant and locally specific homeless 'scenes' – scenes that are both acknowledged and experienced by homeless people, and are performed in material and affective ways in the complex cartographies they generate in the urban spaces concerned. Though rural areas are popularly disconnected from the politics and representations of homelessness, by way of contrast chapter 8 explores the production and consumption of very different homeless services and scenes in four very different rural areas. Here, we chart some of the connections between urban and rural homelessness, but also offer a more nuanced account of the multiple geographies of homelessness in a variated rural space. Drawing these issues together, chapter 9 offers some broader thoughts on the role of the voluntary sector and of volunteers in providing for homeless people, and on revanchism, neoliberalism and postsecuralism in the homeless city.

Chapter Two

From Neoliberalization to Postsecularism

Introduction

It is inevitable that our account of responses to homelessness in Britain over the past 15 years or so will be deeply coloured by ideas about neoliberalism, which has been recognized as 'the dominant political and ideological form of capitalist globalisation' (Brenner & Theodore, 2002: 350) and 'the most successful ideology in world history' (Anderson, 2000: 17). Broadly, as an ideology neoliberalism entails a belief in the market as the most desirable mechanism for regulating the economy. As a raft of policies, neoliberal governments across the globe have promoted supply-side innovation and competitiveness, privatization and deregulation in order to transform not only the economy but also the provision of public services, including welfare. However, to apply neoliberalism as some kind of unified set of top-down explanations for all kinds of social, political and economic change without exploring its day-to-day constitution is to generalize too far. We are therefore interested here in three particular facets of neoliberalism.

First, it is important to recognize the *techniques* of neoliberalism (Larner, 2003) – the seemingly mundane practices and processes through which neoliberalism constitutes itself in different spaces and social networks. Indeed, Brenner and Theodore (2002) refer to 'actually existing neoliberalism' in order to move away from sweeping generalizations and to identify the partial and sometimes tangential nature of any neoliberal transformation. We are therefore fascinated by the techniques of actually existing neoliberalism that lead to the emergence of responsible and irresponsible spaces and subjects in the contemporary city in connection with homelessness, and following Brenner and Theodore (2002) we recognize that these techniques will often be clouded by 'multifarious institutional forms … diverse socio-political effects and their multiple contradictions'.

Second, following Larner (2003: 511) we are interested not just in the creation of particular 'subject positions', but in the 'acting subjects' brought into being under neoliberalism. Accordingly we need to take seriously the claim that governmentality takes a particular form under neoliberalism (Rose, 1996; Dean, 1999), conjuring up a different form of politics in which governmental technologies are used to construct not only different subject positions, but also different *subjectivities*. Rather than placing constraints upon the freedoms of citizens per se, power can be seen as that which 'makes up' citizens who are capable of coping with particular forms of regulated freedom (Rose & Miller, 1992). We therefore need to know both about how different neoliberal citizens are made up, and about the kinds of regulated freedoms they bear. Thus homeless subjectivities will encounter particular techniques that regulate individual and collective freedoms, and bestow political and cultural doxa about how these regulated freedoms should be distributed and endured. Such a making up of homeless citizens (and we note here Mitchell's powerful insistence that homeless people have had their citizenship removed by these techniques) bestows an equally powerful imperative on wider citizenship in its response to the presence of homeless subjectivities in the spatial and social networks they inhabit. As such, the shift to neoliberalism involves the recasting of individual and collective subjectivities as the government seeks to define and shape what is appropriate conduct at these individual and collective levels. Raco (2005: 76) terms this the 'conduct of conduct' – a phrase that neatly summarizes how neoliberal governments seek to establish and build subjectivities in and through which their programmes and strategies can be put into operation. We want to assess how the subject position of 'homeless' is made up and acted out – by both homeless people and others – in an era of neoliberal governance in Britain.

Third, we are interested in neoliberalism as a process rather than as an end state. Temporality is crucial to the idea of actually existing neoliberalism and we want to suggest both that there has been a significant change in the nature and form of welfare policies and practices in Britain since the election of New Labour in 1997, and that this change is evident in the basic rationale of state welfare provision, the practices and technologies of the state through which change has been enabled, and in the attempts by the state to change the subjectivities of welfare providers, welfare recipients and a broader public.

Rephasing Neoliberalism: From Governance to 'Governmentality'

In their analysis of neoliberalization, Peck and Tickell (2002) trace a series of fundamental shifts in the basic structure of neoliberalism as it has unfolded in the advanced economies of the North Atlantic: the first the move from the abstract philosophical project, or 'proto-neoliberalism', of the 1970s to the 'roll-back' neoliberalism of the 1980s (with its focus upon a restructuring of the economy and a rolling-back of the Keynesian welfare state apparatus); the second, beginning in the early 1990s, a shift towards a more socially interventionist agenda (or 'roll-out' neoliberalism) designed to manage and contain the increasingly obvious social costs associated with this earlier restructuring.

In practice, of course, Peck and Tickell's framework is better treated as a useful heuristic rather than a strict chronology, with some of the key elements of neoliberal restructuring they identify evident in more than one of these phases, and suggesting a certain bleeding of categories and phases one into another. Hence, it is indeed clearly possible to read roll-back neoliberalism as mainly characterized by a relatively active role for the state in the *economic* sphere (most obviously, in the careful management of a 'free market') and a progressive *withdrawal* of the state from the active delivery of welfare. But it is equally clear that in Britain as elsewhere successive Conservative administrations throughout the 1980s actually worked quite hard at transforming both public perceptions of welfare and welfare recipients, and the structures of welfare delivery, in ways that did more than simply lay the groundwork for a more active intervention in the social field in the 1990s (Malpass, 1985). Most obviously, a convincing case can be made that a number of the central tenets of the 'welfare settlement' of the 1990s (based around the centrality of paid employment and of the need for systems of income support to help not hinder the development of a more flexible labour market, of individual responsibility for one's own welfare needs within a 'mixed economy' of welfare, and the drive towards 'value for money') were in fact first ushered in as part of a broader transformation of British welfare under the third Thatcher administration of 1986–90 (Cochrane, 1994). As such, though we remain convinced by the general thrust of Peck and Tickell's argument – and in particular, their conceptualization of roll-out neoliberalism as, in essence, a form of *crisis management* – the chronology they develop cannot easily accommodate a more detailed reading of British welfare policy and practice. Nor does it allow for any change in welfare policies and practices within the rather broad periods they identify.

An alternative to Peck and Tickell's chronology is provided by Ling (2000). Focusing more narrowly than Peck and Tickell (2002), Ling has examined changes to British welfare policy and practice over the past 60 years. Like Peck and Tickell (2002), Ling (2000) identifies three ideal typical periods of state welfare provision. In contrast to Peck and Tickell, however, for Ling the most important change relates not to any apparent shift from a period of roll-back to roll-out neoliberalism in the early 1990s, but to the move from what he terms a system of '*governance*' to a system of '*governmentality*' in the mid-to-late 1990s, broadly concomitant with the election of the New Labour government. We should say at the outset that we find Ling's terminology somewhat confusing. While he is not alone in identifying a shift from a system of 'government' to one of 'governance', his use of the term 'governmentality' to describe a particular mode of governing is more problematic (Richards & Smith, 2002). From a Foucauldian perspective, governmentality more properly refers to the *process of governing* itself (Foucault, 1979, 1991; Rose & Miller, 1992; Raco & Imrie, 2000). Such a process takes different forms at different times, as the rationalities and practices of governing (themselves giving rise to particular subjectivities) coalesce to form particular modes of governmentality: 'government', 'governance' and so on (Larner & Walters, 2000; Morrison, 2000). Hence, while it is possible to identify different modes of governmentality, it is not strictly speaking possible to talk of 'governmentality' as itself a mode of governing and attribute it to a particular period of time. It is partly because of this that where others too have identified recent changes in neoliberal welfare state regimes that take these regimes somewhere beyond a system of 'governance', other terms have been used to describe this new phase: ranging from the 'Third Way' to a period of 'de-governmentalization' (see Morrison, 2000; Loughlin, 2004). We remain wedded to Ling's framework (if not his terminology), however, because we are more convinced by his account of the *substance* of recent changes than we are by the more limited changes described in these other accounts. At the risk of generating confusion, we have therefore retained Ling's terminology, while analysing the changes he describes through a governmentality *perspective*: that is, noting the key differences in the basic *rationale* and *practices* of state welfare provision, and in the *subjectivities* such changes give rise to, in the different periods he identifies.

To elaborate, Ling suggests that from 1947 to around the mid-1970s British welfare was characterized by a system of *government*: 'an epoch when, in Kooiman's terms, "Governing was basically regarded as one-way traffic from those governing to those governed"', with the majority of welfare services provided directly by the state (Richards & Smith, 2002: 15). From about the mid-1970s, however, a shift towards a system of *governance* became apparent, as 'the number of actors in the policy ... arena multiplied, the boundaries between the public and private sector ... blurred and central government's command over a more complex policy process ... receded' (Richards & Smith, 2002: 15). Developing this basic framework, then, the shift to a system of governance was associated with changes across three broad domains.

First, with regard to the *rationale* of state welfare provision, responsibility for the delivery of an increasing array of welfare services passed from central and local government to other agencies in the profit but also and especially the not-for-profit, non-statutory sector. While the multiplication of welfare agencies can be understood in part as a response to a recognition of the inability of the state to meet the needs of all, with the election of a Conservative government in 1979 it became tied into a more basic recon-ceptualization of the state's role in welfare provision. As they sought to free the state from its responsibilities for the delivery of welfare, successive Conservative administrations not only encouraged the expansion of the non-statutory sector but attempted to shift the burden of welfare provision away from the state and on to both non-statutory agencies and the shoulders of private citizens themselves.

Second, even while introducing a fundamental split between purchaser and provider, from the early 1980s especially British welfare policy under-went a complex process of spatial reorganization. Part and parcel of a broader attack on the power of the local state, as responsibility for the deliv-ery of welfare was devolved to (non-elected) local bodies in the private and not-for-profit sector, responsibility for the regulation of those bodies passed from local to central government. Throughout this period, however, the *technologies* of state regulation remained relatively underdeveloped, or better still 'thin'. Hence, while central government showed increasing concern for value for money (ensured through new systems of Compulsory Competitive Tendering and the widespread dissemination of the principles of the New Public Management), such systems had little power to determine *how* serv-ices were delivered.

Third, partly as a result of this limited regulatory framework, both indi-vidual agencies and the non-statutory sector as a whole retained a signifi-cant degree of independence throughout this period, providing an important space for the voicing of dissent when government policy clashed with agency practice or with the ideals of the sector more broadly. With regard to any attempt to reshape the *subjectivities* of welfare recipients and of a broader public, Conservative rhetoric concerned itself mainly with an attack on the idea of state-sponsored welfare per se (frequently casting welfare recipients as a drain on collective wealth) and pushed instead a creed of individualism, within which any responsibility the private citizen might have for the welfare of others was cast as a choice rather than an obligation.

The move from a system of government to governance therefore had a significant impact on both the logic and form of British welfare (see also Rhodes, 1997; Bevir & Rhodes, 2003). For Ling, however, the more recent shift away from a system of governance towards what he terms a system of 'governmentality', around the mid-to-late 1990s, has been equally if not more significant. Though such a shift cannot be directly aligned with the change of government at that time (with a number of the features he identi-fies as articulating a period of governmentality evident in different areas of British welfare policy prior to May 1997), there is little doubt that the changes he describes accelerated with the election of New Labour.

In particular, the new government's much vaunted Compacts with the voluntary sector, announced in 1998 (described by Kendall as 'an unparalleled step in the positioning of the third sector in [British] public policy'), signalled a sea change in British welfare policy and practice (Kendall, 2000: 542). Not least, the Compact articulated a fundamental change in the *rationale* of state welfare provision. Where previous Conservative administrations had turned to the non-statutory sector mainly as a way of off-loading the state's responsibilities for welfare delivery, New Labour described a new vision of British welfare policy: with the state working in partnership with an expanded non-statutory sector (Giddens, 1998; Home Office, 1998). Such a vision speaks of the strengths most usually associated with the non-statutory sector (its 'expertise', 'creativity' and 'flexibility') but also of a renewed faith in the state – whose role, far from receding, is seen as overseeing the work of the sector (so as to ensure issues of quality control, for example) and setting the broader direction of welfare policy. This widening of the idea of partnership opened up the potential for new spaces of welfare and care. While still open to a critique of incorporation – the continuing acquiescence of third sector organizations to the ideologies and techniques of neoliberal workfare and potentially of punitive revanchist urbanisms – the enhanced role of partnership also established the conditions of possibility for new 'third spaces' – or 'border zones' (Vasquez & Marquardt, 2003) – in the city in which messy and contested conditions for the mediation of incorporation in, and resistance to, waves of neoliberalism may have been established.

At the same time, however, it is also clear that to facilitate this new vision, New Labour set about transforming the *technologies* of welfare and embarked upon a complex reorganization of local–central state responsibilities and of state personnel. Most importantly, perhaps, with the introduction of Best Value in place of the previous mechanism of Compulsory Competitive Tendering, New Labour sought to exert much greater control over how non-statutory 'partner' agencies deliver welfare services, with a new tendering process effectively dictating the policies and procedures an agency must follow in order to enter into a service contract. Backed up by the introduction of strict performance targets, the effect has been to channel funding to what Ling calls 'fit partners': those agencies whose ethos and approach is in broad alignment with the aims and objectives of central government policy (Ling, 2000). At the same time, and in contrast to the previous era, under New Labour day-to-day responsibility for the management and regulation of non-statutory agencies has passed (back) to the local state. Given the degree to which Best Value determines the regulatory framework, however, it is difficult to read such a move as evidence of genuine decentralization. Instead, we appear to be witnessing a recentralization and formalization of state power within which, as Maile and Hoggett (2001: 512) argue: 'Local government is increasingly becoming a "policy free zone" … [its role] to deliver centrally determined policies in a strategic way.' Such a process has been facilitated by a complex restructuring of state personnel. Thus, the late 1990s and early 2000s especially saw a rapid proliferation of central government appointed 'special advisors', acting at both the centre (in the form of various 'tsars') and the periphery: chairing the 'local services consortia' that have become a key part of the welfare landscape under New Labour. Seconded from the local state, but funded directly from the centre, the latter in particular represented a significant, if subtle, extension of central government's regulatory reach: disseminating government directives and shaping discussions as to appropriate responses to (centrally defined) local service needs so as to ensure that local authorities and non-statutory agencies alike remain 'on message'.

In stark contrast to the relative independence enjoyed by non-statutory agencies under previous Conservative administrations, then, under New Labour the non-statutory sector has found itself subject to increased central government control. At the national level, in particular, New Labour has been especially adept at setting the limits to debate. By holding out the promise of a greater say in the shaping of government policy, New Labour has increasingly been able to contain the voice of critics fearful of losing their place at the table of government (Newman, 2000). At the local level, hemmed in by new contracts and performance targets but fearful of stepping outside these predetermined limits lest it result in a loss of funding, agencies appear to have embarked upon a process of 'self-regulation': shaping their services and procedures in line with the definitions of need provided by central government (Anonymous, 2001).

Finally, while the shift from a system of governance to 'governmentality' appears to have constructed new subjectivities among welfare *providers*, so too it has seen a transformation of the relationships between the state and the private citizen: both direct welfare recipients and a broader public. Here, New Labour has sought to clarify the rights but also the responsibilities of those in receipt of welfare services. But a broader attempt to 'govern by culture' is also apparent: as central government has sought to delineate the most effective, if not also the 'right and proper', ways for private citizens to provide both for themselves and, in a significant departure from the creed of individualism exposed by previous Conservative governments, for others (Ling, 2000).

At first sight at least, Ling's reading of recent changes in British welfare policy and practice does not sit easily with the chronology of neoliberalization proposed by Peck and Tickell (2002). Given the rather different focus of the two accounts, however, we believe it is possible to accommodate Ling's more specific analysis within Peck and Tickell's broader framework. Here we therefore read the shift from a system of governance to 'governmentality' that Ling proposes as a second, more powerful articulation of the broader programme of roll-out neoliberalization that Peck and Tickell identify. We proceed by carrying this argument over into a reading of central government responses to the crisis of street homelessness in 1990s Britain. We identify the roots of that crisis, the moment at which central government first responded to it (broadly coincident with Peck and Tickell's timing of the shift from roll-back to roll-out neoliberalism) and the point at which the New Labour government initiated a *new* response, formulated around a system of 'govermentality'.

Neoliberalism and Britain's Crisis of Street Homelessness

The crisis of rough sleeping that unfolded in Britain in the late 1980s remains one of the most potent symbols of the social costs of the Thatcher revolution (Carlen, 1996). When examined through the twin lens of roll-back neoliberalism, with its emphasis upon a 'free market' economy and a minimalist state, the roots of that crisis are not difficult to trace. As the Conservative government of 1979–83 embarked upon a radical restructuring of the British space-economy, decimating Britain's traditional manufacturing base and speeding the move towards a high skill/low skill service economy, the British labour market showed the first signs of growing income and occupational polarization (Mohen, 1999). With levels of unemployment reaching record highs, the number of long-term unemployed in particular rose dramatically, especially among the young (Robinson, 1989; Heddy, 1990). At the same time, in line with their desire to 'roll back the state' (and reduce a growing benefits bill), successive Conservative administrations embarked upon a simultaneous and systematic dismantling of the welfare safety net (Cloke, 1995), leading to three especially significant impacts on the emergent crisis of street homelessness (Anderson, 1993). First, with the passage of the 1980 Housing Act and the introduction of Right-to-Buy, local authority housing stocks were significantly reduced at a time when the supply of new social housing was in decline following dramatic reductions in central government's Housing Investment Programme (Forrest & Murie, 1988; Brownhill & Sharp, 1992). Second, faced with the need to accommodate those who a decade earlier would have turned to the local state, Britain's housing associations found themselves increasingly unable to offer accommodation to their traditional client groups. As a result, and at the very moment that the removal of Fair Rents had significantly increased the cost (though not the supply) of private rented accommodation, poorer single people in particular found their access to affordable rental housing severely curtailed (Warrington, 1996). Third, reflecting a disastrous combination of financial pragmatism and neoconservative doctrine, under the 1986 Social Security Act 16- and 17-year-olds became ineligible for Income Support, as the government looked to the family to pick up the mantel of welfare provision for Britain's young people (Hutson & Liddiard, 1994).

Not surprisingly, the changes brought about by Conservative free-marketeering produced an almost immediate and dramatic rise in levels of homelessness of all kinds, and heralded important changes in the characteristics of Britain's single homeless population. Most importantly, perhaps, a traditional population of older, single homeless men was supplemented and eventually surpassed by growing numbers of younger men and women seeking refuge in Britain's shelter system. The visible presence of young people in night shelters and hostels, day centres and soup kitchens challenged popular stereotypes of the 'vagrants' and 'tramps' traditionally understood as making up Britain's single homeless population and considerably raised public sympathy for homeless people (Hutson & Liddiard, 1994). At the same time, as the providers of night shelter and hostel accommodation sought to respond to the needs of new client groups, the shift towards smaller units offering single rooms and increased levels of support rather than basic dormitory style arrangements resulted in a steady decline in the total number of emergency beds available to homeless people across Britain and a dramatic rise in levels of street homelessness (see chapter 6; see also Harrison, 1996). Indeed, by the summer of 1990 the sight of some 3000 people sleeping rough in central London provided the British public with a potent symbol of the costs of Thatcherism and, in combination with that summer's poll tax riots, a serious legitimation crisis for the government (Goodwin & Painter, 1996).

The Rough Sleepers Initiative

According to the revanchist city thesis it might be expected that at this point any response to such a crisis would echo developments in the USA – with campaigns by city managers to clear homeless people from the streets, excising both the subject positions and acting subjects of homelessness from the sites and sights of Britain's cities. In reality the response to this crisis in Britain was far more complex, the result of a complex fusion of ideology, reactionism and politicized 'responsibility' on the part of government that together ushered in new forms of homeless governance at this time.

Most importantly, perhaps, spurred on by calls from an increasingly hostile media and pressure groups such as Shelter, CHAR and Crisis not only to respond but to respond *humanely* to a crisis of street homelessness seen by many as of the government's own making, the British government spearheaded a *two part* response to this crisis – with the introduction of new programmes designed to further the supply of emergency services for single homeless people, and more sustained attempts to 'reclaim the streets' (*Daily Telegraph*, 1990a, b; *Guardian*, 1990).

At the heart of the government's strategy lay the *Rough Sleepers Initiative* (RSI), launched in June 1990 and managed by the then Department of Environment (DoE) with an initial budget of £15 million rising to £179 million through phases two and three (1993–9) (Randall & Brown, 1993, 1996). For the Conservatives, the main appeal of the RSI was that it enabled central government to point to a visible response to the problems of street homelessness (namely, the increased provision of emergency accommodation), without challenging the position of single homeless people more generally as a residual group within the British welfare system – denied the same rights to social housing afforded homeless families (Fitzpatrick et al., 2000). In the first instance at least, the RSI also applied only to central London: where the problems of street homelessness were both most visible and most politically damaging. Importantly, responsibility for delivering the emergency shelters and smaller number of 'move-on' units made available through the RSI fell not to the local state (as was the case for homeless families) but to non-statutory organizations. Indeed, while local authorities played a limited role in coordinating bids for RSI funding on behalf of the non-statutory agencies operating in their areas, they were otherwise little involved in the programme – with the regulation of these organizations passing directly to central government via the DoE. At the same time, though operating under a system of Compulsory Competitive Tendering meant that the DoE showed a basic concern with value-for-money, it otherwise imposed only very 'thin' forms of regulatory control upon organizations bidding for RSI money, with agencies required to provide evidence as to the existence of suitable outreach or resettlement programmes, or of their attempts to engage in joint working with other agencies in their local area, for example, only in the later phases of the initiative.

While the launch of the RSI might well be read as signalling a move beyond an earlier position of 'malign neglect', then, in the light of their fail-ure to reverse the cuts in the supply of social housing initiated in the 1980s, or even to provide for a significant supply of 'move-on' rather than only emergency accommodation, it is clear that the initiative was hardly repre-sentative of a genuine attempt by the British government to solve the prob-lems of single homelessness. Instead, it is perhaps most usefully seen as an exercise in *containment*, designed to render the crisis of street homelessness less visible even as it did little to address the root causes of that crisis. Significantly, exactly this charge was levelled at the government by Britain's homeless pressure groups, as indeed by a number of the organizations con-tracted to supply accommodation under the RSI, a number of whom accused the DoE of overseeing a warehousing exercise (*Guardian*, 1990).

Furthermore, from the outset, organizations such as Centrepoint, Shelter, CHAR and Crisis also voiced concerns over what appeared to be a second arm of government policy. Following the failure of Phase 1 of the RSI to significantly reduce levels of rough sleeping in key areas of central London, for example, in August 1991 the DoE called upon Britain's homeless chari-ties to work with the Metropolitan Police to clear what they termed a 'hard core' of rough sleepers from a number of the capital's 'black spots'. When these requests were turned down, the police embarked upon clearance campaigns of their own, increasing the number of people arrested under the power of Britain's Vagrancy Acts from 192 in 1991 to 1445 in 1992 in central London alone (*Independent*, 1992). As the 1990s wore on the government's position towards street homeless people grew more hostile. In May 1994, for example, John Major launched a stinging verbal attack on Britain's 'homeless' beggars, and in September of the same year the then Secretary to the Treasury Peter Lilley called for the suspension of benefit payments to people selling the street newspaper the *Big Issue*. Significantly, however, the right-wing tabloid press notwithstanding (*Daily Express*, 1994; *Daily Mail*, 1994), as the government sought to further demonize homeless people by conflating the problems of homelessness with street crime and begging, public opinion increasingly turned against the government (*Guardian*, 1994; *Observer*, 1994). Such attacks also significantly soured relationships between central government and the non-statutory agencies charged with the task of delivering central government policy.

With the benefit of hindsight the launch of the RSI and associated street clearance campaigns can quite easily be read as articulating a shift from roll-back to roll-out neoliberalism, as first the Thatcher and then the Major government sought ways of containing a crisis of street homelessness that had its roots in an earlier period of economic restructuring and welfare 'reform'. But it is also clear that this attempt at containment was remarkably ineffective. Having failed to dampen public sympathy for homeless people, and soured relationships with the non-statutory organizations charged with delivering their policies, successive Conservative administrations also failed to significantly reduce the number of people sleeping rough. By the time that New Labour came to power in May 1997, for example, some 2000 or so people remained on the streets of central London, and countless hundreds of others in towns and cities across the country (Brown et al., 1996).

The Homelessness Action Programme

As one of the most obvious symbols of social exclusion, street homelessness was always going to be afforded a high priority by a government pledging a return to a more cohesive society (Fitzpatrick et al., 2000; Jones & Johnsen, 2009). In this sense, it was hardly surprising when almost immediately on gaining office in 1997 the New Labour government announced a series of measures designed to tackle a continuing crisis of rough sleeping, with an extension of the previous administration's RSI (1997–9) and the launch of its own *Homelessness Action Programme* (HAP) (1999–2002). Where the former had (finally) provided funding to just seven towns and cities outside of London identified as having especially high levels of street homelessness, the latter extended central government funding to no fewer than 113 towns and cities across the UK – at a total cost of some £134 million. At the same time, working through the auspices of the newly created *Rough Sleepers Unit*

(RSU), New Labour also promised to transform the apparatus by which problems of rough sleeping might be managed. Most importantly, from the outset New Labour looked towards the creation of closer relations between central government and the non-statutory organizations responsible for the delivery of care and accommodation to single homeless people: part and parcel of the move towards 'active partnership' formalized in the government's Compacts with the voluntary sector (Home Office, 1998). Eased by the appointment of the ex Deputy Director of Shelter, Louise Casey, as the head of the government's RSU and first homelessness 'tsar', Britain's major pressure groups thus began to play a far more active role in the shaping of government policy, feeding in to discussions around the new Homelessness Bill as well as the design of the HAP itself.

Under the HAP, new contracts drawn up under a system of Best Value (the successor to the Conservative's Compulsory Competitive Tendering) sought to correct the shortcomings of the RSI by imposing far stricter conditions upon agencies bidding for government money: shifting the focus from simple value-for-money to a much closer concern with modes of service delivery. In particular, agencies bidding for HAP monies were now required to demonstrate their active engagement with other organizations working with single homeless people in their local area (through membership of local street service consortia, for example); the existence of suitable outreach and resettlement programmes; and, crucially, their focus upon the specific problems of rough sleeping rather than problems of single homelessness more generally (DETR, 2000).

Underpinning these new contractual arrangements were new technologies of monitoring and control, designed to ensure that agencies fulfilled their contractual obligations. Most importantly, perhaps, participating agencies found themselves facing new performance targets that required them to demonstrate a reduction in levels of rough sleeping (assessed via repeated street counts) and a measurable through-put of clients into move-on accommodation. Undermining the notion of an equal partnership with central government, then, voluntary organizations in receipt of HAP funding soon found themselves increasingly subject to what Hoggett (1994) has called control by 'remote control': as new contractual arrangements and performance indicators tied participating agencies ever closer to the approach demanded of them by the RSU. At the same time, and moving somewhat beyond this notion of 'control at a distance', the RSU sought to extend its physical presence, seconding local authority officers in those cities in receipt of a significant proportion of HAP monies to chair the various consortia established to facilitate local joint working. Bringing together both those currently in receipt of central government funding and, crucially, those who might wish to apply for funding in the future, such consortia represented a significant extension of central government power. Not least, while always able to threaten a withdrawal of funding, the real success of the

RSU in this regard was to alter the terms of debate at the local level. With agencies that rejected the approaches of the RSU quickly finding themselves labelled unhelpful or 'unprofessional', and cast outside the loop of future funding opportunities, alternative approaches to the management of rough sleeping became if not unthinkable then certainly difficult to articulate (Anonymous, 2001).

At the same time, the new regulatory regimes introduced under the auspices of the RSU were further complicated by a complex *rescaling* of responsibilities for the purchase and control of services for single homeless people from central to local government. Though through the course of the HAP service delivery agencies remained subject to regulation by central government (in the form of the RSU), with the passage of the Homelessness Act 2002 responsibility for these services passed to local authorities charged with the task of implementing a *Local Homelessness Strategy* (ODPM, 2003). With the implementation of the *Supporting People Programme* the service charge element of the Housing Benefits system (which had been paid direct to service agencies) was replaced by funding from the Supporting People Programme. Under the latter programme agencies providing care and accommodation to vulnerable groups (including but not limited to single homeless people) bid for core funding from the local state, which in turn must present a case to central government for the amount of funding to be made available each period.* Crucially, though subject to a general needs assessment (the number of people found sleeping rough in their local area, for example) the allocation of Supporting People funds also depends upon the past performance of each authority (including any reduction in levels of rough sleeping through the period of the HAP) and plans for future spending, as laid out in its Local Homelessness Strategy. Hence, through the course of the HAP both service agencies and local authorities found themselves playing a complicated game. For the former, while it was important to stay on side with the RSU (to safeguard current funding arrangements) it was also necessary to maintain strong relations with the local state (lest they jeopardize future income opportunities under Supporting People). For the latter, while seeking to ensure the compliance of local agencies with performance targets set by the RSU (so as not to jeopardize future funding allocations under Supporting People) local authorities also found themselves having to tread a careful path with key non-statutory agencies upon whose advice and expertise they often had to rely in preparing their Local Homelessness Strategies.

---

* Importantly, Supporting People funding was ringfenced until 2009, but will be subsumed within local authorities' general-use Area Based Grant from 20 October 2011. While this could potentially lend greater flexibility to the way housing-related support services are provided, there are some concerns in the sector that it could potentially divert funding away from homelessness to other uses (Communities and Local Government, 2008b).

Finally, complementing this reworking of the relationships between central and local government and their voluntary sector 'partners', New Labour also worked hard at transforming public understandings of street homelessness and of street homeless people. Most significantly, in place of the crude attacks on homeless people perpetuated by the Major government, New Labour sought to reconstruct understandings of street homelessness within the broader context of their approach to problems of social exclusion – focusing upon the rights but also (and increasingly) the responsibilities of homeless people to confront the causes of their own exclusion. Hence, in his forward to the initial report on rough sleeping by the Social Exclusion Unit, for example, Prime Minister Tony Blair outlined the government's compact with those still on the streets. Setting their right to access a more extensive shelter system against their responsibility (to both welfare providers and a wider public alike) to take up the offer of accommodation, he noted that: '[while] the Government believes the public will expect hostel places to be taken up as more become available ... the police have [also] often said they would be willing to take a more directive approach with rough sleepers if there was somewhere to take them and a more co-ordinated approach' (quoted in Fitzpatrick et al., 2000).

In contrast to other areas of welfare, however, New Labour also sought to outline the counter side of this compact: setting out the responsibilities of a wider public in tackling the problems of street homelessness. In a powerful example of 'governing by culture', New Labour thus sought to remind the public of their duty to care for street homeless people (see, for example, 'Be a buddy to the homeless, says Blair', (*Daily Mail*, 1998); 'Blair urges public to be "buddies" to homeless' (*Daily Telegraph*, 1998)). Going further, in its *Change a Life* (2000) campaign the RSU sought to define the 'right and proper' mode of caring: urging those who wished to ease the plight of home-less people to give to a number of nominated charities rather than direct to people on the streets. Importantly, even while it conflated the problems of rough sleeping with the problem of begging, one of the most notable aspects of the Change a Life campaign was the limited criticism it attracted from those working in the field (Fitzpatrick & Kennedy, 2001). Certainly, where similar such moves by the previous Conservative government had quickly attracted the wrath of Britain's main homelessness pressure groups, Change a Life generated little overt criticism from organizations that seemed loath to publicly criticize the RSU lest they jeopardize their ability to influence government thinking on forthcoming legislation: notably, the then forth-coming Homelessness Act (Shelter, 2002).

Tracing the development of the RSI and HAP, then, it is not difficult to read key differences between the two programmes as articulating a number of the features that Ling identifies in his reading of a shift from a system of 'governance' to 'governmentality' (Ling, 2000). Rather than understanding such a shift as counter to the chronology proposed by Peck and Tickell

(2002), however, it may be more instructive to read it as indicating a second, more powerful articulation of the move to a programme of roll-out neoliberalism. While such a programme was initiated by the RSI and associated street clearance campaigns under the Thatcher and Major governments, it clearly accelerated under New Labour, as the government attempted to find *new* ways to confront and contain a still visible crisis of street homelessness that has its roots in an earlier period of economic restructuring and welfare 'reform'.

Revanchist Neoliberalisms?

But, to what extent can these periods of governance really be understood in terms of the conceptual frameworks presented by revanchism and neoliberalization? A definitive answer to this question is extremely difficult on a number of counts, but principally because of the problems endemic in untangling theory-led neo-Marxist critiques from the possibility of well intentioned (and context-specific) progressive government policy-making. From the former perspective, any attempt to provide welfare relief to homeless people within contemporary systems of governance is easily dismissed as irrelevant tinkering within a flawed and inevitably regressive collusion between capital and the state. By this token it would be extremely difficult, if not impossible, to recognize anything other than punitive techniques of control and containment of homeless people in Britain over the past 15 years. All else may easily be dismissed as mere legitimation. In terms of the potential for more progressive political intentions, how do we begin to recognize an empowering politics of social welfare in these circumstances, when possibly laudable objectives of eradicating homelessness by providing appropriate care, welfare and rehabilitation in specialized facilities (night shelters, hostels and 'move-on' housing) are in practice extremely difficult to disentangle from more sinister ideologies involving the clearance of homeless people from public spaces and thereby the annihilation of the active homeless subject?

We want to argue that such complexities are part and parcel of the multifaceted layers of governance in operation in the welfare sector, and that narratives of responses to homelessness must always be kept open to these multiple and overlapping interpretations. It is clear to us, for example, that the *rationale* for neoliberal governance was significantly different in the New Labour era – in the early years of the administration at least (see below) – than in the era preceding it. This difference is manifest in the rhetoric associated with 'dealing with' homeless subjectivities:

> I think we've been through a period where too many people have been given to understand that if they have a problem, it's the government's job to cope with it. 'I have a problem, I'll get a grant.' 'I'm homeless, the government must

house me.' They're casting their problem on society. And you know, there is no such thing as society. (Margaret Thatcher, *Women's Own Magazine*, 3 October 1987)

The sight of a rough sleeper bedding down for the night in a shop doorway or on a park bench is one of the most potent symbols of social exclusion in Britain today. (Tony Blair, Social Exclusion Unit, 1998: foreword)

Social exclusion is an extreme consequence of what happens when people don't get a fair deal throughout their lives. (Social Exclusion Task Force, 2007: http://www.cse.cabinetoffice.gov.uk/getDynamicContentAreaSection. do?id=15, accessed 9 June 2009)

The deep-seated hostility of the Conservative government to the collectivist nature of the welfare state is evident in the highly politicized framing of deviant homeless people as a problem of welfare dependency (Carlen, 1996). The rationale deployed by New Labour is quite different. For New Labour homelessness is understood as part of broader processes of social exclusion; hence the government's determination to provide support that enables homeless people to reach a 'level playing field' with the rest of society (Pleace, 1998; Deacon, 2000). While cognizant of critiques of the construction of 'social exclusion' drawn upon by New Labour (with its focus on opportunity rather than redistribution, and the reduction of 'inclusion' to inclusion in a (highly polarized) labour market; Levitas, 2007), we would nonetheless argue that the concept of social exclusion underpinning New Labour's rationale for welfare provision more broadly is also evident in its approach to the governance of homelessness; and that this drive to combat social exclusion is difficult to square with a characterization of New Labour's response to homelessness as being only (or even mainly) revanchist. Instead, this rationale has embraced (or at least provided space for) an ethics of welfare and care, sponsored new subjectivities of third sector involvement and volunteering, and provided a new emphasis on the prevention of homelessness. Moreover, on the face of it at least, these policies have been remarkably successful in reducing levels of rough sleeping (though see Pawson, 2007).

However, there are three immediate and important caveats to this evaluation. First, as we explore in chapters 5 and 6, the apparatus put in place by New Labour in an effort to tackle problems of homelessness and social exclusion has in some instances been damaging to the voluntary sector 'partners' New Labour has turned to in an attempt to prosecute its policies and, ultimately, to the welfare of homeless people themselves. Most obviously, New Labour's insistence on the introduction of the market, and the disciplining technologies of performance targets, into the homelessness sector has in some regards undermined the work of service agencies. Such agencies must now compete one with another to secure funding, with the terms of competition set around a number of targets (the speed with which a person is taken from the streets, through a day centre and hostel into 'supported accommodation' of their own, for example) that might in fact hamper the chances of a person making a successful exit from homelessness. In short, while in a broader sense the 'actually existing neoliberalism' articulated by New Labour homelessness policy may have opened up a space for an alternative ethics of care, the insistence of New Labour in running homeless welfare provision along neoliberal lines has simultaneously undermined such an ethic.

Second, as we explore in chapter 6 and as other reports on the challenges still facing British homelessness policy confirm (see, for example, the Salvation Army, 2008), it is clear that this apparatus may in any case not be as coherent, or effective, as has been claimed. There is now considerable evidence, for example, that the target-driven culture introduced by New Labour encouraged the engineering of artificially low counts of the rough sleeping population (Cloke et al., 2001a; Shapps, 2007). Furthermore, continuing shortages of rehabilitation facilities for homeless people with alcohol and drug dependencies, and of affordable and supported move-on housing, mean that the 'helping hand' put in place by New Labour often leads only to the 'warehousing' of homeless people in hostels – a phenomenon that invites critique as part of a punitive politics of containment.

Third, and relatedly, it is clear that the rationale underpinning New Labour's homeless policy has changed in recent years. As Johnsen and Fitzpatrick (2007, 2010) have documented, with the winding down of the HAP in 2002–3, the focus of government began to change from a concern with the provision of services for homeless people to the control of the 'conduct of conduct' of homeless people. In a telling shift in departmental responsibilities, for example, in 2003 the Home Office's Anti-Social Behaviour Unit took up the issue of 'problem street culture' – advocating the use of Anti-Social Behaviour Orders (ASBOs) against those who 'persistently' beg. The same year also saw begging made a recordable offence in Britain for the first time. To some extent, a certain intolerance of those who 'chose' to remain on the streets (rather than take advantage of the services on offer to them through the auspices of the HAP) was always evident in the approach of the RSU, as Blair's foreword to the unit's inaugural report into the problems of street homelessness in 1998 made clear, and as we document in relation to the criticisms directed towards Britain's soup runs in chapter 4. But it is also clear that the past few years have seen a strengthening of the government's resolve to take 'control of the streets'. Moreover, it would appear that the harder line taken by central government against members of a 'problematic' street population has often found support at the local level and chimes with broader changes in the policing of public space in Britain's city centres over the past few years, when the growth in, for example, Business Improvement Districts has seen the reshaping of Britain's town centres around the logic of 'apodictic' spaces (Ruddick, 1996: 198) – spaces in which forms of privileged inclusion (built around retail and consumption) effectively dictate the exclusion of any attempts by homeless people to appropriate those spaces for their own use (see also Doherty et al., 2008).

If the *rationale* of New Labour's neoliberal governance suggests complexity in the understanding of responses to homelessness, then so too does the making up of homeless *subjectivities* under this regime. To some extent, the neoliberal homeless subject varies according to its status as 'insider' or 'outsider' *vis-à-vis* the systems of response provided. That is, homeless people who are brought inside these systems, either at preventative stages or as part of the newly joined-up governance of rough sleeping, can become part of the supposed success-narrative of rehabilitation. This subject position is easily represented in terms of prevailing cultures of targets achieved and cleaned up streets, even if the acting subjects involved may lead more messy lives – sometimes articulating something more akin to a revolving door existence than any genuine 'rehabilitation' or 'reintegration' into 'mainstream' society. However, many homeless people fall outside of these response systems, and are thereby attributed made-up subjectivities that reflect their outsider status. Alongside the criminalization and victimization of (some) homeless people discussed here, there are also a range of 'invisible' homeless subjectivities in play in the contemporary city: those who do not meet statutory criteria for acceptance as homeless, those who choose not to declare themselves as homeless, those – such as asylum seekers – who by definition are prevented from being regarded as homeless, and so on.

There is an interesting parallel here, of course, with the subject-status given to non-statutory organizations providing welfare services for homeless people. As we detail in chapters 4, 5 and 6, organizations working in partnership with government (and thereby viewed as 'fit' for inclusion in governance at a distance) are granted at least a temporary legitimacy in terms of their apparent professionalism and suitability to engage in the wider responsibilities of citizenship. These insider organizations can be contrasted with those working outside of partnerships with government, who often rely on charitable giving and volunteer labour and are thus often less well placed to provide a high standard of specialist service. Some such outsider organizations are often subjectified as deviant and unprofessional because their activities involve serving homeless people on the streets, and therefore effectively oppose government-led orthodoxies geared towards removing homeless people from sight. Actually existing neoliberalism, then, works in parallel to enact ethical codes and subjectivities of welfare for compliant insiders while imposing more punitive codes of deviancy on uncompliant outsiders.

Finally, any reading of British homelessness policy as revanchist neoliberalism also needs to take account of the uneven geographies that form around the reach and capacity of government to affect the conduct of conduct, and around the construction of these parallel insider/outsider subjectivities. Thus, rather than asserting some kind of 'total capture' of the homeless welfare apparatus by central government, we show in chapters 7 and 8 how actually existing neoliberalism leads to the unfolding of different responses to homelessness in different places. For example, there are many smaller towns where there has been a growing crisis of street homelessness, but where voluntary sector organizations have been unable to draw upon the central government funds made available to (some) providers in larger towns and cities in an effort to meet that crisis. At the same time, local homeless service networks in many larger towns and cities are characterized by a range of both 'insider' and 'outsider' organizations – those who have taken the money and, by and large, signed up to the service contracts dictated by the HAP or Supporting People, and those who have either been excluded from or excluded themselves from both this money and these contracts. And there are individual paid staff and volunteers inside these 'insider' organizations who continue to frustrate the efforts of network managers – by refusing to ration hostel beds in accordance with the demands of local homelessness strategies, for example. The neoliberalization of British homelessness policy therefore needs to be understood with full reference to the complexities of 'hollowing out' and the continuing and significant limits to state power even in an era of roll-out neoliberalism, and to the ways in which state power itself becomes transformed in practice by both insider and outsider organizations, paid staff, volunteers and homeless people.

An Emerging Context of Postsecularism

Thus far, our exploration of responses to homelessness in Britain has been restricted to ideas that prioritize and valorize the ability of the state either to engineer punitive mechanisms of containment and control in order to protect the interests of capital and powerful social elites, or to use political and cultural regulation to influence the 'conduct of conduct' of homeless people, homeless service providers and wider publics in an effort to tackle (particular constructions of) homelessness. In both cases we have expressed the need for caution in accepting wholesale any notion that the actions of the state are without limits, and to take full account of the geographical unevenness and/or susceptibility of state policy to transformation and resistance from the individuals and organizations that populate its insider and outsider subject positions. We now want to expand these conceptual horizons in such a way as to take more significant account of the importance of emergent geographies of care in the landscapes of homeless service provision. In particular we want to explore the place that the motivational forces of ethical citizenship that often underpin such services might play in our understandings of recent responses to homelessness.

The growing role of government/third sector 'partnerships' in the delivery of welfare has tended to be interpreted either in terms of the emergence of some kind of 'shadow state' apparatus (Wolch, 1990) or, more recently, as evidence of the incorporation of third sector organizations into programmes of governance that further state ideology and neoliberal techniques of subject formation (Beckford, 2003; Davie, 2007). There are, however, other interpretative possibilities to add into this mix. Most obviously, recent years have seen increasing interest in the idea that previous stereotypical binaries of public secularism and private religion are being reshaped, particularly in the field of urban welfare. For some, this 'postsecular rapprochement' represents a moving away from the fundamentalisms of secularism and religion and a moving into new forms of collaborative ethical praxis capable of fashioning new geographies of welfare and care in the urban environment (Farnell et al., 2003; Baker, 2007; Taylor, 2007; Beaumont, 2008; Berger et al., 2008; Scott et al., 2009). If so, there is an intriguing possibility that these postsecular movements may be co-constituting different spaces and forms of resistance to the rolling out of neoliberalism, both from within and without formal positions of government/third sector partnership.

Beyond Secularism

Put crudely, our suggestion is that there may be connections between this broader postsecular rapprochement and the crucial role that faith-based organizations (FBOs) and faith-motivated people in particular continue to play in the provision of welfare services, and associated logics of care and compassion, for homeless people in Britain. There are a number of ways in which this postsecular reapproachment might be traced, of course. One way would simply be to note the increasingly prominent role that FBOs are now playing in urban social welfare provision more generally (Beaumont, 2008; Dinham et al., 2009). In fact, in the homelessness sector this role is hardly new, with organizations like the Salvation Army testament to the work of FBOs in this field for more than a century. Indeed, it might even be the case that through the 1970s and early 1980s at least the relative importance of FBOs in this field declined, as the emergence of a number of new secular organizations such as Shelter and the Simon Community was inspired in part by a desire to challenge the approach to the accommodation and care of homeless people then articulated by more traditional, faith-based, organizations (Foord et al., 1998). Yet it is also clear that the very rapid growth in the number of non-statutory organizations engaged in such work in the 1980s and 1990s also included many new FBOs; that FBOs are currently strongly represented in the provision of services for homeless people and are in fact the dominant group in some sectors, such as soup runs (see chapters 4, 5 and 6; Johnsen with Fitzpatrick, 2009).

Another way would be to point to other new and rather different kinds of interconnection between faith and secular interests. For example, faith groups have been shown to act as umbrella organizations for different kinds of collaborative activity, motivated by secular social justice ideals as well as by faith. This umbrella function certainly occurs (as we shall see) in the provision of services for homeless people, but other examples include the promotion of fair trade and other aspects of ethical consumption (Cloke et al., 2009). Sometimes such partnerships form around ethical positionings in which secular and faith-motivated ideologies converge, as in the holistic approach to serving homeless people, and in responding to the needs of distant others through consumption of fairly traded goods. Elsewhere, for example in the work of organizations like London Citizens, faith-based and secular organizations that bring very different ethical and moral positionings to the table are coming together under the auspices of secular umbrella organizations and agreeing to put such differences 'on hold' in order to make common cause on specific demands – for a living wage, or the regularization of migrants, for example (Wills et al., 2009a).

Finally, we might point to more complex changes in the ethos of different welfare organizations. Thus, in chapters 4 and 5, for example, we demonstrate how some secular organizations involved in running day centres and soup runs have begun to embrace an ethos of holistic care that might previously have been considered as rooted in the principles of Christian faith. In contrast, throughout this book we offer examples of how many Christian organizations in the homelessness sector have moved away from any attempt to use service provision as an opportunity for evangelistic conversion and to offer instead a 'service without strings'; an approach that can perhaps be equally convincingly read as articulating a particular form of caring for others rooted in Christian belief (and in particular, the concept of agape) or as rooted in approaches to the care of others more commonly associated with secular ways of serving.

In the remainder of this chapter we explore this emerging context of postsecularism in two main ways. First, in conceptual terms we trace shifts in *reflexivity* and *praxis* that underpin these new postsecular spaces. Critiques of secularism have led thinkers and actors into new engagements with, and explorations of, ethical frameworks and actions that are more tolerant – even welcoming of – aspects of religion and faith in circumstances previously assumed to be secular. Here, homelessness has served as a highly visible example of the inability of secularist ethics alone to prevent or deal with social exclusion in contemporary society, and the serving and caring for homeless people has emerged as a key arena in which postsecular praxis has developed. Second, we investigate the ethos of organizations providing services for homeless people, tracing signs of the emergence of a postsecular ethics in these service spaces.

The ebb and flow of secularism

Many of the key aspects that underpin the contemporary movement beyond secularism are charted in Blond's (1998) disquieting critique of the principally secular basis of public society and space. First, he claims that secularism has permitted religion to be sequestrated by fundamentalist elements, who – in what Hedges (2006) regards as a form of fascism – have demonstrated a dangerous capacity to ostracize and condemn 'others' who are variously deemed unworthy of moral consideration. A move towards postsecularism therefore represents an exploration of the possibilities of mutual acceptance of social difference, and mutual acceptance of and respect across the secular/religious divide, thus undermining religious fundamentalists, but also requiring recognition from secular groups of the potential value of non-fascist spirituality. Second, secular narratives have often assumed that the kinds of advances achieved by science can be reproduced in ethical and political fields, especially those related to welfare. Blond asserts that a secularism based upon the individualist and market-orientated politics of contemporary political economy can, unless referenced against other codes of morality and ethics (relating, say, to justice, community and mutual responsibility), simply valorize selfishness, individual acquisitiveness and a more general punitive blaming of social victims such as homeless people for their own plight. A more postsecular approach, therefore, is likely to espouse a going-beyond-the-self, and to find more communitarian routes to tackling ethical issues. Third, secularism has been at least partly responsible for producing a vacuum of hopelessness in a society that is becoming characterized by myriad self-serving acts of denial and negation that have served as the weak mysticism of the age. The ideological narratives of neoliberalized governmentalities of state and market have spawned a society that often seems shot through with cynicism and lack of hope – resulting in pessimistic doubts about whether people can change things or make a difference, and a loss of capacity to participate, be inspired or enchanted (Bennett, 2001). As Blond points out, secularism has implied a broad disavowal of any possibility that social melancholia and desperation can be dealt with in any way that could transfigure individuals and their world. Postsecularism by contrast invites a going beyond what is rational and immediately visible in order to explore the possibilities of the invisible in whatever form.

This reflexive territory of postsecularism is evident in how some of the key thinkers of materialist socialism have been drawn to ideas from the contexts of religion and faith in their search for a renewed sense of justice and hope in contemporary society. This is not to suggest that Marxist atheists are suddenly converting to religion, but rather that the philosophical search for answers to the questions posed by secularized individualism has been attracted towards implicit horizons of faith and belief, albeit in a rather fragmented and partial manner. Thus, Habermas (2002) and Matustik (2008) have emphasized the emergence of a postsecular society in which secular institutions have been infused with varying forms of spiritual prompts to politics and ethics, and other leading socialist philosophers have begun to invoke theological precepts in order to visualize appropriate philosophies of hope. As Milbank (2005: 398) has put it:

> Derrida sustains the openness of signs and the absoluteness of the ethical command by recourse to … negative theology; Deleuze sustains the possibility of a deterritorialisation of matter and meaning in terms of a Spinozistic virtual absolute; Badiou sustains the possibility of a revolutionary event in terms of the one historical event of the arrival of the very logic of the event as such, which is none other than that of Pauline grace; Žižek sustains the possibility of a revolutionary love beyond desire by reference to the historical emergence of the ultimate sublime object, which reconciles us to the void constituted only through a rift in the void. This sublime object is Christ.

These kinds of philosophical attempts to re-form the foundations on which future socialism might be built are drawing on idealist visions but also on a range of what might be regarded as 'theo-ethics' (Cloke, 2009) of otherness, grace, love and hope that constitute an excess beyond material logic and rationale. Thus, both Žižek (2001) and Badiou (2001), for example, express anxiety that contemporary concerns for 'otherness' often result in other social groups (such as homeless people) being kept at a geographical and representational distance, attributed the role at best of victim and at worst of criminal, and observed too often through a societal lens of moral detachment and ethical indifference. In contrast, theo-ethical collaborations between philosophy and theology invoke a call to love that involves 'the mutual recognition of our positive realizations and capacities' (Milbank, 2005: 399), and have begun to offer prospects for envisaging equality with difference through an ontological lens of faith, hope and charity. Moreover, these ideas are not confined to any particular organizational form or expectation of specific belief. For Derrida (1996) the appeal is to a postmodern, nomadic form of theology that involves a deconstructive grasp of religiosity that represents a radical departure from traditional religious movements. Alternatively, for Žižek (2001) Christianity presents the framework for an idealist materialism.

We want to suggest that both of these philosophical traces are becoming evident in emergent postsecular spaces associated with homelessness in the city. Indeed, we want to suggest that neoliberalism itself has opened up spaces and opportunities for an enactment of this movement beyond secularism in the political arena, and that in particular the deployment of neo-liberalizing technologies and the potential for a recasting of appropriate subjectivities have enabled the establishment of postsecular footholds in the city. Most obviously, the age of neoliberal governance has released a resurgence of faith-based activity into the public sphere (see Beaumont, 2008; Beaumont & Dias, 2008; Cloke et al., 2008) as the disappearance or contracting out of services previously provided by the state has created opportunities for faith-groups to fill the gap, with the result that FBOs have become increasingly influential as part of the wider incorporation of third sector organizations into the arenas of welfare policy and practice, including (and especially perhaps) homelessness.

While we recognize that for some the concept of 'incorporation' is suggestive of a tendency for FBOs to forsake their theo-ethics and independence in order to take on their role in the (neoliberal) state apparatus, we want to explore the possibility that such incorporation also allows an infiltration of these very theo-ethics and postsecular possibilities into the public arena. Thus, our analysis of New Labour's Compacts with the third sector, for example, suggests that these Compacts went beyond a desire simply to offload the responsibilities (and resources) for welfare provision from the state to third sector providers, and involved instead a recognition of and genuine commitment to the apparent strengths of these groups, including FBOs, in terms of local awareness, expertise, creativity and capacity to care. Furthermore, by establishing (some) third sector agencies as appropriate and 'fit' partners in governmentality, such Compacts opened up the possibility that the theo-ethical perspectives held by some of these organizations might be introduced into government and a wider public; promoting practices of charity and care and a renewed culture of active community.

Of course, we would also note that any such formal introduction of a theo-ethics very often leads to conflict in a context where the tendering process at both national and local levels remains suffused with secularist attitudes. Thus, as we show in chapter 5, for example, many local authorities clearly remain suspicious of, if not openly hostile towards, FBOs operating in the homelessness sector – mainly because of a fear that such organizations have not yet renounced the desire to proselytize. Questions also remain over whether the willingness of other local authorities to work with FBOs is representative of a new recognition of the additional and intrinsic values that a faith-based approach brings to the work that such organizations do, and the care they offer to homeless people, or a more cynical requisition of the resources (infrastructure, expertise and – volunteer as well as paid – labour) FBOs can offer the local state.

These questions notwithstanding, it is clear that within a new neoliberal framework of governance, FBOs now play a prominent role in different areas of welfare provision, especially for homeless people. Moreover, despite the very real risk that the incorporation of FBOs into such a system will reduce their ability to protest against that system, there is also evidence (see Cloke et al., 2008) that in some sectors at least FBOs have developed significant roles in related capacity building, lobbying and political protest. Thus Lowndes and Chapman (2005), for example, suggest that such groups

have significant motivational linkages to their communities, and are more
generally seeking to translate normative religious values into ethical impulses
of love, joy, peace, charity, equality and so on, which can then be harnessed
in areas of welfare, community cohesion and ethical citizenship. FBOs can
also be recognized as some of the last remaining islands of social capital in
some urban communities (Baker & Skinner, 2006) and bring potential
resources (buildings, volunteers, social leadership and so on) to bear in local
welfare activity.

Our argument here, then, is not that FBOs have suddenly introduced
wholesale new values and ways of working into the welfare system. Clearly,
involvement in partnerships of governance may well dilute or force into the
background the very theo-ethical faith motivations that formed the basis of
their existence. FBOs can find themselves locked into centrally controlled
ways of operating, becoming 'insider' organizations by accepting government funding, along with the strings attached to that funding, and in so
doing they can find that their ethos and their character can change.
Alternatively, FBOs can operate as outsider organizations, working on shoestring budgets and relying heavily on volunteers, and thus finding themselves dismissed as amateur players in the new professionalized world of
service provision. We do argue, however, that the foothold established by
FBOs in the field of urban welfare, and homelessness in particular, offers
two kinds of postsecular possibility.

First, although organizations can be incorporated into neoliberal governmentalities, individuals within those organizations are often less bound into
the technologies and ideologies of these governmentalities, while the very
presence of FBOs permits new ways of performatively bringing care and
welfare into being at ground level (see also Conradson, 2003). Thus new
spaces of care can emerge out of seemingly incorporated partnership.
Second, as well as at the level of state and society, FBOs open out the possibility for local-level rapprochement between the secular and the religious.
Here, we refer to the ways in which faith-motivated organizations will often
come to form a nexus of participation that embraces a range of different
people with different motivations across the faith/non-faith divide. Spaces
of care can represent literal spaces of rapprochement, as people of many
faiths or none work alongside each other in particular projects of ethical
citizenship. These comings together may be pragmatic or deliberately collaborative, but they nevertheless open out possibilities of performatively
bringing the postsecular into being as previously divisive barriers between
secular and faith approaches are broken down. Such rapprochement
demands not only new respect for faith motivation among secular society,
but also a willingness among faith communities to embrace new forms of
postsecular faith-ethics, reflecting an 'overt metaphysical/religious pluralism' in public life so as to forge a 'positive engagement out of the multicultural plurality of contemporary life' (Connolly, 1999: 185). At the local

level, then, and perhaps in more aggregate form, this collaborative activity can lead to a shift in the state's 'secularist self-understanding' (de Vries, 2006: 3). Much, however, depends both on the willingness of secular groups to accept faith-based responses, and on the willingness of religious groups to embrace new forms of faith-motivated praxis, which can equally reach out across the divide between faith and the secular.

The ebb and flow of faith praxis

The idea of postsecular rapprochement suggests that there are new opportunities for faith groups to bring their own brands of salt, light, fragrance and flavour back into the heart of the polity provided that they too are willing to embrace the demands of postsecular faith-ethics in which virtue is placed in a new and positive relation to difference, such that faith-motivated service is characterized by the performance of caritas without strings (Coles, 1997) rather than by conversion-oriented evangelism. Here we illustrate the religious side of the postsecular rapprochement with reference to Christianity – currently the most prevelant religious influence in providing services for homeless people in Britain (Johnsen with Fitzpatrick, 2009). But we freely acknowledge that the multicultural nature of the contemporary city requires that discussion of the public positioning of faith needs to take account of a range of different religions, and of the various ways in which the fundamentalisms induced during the secular era have been transformed into wider, more plural, theo-ethics through which the punitive handling of social 'others' can be transformed into a more humane recognition of the needs of different groups of people. Christian adaptations to and for the post-secular are themselves also manifold, but we focus here on two particular attributes that help to define the Christian response to practising faith in post-Christendom in such a way as to contribute to the postsecular rapprochement and its critique of fundamentalism: the search for the hyperreal; and theology through praxis.

First, the search for the possibilities of what is *invisible* rather than visible has in part entailed a seeking out of aspects of faith, religion and spirituality that offer what Caputo (2001: 91) has termed the 'hyperreal' – a reality beyond the visible, extending out from the restricted range of possibilities recognized within modernity. Caputo has argued that the search for the hyperreal will be frustrated among what he describes as the all-knowing, God-substituting certainties of fundamentalist religion, and suggests that instead some faith-motivated people are embracing a more 'not-knowing' outlook to faith, involving endless translatability between God and love, beauty, justice and truth, in which worship is integrally interconnected with transformation – both of the individual worshipper, and of the society in which they are placed. In Caputo's terms, then, faith is an enactment – a leap of love into this hyperreality – and finds its shape in the contradiction and reversing of human and cultural drives, in drawing on invisible powers and being 'left hanging on a prayer for the impossible' (Caputo, 2001: 136). It is interesting how the critique of secularism in terms of an inability to grasp the invisible can be connected with a renewed interest in 'spiritual landscapes' (Dewsbury & Cloke, 2009) and the emergence of a new sense of sacred within the postsecular, to be found in

> anarchic effects produced by re-sacralizing the settled secular order, disturbing and disordering the disenchanted world, producing an anarchic chaosmos of odd brilliant disturbances, of gifts that spring up like magic in the midst of scrambled economies. (Caputo, 2006: 291; see also Bartley, 2006)

Moreover, when Caputo illustrates the enactment of these uncertain leaps of love into the hyperreal, he is drawn to the ways in which faith-motivated people serve the excluded and the marginalized:

> Religious people, the 'people of God', the people of the impossible, impassioned by a love that leaves them restless and unhinged … are impossible people. In every sense of the word. If, on any given day, you go into the worst neighbourhoods of the inner cities of most large urban centres, the people you will find there serving the poor and needy, expending their lives and considerable talents attending to the least amongst us, will almost certainly be religious people – evangelicals and Pentecostalists, social workers with deeply held religious convictions, Christian, Jewish and Islamic, men and women, priests and nuns, black and white. They are the better angels of our nature. They are down in the trenches, out on the streets, serving the widow, the orphan, and the stranger, while the critics of religion are sleeping in on Sunday mornings. (Caputo, 2001: 92)

Of course, this picture needs to be made realistic. Caputo also shows us how faith motivates people who are lovers of the impossible, and who will often be led to practise their passion in situations of social, economic or political need, but who in the process can become impossible people capable of imposing their knowledge of God on others, and in so doing potentially compromising the freedoms of people who disagree with them. However, his identification of an active search for the hyperreal seems to us to conjure up one of the forces that underlies the attractiveness of spirituality in key postsecular spaces, especially those spaces of service to disadvantaged people of whom those suffering homelessness have become iconic.

We need to emphasize here that there is much more to contemporary religion than a search for the hyperreal. Indeed, it would be foolish to minimize the huge diversity of theology, ritual and culture at work here. However, there is a second trend of some current religious practice that we believe is helping to contribute both to faith-motivated service in society and to the emergent conditions for postsecular spaces in cities. This is the growing importance of *praxis* as a central facet of the expression of faith. Oakley (2005) argues that an intrigue with the possibilities of the invisible will often be interconnected with an intrigue with the possibilities of ethical practice – many faith communities are realizing more than ever that theology per se is inaccessible without attention to the key practices that constitute and realize that theology (Hutter, 1997). As a result, some sections of the Christian church, for example, are becoming more radicalized by intentional forms of discipleship based on the theo-ethics of praxis. Dissatisfaction with how the church can be drawn into the worldliness of individual self-centredness, excess and unthinking consumerism, and uncaring globalization, has led some faith communities to live out a rediscovery of Jesus-values as self-imposed 'exiles' within the 'empire' of secularized political economy and culture. As Frost (2006) has argued, old-fashioned church cultures of respectability and conservatism remain, but some Christian communities – across the spectrum of denominations and settings – have become uncomfortable with these cultures and have embraced more radical forms of discipleship and pursued new agendas for 'exile' faith-praxis.

As we have discussed at length elsewhere (see Cloke, 2009), there is no clear pathway from these biblical foundations and understandings of Jesus-values to a particular ethics of contemporary praxis. Overrigid foundationalism can lead to tyrannical and dangerous fundamentalism, while extreme postmodernism can lead to uncompromising relativism. However, there is evidence that the formulation of contemporary faith practice is increasingly leaning on a mix of tradition and immanence in the form of virtue ethics. In philosophical terms, the contribution of faith-ethics to the postsecular compact is at least in part that 'the Christian mythos is able to rescue virtue from deconstruction into violent agnostic difference' (Milbank, 2006: 380). In practical terms, virtue has been placed in a new and positive relation to difference in order to validate liberty and equality. Christian charity is being reproduced as relational love and friendship, a gratuitous and creative practice of service without strings, rather than with proselytizing as the core purpose. This focus on the counter-ethics of duty, virtue and service means that faith-motivated practice – for example, in the provision of services for homeless people – becomes less exclusive and exclusionary, and opens up possibilities of joining with other ethically motivated groups of people in a common cause of service, once again enhancing the possibilities of emergent spaces of postsecular rapprochement.

We need to express two brief caveats here. First, we do not suggest that faith-motivation is somehow dumbed down by engagement in postsecular partnership. On the contrary, Christian theo-ethics of hope present particular imaginative manoeuvres – including the possibility of the prophetic, the possibility of engaging spiritual interiority and the possibility of alternative discernment (see Cloke, 2009) – that prompt particular illumination of current landscapes, practices and circumstances, and release particular poetics of resistance into postsecular rapprochements. These specificities can in some circumstances also continue to present an air of exclusivity that can hamper alliances with potential partners. Second, it would be erroneous to suggest that there is any homogeneous positioning of faith and faith groups in urban landscapes of postsecularism. Within the wide variety of faith-practice in the city, there will be many religious manifestations that have little to do with the possibilities of hyperreality, or of ethical and prophetic praxis, let alone the resacralizing of the settled order via anarchic disturbance. Indeed, outworkings of traditional fundamentalist faith within an emerging postsecular environment will quite correctly be subject to continuing wider critiques of fundamentalism in religion (see Herriot, 2008). Some faith groups, then, will not display the kind of 'no-strings' generosity and service that might otherwise mark them out as formative to a new and more postsecular way of working. So what we are pointing to here is a partial, uneven and variable possibility that faith-motivated groups will join with others in third spaces in the city where a common ground can be established in the pursuit of ethical ideals and practical service. While such rapprochements have existed in the past, they may now be more widespread and centrally positioned in the formal and informal landscapes of welfare provision in the city.

Postsecular Caritas and Serving Homeless People

We have explored the possibilities of emergent postsecular spaces in the city at some length because we believe that they point to a missing link in the conceptualization of contemporary homelessness in Britain. Any picture of vicious or uncaring control and containment of homeless people by political and social elites must be tempered by recognition of an opposing social and political urge to care for and serve homeless people in recognition of their plight as 'the least of these', as the most clearly indicative victims of the current societal malaise. Postsecularism begins to identify the reasons why individuals and organizations become involved in the task of caring for, or serving, homeless people, but further substantiation is required of the degree to which the motivations of ground-level service providers match with this postsecularization thesis. As an aid to this process of substantiation, we sought information from managers involved in running day centres and hostels for homeless people about the mission statements and motivational frameworks that applied to their organizations. A full account of this part of our project is provided elsewhere (Cloke et al., 2005), but here we summarize the findings in terms of how they reflect the components of a potential emergence of postsecular spaces.

It seems to us incontrovertible that non-statutory organizations are of crucial importance in the landscape of services for homeless people. It is equally clear from the materials sent to us that the involvement of these organizations, and of the professionals and volunteers associated with them, is undergirded by strong and deliberate statements of 'mission' or 'values'. Thus this crucial segment of welfare services can be seen as being upheld by organizations and individuals who, at least on the surface, are working with clear, but interestingly divergent, discourses of *ethos*, which present ethical bases for involvement and action.

In focusing on the ethos of organizations serving homeless people we are immediately aware of the potential pitfalls inherent in any universalist assumptions about accepting expressions of ethos at face value. Statements of ethos from organizations will be designed for external consumption, will attract widely varying levels of allegiance from staff and volunteers, and therefore will not necessarily be carried through into the spaces of care that are formed by the activities of the organizations and those who are served by them. Indeed, and as we show in chapter 4, there is considerable evidence of significant diversity between organizational mission statements, the reasons why individuals participate and the characteristics that shape an individual's day-to-day involvement. As Scott et al. (2000: 18) argue in the case of voluntary participation more generally:

> volunteering is a complex matter ... it may not even be very voluntary in many situations. The contingencies of how people become involved in voluntary groups, and stay involved or leave, are likely to be different in different circumstances and for different people. Volunteers are not all the same, and the immediate social context or milieu will also be different.

We are equally aware that statements of corporate positionality can only ever be a partial recognition or knowing of subjectivity (Rose, 1996), and may even represent a deliberate attempt to fashion an artificial and often flattering image of the self (Pile & Thrift, 1995), thus conjuring up moral rhetorics where in reality actions and affects may be more knowingly self-serving or instinctive. Nevertheless, we believe that the discourses of ethos presented by organizations providing services for homeless people both present important insights into contemporary charitable assemblages of ethics-at-work and more specifically present important articulations of how the 'self' of the service-provider relates to the 'other' of homeless people.

Recent ethical cartographies (for example, Sack, 1997; Proctor & Smith, 1999; Smith, 2000) have mapped out a range of moral terrains in which the self is related to the other in contexts such as providing services for homeless people. Such landscapes are waymarked by key differentials; for example, between caring 'about' and 'caring for', and between 'caring for locally' and 'caring at a distance'. To some extent, in what appears to some as a world of increasing self-preoccupation, issues of justice and ethical responsibility are brightly illuminated both by the suffering of the marginalized and oppressed and by evidence of responses to such suffering that demonstrate a 'going-beyond-the-self' (Cloke, 2002). Thus in the homelessness sector, it would seem that new forms of selfless responsibility, freedom and resistance are being expressed for the benefit and inclusion of homeless people in the form of recognizable collective action, fuelled by ideological, charitable, spiritual and volunteering motives.

However, such exhibitions of going-beyond-the-self can be subjected to a range of analytical interpretation. At one extreme the self–other relations involved can be viewed through the lens of what Allahyari (2000: 4) has termed 'moral selving'; that is, the work of 'creating oneself as a more virtuous, and often spiritual person'. In this way, what seems to be a going-beyond-the-self is more properly explained as a reinventing of the self, with resulting charitable effects. An alternative interpretative perspective is to regard charitable or caring involvements as a reasoned or instinctive reaching out beyond self-interest – what Augé (1998) terms a 'sense *for* the other' via an appreciation of otherness that is emotional, connected and committed. Any such sense for the other may involve attempts to achieve partnerships of solidarity via participation and involvement in the world of the other, as well as the establishment of spaces of care in which the other is expected to come into the world of the self. Gutierrez (1988: 73) has even suggested that this kind of going-beyond-the-self should be interpreted in terms of whether the self is attempting to convert the other into the world of the self, or whether the self is willing to be converted by the other, through a commitment 'to enter and in some cases remain in the universe of the poor with a much clearer awareness, making it a place of residence and not simply of work'. In other words, solidarity with the other may require a deprivation of some of the normal comforts of the self.

Drawing on Coles's (1997) rethinking of the politics of generosity, we conducted discourse analysis to examine organizational statements of ethos in terms of three ideal types – Christian caritas, secular humanism and postsecular charity – in an attempt to examine evidence of emergent postsecular spaces in the city. We looked at ethical discourses found in information provided by the surveyed organizations running 101 hostels and 48 day centres in England, Scotland and Wales, recognizing these not as a statistical sample (as there is considerable variation in the likelihood of different kinds of organization producing literature and publishing their ethos or mission statement), but as an indicative grouping demonstrating qualitative insight into the discourses concerned.

Christian caritas

In his exploration of the possibilities for an ethics and politics of what he calls 'receptive generosity', Coles argues that there have been two principal pathways to the ethical prompting of charity. The first stems from movements rooted in various forms of Christian religion that have acted out love (agape) and charity (caritas) as God-ordained principles and God-given gifts that provide a key ethical framework for living in the world of the self and the world of the other. Coles (1997: 2) characterizes these Christian roots thus:

> God is the very movement of *caritas* and *agape*, and these qualities infuse the being of his gift: namely, all of creation as the temporal elaboration of his word. We, of his loving gift, have been given his Son, who through the Gospels exemplifies the incarnation of *caritas* and teaches us how to receive God's love and in turn proliferate giving. To receive and follow this path, to faithfully interpret God's signs and love one's neighbour, is to 'be fruitful and multiply'. ... It is thus through receiving and giving that we participate in the unfolding of his gift and being, whereas to reject the flow of *caritas* is to tend towards nothingness.

The outworking of this theology of caritas can take many forms, and here we wish to highlight some frequent misunderstandings of terms such as proselytism and evangelism (see also chapter 4). FBOs are often accused of *proselytizing*, which we would define in terms of a strategic and tactical intention to convert the other into a new set of religious beliefs, rituals and practices. In fact, they might more accurately be analysed in terms of varying approaches to *evangelism*; that is, the sharing of the Christian faith. Evangelism can involve varying forms of relationships with service users, ranging from an overt emphasis on soul/spirit as essential facets in the practice of a regime of care, through an open sharing of a faith-motivation that explains involvement in service provision, to an outpouring of unconditional love and care – a living out of faith that produces 'service without strings'. Different strategies of evangelism and service are further complicated by cross-cutting variations in attitudes towards the causes of social problems, ranging from an emphasis on the individual's responsibility for their own situation to a focus on the structures that entrap the individual. To some extent the jumbling of the three categories of ethical impulse discussed by Coles means that using these categories as analytical frames is somewhat artificial. However, as Coles (1997: 5) himself recognizes, the contemporary charitable terrain is 'deeply permeated' by Christianity and modern autonomous subjectivity, and our surveys do demonstrate clear evidence of organizational mission statements that declare elements of Christian ethos. For example, 40 of the 101 hostels and 20 of the 48 day centres for which detailed information was available presented an unambiguous Christian basis for the service being provided.

In summary, we found that these discourses of Christian faith-in-action point to a significant and characteristic involvement in contemporary charity. It is clear that a considerable segment of the landscape of emergency services for homeless people is motivated by Christian caritas, and that charity is predominantly associated with different forms of evangelism in terms of the connections made between biblical precepts of love and care, and the practical need to serve homeless people. However, the terms charity and caritas are themselves unpopular in these discourses, with expression of agape/love being far more appealing to the organizations concerned. This distinction of appeal is not explained by the organizations concerned but on this evidence it would appear that so far as contemporary Christianity is concerned, generosity is constructed as far more love-orientated than charitable, perhaps indicating either some acquiescence to the secularization of 'charity' and the recasting of generosity around the more exclusive Christian prompting of agape-love, and/or an unease with the ways in which Christian caritas may be perceived by others as necessarily associated with 'strings'.

It also seems inevitable that people concerned with establishing, managing and volunteering in these organizations will to some extent be involved in moral selving, but the scale and intensity of involvement required to run these services suggests a very significant going-beyond-the-self, with the giving of finance and time representing responses that are not without cost to the giver. This going-beyond-the-self in order to prioritize the needs of homeless people suggests a strong sense of homeless people as other, and the ways in which those involved are prompted to act – often in a sustained fashion – suggests at least a partial sense *for* the other that is committed, connected and emotional as described by Gutierrez (1988) (and see chapter 4). The involvements of service providers will range from short-term low-cost, to life-changing self-commitment, and where the latter occurs there may well be indications of some conversion *for* the other. However, any such self-conversion on the part of service providers does not seem to involve a downplay of their underlying faith-based ethos.

For some, but by no means all, FBOs the moral impulse of Christian caritas can be to elevate spiritual needs alongside more commonly recognized physical and emotional needs. In one sense this represents a non-recognition of alterity – a potential imposition of the Christian worldview onto homeless people – although most organizations emphasize the non-discriminatory and individual sensitivity of their work. To some extent Christians reflect a sense of receptive generosity, in their claim to enhance homeless people's capacity to receptively and generously engage the world, although their faith-based action inevitably treads a fine line between caring enhancement and oppression – as the faith ethic leads to a being commanded by a receptivity to the spiritual as well as the physical needs of the other, and thereby risks the enforcement of the spiritual onto the other.

Secular humanism

Coles's (1997) second pathway to the ethical prompting of charity arises from the replacement of God-centred philosophies with those which centre on human beings and their political and economic institutions. This excision of biblical influence has not been as easy as it might seem, as 'secular efforts adopt many of the contours of the very religion that provokes the crisis to which they are a response' (Coles, 1997: 8), and we can assume that many organizations and individuals prompted by humanist motives and ethos will be influenced by, and sympathetic to, Christian principles of giving, justice and mercy, even if refusing to accept the 'God-trick' that sources these principles. The core of a secular humanist approach is reasoned altruism that conjures up justice-based understandings of charity and philanthropy. In different ways, secular humanists display a reasoned acceptance of beneficence and benevolence both as a disposition or virtue and as a principle, rule or ideal. As Frankena (1987) suggests, this essential difference allows charity to be underpinned by moral value judgements, or by character and instinct, according to the preference for principles, and dispositions.

Again it should be emphasized in this context that the separation of the Christian and the secular is often indistinct in organizations offering emergency services to homeless people. Several of the statements of ethos received in our surveys indicated a deliberate partnership of church, state and voluntary organizations coming together with a more general ethos of service for homeless people (see also chapters 4, 5 and 6). This may partly be due to a gathering of interested groups and individuals in a particular locale, and partly because individuals often look to an existing project as a vehicle for their involvement even if the specific ethos of that project does not provide an exact match for their personal motivation. As a result, it is often difficult to disentangle Christian and secular ethos in the organizational statements surveyed. The overtly Christian philosophy discussed above is clearly non-secular, but many of the strands of seemingly secular ethos in these statements apply to a range of organizations – non-Christian, Christian and partnerships between these categories. Indeed, we suggest that Christian and secular ethos will often invite similar views about the rights of the individual and the provision of services to the needy (see also Johnsen with Fitzpatrick, 2009).

Discourses of secular charity-in-action suggest that much of the underlying ethos of services for homeless people relies on 'given' notions of basic human rights and rules of social justice that are fashioned into the provision of safe shelter for individuals who are to be accepted as themselves, nonjudgementally. Within these services there is a range of approaches to realizing the potential of the individual for self-sufficiency, with some sense that individuals need to be helped or empowered to solve their own problems, but a wider rationale of easing the marginalized back into the system which has previously failed them. These approaches appear similar to those adopted in avowedly Christian organizations, save for the absence of a spiritual dimension in holistic recovery. Indeed, it is clear that there is substantial overlap between humanistic and Christian ethos here, with the different philosophical roots often producing similar values. These statements of ethos convey a strong sense *of* the other, and equally a substantial suggestion of being *for* the other to a degree that cannot simply be explained by moral or social selving. There is clear scope here for the kinds of postsecular rapprochements discussed above, perhaps revolving around particular understandings of, and strategies for, empowerment and acceptance of homeless people.

Postsecular charity

Coles's critique of both Christian caritas and secular charity centres on their roots of self-identification of what is true, just, valuable and right. Whether inspired by God, or encased in modern rational subjectivity, the 'giving' of charity originates from the self and thereby often discriminates against the recipient. Coles (1997: 2) puts it like this:

> Perhaps this self-origination is sometimes understood better as an internally differentiated dynamic flow, a giving always moving beyond itself, and in this sense less stable than a self-identity. Yet even as in some sense dynamic, *even in its movement*, the fount of giving is self-identical insofar as this flow does not receive – and even precludes reception of – alterity. The archetypes of giving have been profoundly divorced from receiving. Many understandings do not admit the possibility that God or the transcendental subject can receive anything radically other.

Thus, for Coles, Christian caritas is in fact regarded as inextricably bound into an imaginary frame that is unable to recognize the radical alterity in those who live beyond, or reject, the Christian metanarrative. Conversion of, rather than conversion for, is the apparent motif of caritas. Recent reworkings of the ideas of caritas and agape (see Vattimo, 1999; Žižek, 2000) try to answer exactly this charge, by insisting that charity and love should be seen as self-suppressing duties, which represent hard work rather than soft romantic notions (see Cloke, 2002). At a more practical level, a common critique of charitable Christian organizations such as the Salvation Army is that they represent institutions of oppressive social control (see, for example, Anderson, 1923; Wallace, 1965; Spradley, 1970; Wiseman, 1979; Snow & Anderson, 1993). Staffed by supposedly zealous proselytizers, and used only as a place of last resort by homeless people themselves, the Salvation Army's caritas can be presented as a giving that is totally self-identical, and blind to the alterity of its receivers. Such stereotyping often reflects the historical circumstances of the Salvation Army, which has in many ways reinvented itself in response to such critiques. As a result these lingering stereotypes have been strongly challenged; for example, in Himmelfarb's (1991) account, which articulates the Salvation Army as a site of radical inspiration as well as social regulation, though the emphasis remains on what can be given rather than on receptivity to otherness.

Equally, secular humanism is regarded by Coles as providing the moral foundational narratives that underpin the failures of modern liberal societies to deal adequately with otherness. Charitable giving centred on the identity of the rational subject can be linked to the civilizing of the uncivilized, the making respectable of the irresponsible, and the fetishization of moral righteousness and autonomy, and as such can be oblivious to the need for receptivity of alterity. The very reasonableness of justice and charity can obscure the fact that underlying judgements are allied to the reason of the time and place concerned, which may well neglect those – such as homeless people – who somehow fall outside that reason. In Connolly's (1999) critique of Rawls, for example, he asks the question: how is reasonableness attained, and on what logic is it grounded? His answer in reading Rawls is that 'Rawls says the disposition comes from a fortunate cultural tradition that already embodies it' (Connolly, 1999: 144). That is, what is reasonable is grounded in itself, when that sense of reason is widely shared in a culture. In such circumstances, access to the other of the other (Doel, 1994) is blocked by the targeting of reason to the other of the same. These issues of justice and reasonableness are key factors in charitable responses to homelessness. Recent debates over whether it is reasonable and just to get homeless people 'off the street' (Fitzpatrick & Jones, 2005), for example, identify potential discrimination against the other of the 'on-street' other (often excluded both regulationally and representationally in terms of begging and criminality) as opposed to the other of the 'off-street' same (the compliant homeless person engaging with the services provided to keep them off the street).

Given these presumed failures of Christian caritas and secular charity to deal with alterity, Coles proposes a postsecular charity that encompasses a receptive generosity, whereby giving involves the ability to receive the specificity of the other and to be generous in the context of that specificity rather than in the context of the self. This he explains as follows:

> Giving must navigate the tensions between receptively addressing the other's extant perspectives, desires, and joys, on the one hand, and responding to them in ways that might enhance the other's capacity to receptively and generously engage the world, on the other. Ignoring the former imperative leads to blind imperialism; ignoring the latter leads to a slackening of the will to resist and move beyond the life-stunting limits of present beings. (Coles 1997: 105)

Postsecular charity is thus distinguished by its rejection of universalist reason, and its espousal of more phenomenological appreciations of what is ethically right, good or sound in particular circumstances. In the terms argued by Levinas (1994, 1998), the ethics of these rights, wrongs and soundnesses arise from the interconnectedness of responsibility between self and other. Lives lived in social interaction with the other will produce intersubjective ethics prior to any mediated rules of social justice (Popke, 2003). Bauman (1993) draws on Levinas in his account of the postmodern moral crisis and emphasizes both a loss of faith in traditional ethical networks and the importance of the ability to choose between differing ethical systems. In understanding choice as an innate human capacity, Bauman also urges the deployment of asymmetrical moral stances involving an active being *for* the other regardless of whether the other is for us. As such there is no expectation of reciprocity. In one sense, the unconditional responsibility seems to free the moral self from heterogeneous laws and reciprocal expectations, but in another sense the moral self is commanded by the other.

Bauman exposes here the intricate balancing act inherent in Cole's proposal for receptive generosity. Being for the other, if advanced with undue vigour, can become tyrannical and oppressive; non-discrimination can be seen in some senses as a neutralizing of the other, involving failure to take full account of the otherness of the other to influence pre-existing categories of deservedness. Thus, being commanded by the other demands an interpretation or translation of the needs of the other, which can lead to personal moral impulses being enforced on the other. Generosity in the context of being for the other means treading a fine line between care and oppressing, especially when practical enactments of being for the other are rationalized from the perspective of the self.

Conclusions

Perhaps unsurprisingly, the ethos statements of organizations providing emergency services for homeless people show little sign of the depth of postsecularism for which Coles (1997) argues. In one sense, it is to be expected that organizational statements will tend to universalize their attitudes towards avoiding discrimination and recognizing the importance of alterity, but these certainly do not reflect empirical evidence of the relational and reciprocal form taken by alterity. Of course, any move towards postsecular charity is anyway most likely to be witnessed and analysed at the level of day-to-day performances and interactions between staff, volunteers and homeless people. Although there are reasons to suggest that the sacrificial giving of self and time by paid and voluntary workers in hostels and day centres is likely to represent something more than moral selving, at least in some cases, it is only in these human interactions, and the spaces of care they produce, that any assessment can be made of the degree to which workers are attempting to convert the other (to their sense of rationality, respectability, responsibility and so on), or conversely are converting themselves to other ways of seeing the world. The fine line between care and oppression cannot be judged by organizational ethos; instead it will only be evident in the smaller-scale ethical practices brought into being in the various spaces of care that populate the homeless service landscape – hence our exploration of exactly these spaces in chapters 4, 5 and 6.

Furthermore, the discursive accounts of organizational ethos outlined here and in subsequent chapters anyway call into question whether Coles's (1997) three categories of generosity accurately reflect the principal fault lines that differentiate between the approaches to providing services for homeless people in contemporary Britain. In our work we have discovered Christian organizations functioning in a secular humanist world, sometimes appearing to reflect varying degrees of alterity, working alongside partnership projects involving both Christian and non-Christian organizations and individuals, working alongside secular organizations that often draw (implicitly at least) on principles comparable to those expressed by Christians, and displaying wide variations in terms of professionalism, expectations of social responsibility on behalf of clients and rules-based regimes. Viewed in this way, the historically ordered categories advanced by Coles seem to have become rather jumbled in the postsecular arena. So while, for example, there appear to be obvious distinctions between organizations that are avowedly Christian and those that are not, the significant diversity within the 'avowedly Christian' grouping may in some cases be of greater significance than differences between Christian and non-Christian organizations.

As we show, rather than Coles's ideal typical formations, the principal fault line evident in this book appears to reflect the divisive moralities that desire or expect particular behaviour on the part of the homeless recipients of service. We recognize two main types of service that encapsulate an expectation that homeless people will change their way of living. The first (and in our experience rare) type, associated with an ethos that involves overt faith-sharing, unashamedly signals the purposeful conversion of the other, as spiritual needs are elevated alongside more commonly recognized physical and emotional needs. Here Coles's (1997) critique of potential oppression and tyranny is inherently challenged because this holistic response is believed by its advocates to be the most suitable way of enhancing the capacity of the other to engage receptively with the world. The second, which is evident in both secular and Christian organizations, reflects an expectation that homeless people will raise their levels of self-endeavour and self-responsibility, and represents an ethos where care is only given in return for deliverable changes in attitude and lifestyle.

Both of these forms of expectation levied on homeless people contrast markedly with an alternative form of service, drawing on secular and Christian participation, which lays no moral expectation on service clients. Here, care is provided regardless of individual response – there is no underlying motive of conversion to Christianity or of enforced abandonment of particular aspects of a homeless lifestyle – and it may well be that such services are better equipped to recognize, rather than subdue, the alterity of the homeless people concerned. It is this last category that particularly reflects emergent spaces of *postsecular* care in the city. Nonetheless, in all cases we can begin to discern a praxis of care that counterposes any conceptual assumptions about punitive urbanisms and vicious geographies of control and containment, and repudiates the universality of conceptual frameworks of revanchist and postjustice urbanisms.

Chapter Three

Tactics and Performativities in the Homeless City

Introduction

In this chapter, we want to provide a rather different context for under-standing homelessness from that underpinned by the explanatory power of revanchism and neoliberalism. According to these concepts, to study home-lessness is to be concerned with the strategies by which spaces of homeless-ness are disciplined and organized. Though attention has been turned to the tactics deployed by homeless people in order to negotiate these regulated spaces, such issues tend to be of secondary importance in accounts of urban homelessness underpinned by these concepts. Such perspectives thus tend to reconstitute the city as a 'homeless city', the contours of which are shaped by institutional (and some non-institutional) places such as shelters, hostels and day centres, where the necessities of everyday life can be accessed. In this way, the homeless city becomes reduced to a kind of time-space dia-gram of regulatory staging, punctuated by nodal service spaces such as hos-tels and drop-ins, but also by less formal but still regulated places such as parks and squares. In turn, the experience of homelessness becomes a story of how homeless people negotiate the various forms of regulation and con-trol they encounter as they move within and between these spaces.

Such accounts are in an important sense framed within a powerful and particular logic of *rationality* – the rationalities of disciplinary space, and the tactical rationalities deployed by homeless people in order to 'get by' in an increasingly restrictive urban order. While we recognize the value of this work, the problem with such accounts is that they leave little room for exploring other aspects of homeless people's lives – such as care, generosity, charity and anger. Though not necessarily governed by such rationalities these *emotions* nevertheless shape both the lives of homeless people and, as a consequence, the contours of the homeless city.

In this chapter we argue that there is a need to move beyond this rationalist reading of the homeless city, in order to recognize the importance of emotion and affect in the lives of homeless people, and the traces such emotions and affects leave on and in the homeless city. Such a move entails an exploration of the maps of the homeless city drawn up by homeless people themselves, identifying practices that transcend these better known tactics of negotiation and opening out a geography of performativity and affect as well as of regulation and resistance.

Drawing on our conversations with homeless people in a large city in the south-west of England (Benington, population 381,618), here we reenvisage the experience of homelessness in three main ways. First, we demonstrate that the nodal territory of the homeless city is in fact constituted by a complex assemblage of places to sleep, eat, earn and hang out, which mix traditional nodes with other less visible – but equally significant – spaces of homelessness in the city. The cartographies of homelessness that subsequently emerge from this remapping exercise can thus best be understood in terms of the journeys and pauses of homeless people, which are bound up in complex ways with these different spaces. Second, these journeys and pauses are punctuated by different kinds of performativities. The performance of impression management – presenting an identity of supplication when in a shelter, but as far as possible one of 'normality' when on the streets, for example – has long been recognized as a tactic that is regularly used by homeless people in their day-to-day lives (see, for example, Knowles, 2000). In this chapter, however, we argue that the journeys and pauses of homeless people are also characterized by other performativities, both routinized and more immanent, which are best understood not as a means of 'getting by', transgression or resistance, but as indications of more ephemeral emotional affects. These other performativities leave traces in and around the city omitted in most accounts of the homeless city, but that in fact reflect some of the most significant moments in a homeless person's day, and present significant markers of the *active* presence of homeless people in the city.

Third, we show how this performativity is in turn bound up in complex ways with the architecture of the city itself. Amin and Thrift (2002) have argued that we should do more to name the 'neglected' spatialities of the city and to edit back into our accounts of urban space the 'strange maps' of city life. Their focus is directed to 'the intermesh between flesh and stone, humans and non-humans, fixtures and flows, emotions and practices' (Amin & Thrift, 2002: 9) that characterize urban life, and to the multitude of spatial performances and practices that bring the city into being. Together these relational hybridities (Whatmore, 2002), performativities and affects point to the capacity of the city to act as a space where a multitude of rationalities and non-rationalities are played out, and to the potential for remapping the city in ways that move beyond orthodox theoretical order. Here we explore this potential for remapping the homeless city, investigating the idea that an understanding of the performative and affective geographies of homelessness can breathe new life into understandings of homelessness.

As Howley (2001) has argued, the urban environment both shapes and is shaped by all those who inhabit it. In this sense, new cartographies of homelessness need to be placed alongside a range of other practices that also re-order and re-encode city space – for example, some of those associated with youth culture such as skateboarding (see Borden, 2001). Yet we would argue that the spatialities of homelessness convey political and social significance that transcends some of these other urban practices more obviously related to the politics of pleasure. The huge weight of resource that has been deployed in response to the problems of homelessness in North American and Western European cities in recent years – much of it in an attempt to clear homeless people from the streets – is testament to the symbolic weight that homelessness carries in the urban imaginary: as the visible presence of even quite small numbers of homeless people comes to stand for much deeper failings – of the welfare contract, for example, or of the vitality and wealth of the post-industrial city. Understood in this way, our interest in the performative is far from playful. By emphasizing questions of performativity we seek to draw attention to some of the ways in which homeless people themselves, rather than others, make sense of and in turn remake the homeless city – a cartography that gives rise to a geography of homelessness that may indeed appear 'strange' in relation to more familiar, hegemonic mappings of urban homelessness.

Strategies and Tactics in the Homeless City

As outlined in chapter 1, the spatial imaginary of urban homelessness has been carefully accumulated through a series of seminal studies, many of which have been conducted in the United States. For example, Duncan's (1983) recognition of 'prime' and 'marginal' space firmly places homeless people in peripheral urban spaces that are of little value to mainstream society and where their performance of 'spoiled' identities (Goffman, 1968) is least in conflict with the experiences of ordinary, 'normal' people. Research into one of the principal sites of such marginality – the service-dependent ghetto (Dear & Wolch, 1987, 1994; Rowe & Wolch, 1990) – has charted how these marginal spaces are regulated to become the 'natural' habitus of homeless people. In de Certeau's (1984) terms, the institutional support but also containment of homeless people in such spaces represents a *strategy* by which power is imposed through the organization and disciplining of space, with the effect that the geographies of service provision significantly shape the geographies of homelessness in the city (Takahashi, 1998). According to such accounts, homeless people develop specific routines around these service nodes (Wolch et al., 1993) as these service spaces come to provide a source of both the material and, to a lesser extent perhaps, emotional sustenance and support necessary to make the adjustment from 'housed' to 'homeless' (Rowe & Wolch, 1990). As Rahimian et al. (1992) emphasize, the necessary and regular movements between service spaces in turn emerge as a key facet of the formal, and formally regulated, landscape of homelessness in the city (see also Snow & Anderson, 1993).

Accounts of urban homelessness have also embraced cartographies of mobility within prime city space, and of interstitial places (Wardhaugh, 2000) within prime space, where public spaces are effectively commandeered for private use by homeless people. These niches have been identified in varying shapes and sizes, from sleeping in public beach lockers (Wolch & Rowe, 1992) and shop doorways (Smith, 1993) to the use of railway stations or even airports (Hopper, 1991). Homeless people's use of these interstitial spaces will often provoke a sense of dis-ease (Kearns, 1993) undercutting the symbolism and orderliness associated with these spaces and thus threatening the 'proper' meaning of the places (Mair, 1986; Cresswell, 1996). Accordingly, the out-of-placeness of homeless people has often led to a 'purification' of urban space (Sibley, 1995) by which homeless people have been increasingly excluded from key public sites (Davis, 1990; Blomley, 1994; Mitchell, 1997). Indeed, as we argued in chapters 1 and 2, there is increasing evidence that the regulatory environment in which homeless people live has become more restrictive, and in some cases punitive, over recent years. As key businesses have moved out from the urban core and relocated in newly purified peripheral spaces, for example, the city centre has increasingly become constructed as a 'site of danger and a repository for urban fears and unease' (Wardhaugh, 2000: 102). At the same time, a revitalization of 'urban living' in downtown areas has often involved attempts to clear the central city of homeless people, panhandlers and beggars (Mitchell, 1997, 2001). Though not producing the same spatial configurations in all places (MacLeod, 2002), the general logic of these changes suggests increasing levels of surveillance over the movements of homeless people in the city, and increasing prohibition of their use of both prime and interstitial spaces.

The above picture emphasizes the regulatory control of the spaces in which homeless people dwell and move. Others have emphasized instead homeless people's attempts to negotiate, or resist, such regulation. As Lees (1998) argues, the street is a complex space that tells a variety of stories. While most constructions of homeless people emphasize deviance (Erikson, 1996; Phillips, 2000) or vulnerability (Mair, 1986; Deutsche, 1990), such constructions give little insight into how homeless people exercise autonomy within the wider constraints of social and cultural regulation. In contrast, Ruddick (1990, 1996) draws attention to a vision of homeless people as social subjects who both shape and are shaped by the new social spaces of the city. Here she contrasts understandings of the victimization of homeless people with their individual and collective tenacity and creativity in coping with that victimization – resulting in a series of 'tactics' (de Certeau, 1984) that sometimes transgress and sometimes articulate more conscious resistance to the hegemonic meanings and orthodoxies of particular urban spaces (on the distinction between 'transgression' and 'resistance' see Cresswell, 1996). Thus, she points to the continued presence of homeless people in prime urban parks as undermining the imaginary and wealth of the postindustrial city, for example, as well as to more obviously resistant practices such as street weddings.

This acknowledgement of the tactical rationalities of homeless people contributes significantly to the 'strange maps' of urban homelessness. But we need to go further. For some (see, for example, Cooper, 2001), homeless people's journeys through the city suggest a literal and metaphorical redistribution of the spaces and uses of 'home' across the wider scale of the city. Thus homeless people will journey to meet basic survival needs, but also to earn money or to seek leisure and restful pauses in their daily practices, sometimes gathering communally, sometimes seeking solitude. For us, it is clear that these routines of movement and pause are intimately associated not only with the wider geographies of service provision or the continuum of prime and marginal space, but also with a practical knowledge of the micro-architectures of the city (Crang, 2000). In this way, small back streets and alleyways provide channels for relatively 'invisible' movement through the city; recesses and doorways in buildings can provide shelter and relative warmth; enclosed public spaces offering formal seating or informal surfaces (walls, ledges, steps) on which to sit provide communal resting places; and so on. Such routines involve not only an understanding of socio-spatial possibilities in the regulated city, but also a re-reading of the homeless city in terms of the possibilities of counter-inscription, of tracing over the formal understandings of city space and registering alternative signs and markers with which to re-edit the geography of the formally constituted homeless city. For example, shop doorways become sleeping places, public lavatories become bathrooms, underground walkways and concourses become gathering points, with blankets, needle disposal bins and specific graffiti each serving as signs by which this other homeless city is variously marked out.

Yet our argument here is that the acknowledgement even of this re-inscription continues to miss out on other aspects of homeless people's lives and of the homeless city not governed by the rationalities of either regulatory strategies or the tactical rationalities of re-inscription, transgression and resistance. Maps of the homeless city need also to reflect the affective worlds of homelessness, as homeless people co-constitute places of care, generosity, hope, charity, fun and anger in both the better known spaces of homelessness and in those spaces that homeless people bring into being as 'homeless places' through practices of re-inscription. Yes, maps of the homeless city are punctuated by sleeping places, eating places, resting places, panhandling places and toilet places (Kawash, 1998). Such places may reflect the regulatory strategies of city authorities, the tactical rationalities of homeless people themselves, or a combination of the two. But such places are only made *meaningful* by the embodied and emotional interactions of homeless people. We argue that it is these geographies of performativity and affect that construct key traces of homelessness in the city – some permanent, others transient; some visible, others largely invisible to the public eye. By recognizing emotion and affect in the lives of homeless people we can begin to build a more nuanced account of the homeless city.

The Performative and Affective Geographies of Homelessness

An awareness of the tactics homeless people deploy in their negotiation of the homeless city contributes significantly to re-establishing a sense of homeless people's own agency. But we want to suggest that not all the journeys or pauses made by homeless people in the city, or the traces they leave behind, are tactical in nature. As we have argued, the tactical negotiation of regulated space can result in a re-editing of the spaces of the homeless city. Yet it seems likely that other, less tactical, agency also serves to leave traces of homelessness in and around the city – traces that are perhaps more obviously emotionally constructed, and that may be articulated in either routinized or improvised behaviours. Such traces can be permanent or transient, visible or largely invisible, solidly connecting with the materialities of particular places, or leaving the merest wisp of a vapour trail.

Here, an acknowledgement of different forms of performativity and affect offers a parallel framework for charting the lives of homeless people and the marks they leave on city space. There are in fact three, rather different, sets of ideas that can be brought to bear on the practices of performativity in the context of homelessness. The first draws on Goffman's (1959) emphasis on the management of impressions. His conceptualization of social interaction related to engagements between individuals and their audiences, and envisaged deliberate performances drawing on particular props and resources, both visible and spoken about and invisible and silent. Such performances are often deliberately scripted, staged and consumed, and are designed to create a particular impression. The second set of ideas stems from Butler's (1990, 1993, 1997) understanding of how practices enact identities. In contrast to Goffman's vision of the active, conscious performance, Butler's interest is in 'doing discourse' (Gregson & Rose, 2000: 433), in the way in which identity formation is inscribed both by the routinized iterative performances of sedimented forms of social practice and by the regulatory power of the discourses that are thus also sedimented. In this coincidence of enacting and signifying, discourses discipline their subjects even as they produce them.

Third, Thrift's (1996, 1999, 2000, 2004) theorization of the non-representational (see also Dewsbury, 2000; Thrift & Dewsbury, 2000) emphasizes 'the flow of practice in everyday life as embodied, as caught up with and committed to the creation of affect, as contextual and as inevitably technologised through language and objects' (Thrift & Dewsbury, 2000: 415). Performativity, in this light, is the ongoing creation of affects, of unplanned and unaccountable outcomes of relational encounters that are 'only rendered visible in the act of doing' (Dewsbury, 2000: 472). These manifestations of everyday life suggest an immanent rupture in space and subjectivity that at any moment allows change to happen. Performativity is thus a becoming practice, most easily (though perhaps inaccurately) visualized in metaphors of theatrical improvisation (Nash, 2000).

Each of these three strands offers scope for better understanding homeless people's lives and the geographies of the homeless city. Different performativities cross-cut the notion of tactical agency, and leave different traces of homelessness capable of re-inscribing the city in different ways. Goffman's conceptualization of deliberately staged performances, for example, is useful in understanding the tactical management of impressions in situations where homeless people choose to play to an audience – for example, when begging or busking (Dean, 1999). Here some of the main thoroughfares of retail and leisure in the city are re-marked as places of encounter with homelessness, engendering feelings of charity, fear, avoidance or loathing on the part of the housed public. Traces here can be visual/material (cast off blankets or worn clothing) or sonic (the spoken or shouted markers of begging or *Big Issue* selling), as the props used to attract attention and generosity leave a mark on these spaces. Butler's notion of 'doing discourse' resonates well with the well worn everyday routines that can characterize how homeless people receive welfare in the institutional spaces of the hostel or the day centre – routines that are often underpinned by disciplinary discourses of what it is to be homeless (Veness, 1994; Williams, 1996). Thrift's non-representational practices of being-in-the-world can be traced most effectively in those less frequently remarked moments brought into being by the interactions of homeless people, and between homeless people and members of the housed public, which move around momentary and pre-discursive outbursts of generosity, anger and unrehearsed sociability: in street gatherings, in day centres, in hostels or in begging encounters, for example.

As should be clear, we do not wish to imply by these examples that there is any static fix between different aspects of performativity and different kinds of spaces. Impressions are managed throughout homeless people's movements across the homeless city; routine performance of identity occurs in and beyond the regulated spaces of formal service provision; and moments of spontaneity erupt throughout the life experiences of homeless people. Indeed, the same spaces, and same encounters, may often be profitably read as articulating – or rather, as being brought into being by – different kinds of performativity.

We do suggest, however, that each of these rather different forms of performativity will leave different kinds of traces in the urban landscape.

Clearly there is a risk in this emphasis on performativity of undervaluing the stubborn and oppressive materialities of homeless people's experiences. Indeed, in Nash's view, some non-representational approaches risk a retreat from material politics into 'the individualistic and universalising sovereign subject', with a consequent inability to combine theoretical insights with 'detailed attention to the political, economic and cultural geographies of specific everyday practices' (Nash, 2000: 662). Certainly, such is not our aim. But we do want to draw attention to the enacted interventions of generosity, care, therapy and charity as well as to the more negative experiences of exclusion, fear, oppression and anger that characterize homeless people's lives.

In what follows we explore these maps of the homeless city as presented to us by homeless people in the city of Benington. We seek to understand the journeys and pauses that make up these maps both in terms of the strategies of spatial ordering and the tactical negotiation of that spatial order, and in terms of the performative and affective geographies that are less governed by such rationalities. We focus our attention on two forms of performativity evident in these accounts, drawing upon both Goffman's (1959) concept of a conscious impression management and Thrift's (1996, 1999, 2000, 2004) theorization of the pre-conscious or unconscious flow of affect in homeless people's day-to-day lives. Insofar as is possible, given our ethnographic methodology our discussion is framed by categories (places to sleep, eat, earn, and hang-out) that reflect the concerns of our interviewees, though we also discuss journeys that were taken as a 'given' by our interviewees but that seemed to us to underpin their accounts of being homeless in the city.

Places to Sleep

Wolch and Dear's (1993) thesis of the service-dependent ghetto rests on the observation that the concentration of welfare services, shelters and hostel accommodation 'remains the prime reason that homeless people cluster in certain areas' (1993: 39). Hostels and shelters are usually sited in the marginal spaces of the city and their location contributes to the regulation and containment of homeless people. The expectation is, then, that the basic geographies of homelessness will be relatively similar in most cities, framed as they are by the sites and activities of non-statutory service providers, and varying only in terms of how the numbers and location of services vary from city to city. In line with a number of other cities across the UK, the number of emergency beds available to homeless people in Benington has in fact declined over the past five or ten years following the refurbishment and 'improvement' of some of the city's larger hostels (see also chapter 6). At the same time, a shortage of 'move-on' accommodation means that many of the city's hostels are 'silting up'. Though Benington has five emergency hostels in total (one of which is a traditional dormitory-style night shelter), four day centres and a number of soup runs, most of our interviewees had experienced a mix of hostel living and rough sleeping over the years.

As might be expected, Benington's homeless services are predominantly located in the marginal spaces of the city represented by the Westhill area, very close to the city centre. The Westhill neighbourhood is also characterized by a concentration of prostitution and drug dealing. These other activities reinforce the stigma many people feel when turning to homeless services in Benington, and is the source of considerable fear for people – especially homeless women – when making their way to a hostel.

Importantly, such fear is intimately interconnected with the physical architecture of the city itself, and with the buildings, squares, (blind) corners and pavements that characterize this part of the city, as Alan explains:

> First of all, you've got to walk through the square where you've got a lot of prostitution. Then once you have got through the square you've got a few little corners where drug dealers are standing, then you've still got to go round the other corner right in front of the **** [pub] (where the big drug problem is) to get into the shelter. (Alan, 43, former rough sleeper and now squatting, Benington)

As we explore in more detail in chapter 6, hostel life is highly regulated both by the formal rules restricting entry and residence (such as no alcohol or drugs, no families, couples or visitors) and by informal codes of practice established among residents themselves and which must be adhered to if a person is to avoid the violence that can sometimes erupt in such places. As a result, though people frequently described the boredom of hostel living, this should not be taken to imply a dampening of emotion. Instead, hostel life was characterized by many as moving around often acute feelings of despair, anger, frustration and fear. More specifically, far from providing for the feelings of safety, comfort and control more usually associated with a sense of 'home', for many hostel life meant engaging in constant and careful impression management in order to gain access to the facility, to supervision and to staff, and more simply to make it safely through the day:

SARAH: So say someone new arrives …

CHRIS: You are likely to get extremely badly hassled. That's the first thing that will happen. … Of course you would, you're not known. All of a sudden you'll be up at the hatch getting a meal, you'll go to sit down at a table and you will find that everyone is just going like that, just looking. No one is saying a word. They're just looking.

SARAH: And what are they looking for?

CHRIS: The way your dress, your stance, the position you are sat in. If you look relaxed they know that you can look after yourself. But if you sit there all timid then you will get preyed on. It's all about observation. When you are homeless and you're a street person or an addict or prostitute, your senses seem to hone in like a knife-edge. (Chris, 53, staying in a warden-controlled bed and breakfast hotel, Benington)

[And] if you have a problem it's no good … talking to a member of staff. … They'll listen to you and it's 'Yes, I'll get someone to help you.' And then they [just] vanish upstairs. … [And] it's no good you getting angry. You can't put your fist through armoured glass. Although I've seen people try. (Colin, 53, resident HAP-funded 'high support' hostel, Benington)

Yet not all hostels were described in the same way. Indeed, homeless men often conferred a clear ranking on different hostels across the city, with one particular hostel regarded as 'the best hostel in town' (Sean) and a 'brilliant place' (John). Going further, while a number of the homeless women we spoke with reported that they tried to avoid the city's hostels, and its night shelter in particular (see chapter 6), for fear of the violence (and sexual assault) that sometimes occurs in these spaces – 'choosing' to sleep rough instead – those able to access Benington's sole women-only hostel, located some way from the city's other homeless services in a quiet, suburban neighbourhood, often described a very different experience. Rather than a place to escape from – as was so often the case in the accounts of male respondents – for Julie the women's hostel provided her with a space both of refuge and, more importantly perhaps, of potential transition; a place from which she felt she might in time be able to move forward with her life. Such feelings were the result of the care and commitment she received from staff, care that became evident in spontaneous acts of kindness and moments of shared laughter as much as through the formal structure of supervision and advice (see also chapter 6).

> SARAH: Most of the hostels and day centres are in town. do you like being out here?
> JULIE: Yes … I feel safer … I've heard about the other places and when somebody said '**** hostel' I thought 'oh no'. And then [when I got in here] I thought 'this is brilliant'. … You can chat to the staff like they are friends and have a laugh with them as well. … [Like] … the other day my support worker, I was having a chat with her and she cut my hair … it was brilliant. … they try to help you as much as they can basically. … [It's like] I was saying the other day. I was walking up on the second floor looking out the window and the sun was shining out on the garden and everything and I walked down to the end and said it feels like I'm on my holiday just walking up there, just seeing all the sun and everything, looking out the window. (Julie, 20, resident at Gateway 'high support' hostel, Benington)

Thus Benington's hostels can be seen as intermeshed with a range of different emotional and affective geographies. For some, they embodied restrictive, uncaring and potentially dangerous environments; for others, places of respite and care (see Philo & Parr, 2000; Conradson, 2003).

Perhaps the most graphic illustrations of places to sleep in Benington, however, related not to hostels and shelters but to the practices and locations of sleeping rough and squatting. Many interviewees were clearly well informed about current squats in the city, for example, squats that once again were largely concentrated in the Westhill area. Chris described one such squat thus:

> It's a disused building that used to be two houses – it's been knocked into one and it's quite a nice squat. … The second window from the top is the entry point. They've got a ladder – bring it out and in you go. There's a lot of prostitution goes on in there. Clients get taken there, ladder 'n' all – they're sorted out with a different room. (Chris, 53, former hostel resident, now staying in a warden-controlled bed and breakfast hotel, Benington)

These and other squats are an essential part of Benington's urban fabric, representative of the kind of marginal spaces that can become 'privatized' by homeless people as places to sleep, and sometimes even to earn. The squats themselves are, however, only one (informal) part of a wider (formal) network of facilities accessed by those sleeping rough or squatting – providing accommodation and a place to 'hang out', with showers and food arranged elsewhere, as Alan explains:

> ALAN: They've got individual rooms that they stay in. Some of them have actually found keys to the rooms so they lock them up. And nobody seems to break into those rooms. There seems to be like a hidden code between them … 'that's now my room' … someone takes you along and says 'look, this is a mate of mine …' and they say, 'right, pick a floor'. And eventually they get to know each other and they all decide to get on one floor. Then you get accepted, if you know what I mean. There is a hierarchy system, obviously. Like in any life. Whether you're living in a house, on the street, when you first move in … after a while you become part of the community …
> SARAH: What would happen if someone just broke in and kind of adopted a room?
> ALAN: They'd probably ask him what he was doing. They wouldn't kick him out. They have their own little government going on in there. With a hierarchy.
> SARAH: Is that governed by access to drugs?
> ALAN: Oh yes. Drugs, alcohol. … There's needles everywhere. You've just got to be careful where you walk. Especially in the social area in the middle … in the middle there's like a foyer on every floor. So that tends to become like the social area. They drink alcohol, sit down talk. Somebody might have a radio which they bring out so they play music and have a chat … it's where we can be private – you know, normal. It's where me and my girlfriend can

be alone, and where you can call in on your mates. But it's still not like a fucking home 'cos you have to go down the **** to get a shower. (Alan, 43, former rough sleeper and now squatting, Benington)

As Alan makes clear, though such spaces are subject to their own informal rules and regulations, such rules move around a very different ethos and are enforced in very different ways from the rules governing life in night shelters and hostels. Prohibited in the latter, drugs and alcohol form the basis of both sociality and the social hierarchy in the former. Likewise, and in stark contrast to formal spaces of institutional 'care' where the threat of eviction looms large for those who break the rules, though there is a clear etiquette to squatting, those who fail to comply will rarely if ever be asked to leave. More than anything, squats provide hidden-from-view places in the marginal zones of the city where homeless people can live the lives of more-than-homeless individuals away from the public gaze and establish something more akin to the usual constructions of 'home' (Veness, 1993). Though lacking several of the material comforts more usually associated with 'home', squats thereby provide homeless people with a space of relative privacy, autonomy and control where they can live according to their own rather than other people's rules; where friends are free to come and go; and where they can enjoy the same kinds of relationships that the housed population takes for granted.

Other sleeping sites involve homeless people moving beyond these marginal areas into the prime spaces of the city. For example, car parks ring Benington's downtown shopping area and represent key sites for rough sleeping. Once again, practices of rough sleeping are intimately interconnected with the micro-architecture of the city. When seeking a suitable site, for example, it is important that people find first an accommodating physical environment – with architecture that offers some protection both from the elements and from surveillance by security and the wider public. Ideally, such a site should also be characterized by a more accommodating regulatory regime, as Rob explains:

ROB: That's the **** [hotel] car park again. Spacious, that. Plenty of space there believe me. Sometimes there were like 15, 20 people'd sleep there. 'Cos it had an 'L' shape, it was out of the wind and everything. I was staying there back last August. ... That's behind the **** [name of another well known hotel chain]. See down here they've got grilled cages and the fans are on top. There's a cooler box. But you see a lot of cardboard in there, right, which everyone'd chuck out? Well, we'd just crash there some nights ...

SARAH: Did the staff know you were there?

ROB: They never bothered us at all. There were only like two or three of us at a time that used to stay there. It was brilliant down there. It was as warm as toast. It was below ground level. And the fence there meant we were out of public view. (Rob, 47, hostel resident, Benington)

Figure 3.1   Hotel car park

Rob: That's behind the **** [well known hotel chain]. See down here they've got grilled cages and the fans are on top ... you see a lot of cardboard in there, right, which everyone'd chuck out? Well, we'd just crash there some nights ...

Sarah: Did the staff know you were there?

Rob: They never bothered us at all. There were only like two or three of us at a time that used to stay there. It was brilliant down there. It was as warm as toast. It was below ground level. And the fence there meant we were out of public view. (Rob, 47)

Not all such sites offer such an accommodating regime as that of the hotel. Benington's downtown indoor shopping mall, for example, is tightly policed against homeless people during the day, and its car park similarly closed off at night. Thus the city's car parks are in fact subject to differing levels of security and are more or less likely to attract attention and interference from people using downtown centres of entertainment. Describing this variegated landscape of regulation and control, Chrissie says:

We used to use the car parks there, but then they got pretty funny about [it]. ... They spread the steps with tar and stuff and all sorts of black gooey horrible stuff [to keep us out]. ... But in the NCP (National Car Parks) at ****, the staff are lovely there, real nice. They tell us where to sleep and where to put your stuff. But only if you've got their respect and you keep the place tidy. I always instigate a tidy up where we've stayed. I won't let people leave a mess. (Chrissie, 46, hostel resident, Benington)

These accounts reveal some of the different layers of performativity and affect associated with rough sleeping. In places such as the NCP car park, homeless people are only 'accommodated' if they perform in certain ways. In particular, they perform impression management in order to gain 'respect' and to keep the space tidy, ensuring that the staff of the car park can open it up the next morning with other users unaware of the night-time presence of homeless people. Within such sites, homeless people gather together, finding protection in numbers from the wider public, offering protection to the more vulnerable among them (especially women) from others on the streets, and enjoying the physical and emotional comfort that snuggling up against another warm body can afford. Through such practices, interstitial places within the prime spaces of the city are re-inscribed by homeless people as places of possibility and affect:

> Rob: We used to sleep in the bandstand – four or five of us. It was bitter. ... But if you cuddle up together, you can keep warm, like body heat and all that. ... We used to get a lot of drunks come through, throwing abuse and chucking stones and bottles. But there was never any bad violence there. ... That was a girl I met when I was sleeping rough, Jane. ... When I met her she was sleeping one place where I went and we just latched onto each other basically, company for one another. Nothing sexual like, just friends. She'd help me out, I'd help her out.
> Sarah: I guess she'd have felt safer with you around too?
> Rob: Yeah, because people take liberties with girls on the street. It happens quite a lot. (Rob, 47, hostel resident, Benington)

Thus far our account suggests a rather static series of 'places to sleep', but the experiences recounted by other interviewees involved considerable and often continual movement, both between using hostels and rough sleeping, and in order to find safe sites during periods of rough sleeping. Homelessness often has a mobile housing path (May, 2000a, b, 2003a) and rough sleeping is also often a mobile practice. Describing his time camping in the city, Alan, for example, told us: 'I used to move around every second day, to stop the ground showing marks of somebody being there, where somebody would follow ... you just keep moving.' Elaborating, Alan showed us a photograph that explained the logic of his movement. It was of:

> some poor devil's tent that's been wrecked – up by **** [a tourist landmark in a very affluent suburb, two miles from the city centre]. That's where he was living. You can see his ketchup there where they've thrown it. His razors, the battery for his little torch, a tin. They've thrown everything everywhere and totally wrecked it. (Alan, 43, former rough sleeper and now squatting, Benington)

Although sleeping in a tent is not normally associated with city life, we were assured that 'loads of people do it', and indeed in our research in day centres

Figure 3.2   Tent

This is some poor devil's tent that's been wrecked by . . . we don't know who . . . That's how he was living. . . . You can see his ketchup there where they've thrown it. His razors, the battery for his little torch, a tin. They've thrown everything everywhere and totally wrecked [it]. . . . I used to find secure places [when I slept in a tent]. Camouflage it. I mean . . . he made a mistake. His canopy was orange, so it was quite visible. . . . [And of course] you don't normally go there during the day. You go there when it's dark so that nobody can see you going there. So if you've got no way of lighting the place, you can't see nothing. And in these tents, it's too dangerous to put a candle. I've seen so many people burn their tents down and nearly kill themselves. (Alan, 43)

it was not uncommon to see people carrying their tents around with them, never putting them down for fear of them being stolen. Alan keeps his 'luxuries' buried in a box (cf. Cooper, 2001) for fear of the kind of destruction that ensues when tents are found, and lives a transient life of journeys in and between the green spaces of the city. Like those using Benington's car parks, however, he too is careful to remove any 'marks' – a practice that often leaves homeless people's presence in the city difficult to trace (cf. similar such accounts of the tactics of homeless people in the countryside: Cloke et al., 2000b).

As Joan Smith has argued, rough sleeping presents particular difficulties for women, not least because of the increased danger of sexual harassment and abuse from both members of the housed public and other homeless people (Smith, 1999). Not surprisingly, then, although, as Chrissie's account above makes clear, women did sometimes join other rough sleepers in the city's better known rough sleeping spots, others avoided these sites for exactly the reasons Smith notes. For example, echoing Alan's experiences, Mandy spent two and half years sleeping deep in the forest a few miles from the city centre, while Sharon bedded down in the doorway of a synagogue in a suburban neighbourhood that 'was away from town and stuff [so that she] felt quite safe there'.

These gendered geographies of rough sleeping raise particular issues for service providers, of course, who will often have difficulty in locating and making contact with women on the streets. But more generally, it is clear that these tactics of movement, sometimes visible, sometimes largely invisible, present traces of homelessness, however faint, beyond the service-dependent ghetto. Though Benington's hostels and night shelter continue to reflect key nodal points where many journeys begin and end, many other forms and maps of homeless mobility criss-cross the city. These movements are 'tactical' in the sense that they reflect the art of making do and using what is there (Crang, 2000) to pass through and temporarily occupy city spaces. They reflect practical urban knowledges, and they create new linkages between city sites. But the traces of homelessness thus marked are more than *only* tactical. These sites and these journeys are enacted performatively, placating pseudo-regulators here, cuddling up warmly and defensively there. Such practices reflect a logic of impression management but also of affective co-constitution that translate the seeming rationalities of regulated space and tactical response into emotionally laden intensities and moods of fear, solidarity and care.

Places to Eat

Our interviewees' accounts of places to eat reinforce both the centrifugal pull of homeless services located in the marginal spaces of the city, and the mobilities of homeless people as they journey into prime city spaces in search of alternative sources of food. Previous research (Rahimian et al., 1992; Wolch et al., 1993) suggests that formal emergency services such as day centres, which provide free or inexpensive food for homeless people, act both as significant nodes in the daily journeys of homeless people in the city and as strong regulatory influences on such movements. In line with such work, the homeless people we talked with also had a good understanding of a commonly known and widely used 'food route'. Such a route depends upon mutual information networks that enable people to journey to particular services offering food at particular times of the day. Thus people know of the different day centres offering free tea and coffee at different times of the day, and they deploy detailed knowledges concerning not only where to get a meal but what kind of experience is likely to be served up at the place concerned (Johnsen et al., 2005a). Here is how Frank describes Benington's food route:

On a Sunday at 12 o'clock up in Westhill's ****, you get a Sunday dinner, you know, it might only be fishcakes and chips or sommat, but there's a meal … and when you leave you always get a loaf of bread and some cakes. … At 3.30 the **** opens so you can go up there between 3.30 and 5.00. So that's your Sunday taken care of, and then obviously if you wanna go to the night shelter [it] opens at 10 o'clock so you've only got a couple of hours – like Saturday's the worst day of the lot to be on the street 'cos there's nothing open … unless you've got money, there's nothing to do. (Frank, 43, service user, Help Day Centre, Benington)

But it is clear that 'places to eat' are also inscribed with other functionalities and affective characteristics. Most obviously, as we explore in further detail in chapter 5, day centres can be understood as providing homeless people with an important space of sociality. The chatter that pervades meal times and other activities in a day centre might in one sense, of course, be understood as representative of nothing more than the performative sociability that often accompanies eating with others (Bell & Valentine, 1997). But for homeless people, such 'chatter' – and the day centre more widely – offers more. For those housed in temporary accommodation, for example, day centres may provide their only means of alleviating loneliness and social isolation; for those sleeping rough they can offer shelter from the ongoing threat of violence on the streets (Ballintyne, 1999; Dean, 1999). More generally, day centres can most usefully be understood as key sites in a wider 'geography of licence': a space where an individual's homeless status – conferred 'other' in most contexts – becomes the norm, and where bodily appearances, odours and certain behaviours (for example, talking to oneself or sleeping under a table) that might be deemed 'odd' or 'inappropriate' elsewhere are accepted (Goffman, 1961; Parr, 2000; see also chapter 5). As a result, even the most basic services offered by day centres (for example, showering facilities) can and should be read not in simple functional terms but with regard to their transformative effects on people's sense of self, and the very real emotional responses they can engender. For Carl, for example, showering provokes a genuine and joyful lifting of the spirits. As he puts it, to shower at the drop-in café is 'the best fucking feeling of the week – it's like you can *almost* be normal again' (emphasis added).

But it is also important not to offer too romantic a view of such spaces (Johnsen et al., 2005a). In part precisely because operating as a space of licence, day centres are also often volatile places. As a result, for some, and women in particular, day centres are often avoided altogether, or necessitate that a user engages in careful impression management (for example, not catching other people's eyes, or affecting the easy familiarity with such environments described by Chris in the case of hostels) so as to avoid the trouble that can sometimes flare in such places (see May et al., 2007). An extract from our field notes in another city captures these dynamics:

> Returned to St Barnabas just after 12:30 p.m. Simon and Paddy were standing in the foyer, shouting drunkenly through the side window at a service user inside. ... They've both been serving bans for about a week now. Simon started yelling aggressively as I approached the door, 'Hey you, lady, can you get me some food from in there, I'm fucking starving and those fuckers won't give me any.' Very intimidating – especially given that several staff members and service users have already warned me about Simon's tendency to resort to violence with little provocation. Needless to say, I was more than a tad relieved when Dan (a staff member) responded to the doorbell and let me in. (Field Notes, St Barnabas Day Centre, Wimpster)

Once again, in the current context almost all such services are located in the more marginal neighbourhood of Westhill, and the routes between these services do not necessarily intrude on prime public space. But on days when services are closed, or if one wants to avoid such services in the first place, it is necessary to move beyond the usual routes and venture into other parts of the city in search of food, as Frank explains: 'The only day in Benington you can't get free food is a Saturday ... so Saturday you go and do the skips behind the shops ... live out of them 'cos you get to know where all the good ones are' (Frank, 43, service user, Help Day Centre, Benington). Though it is only on a Saturday that Frank ventures into the prime spaces of the city in search of food, it is clear from our interviews with others that the usual food route is often punctuated by other journeys and other performances that bring homeless people into prime downtown space. As well as the pickings from discarded food from skips, for example, people often told us of particular commercial outlets they had nurtured as a source of inexpensive food, as Chrissie reveals:

> That's the burger truck where they give me free food at night-time and I pick up their rubbish and stuff. Why they give me free food is because when they first went there I went up and welcomed them into the area and I told them where the best places for them to park would be. ... [And] That's a kebab van on ****. ... Sometimes they give [me] them for free. ... We have a standing joke me and **** [owner] that ****'s my boyfriend! They ask me to give him a kiss and I chase after him trying to kiss his cheek. (Chrissie, 46, hostel resident, Benington)

Here, it is clear that Chrissie has cultivated a range of performative relationships with potential food providers. Some revolve around careful impression management: presenting herself as a source of local knowledge, or creating the impression of need/hunger, for example. Others are more creative performances in which light-hearted flirtatious exchanges become almost routinized ('a standing joke') within the overall context of small acts of kindness by the vendors concerned. In such ways, these food-sites become spaces of affect: with outbursts of hospitality, generosity, laughter and care interspersing a more conventional commercial presence. Such interactions

Figure 3.3   Kebab van

That's a kebab van on ****. That's **** who works there. I've known him for a couple of years now. I buy kebabs there for £1.50. Normally they're £3. . . . Sometimes they give them for free. Or if I hold my hand out and I've only got a pound of change in my hand, sometimes he says 'no, you've made more money than that' – if there's lots of people about. If there's not many people about sometimes he'll just say 'keep it'. . . . We have a standing joke me and **** that ****'s my boyfriend. They ask me to give him a kiss and I chase after him trying to kiss his cheek. The other two people that work there egg me on. It all started because a whole kebab is too big for me. I wouldn't mind paying the three pounds, but it's just that I wouldn't eat it. I mean I can give half away which I don't mind, but sometimes I can't always afford it. (Chrissie, 46)

bring into being a quite different cartography of the 'food route', a cartography that is often related to other key sites in the homeless city, such as places to earn or to 'hang out'.

Places to Earn

The expectation arising from the revanchist city thesis (see Smith, 1996a; Mitchell, 2001) is that the ability of homeless people to beg or 'panhandle' in the prime spaces of the city is increasingly being restricted both by stricter policing and regulation, and by the shifting boundaries of gentrification. Benington has also been subject to periodic police sweeps to clear beggars from its streets, often accompanied by frenzied media campaigns. There is also no doubt that over recent years homeless people on the streets are more likely to be known as individuals to the police, and are less free to remain uninterrupted in prime city spaces (Fooks & Pantazis, 1999). Nevertheless, many of the significant places on the 'strange maps' of Benington related by homeless people relate to particular begging 'pitches' that offer what are perceived to be good begging opportunities. Most obviously, people talked about the opportunities for begging by the city's cash machines. Other prime pitches are places where people may emerge from an evening's entertainment feeling well fed, well watered and generous, as Kate explained:

> You tend to go where other people are begging ... on a Friday and Saturday night when all the pubs and clubs are kicking out ... you pick a spot round there, really either by a food place where they're all coming out afterwards to get something to eat, or along the way to the club, or whatever. (Kate, 24, Traveller, Benington)

In Benington, as elsewhere, to beg in prime urban spaces does indeed increasingly require that homeless people negotiate formal surveillance and regulation by both the police and private security. Such a process necessitates careful and routinized performances of impression management, as Ralph explains (and see figure 3.4):

> The guy on the right is a beggar and that's my two bouncer friends. That's ****, and I think his name is **** ... I used to dance outside the **** [club]. They're the guys who've said they'll give me work if I clean myself up. Everyone down at the **** knows me. If you treat them with respect then, you know, you get the same respect back. I'm always polite, and I always clean up after myself. And not just my own stuff, but like if there's a load of rubbish I'll pick it up and put it in the bin. (Ralph, 35, hostel resident, Benington)

There is also clear evidence of informal regulation of on-street practices. Thus we were told how use of a particular pitch is founded on clearly understood social rules, which are enforced both by a kind of begging etiquette and by threatened or actual violence. Anne and Ray, for example, explained to us how the 'ownership' of a pitch actually works, while Alan explained the operation of the local 'rental market':

> Gerry does NatWest [i.e. begs by the bank cashpoint] and he has done for about 17 months. ... When Gerry turns up you leave. That's what the majority of them do, they turn up and then you have to go. ... Sometimes you have to defend your pitch. Your worst enemy is your own kind. Most people know it's my pitch and bugger off when I show up, but there's a few people with no respect, no respect for begging etiquette. (Anne, 31, day centre user, Benington)

> Well if you do it [beg] prolonged in a month and it's classed as your pitch, any newcomer that come to town that tries to take it off you, you just batter the

Figure 3.4   Bouncer friends

The guy on the right is a beggar and that's my two bouncer friends. That's ****, and I think his name is ****. .... I used to dance outside the **** [club]. They're the guys who've said they'll give me work if I clean myself up. Everyone down at the **** knows me. If you treat them with respect then, you know, you get the same respect back. (Ralph, 46)

shit out of 'em and tell 'em to move on, because you get regular customers that will give to you ... and if other people start begging there it fucks it up for you, and then you stop getting drops. (Ray, 35, hostel resident, Benington)

Like it's always someone's pitch. If he's not there someone can sit there, but as soon as he comes back ... he might say 'look do ya want to use the pitch for a couple of days because I've got to go somewhere, well it'll cost X amount per day.' (Alan, 43, former rough sleeper and now squatting, Benington)

Though the temporary inhabitation of prime city spaces by homeless people is dynamic in terms of the individuals involved, then, it also seems to rely on particular routine doxa (Cresswell, 1996) concerning the allocation of space in the homeless city. Thus, though rarely noticeable to the non-homeless population, processes of spatial subdivision are clear. Particular spatial units are delineated, prompting a language ('pitches', 'drops') of their own and a system of regulation that dictates their use. Regulation by institutionalized policing defines no-go areas (such as in the downtown shopping mall), but informal regulation via etiquette backed up by violence is equally capable of

Figure 3.5   Begging pitch

> I was talking to a gentleman at the waterfront begging. I said 'Do you mind if I take a photograph?' He said 'I don't really want my photo taken.' I said 'Well, can I take your pitch' – what they call their pitch, their begging pitch. All the beggars have got their pitches. Nobody will go to another beggar's pitch otherwise . . . fight time! So he said 'OK'. So he left his sleeping bag in there. Even though a lot of them are living rough or in a tent or whatever they'll take their sleeping bag with them in case it gets stolen. . . . Anybody can sit there. But when he turns up . . . they . . . move. There's no argument. . . . Like it's always someone's pitch. If he's not there someone can sit there, but as soon as he comes back . . . he might say 'Look, do you want to use the pitch for a couple of days, 'cos I've got to go somewhere, well it'll cost X amount per day.' (Alan, 43)

structuring the use of space, leaving temporal niches for secondary use of pitches but allocating a sense of 'ownership' for prime time-spaces.

Certainly, the use of these pitches involves particular kinds of performances designed to result in money being earned. These performances are rather different from those in places to sleep or to eat. Here, there can be costumes and props (such as blankets, dogs, signs), and prepared scripts (such as hard luck stories, or mumbled reference to 'sparing change'). Our interviewees drew a clear distinction, for example, between polite and aggressive begging:

> People have got to stay polite really. I mean I can understand ... because I've done it myself ... been really desperate for the money to get gear [heroin]. But I've never aggressively begged anyone. No matter what, I've always stayed

polite. Because you do get people who get aggravated ... now that's what I call begging ... someone *pleading* with someone. (Chrissie, 46, hostel resident, Benington)

Building up a regular clientele or generating appeal to passers-by necessitates polite performance, often using a dog to win public sympathy, or perhaps involving some degree of temporary abstinence from drink or drugs in order to perform sensitively to one's 'public'. In a slightly different context, James – who told us 'I've never begged in my life', but who occupies a regulated pitch selling the *Big Issue* magazine – emphasized that 'I don't drink during the day if I'm doing the *Big Issue*.'

In some cases, however, the performance of homeless people in such places transcends these rules of self-presentation and constitutes a more active and theatrical show of humour, music or dancing – as Chrissie explained:

I never sit down. And I don't carry a blanket with me either ... I sort of entertain people rather than just [sitting] out there saying 'spare some change please'. At the **** [a club] where they know me, they call me 'the little legend'. I sing songs. One guy always sings '*Amore*' with me ... and he gives me some change. (Chrissie, 46, hostel resident, Benington)

Other interviewees used dancing or drawing to perform to people passing their pitches. In these cases the performances of homeless people can be interpreted in terms of begging as al fresco street entertainment, capable of being read as spontaneous becoming but also as a more obviously scripted, self-reflexive and conscious act of impression management designed to engender charity from the housed public and reduce levels of attention from local police. Similarly, if the geographies of begging reflect in part a tactical mapping of the homeless city that depends upon a detailed knowledge of the earning potential of different sites across the city (sites that may change on a diurnal or seasonal cycle), they may also be understood as articulating a geography of generosity and affect: where need and charity, threat and anger intersect on a regular basis. However conceptualized (and on the gendering of these begging encounters see May et al., 2007), it is clear, as Chrissie suggests, that this geography and these performances give rise to a rather different understanding of the homeless city: one in which the 'spaces of homelessness' are brought into being by the embodied performances of homeless people themselves and their interactions with others, rather than constituted by pre-existing and officially designated spaces of homelessness that require only to be filled by 'the homeless':

SARAH: So where are the best places to beg then?
CHRISSIE: There are no best places. Because you get a place and you make it your own. So that that then becomes a good place. (Chrissie, 46, hostel resident, Benington)

Places to 'Hang Out'

Finally, in among the networks of movement and pause connecting places to sleep, eat and earn, our interviewees identified other spaces in the city in which they could simply 'hang out' – sometimes alone, sometimes in groups. Representations of homelessness often neglect these aspects of the life of homeless people, preferring instead to emphasize stereotypes of sleeping rough or of begging (see, for example, Daly, 1996). But for a number of our respondents, 'time away' from the institutional spaces in which they spend much of their day, and from other homeless people, played an important part in efforts to reclaim a 'more-than-homeless' identity, as they sought in fact to 'pass' as members of the housed public and make use of other parts of the city (see also Knowles, 2000). For Don, for example,

> The library's a good haunt as well, if it's raining and you've got nowhere to go. ... Go in there, read a book, get out of the rain, out of the weather, out of the frost, snow, wind, whatever ... [and of course] ... they don't know I'm home-less, sort of thing you know. You don't get out, sort of 'Oh I'm homeless' sort of thing – carry an enormous balloon or summat. I prefer to go incognito on that one, low profile it and act like you're not really homeless. (Don, 52, hostel resident, Benington)

Such spaces are not equally accessible to all, of course. In common with others who have traced the growing exclusion of homeless people from such sites (Lees, 1997), our interviewees too suggested that mainstream public spaces such as the library and the museum are less accessible to those more obviously and visibly marked as 'homeless': people whose drug or alcohol dependencies, for example, render them more likely to disturb the expected rules and aesthetics of such spaces. Such social differentiation also occurs in a self-regulated manner, as different public places are used by different sub-groups among the wider 'street homeless' population. As Anne explains,

> You get pissheads, smackheads and straightheads ... some pissheads are junk-ies and some junkies are pissheads, so those lot will interact, but it's very rare you get straightheads and junkies interact. You might get pissheads and straightheads but you won't get straightheads and junkies interacting. (Anne, 31, day centre user, Benington)

As we explore further in chapters 4, 5 and 6, though drinkers, drug-users and other homeless people will often be found using the same services, or begging in similar places, there is little intermixing within these spaces. Socially, the divides between these groups can be strongly defined, serving to marginalize intravenous drug-users especially. Thus a picture emerges here of intense fields of intersubjectivity within and between different groups of homeless people. Trust, solidarity and friendship are fostered within groups, while threat and animosity can arise between them (on the gender dynamics of these various sub-groups, and women's role within them, see May et al., 2007). Such networks map out on to equally differentiated social spaces across the wider city. Such spaces, largely invisible to the housed public outside of times of congregation, serve partly as places of information (providing people with knowledge of the best places to sleep rough, or to beg, for example), partly as places of companionship and sociability. As Chrissie explained of one such space – a set of steps on one of the main arterial roads heading north out of the city centre, for example:

> That's **** on **** street where we all sit to have a drink. Lots of people going past those steps stop and have a drink and that sort of thing. It's quite a social gathering point. ... If you want to find someone they'll be there or in The Pit. (Chrissie, 46, hostel resident, Benington)

Pressed further on why that particular spot had become a key place to hang out, she told us:

> It's opposite the off-licence – a lot of drinkers go into that offy – they've got a slate in there. They can go in six days out of seven and get their stuff on tick and when their payday [benefits day] comes they just hand their giro [benefit cheque] over.

Thus, 'the steps' are widely known as a gathering place for the drinker/pisshead sub-groups of homeless people in Benington. Fuelled by nearby and readily available alcohol, the steps have taken on a life of their own, re-inscribing the micro-architecture of the space as a gathering place where homeless people enjoy the imminent pleasures of company, laughter and friendship (see figure 3.6).

Where gatherings occur in prime city spaces the meaning of those spaces is therefore re-inscribed by homeless people, if only for a while and in ways that – outside the hours of congregation – may remain invisible to the housed public. By contrast, other gathering places are more visible and the re-inscription that occurs there both acquires a greater permanence and becomes more threatening to the hegemonic meanings and mappings of the city. One such example of a visible place to hang out in Benington's downtown area, referred to by Chrissie, is more usually associated with drug-user/smackhead sub-groups. A roundabout just beyond the major shopping centre provides a sunken circular space criss-crossed by pedestrian walkways and ringed by underpasses via which shoppers and downtown workers journey from the centre to nearby car parks. Commonly know as the 'Bear Pit' (or simply 'The Pit') but also (with allusions to hallucination) the 'Magic Roundabout' or 'Magic Circle', this place is a very significant

Figure 3.6   The steps

> Lots of people going past those steps stop and have a drink and that sort of thing. It's quite a social gathering point. ... If you want to find someone they'll be there or in The Pit. ... **** is a saxophone player who can be the most annoying person. But he is a good geezer. **** is always going into detox and she's got a pal that pays for her to do detox. Then she comes out and uses again. ... Oh, [that's] ****, a fellow beggar on **** [a main road leading from the city centre]. (Chrissie, 46)

chill-out zone for homeless people during the day. Although because of its proximity to the shopping centre it is subject to periodic police purges in an attempt to purify the space, it is known by homeless people as a place of tolerance in which to score drugs as well as to gather with mates, and engage in mutual entertainment, often involving some form of music.

Not 20 metres from one of the major department stores in Benington's downtown area, then, a key public space sees the very obvious interaction of shoppers, workers and homeless people. For the former, the Bear Pit can be a place of fear, not easily avoided because of difficulties crossing heavy traffic at street level. But it also becomes a place of compassion, when passers-by respond to beggars, and when the place is routinely used as a serving site by local soup kitchens. For homeless people this is a well known place to chill. It has its own micro-architecture of seats and toilets, variously used for sleeping, drinking and injecting, and it is sunken away from the view of the general public. The Bear Pit can thus be recognized as articulating a number of the key characteristics of the (reconfigured) homeless city: (re-)inscribed as a site of civic and commercial importance and of homelessness; of fear and avoidance and of charity and care; of (occasional) purification and of friendship and association. As the city's homeless and housed populations alike learn and enact its complex and contradictory geographies, so the performative and affective geographies of homelessness leave their mark on the city.

Conclusions: Remapping the Homeless City

Though our remapping of the homeless city has drawn directly from the experiences and practices of our interviewees, it can only ever be a partial account. Not least, our research put us in contact with only a particular segment of Benington's homeless population. In tracing the understandings and practices of those using the city's night shelters, hostels, squats and rough sleeping sites we can say little about the understandings and practices of a more extensive 'hidden homeless' population about whom we know remarkably little (Crisis, 2004; see also May et al., 2007). In one sense, such a focus is entirely understandable. As representatives, variously, either of a key threat to the core values of the post-industrial city or of the group most 'deserving' of our sympathy and aid, it is the city's 'visibly homeless' who carry with them the most ideological weight in the urban imaginary, and thus whose practices rework that imaginary in the most powerful though not always immediately obvious or visible ways.

Yet it is clear that other cartographies must also be in play. Such cartographies may describe the understandings and practices of the hidden homeless, or the still hidden practices of the visibly homeless. Indeed, many of the pathways and places inhabited and acted out by the homeless people we talked to were either kept secret from us or have necessarily been kept confidential here. For example, we were told about several hiding places where rough sleepers 'stash' their sleeping bags and other precious belongings – but were asked not to reveal such sites lest they be discovered by others (for further discussion of such issues see Johnsen et al., 2008). The well worn contours of the 'food route' are also testament to the priority many of our respondents gave to the procuring of free or inexpensive food – a priority relating, for some, to the need to set aside their money for the procurement of drugs or alcohol instead. Indeed, overlaying the journeys and pauses outlined here were other places and pathways, sometimes spoken about in confidence, sometimes only alluded to, structured around places to score or to deal drugs or to steal (see also Wardhaugh, 2000). The mapping of such places invokes in us particular ethical concerns, yet the significance of secret places and secretive practices and performances should by rights be considered as highly significant in the 'strange maps' of homelessness in the city. This is particularly so since by definition secretive and therefore safe (or indeed unsafe) places are not clearly inscribed by markers and signs, and may therefore purposefully be hidden from routine cartographies of the homeless city.

More generally, our account offers clear parallels with, but also important distinctions from, existing studies of urban homelessness. It is clear, for example, that the strategic regulation of the lives of homeless people occurs through both direct policing and the concentration of institutional service nodes in marginal spaces of the city. Hostels, shelters, day centres and drop-ins represent key homeless spaces, and much of the day-to-day life of the homeless people we spoke with is spent in them, or walking between them. Indeed, the relatively high levels of service provision in Benington are associated with its history as a place that attracts homeless people from other parts of the country. Thus, some homeless people, including several of our interviewees, had travelled to Benington from elsewhere at least in part because of the services available, but also for other reasons, including perceptions as to the greater availability and cheaper price of narcotics there.

Yet many other places lack the formal spaces catering specifically *for* homeless people that dot Benington's service landscape. As we show in chapters 7 and 8, for example, other cities have no day centre, so that homeless people must find alternative means of accessing food, laundry and bathing facilities. In such places, informal sources of food (for example, donations from bakery staff) become increasingly important, as does access to public toilets (in shopping centres or train stations, for example) for ablutions (Johnsen et al., 2005a). In contrast, other towns and cities have day centres but no emergency hostel accommodation, meaning that safe places to sleep rough are at a premium. Not all or even the majority of homeless people in such places migrate to other centres where more services exist (May, 2003a). Instead, each place reflects its own patterns of journeys and pauses, sometimes supplementing, sometimes replacing the institutional service nodes of the formally constituted homeless city with more covert sojourns in that place.

It is also clear that even in places of relatively 'high' service provision such as Benington, homeless people are able to escape being penned into the marginal spaces occupied by such services and undertake considerable movement through and pauses within the prime spaces of the city in their efforts to find places to sleep, eat, earn and hang out. Consider, for example, Chrissie's regular night-time routine:

> I start off on ★★★★ ... get enough money for a drink. ... Then I go to ★★★★ Street. The ★★★★ Street shop shuts at half past 10. I work for an extra 10 minutes or so ... get my drink at the end of the night for through the night. So, I usually have two bottles. Then I carry on walking and go down the bottom of ★★★★ and start asking for change down the bottom there ... I end up going into the ★★★★ or ★★★★, clubs like that. Then I go through the Bear Pit. Or over it. Usually over it in the night-time. ... For safety. ... It's just the lager louts that are a nuisance. They are the ones that say ridiculous, dirty, horrible things to

you. They say, you know, 'I'll give you a quid if you suck me cock. Ha ha ha …' They think they are bloody hilarious! [Laughs] And so I say 'oh my love, I'm ever so sorry, but I'm vegetarian!' … And all their mates laugh and nine times out of ten that's got me change! … Anyway, and then I walk down *** Street … turn onto where the police station is … because that's a popular pitch. … No one used to bother with it because it's opposite the police station. But I started doing it … used to do well there … never been taken in for begging … never really been outright accused of begging. I haven't got my photograph in the begging book. … Then … across town and sometimes hang about here in the centre … do a left to the **** and then I stay at the **** until half past two, three o'clock … walk about in front of the … kebab van … then down **** Street and sometimes I do the ****. I sit outside the **** and read my book because that's a café and they like me there. They give me Easter eggs at Easter and stuff like that … after [that] … I might get back to where I'm staying at about five [in the morning]. But often on Fridays and Saturdays I very often don't get to bed at all because I'll be out until half past five, six o'clock. Busy, busy! (Chrissie, 46, hostel resident, Benington)

Chrissie's journey traverses Benington's downtown and maps out places to buy drink, to beg, to meet friends and finally to sleep (more usually through the daytime when back in the hostel where she 'lives'). Her journey is replete with tactical assessments and choices about how long to stay where and how profitable a place might be, and with performances of impression management that variously deflect and attract attention from people who she fears and begs from respectively. It is also a journey punctuated with spontaneous outbursts of laughter/happiness and of anger/fear as she interacts with different people in different places. It routinely uses particular buildings, roads and areas as waymarkers, and embodies walking considerable distances and standing around for considerable periods of time and, although expressed as a nightly routine, Chrissie explained to us that she changes her route according to the season and the weather. Such journeyings are replicated in complex fashion by very considerable numbers of homeless people in the city, and maps of the homeless city must necessarily recognize these flows as being as significant as the nodal spaces that are linked by them (Crang, 2001; cf. Wolch et al., 1993).

Thus, Chrissie's account and those of other homeless people in Benington belie any simple models of urban homelessness that emphasize the policing and clearance of homeless people in a 'revanchist' city, or the regulatory concentration of the service-dependent ghetto (Wolch & Dear, 1993; Smith, 1996a). These movements, and pauses, transcend regular and regulated routes, and reflect a tactical criss-crossing of the city to connect up a range of differently significant places. In so doing they begin to re-inscribe sites and connections in the city with meanings associated with homelessness. In a further departure from existing models of urban homelessness, however, we would argue from the accounts of our interviewees that the movements and pauses of homeless people in the city can also be understood in terms of issues of affect and performativity that are not obviously governed by the rationalities of regulation or tactical response. Homeless journeys are interspersed by particular embodied geographies, as homeless people sleep, eat, deal with cold and wet weather, arrange their ablutions, deal with addictions and relate to each other in ways that incorporate 'bad violence' but also fun and association. Such flows are often the result of deliberate interventions, as people set up 'home', make friends, ensure security and seek money and entertainment, but they vary in the ways in which they present themselves as performative. In the accounts of our interviewees we recognize the staging of performances to produce a particular kind of impression, as when begging or securing the goodwill of night-time car park attendants, for example, but also – as Chrissie's account demonstrates – other geographies of performativity less often traced in accounts of the homeless city: moments of pre-conscious and unplanned outbursts of anger, fear and laughter that remake, if only for a moment, the spaces in which they burst forth.

For those not caught up in their immediate effects, such moments often go unnoticed and unremarked. But they leave traces upon the city that reach beyond those involved in the original encounter and shape subsequent interactions among homeless people and between homeless people and others. They are, in this sense, anything but momentary or ephemeral. Similarly, the oft unremarked and transient spaces of homelessness brought into being through the practices of homeless people and others – the steps upon which homeless people gather to drink and to socialize, for example – are constantly reproduced. As some (including some of those we have tried to give voice to here) leave the streets, others take their place: learning from those around them the 'secret' as well as the better known pathways and places of the homeless city.

This remapping of the homeless city matters. Drawing attention to the knowing and creative deployment of impression management, but also to the pre-discursive and emotional aspects of homeless people's lives, gives back to homeless people not only an agency but also a humanity that is too often lacking in accounts that stress only the strategies by which homeless people are controlled and contained, or the rational tactics through which homeless people resist that containment. This sense of humanity is crucial. Most obviously, as Feldman (2004) argues, those who would deny homeless people the same rights to the city enjoyed by others must first deny their shared humanity. It matters in more immediate, more practical, ways too. To better serve the needs of homeless people we need a better understanding of the geographies of the homeless city. In the simplest of senses, to reach those sleeping rough, for example, we must first understand where it is they are likely to be sleeping (see also May et al., 2007).

Of course, such knowledges may also be used in other ways – most obviously, in attempts to first locate and then remove (sometimes forcibly) homeless people from the streets. Re-imagining the urban is and never can be a politically neutral manoeuvre. Nevertheless, and building on the remapping of the homeless city attempted here, we would also argue that these risks associated with the idea of a revanchist or postjustice city have to be set alongside very considerable evidence of a propensity to care for homeless people, seen especially in the 'spaces of care' represented by hostels, day centres and soup runs. As we show in chapters 4, 5 and 6, by and large these are places in which the humanity of homeless people is respected, and where the emotional and affective landscapes of being homeless are matched by the emotional as well as practical concerns of professionals and volunteers who choose to get involved in responding to the needs of homeless people. In many ways, then, it is in these service spaces that the idea of a postjustice city is most obviously refuted – replaced by something else more aligned with ideas of the postsecular city and ethical citizenship (Cloke et al., 2007). It is to these spaces of care that we now turn.

Chapter Four

'He's Not Homeless, He Shouldn't Have Any Food': Outdoor Relief in a Postsecular Age

Introduction

Having remapped the geographies of street homelessness, in this and the following two chapters we consider the complex geographies surrounding efforts to provide for street homeless people. We begin, here, with a consideration of the geo-ethics of the 'soup run', connecting arguments about homeless service provision to wider debates around the postsecular. At the most obvious level, perhaps, Britain's soup runs challenge assertions as to the recent decline in faith-based collective voluntarism (Eckstein, 2001; Meijs & Hoogstad, 2001) and confirm that responses to urban homelessness cannot sensibly be understood only with reference to the pernicious logic of revanchism. Thus, the vast majority of Britain's soup runs are provided by faith-based organizations. Most draw heavily on volunteer labour, and many rely almost exclusively upon public donation for their continued survival (Johnsen et al., 2005b). Indeed, and contrary to visions of a city populace consumed with the desire for revenge, the flow of donations to such organizations is evidence of the continuing concern for homeless people held by wide swathes of the British public (cf. Pleace, 1998).

The volunteers staffing Britain's soup runs are in turn perhaps one of the most obvious expressions of that sense of 'active citizenship' championed by New Labour as a key component of a new 'Third Way' (Fairclough, 2002). Yet far from celebrated, soup runs – and soup run volunteers – have recently been the target of vigorous criticism from both central government and a number of Britain's larger homelessness charities (ODPM, 1999; Randall & Brown, 2002). Constructed on the one hand as unnecessary – because perhaps providing services to those who may in fact not be 'homeless' at all – they have also been castigated for helping to sustain a street lifestyle among those who obviously are: because apparently making it possible for people living on the streets to get by without engaging with mainstream services, or enabling those with addictions to use money that might otherwise have been spent on food to service their habit instead.

The reasons why soup runs provoke such strong reactions – with the efforts of thousands of volunteers more than matched by the criticisms of this voluntary effort – are not difficult to disentangle. For those wanting to do something to counter the problems of street homelessness, soup runs offer an immediate and highly visible expression of their desire to help. By contrast, for central government, local government officials and city managers the visible congregation of large numbers of people at a soup run is evidence of continued poverty in the 'postindustrial' city, and of the failure to tackle the problems of homelessness and social exclusion.

Such tensions are by no means new. Historically, the provision of alms in Britain has taken two forms: 'outdoor relief' (food) and 'indoor relief' (food and shelter). While the former has tended to be given freely and unconditionally, the latter has usually been made conditional upon the recipient completing a variety of 'rehabilitative' tasks (Driver, 1993). This division has always been a subject of contention, because so closely associated with debates regarding individual culpability (Wardhaugh, 2000). For example, in the sixteenth century the division between indoor and outdoor relief became superimposed upon a moral distinction between the 'deserving' and the 'undeserving' poor. In sixteenth- and seventeenth-century Britain, this distinction took the form of a division between disabled people, the very elderly, widows and children on the one hand, and the 'able bodied' poor on the other. While the former were adjudged to have been stricken by poverty through no fault of their own, and were thus deemed eligible by the state for outdoor relief, the latter came to be viewed as a threat to the work ethic and wider moral order and were consigned instead to the oppressive environments of the closed hostel or, later, the workhouse (Pound, 1971; Leigh, 1979; Driver, 1993; Davis-Smith, 1995). When the provision of outdoor relief by private citizens and local charities increased in response to the rapid rise in poverty and homelessness in the mid-to-late nineteenth century, disputes over the most appropriate way of providing for the poor re-emerged (Humphreys, 1999). The then newly formed Charity Organisation Society (COS), for example, argued that far from ameliorating homelessness, the haphazard nature of public charity exacerbated problems of vagrancy and pauperism. In an attempt to curb such practices the COS came up with a number of schemes designed to regulate this charitable impulse and drive recipients into the hands of more 'suitable' providers such as the Salvation Army. Their efforts failed, with both local charities and private individuals continuing to give directly to people on the streets rather than only through the auspices of the COS and more established charitable groups (Davis-Smith, 1995).

These earlier struggles between those providing outdoor relief and those who would seek to regulate it – and the distinction between the 'deserving' and the 'undeserving' poor underpinning such divisions – have continued relevance in the contemporary era. Most obviously, a basic distinction between the 'deserving' and the 'undeserving' poor continues to shape Britain's homelessness legislation (Beresford, 1979; Neale, 1997). Thus the 1977 Housing (Homeless Persons) Act, for example, drew a clear distinction between the 'unintentionally' and 'intentionally' homeless in England (with only the former extended a statutory right to rehousing), with this distinction remaining in subsequent revisions to the Act (Lowe, 1997).

In a similar vein, when launching its *Homelessness Action Programme* central government made clear that homeless people should take up the new opportunities the programme offered or risk being apportioned blame (found culpable) for their continued presence on the streets (Fitzpatrick et al., 2000), with the Social Exclusion Unit noting that though the 'Government has no present plans to ... make it an offence to sleep rough ... since the explicit intention of the policy is to deliver clear streets, the Government believes that the public will feel they have a right to expect hostel places to be taken up as more become available' (Social Exclusion Unit, 1998: 20). Turning its attention to soup runs themselves, rather than to their clients, the Rough Sleepers Unit also made clear the government's commitment to pursuing 'approaches which help people off the streets' rather than those (notably soup runs) 'which sustain a street lifestyle' (ODPM, 1999: 4). Indeed, echoing the work of the COS more than a century earlier, in July 2000 the then Office of the Deputy Prime Minister commissioned the Salvation Army to put together the London Soup and Clothing Run Co-Ordination Project (LSCRCP) – charging it with the task of radically reducing the number of runs operating in central London (Moore, 2002). Responding to concerns about the lack of 'supportive interaction' between volunteers and service users, and the impression that most of the people served by soup runs were not in fact rough sleepers at all but the 'unsettled resettled' ('socially rootless' people who seek 'the camaraderie of the soup runs for support'), the LSCRCP set about 'encouraging' 'excess' groups either to stop serving altogether or to redirect their efforts into other activities, such as night shelters or tenancy sustainment programmes. The target of reducing the number of soup runs operating in central London by two-thirds (not coincidentally, perhaps, the same target that had been applied to levels of rough sleeping) was achieved by mid-2002, by which time 50 different soup runs had either halted their activities entirely or redirected their energies elsewhere (Moore, 2002).

As we show later in the chapter, attempts to close down soup runs have by no means been limited to central London. But as we also show, Britain's soup runs remain – if hardly in a state of 'rude health' – remarkably resilient. Focusing mainly on the experiences of the volunteers providing these services, this chapter explores what drives people to work on soup runs, the characteristics of the organizations providing these services, and what they provide.

The account that emerges speaks to the continued importance, but also remarkable complexity, of this response to the problems of homelessness.

Sustaining Street Lifestyles?

As we have already suggested, our survey of Britain's soup runs makes clear that accounts of the decline in faith-based collective voluntarism are over-stated (Eckstein, 2001; Meijis & Hoogstad, 2001). Some 55 per cent of Britain's soup runs are run by charities, the vast majority of which are faith-based or have links to a larger faith-based organization, such as the Salvation Army or St Vincent de Paul Society. A further 37 per cent are provided by local churches. Though approximately one-quarter (26 per cent) of these projects employ one or more paid coordinators, 74 per cent are run entirely by volunteer staff, with the pools on which organizations draw their volunteers varying in size from as few as two to over two hundred people (Johnsen et al., 2005b). The majority of such projects run on extremely small budgets. Almost four out of ten (39 per cent) survive on less than £500 a year, and half on less than a £1000 per annum. Without recourse to statutory funding, soup runs are almost entirely reliant upon donations; from either their church or parent organization (25 per cent) or the wider local community (members of the public, other churches, schools and local businesses). For many, gifts in kind are as important as any financial contribution, with 38 per cent of projects relying entirely on donated food, and 66 per cent on the donation of bedding and clothing materials, for their continued survival (ibid.).

While this survey offers some indication of the type of organizations involved in soup runs, it also sheds light on recent debates concerning exactly what soup runs provide, and to whom. For example, 70 per cent of Britain's soup runs provide clothing and bedding as well as hot drinks, sandwiches and soup. More importantly, perhaps, far from mainly used by the 'unsettled resettled', soup run coordinators estimate that the majority of people they serve are indeed 'homeless': either sleeping rough (36 per cent of clients) or staying in night shelters or hostels (17 per cent) (ibid.). Though project leaders also estimate that a significant proportion (23 per cent) of clients may well be part of a broader 'hidden homeless' population (that is, people staying in bed and breakfast hotels, in squats, or sharing floor space at a friend's or relative's), they also defend the continuing need to provide for such people – with a project coordinator from Wimpster in the west of England constructing the argument as follows (for additional support for the argument as to the importance of food provided by soup runs in the diets of those in poor housing, see Evans & Dowler, 1999):

> [The thing is,] the system is always gonna fail somewhere, and there is always gonna be a need for people to provide for the gaps when people do fall through

the system. That's my argument against that lady's [Louise Casey, then head of the RSU] view of getting rid of all the soup runs and things. If there wasn't a need we wouldn't do it. The need is still there, and at the end of the day if the need isn't supplied, people will die. (Albert, paid soup run coordinator, Wimpster)

Countering claims that soup runs reduce the likelihood of those already on the streets approaching mainstream services, project coordinators also stress the role that soup runs play in facilitating people's access to other services. Thus, while 70 per cent of projects offer information and advice (on the location and opening hours of local hostels and day centres, for example) as well as food (Johnsen et al., 2005b), homeless people themselves explain how it is often soup runs that steer them towards other services when they don't know where to turn, as Tanya and Kate recall:

[When] I got off the bus ... I was completely lost ... [But] I managed to wander down to what I now know is **** Green ... and then I found the soup run ... and I learnt a lot from the people who were there that night about where to go ... where the *** Centre was ... where the night shelter was. (Tanya, 45, ex rough sleeper, Benington)

I was begging up by the **** and I had some outreach people ... approach me. But I also heard of a load of different places because of the soup runs, people on the soup runs have got the information – they know. (Kate, 24, Traveller, Benington)

Soup runs also clearly provide vital support to those who – for whatever reason – can no longer access mainstream services. Reflecting on their client base, for example, the team in Benington estimate that 'about half of them I would have thought have been banned' from the city's day centres and hostels – leaving the soup run as their only (legal) source of free food and other essentials. Nor can soup runs sensibly be viewed as perpetuating a cycle of homelessness and addiction. Indeed, to frontline workers such arguments seem naive. As the outreach workers below explain, faced with a choice between food or drugs the addict will always choose the latter:

WORKER A: Most of those are people who are out on the street or people who are begging ... they do spend all their money on drugs. That's why they're begging, in most cases, and ...
WORKER B: They don't even want food.
WORKER A: ... food is somewhere over there in their priorities. It's just not – they're not going to spend hard-begged money on food, simple as that. And then that's probably the only food that they get, really, from the soup runs and the night shelter. (Paid staff, local authority street outreach team, Benington)

As these workers explain, closing down a city's soup runs will not result in addicts buying food rather than drugs, only in the likelihood that they will go without food entirely – with obvious consequences for people already in a very poor state of health. Or they will find other ways to procure something to eat, as those with the misfortune to find themselves homeless in a city without such services sometimes do:

> SARAH: [So] when you were sleeping rough, how did you survive on a day-to-day basis? … Because there's not much in **** – soup kitchens and things like that.
>
> PAUL: I was a thief. I was pretty good at it I thought – until I got caught. But yeah, I mean I used to steal tins of soup, things like that. That's the only way I could survive. (Paul, 52, hostel resident, Steeltown)

Far from being the relic of an earlier age, then, it is clear that soup runs remain a vital part of Britain's welfare landscape. They provide an important first point of contact for many on the streets. They offer sustenance to those who, even if in housing of their own, may not be able to afford enough to eat, and give those with serious addictions and those unwilling or unable to access other homeless services at least one (relatively) nutritious meal a day (Evans & Dowler, 1999). They also reduce the (already heightened) likelihood that homeless people will move from the streets into the criminal justice system, by lessening the need for what Pat Carlen (1996) calls 'survivalist crime'.

It is also clear that homeless people themselves value such services. For those sleeping rough especially, as Darren (in his early thirties) explains, a soup may well provide 'the only meal you [have] hot. Just what you need at seven thirty at night'. Less clear is what drives these organizations to action in the first place, and what motivates the many thousands of volunteers still providing these services each night across Britain to continue their work in the face of such hostility not only from government but from other homeless agencies.

Extraordinary Acts of Kindness

In attempting to chart the process by which the 'ordinary' ethics expressed in routine activities of care (for friends, family or neighbours, for example) come to be transformed into an 'extraordinary' sense of ethical commitment to the other, Barnett et al. (2005) point to the role that an accessible or appealing 'device' plays in bridging the gap between ordinary ethics and a more deliberate performance of 'ethical citizenship'. Such devices may take the form of already existing voluntary organizations (which provide potential volunteers with the opportunity to volunteer) or an especially powerful event that sparks a sudden awareness of need. While we have already explored the role of such devices in the prompt to volunteer (Cloke et al., 2007), they can also be used to explore the dynamics shaping the founding of voluntary organizations themselves.

In the case of soup runs, very often this device simply takes the form of an encounter with a homeless person, an encounter that leads people to question what if any provision exists for homeless people locally and, if – as is so often the case – finding the answer to be very little, attempting to fill that gap themselves:

> SARAH: What inspired the development of the soup run?
> ALBERT: The basic problem was very obvious. It's not so obvious now. But then a lot of the rough sleepers were sleeping round the back of our building there, and they used to come – they still do ... to the back door for food and stuff. (Albert, paid soup run coordinator, Wimpster)

For many, this prompt to an extraordinary ethics of care is described in terms of a sense of individual moral responsibility that others no longer seem to recognize. More often, this individual response is framed within wider ethical systems – most commonly (though not exclusively) moving around a Christian ethos. As one project coordinator explains, 'If the council and the government aren't going to provide the services then that's our moral responsibility as a church, to be looking to meet that gap' (Caroline, volunteer soup run coordinator, Benington). And Albert adds:

> [I just] thought that there was a need, that there were people that were really lost, and nobody really cared about them. They were damaged people, homeless people, and nobody cared a sausage about them really. And I really felt that God wanted me to do something about it ... (Albert, paid soup run coordinator, Wimpster)

In light of the preponderance of faith-based organizations in this field, Britain's soup runs might best be understood as emerging out of a complex amalgam of motivational and ethical prompts. Most obviously, while it is often assumed that Christian participation in 'social action' schemes such as soup runs draws upon a basic desire for evangelism (the witnessing of faith to others), in our experience participation in running services for homeless people is rarely fuelled only or simply by evangelism. Instead, participants seem more obviously to subscribe to an ethic of *serving* others, and in particular disadvantaged others. Of course, just as different Christians will express widely differing views as to the causes of homelessness and poverty (ranging from the outcome of individual failure (Steinfels, 2001) to the result of unjust social, economic and political structures and life circumstances (Wallis, 2001)), both evangelism and service can also take a number of different forms. For some, work on a soup run almost always involves some kind of attempt to communicate their beliefs – though it is clear that these acts of witnessing rarely take the form of the aggressive proselytizing for which Christian organizations in this field have been so heavily criticized in the past. For others evangelism is understood as articulated through actions rather than words, quiet service rather than preaching (for accounts of aggressive proselytizing in Salvation Army projects see Anderson, 1923; Wallace, 1965; Spradley, 1970; Wiseman, 1979; Snow & Anderson, 1993; for an account of more recent changes to the Army's ethos, see Himmelfarb, 1991):

> Well, we don't kind of talk about God necessarily: we won't force it on to people, put it like that. Our approach is that if we feel it's right to share about Jesus and it's right to share about our faith then we will. And quite often we will offer to pray for people … But if they're … clearly … [not] interested, then [we] don't bother [them]. (Caroline, volunteer soup run coordinator, Benington)

> I think … we can be a little bit more [of] an evangelical exercise. Whilst we're not preaching with words, we're certainly preaching with our actions. (Albert, paid soup run coordinator, Wimpster)

The idea of Christian charity often seems to carry with it the suggestion of a group of God-fearing do-gooders whose response to marginalized people is wrapped up in a self-identity of faith-virtue, and an other-identity that positions service users as little more than fodder for evangelism. In stark contrast, our research suggests that such individuals – and the organizations in which they are placed – might be much better understood as attempting to articulate a theo-ethical sense of *agape* and *caritas*, a genuine openness to and an outpouring of unconditional love towards the other. Though a Christian concept, such an ethos can be seen in the mission statements of secular as well as avowedly Christian organizations in the field, as this mission statement from a Simon Community in the north of England (2001) illustrates:

> It is often when people are living on the streets that they are in their most vulnerable and lowest states. Desperation and fear are exacerbated by exhaustion, cold, and anxiety, leaving a person with numb resignation and despair; preferring to stay on the street, knowing the score, than daring to hope or try for anything else. At this point, making the most immediate and concrete gesture of caring, without conditions, questions, or demands, is the soup runners' work.

The expression of agape thus means adopting what Augé (1998) has termed a 'sense *for* the other': an emotional, connected and committed orientation towards the needs of others based upon an unconditional acceptance of (rather than desire to change) the other. The aim is to be non-interventionist, accepting of difference, and to bestow upon individuals the dignity to just 'be' without demanding anything in return. At a practical level, as one project manager explains, this may mean reminding volunteers that 'sometimes it's just about listening, it's not about having the answers'. On the streets it means providing a service open to all (whether 'housed' or 'homeless') where 'all are welcome – no judgements made', and where 'hospitality is offered to anyone who wishes to avail of it (and who obviously has some kind of need or wouldn't turn up!) without prejudice'. Integral to such an ethos is a 'no questions asked' policy, described in the following way by a Salvation Army officer:

> You see, [on the soup run] we don't ask any questions, we don't ask – like, if somebody came here [to the Salvation Army Corps] for a sleeping bag or for a food parcel, I start asking, 'What's your name, what's your National Insurance number, where do you live?' ... but on the soup run you ask no questions. We just give, and it's very different.

Yet, notwithstanding the fact that many of those working on soup runs also come through church networks, it does not necessarily follow that soup run volunteers are driven by the same motivations as those founding a project, or that the ethos set out in a project's mission statement will be articulated in the understandings and actions of volunteers when on the streets. Indeed, if asked to elaborate on what first motivated them to get involved with a soup run, volunteers will proffer a wide variety of reasons. For some, the initial decision to volunteer is driven by faith. For others, volunteering has more to do with changes in their own life circumstances and, over time, becomes more obviously explicable in terms of simple routine. Ryan (aged 55) began volunteering when his marriage broke up, for example, and has continued – partly out of habit – for more than a decade.

In light of this variety we would suggest that it is sensible to interpret volunteering not, as is so often the case (Van Til, 1988; Clary, 1996; Nylund, 2001), through the apparent polarities of altruism and egoism, but as both a self-oriented 'filling of the gap' and an 'other-oriented' making good use of unanticipated available time. This pointer towards a *didactic* relationship between selflessness and self-fulfillment – in which giving and receiving become inseparable (see also Bloom & Kilgore, 2003; Yeung, 2004) – is supported by seemingly oppositional discourses of camaraderie and diffi-culty that punctuate accounts of soup run volunteers. Certainly, many vol-unteers confirm that their volunteering brings them positive benefits: Ryan's efforts, for example, are clearly sustained by a mixture of a (rather vague) desire to 'give something back to society', habit and his commitment to col-leagues on the team. Although he finds it difficult to admit that he enjoys his volunteering (perhaps because he does not want to be seen as a do-gooder), this enjoyment principally comes from an obvious camaraderie with other volunteers that (partially) compensates for the stress of working with such vulnerable people in often distressing circumstances.

For others the decision to volunteer is indeed mainly a product of the desire to bear witness to their faith. Such a position is often viewed with suspicion. Rather than the selflessness implied in an ethics of agape and caritas, for example, Allahyari (2000) suggests that those motivated by faith act out of self-interest. Thus she documents how Christian volunteers often engage in a process of what she calls 'moral selving' – the attempt to create a more virtuous, more spiritual self through the act of working *'on'* (and attempting to convert) rather than *for* others.

Though it is perhaps not surprising that volunteers themselves vigorously reject any notion that they are some kind of 'Christian do-gooder' (a charge they do occasionally level at other volunteers, it should be noted), it is in fact very difficult to interpret the actions of soup run volunteers through this kind of lens. Far from struggling to hold back a ready pool of those anxious to prove their spiritual virtue, for example, soup run coordinators often describe the difficulties they have in persuading people to get involved with the soup run – a reluctance one project leader puts down to a sense of 'guilt – [that's] probably a strong word, but I think it's an element of "how can I go and talk to someone [when] I have so much and they have nothing"'. Some volunteers never get over this sense of discomfort. Yet rather than turn their back on the soup run, these people find other ways to serve: shying away from any public expression of virtue, and taking on the less often remarked but nonetheless vital tasks of planning and food preparation instead, for example.

This last example suggests a certain slippage between understandings and actions. Even if some volunteers view 'the homeless' with disquiet (whether out of guilt or fear) they continue to volunteer their time and energies on behalf of homeless people. Similar such slippages are sometimes apparent in the gap between the ethos of the organization for which a person works, a volunteer's own understandings of homelessness and homeless people, and their interactions with homeless people on the streets.

A Performative Ethics of Care

As we noted in chapter 2, any organizational ethos is of course likely to attract widely varying levels of allegiance from the staff and volunteers who represent that organization. As well as being stretched and transformed by individual ethics, organizational ethics can in any case never simply be 'read off' from expressions of that organization's ethos (as presented in its mission statement, for example) because these ethics only properly come into being through practice. Put another way, organizational ethics are a performance of organizational ethos, and these performances emerge differently in different situations depending upon the individuals (paid staff, volunteers and service users) involved in any particular encounter (Cloke et al., 2007).

There are, however, a number of ways in which an organization can seek to align its organizational ethos with the ethical frames and practices of its volunteers. Most obviously, organizations can seek alignment of their overall goals and ethical proclivities through selective recruitment of volunteers. Thus, if drawing on a pool of volunteers from their own church, for example, a project coordinator might reasonably assume that volunteers will bring with them certain key values that align with their own. While this may be the case with projects run by a single church, however, soup runs often draw volunteers from a network of affiliated churches and other groups. In these circumstances it is much more difficult to instill a common ethos, as a representative of this (secular) organization explains:

> To be frank, every night is a separate entity, separate churches. One might be Church of England, one might be Baptist, one might be a Community Church. There are some independents ... I'm independent of the church. I've got other nights independent ... it's very hard to keep them all together. (Lloyd, volunteer soup run coordinator, Benington)

Nor can such organizations necessarily rely on shared training to instill a common ethos. In fact, though project coordinators will often express a desire for some kind of training for their volunteers, they also recognize that in practice any kind of training is hard to organize – with volunteers lacking either the time or the inclination to engage in formal training sessions. They also recognize that, though they might produce a common code of practice, individual teams often desire a certain level of independence to structure their service as they feel best:

> All we can do is bring them out on the first night and just leave them [really]. You've got no other organization. Invite them along to the bi-monthly meeting. I ring them up, all the groups: 'Have you seen this person? How are they getting on? Any agro?' That's the only way you can coordinate things. ... We've got to be independent. We're a very loose collection of people each night. It's hard to get some of the nights [teams] to come to the regular meetings, to keep it together as an organization, and produce the literature, which I've given to you, the code of practice and brochure. (Lloyd, volunteer soup run coordinator, Benington)

Whatever the formally articulated ethos of these organizations, then, in practice the organizational ethics structuring their activities on the streets are liable to shift and change in accordance with the understandings and ethics of individual teams and team members.

In fact, it is clear that volunteers themselves do mainly ascribe to the non-judgemental ethos of open acceptance articulated in project mission statements. For example, rather than questioning whether or not such people are 'really' in need or are 'deserving' of their services, volunteers tend to take a person's presence at a soup run as itself evidence of their need, and thus their 'deservedness':

It's so basic what we actually give them, that if they want to queue up or actually wait for us to give them basics, then they must be desperate ... I tell you what, I wouldn't do it, I can assure you. ... Hanging around just to wait for a bit of soup and a few sandwiches. I wouldn't. You know, you've got to be quite desperate to actually do that. (Richard, soup run volunteer, Wimpster)

But volunteers also sometimes express more ambiguous views about those they serve. Most obviously, some continue to construct distinctions between the 'deserving' and the 'undeserving', distinguishing between those in hostels and the 'genuinely' homeless, for example, or between a newer and more aggressive clientele and older, more romantic figures:

RYAN: [That was the time] I was giving it up. Because I felt that the people that were out there wasn't actually homeless, and that the needy ones wasn't getting what we were hoping they were going to get. So, we bailed for a couple of months ...
MALCOM: Yeah, yeah. You were giving it to the hostel people, which really don't need it.
RYAN: In the early days. When I first started with Brian [it] was the older ones, which were ...
MALCOLM: Yeah, 'gentlemen of the road' ...
RYAN: ... which were on the, you know, had a real drink problem, but had a different character, different way to 'em and they would always be able to tell you a story ...
SARAH: So, some of these younger guys ... are ... harder to deal with? ...
RYAN: [Yeah, you've got to] ... be slightly a bit careful, because you're not quite sure what they're going to do, in effect. You know, they could have a needle in their pocket and, sort of, because you've said something wrong they'd ...
MALCOLM: ... have a go at you. You just don't know. Yeah. (Ryan and Malcolm, soup run volunteers, Benington)

Sparked in part by such experiences, people often reflect upon how their views of homeless people have changed over the course of their time with a project. For many, early experiences on a soup run may lead them to challenge their own, rather stereotypical views of 'the homeless' and to begin to engage instead with service users as individuals, increasing the sympathy they feel for such people. Over time, however, this sympathy may be replaced by a certain 'hardening' of the spirit, as continued exposure to the realities of homeless people's lives leads to a 'waning of effect'.

SARAH: Have your views on homelessness and your perceptions of homeless people altered since you've been working on the soup run? ...
MALCOLM: Yeah, I think it has actually. I think ... I think you basically have this idea in your mind about what a homeless person is, and it tends to be someone who's completely alien to you. But when you actually start to talk

to them you can relate to them … [as] individuals rather than a homeless group. Like I say, in those early days, I used to visualize exactly what homeless people are like. Once you actually start talking to them, they're all individuals at the end of the day and you start to relate to them and I think that makes you much more wanting to … to help. … [Then] you get hardened. (Malcolm, soup run volunteer, Benington)

Working on a soup run is therefore not only physically but emotionally demanding. Serving in all weathers, often late at night, volunteers may find themselves constantly on edge, having to make assessments as to whether or not a person may represent a threat to other users, themselves or members of their team ('because you've said something wrong they … have a go at you, you just don't know'). It can also invoke painful self-reflection, as people confront their own prejudices and perhaps question their motives for getting involved with such work. Different volunteers come to terms with these issues in different ways. For some, such work is only sustainable because of the way in which sudden, unexpected encounters lead them back to the emotional, connected and committed orientation towards the other that Augé (1998) speaks of – moments when a more abstract and fragile sympathy *for* the homeless other is replaced by a more immediate identification and empathy *with* that other:

MALCOLM: Do you remember that girl? … that knocked me for six, didn't it, the other week.
RYAN: Very pretty girl she was, very soft talking and that.
MALCOLM: Very soft talking … public school. … That brought it home to me, didn't it, last week. You get hardened and then you thought 'Oh, crumbs, that could have been your daughter.' (Ryan and Malcolm, soup run volunteers, Benington)

For others, an ethics of open acceptance involves instead a certain distancing of the self from the other, in which the acceptance of alterity on its rather than one's own terms also provides a certain protection for the self from the pain this emotional connection may bring. Only when these barriers are raised is it possible to continue such work:

I guess for me, it's that I recognize that I cannot solve all of the problems of the homeless in Benington … I see that people are heroin addicts or whatever … [And] I can't make people stop being an addict – they have to want it themselves … I guess in a way it gives me a kind of self-protection. … As a Christian it would break your heart every time you walked away, and sometimes it is really, really hard to walk away … you do get emotionally involved, and it is hard to walk away.. but generally speaking … you do put up barriers a little around yourself to try and shut down. Because, like you said, otherwise you just wouldn't be able to do it. (Caroline, volunteer soup run coordinator, Benington)

Openness and Difference, Inclusion and Exclusion

The ethics of open acceptance practised by soup runs marks them out (on the surface at least) as the most inclusive of all the services available to homeless people. Soup runs are open to anyone, do not require referrals from other agencies, do not question the 'deservedness' of those served and, most importantly perhaps, do not place conditions upon the receipt of services. Yet this very openness also means they are extremely volatile, sometimes violent environments. Soup runs are geared towards the needs of all, including those barred from other services and people with complex needs (those suffering from mental illness, or drug or alcohol dependencies, for example). Such people can behave in unpredictable ways, and on rare occasions a soup run can be disrupted by verbal or physical attacks – directed at other services users, but also staff and volunteers, as one soup run coordinator recalls:

> one time ... we just had a really, really drunk guy who – don't know who he was, don't know where he was from, haven't seen him since – but he did verbally lash out at us quite heavily, and that was not particularly nice ... he was saying that he was from **** [a poor neighbourhood known for high levels of drug dealing and prostitution] and he operated **** and he called the shots in ****, and it was funny because initially he was really nice and fine. And then he just flew off the handle because we were speaking to this [other] homeless guy. Then he apologized, and then flew off the handle again. (Lloyd, volunteer soup run coordinator, Benington)

Project coordinators are aware of the risks that new volunteers especially face in such an environment. But they also accept that – in the absence of better training – there is very little they can do to minimize these risks, other than try to quickly develop what Goffman (1971) would call the 'scanning skills' (or 'street smarts') of those new to such work:

> A lot of the team members that we have with us, maybe they've only done this once or twice, so they really have no understanding of where some of these guys are coming from. I guess, for us, we get to know faces and get to know people and get to know different looks and the different – you know. ... So ... I'm very conscious of the team leaders, that we have a responsibility for safety as well. ... It's just common sense really. (Caroline, volunteer soup run coordinator, Benington)

Such environments can clearly be intimidating to the newly homeless too, and to homeless women especially (Rowe & Wolch, 1990; May et al., 2007). Indeed, the very openness that characterizes soup runs can present a barrier to other (potential) service users, suggesting that attempts to include will also, inevitably perhaps, exclude. For the young woman below, for example, the local soup run was perceived as an unsafe, threatening space – leading her and her sister to avoid it all together:

> We started chatting to some people and we were asking them about places to stay and stuff and they said that things have happened there [at the soup run] ... if you don't look scared then nobody is going to hurt you or anything. But we were two girls, and me and my sister got scared really easily so we didn't want to go. (Julie, 23, hostel resident, Benington)

Such volatility is heightened by the often fragmented nature of these organizations – in which different teams may follow rather different practices – and the peculiar spatial politics in play when services are offered in public space. In day centres and hostels, for example, formal rules provide staff with an explicit codification of what constitutes 'acceptable' and 'unacceptable' behaviour on the part of service users. To some extent at least, these rules relieve staff and volunteers from the need to make personal judgements about the actions of their clients. Thus, while individual members of staff might interpret and implement these rules in slightly different ways, the defining line between what is and is not acceptable is at least relatively clearly defined – and usually tangibly expressed in signs adorning a building's interior. As a last resort, individuals exhibiting 'inappropriate' behaviour may also be denied access to the space by 'gatekeepers' in the reception area or, once inside, forcibly removed from the premises (Waters, 1992).

In contrast, while most soup runs have a basic code of practice, individual teams and volunteers have far more leeway in how exactly they choose to operate. One result of this is that the question of what is or is not acceptable behaviour tends to fall to the volunteers on duty. While service users are aware of this, they may also (quite reasonably) protest about a lack of consistency in the application of the 'rules' – claiming that what is deemed acceptable by one team should be acceptable to another, or indeed that the kind of services offered by that team should be made available by the other. A typical example might be the question of whether or not to allow a service user to pick up food on behalf of a friend, or whether an unexpected supply of cakes should be given out at all, if there are not enough for different teams to distribute. Though such issues might seem trivial, they can quickly lead to distrust and resentment on the side of service users if they perceive they are missing out, and can encourage the move towards an ethos of 'less eligibility' on the part of service providers if volunteers deem that any 'extras' only make their work too difficult.

Further complicating these dynamics are the particular spatial politics of the soup run. In contrast to day centres and hostels, soup runs typically operate in outdoor public space – over which service providers have no 'ownership' and which, importantly, has few (obviously tangible) boundaries. Thus, while volunteers may occasionally refuse to serve someone, it is not possible to actually remove that person from the 'premises'; at least, not without enlisting the assistance of the police – a move that will almost certainly undermine the project's relations with service users. As a consequence, if they deem either themselves or other service users to be at risk, volunteers have little option but to close the service down. Such responses are rare, and normally only apply to the night of the incident. But projects may close for longer. For example, a soup run in the north of England halted serving for one month in 1995 'as a warning' to service users because 'it had got more dangerous on the streets'. Safety concerns arising as the result of an 'act of violence' committed by a service user at a south coast soup run meant that the organizers there abandoned the service entirely in 1989, only reinstating it two years later, under the auspices of a different organization.

Given the lack of rules governing soup runs and the risk that the service may be terminated should the situation become too volatile, it is not uncommon for service users to try to 'police' these situations themselves, restoring 'law and order' if and when they deem it necessary. Indeed, service users may in fact be far less tolerant of 'deviant' behaviour, or behaviour that transgresses normal conventions of etiquette, than are volunteers. Thus, as a rule, service users tend to expect everyone being served to abide by orthodox practices of queuing, being polite and expressing gratitude to volunteers for the services received, for example. And they are highly disapproving and unforgiving of those who fail to adhere to such conventions, most especially individuals who are rude to or threaten volunteer staff:

> The night shelter, soup van, it's all the same. If the soup van turns up and has got no sandwiches they [the other service users] go on and on. At least they're getting a cup of coffee and a fag, but that's not good enough. … It pisses me off when I go there and hear people knocking them [the volunteers]. (Charlie, 38, hostel resident, Benington)

> A few weeks ago one of our workers … left her handbag on the front seat of the car. She went to give out soup, one [service user] came along and tried to grab the handbag. Luckily the other guys stood up for them. (Lloyd, volunteer soup run coordinator, Benington)

Service users also tend to construct the same demarcations between the 'deserving' and 'undeserving' as do some volunteers, drawing strict distinctions between those in 'genuine' need (because living on the streets, for example) and those in less obvious need of such services (those with a hostel place, or accommodation of their own):

> There are a few scroungers that don't need to be using it … It saves them money for their beer and everything. … Although I'm going because I'm hungry, I don't believe in going somewhere because I would be taking a meal

from somebody else who might need it more. ... [For example], the first time I was in the night shelter I hadn't eaten a decent meal in six days, so I figured I was property qualified to go and have something to eat. (Dave, 39, hostel resident, Benington)

ALBERT: Anyone who comes to the serving hatch can have anything. We've had lorry drivers who have been sleeping overnight on the main car park – 'yeah sure', you know. You can't be selective because you can't tell by the person whether they're rough-sleepers, unemployed, well off or what.
JEAN: [But] The men are selective and they have a word with you about the fact that that person's not actually homeless [don't they]. They'll say to you, 'Oh, he's not homeless, he shouldn't have any food.' So they can be quite selective. (Albert, paid soup run coordinator, and Jean, volunteer, Wimpster)

Just as with people who beg, such assertions are permeated by questions of legitimacy, with only those sleeping rough often deemed to be 'genuinely' homeless by both volunteers and service users alike (Dean & Melrose, 1999; Fitzpatrick & Kennedy, 2001). Where for volunteers these distinctions may play a role in the decision of whom to serve (even if in practice, as we have seen, services are normally extended to all), for service users they are better understood as relating to attempts to justify their own greater deservedness of the services on offer by undermining the claims of others.

There is a spatial politics at play here too. Expressions of the codes of conduct governing soup run use vary significantly according to the location and method of serving. When service users have gathered at a regular site specifically for the purposes of receiving food, the rules of engagement seem to be determined by mainstream social norms (a civil demeanour and queuing, for example). But when volunteers go in search of potential clients – for example, a person bedded down in a shop doorway – these codes change. Though still serving in a public space, volunteers are aware that they are in effect entering the personal space of the individual concerned, a space that will very often have been 'privatized' via the placement of personal effects such as bedding or other possessions (Lofland, 1973). As a result, they must do so on terms determined by that individual, lending these encounters a less predictable quality. Volunteers generally understand this sense of 'ownership', and of the different conventions that apply to different spaces (Cresswell, 1996). As one project coordinator explains, she became acutely aware of such issues when the team moved from their regular serving site in the centre of the city to a poorer neighbourhood where a number of the city's homeless services are located – thus moving out of their own and into their services users' normal territory:

I don't know, just as a team we felt more on edge. ... We all felt so much more that we were – on their territory, and we therefore had to really play it by their rules. And it just didn't feel particularly brilliant being there ... I don't know how to explain it really – just like 'yeah, this is our space' and when you're in it, you have to behave according to their rules. (Caroline, volunteer soup run coordinator, Benington)

The Politics of Visibility

Serving on the streets, soup run coordinators must also negotiate a complex politics of visibility. It is, of course, the obvious visibility of soup runs that often leads to such virulent opposition to their activities by city managers, government and the wider public. For city managers and government, soup runs are an uncomfortable reminder of the poverty that still exists in cities that must now more than ever attempt to project an image of prosperity (Mitchell, 1997), and of the failure to tackle 'social exclusion'. For members of the public, soup runs pose the most obvious challenge to what Jordan (1999) has described as the 'negative rights of citizenship'. That is, rather than passing up the decision as to who might be deserving of help to welfare professionals paid for through the taxation system, soup runs demand that citizens continue to negotiate these difficult moral dilemmas for themselves.

On rare occasions soup run coordinators might choose to confront this politics head on. In what must be considered a highly politicized act, one of the soup runs we worked with, for example, has chosen to visibly proclaim homeless people's 'rights to the city' (Mitchell, 2003) and to invert normative understandings of homelessness and poverty by hosting regular 'banquets' for homeless people, complete with music, in a central city shopping precinct (on the politics of inversion see Stallybrass and White, 1986; for an example of similar challenges to homeless people's exclusion from prime city space and public life, see the discussion of homeless weddings in Ruddick, 1996).

Though issuing a powerful symbolic challenge to homeless people's more usual exclusion from prime urban space, and an important reminder of the continuing problems of homelessness in the city, such events may be far from liberating for homeless people themselves. Most obviously, perhaps, those attending a banquet must bear the shame that so public a proclamation of their need may bring. Speaking of the stigma associated with the use of homeless services more generally, for example, Robin described why he rarely leaves his hostel (see also Takahashi et al., 2002):

I don't think people wanna be seen to go into them [day centres]. Even now I'm embarrassed when I go out [from the hostel] to walk back in, in case anybody sees me walking through the gate. I still have that feeling. I think that's probably got something to do with the reason I don't go out too often as well, because I don't want to bump into somebody I know and they say, 'What are you doing now?' and I've gotta say, 'I'm living in ★★★★.' (Robin, 54, hostel resident, Wimpster)

Too visible a presence on the streets is also liable to draw the attention of those opposed to a soup run's activities. Certainly this soup run's banquets have attracted considerable opposition from local businesses. In a similar vein, a soup run operating on the south coast of England was forced to move its serving site from a residential square to an area of the seafront 'where there were no residents to object'. By way of contrast, attempts to set up a soup run on the sea front in Sandstown have been consistently blocked by the local authority, fearful that its activities would be bad for the tourist trade:

> We're a tourist town, [so] it don't look good if people are queuing up at a soup caravan for a night, you know, when families have been to pictures or have been on sea front or what, and you get all these homeless people queuing up at a Sally Army van. It don't look good does it, as far as the council are concerned. (Housing advisor, Sandstown)

In an attempt to both limit such opposition and minimize the stigma those using their services may face, soup run coordinators therefore more usually mimic the tactics of homeless people themselves, seeking to reduce their visibility by confining themselves to the more marginal spaces of the city – car parks and side streets, back streets and alleyways within or near to the central city (so as to maximize accessibility) but away from the main thoroughfares (Duncan, 1983; Cloke et al., 2008). Such tactics seem broadly successful, at least in minimizing public opposition, as Albert and Richard remark:

> ALBERT: I would think – my personal view … is it's very low profile. The only people that really know it's going on apart from our own organization is probably the people that make use of the facility, and the odd passer-by who walks by and says, 'Ooh', you know … I'm not aware that we've ever had anything in our local paper about it.
> RICHARD: [And] That's the best way to be really. I mean, it's nice to have some finance [from public donations] towards it, but I'd rather have it that way really. (Albert and Richard, paid soup run coordinator and volunteer, Wimpster)

But these more marginal locations also present difficulties. As Albert points out, moving too far from the public eye can pose a risk to the safety of both service users and volunteers. It may also make it difficult for potential clients to find them:

> [We serve in] the college car park, partly because that is near the **** Day Centre and a lot of them [the service users] know that. We used to go down by outside **** but it's a bit off the beaten track, and security for us apart from anything else. … You couldn't be seen – if anything happened down there you couldn't be seen, so we have okayed it with the college who are only next door to ****, but we use their car park, which is more visual to be seen and is far more convenient all round. (Albert, paid soup run coordinator, Wimpster)

SHARON: I've heard about things like that [soup runs] but I've never actually gone to them.

JULIE: And it's not every day. They're at weird times, and you have to catch them at the right time. I've never found any of those. (Sharon and Julie, aged 20 and 23, hostel residents, Benington)

Thus, like homeless people themselves, soup runs attempt to traverse the 'path of least resistance' (Cooper, 2001), negotiating what Sibley (1995) has referred to as varying 'contours of tolerance' across the city. They must operate in spaces that are marginal enough to minimize the stigma associated with the public provision of alms and conflict with those that oppose their activities, but not so marginal as to render them invisible to potential clients and compromise the safety of volunteers and service users. Projects must also tread a careful path when negotiating their relations with other service agencies, as we explore below.

Survival at the Margins

If soup runs tend to operate in the marginal spaces of the city, they also occupy a marginal position in most local service networks. Indeed, while soup runs have been the target of significant criticism from central government in recent years, they have also had to contend with increasing criticism from other homeless service providers. Summarizing this critique, the manager of an RSU-funded local authority street outreach team castigated the soup runs operating in her city on the basis that:

There are a huge number of cross-agency meetings facilitated by the local authority. [But] the biggest problem comes with the what I call 'ad-hoc' agencies, not in receipt of funding, for example ... the soup runs ... agencies like that ... who are sort of out of the loop. In my role as CAT ['contact and assessment', or street outreach, team] manager I've tried to give those organizations an opportunity to feed into the RSI consortium ... share best practice, etc. ... But it's a hard slog sometimes, because I think people choose not to accept funding for a variety of reasons, and it can be quite difficult getting these agencies ... on board in terms of ensuring a professional approach to the work that they're doing; not just in health and safety and training issues, but more particularly, helping clients move away from a life on the streets – giving people opportunities to move forward in their lives. I think very often that is missing in some of those voluntary organizations ... they're not challenging them [homeless people]; they're not offering them opportunities, and I think they're also to a great degree putting their staff at risk because they don't know who they're taking and they don't know what they're up against. (Manager, local authority street outreach team, Benington)

There are a number of charges here. Soup runs are criticized for being over-reliant on volunteers, for failing to liaise with other agencies in a properly 'joined-up approach', for a lack of staff training (that puts both their volunteers and clients at risk) and, most damningly, for failing to provide people with an 'opportunity' to move forward in their lives. Deploying the rhetoric of the New Public Management, such organizations are thus denigrated for being 'unprofessional' and ignoring 'best practice'; qualities that can no longer be accepted in the new world of corporate voluntarism (for a similar account of the way in which opponents of New Labour's welfare 'reform' are automatically positioned as anti-modernization, see Newman, 2002).

But the conflict between soup runs and other agencies articulated here as a conflict over 'best practice' can be viewed somewhat differently, of course; that is, as a conflict over how one might best define a relationship of care. As one soup run coordinator put it, 'Care is such an open-ended word.' The problem faced by Britain's soup runs is that such open-endedness is no longer tolerated. Under New Labour, 'best practice' – or the 'right and proper' way of caring – has come to be defined in very particular ways (see also Maile and Hoggett, 2001). In its Change a Life campaign, for example, the government has attempted to dictate to members of the housed public the right and proper way to respond to the problems of homelessness – by donating to designated charities rather than giving directly to those on the streets (Fitzpatrick & Jones, 2005). While such a move denies the right of members of the housed public to choose how to give and who to give to, it also denies the possibility of positive agency on the part of homeless people themselves, assuming that they cannot be trusted to spend such money in their own best interests. Similarly, for the RSU and some of the organizations in receipt of Homeless Action Programme funding, 'best practice' equates to a highly interventionist approach – or 'active rehabilitation' (Waters, 1992) – focused on proactive outreach and resettlement schemes in which professionally trained staff, rather than homeless people themselves, determine how best a person may be helped (May et al., 2005). Indeed, 'active rehabilitation' demands that homeless people change aspects of their behavior and lifestyle if they wish to access the services that have been made available to them – whether a shelter bed or a place on a waiting list for subsidized housing (ODPM, 1999). Within such an approach there is no more room for an ethos of open acceptance than there is for homeless people's own agency. And, just as members of the housed public must be dissuaded from giving directly to homeless people lest their money be used inappropriately, so too soup runs must be 'dissuaded' from their activities lest their practices undermine these more 'proactive' attempts to tackle homelessness.

At a philosophical level an ethos of open acceptance and an ethos of active rehabilitation are completely incompatible. At a practical level, this disjuncture means that soup runs do not have access to the statutory funding made available to other homeless services. In fact, in the light of the obvious gap between the government's stance and their own non-interventionist ethos, many soup run providers have actively resisted attempts by their local authority to bring them into line with central government directives – thus turning their backs on any such funding. Though soup run coordinators may well wish to build better relationships with other local service providers (so as to further their signposting work, for example), they also have an ardent desire to maintain their autonomy, as one project coordinator explains:

> [We are] certainly not in the loop ... I think we'd like to try and get a little bit more involved, or at least network a bit more across what people are doing, or what other churches and other organizations are doing, so I think it is a bit unfortunate that we are on the periphery. [But] we do our own thing. And that's not because we want to be elitist in any way, it's just because ... we want to be very much – our real thing is that we want relationships with the people that we meet on the streets, and we want to be able to maintain those relationships, so that's why we very much do our own thing. (Caroline, volunteer soup run coordinator, Benington)

Others have instead more carefully differentiated between the approaches taken by different arms of their organization, taking advantage of the additional statutory funding now available to the 'professionalized' wing of their service, but retaining the independent – and more obviously 'evangelical' – ethos of their soup run:

> I suppose in many ways that – we've seen it in the **** [major homelessness provider] how we have professionalized our social work and in effect now we have a separate company, the **** Housing Association, which deals with all our hostels and our work outside of the church setting. I suppose they have to be less evangelical in their nature because of the government money that's provided to them, and I think that's dictated to them also really. Whereas we can be a little bit more – what's seen as an evangelical exercise. (Albert, paid soup run coordinator, Wimpster)

While such a stance may enable soup runs to retain their independence, it also means that they must continue to operate on very limited budgets. Indeed, many organizations face a continual challenge to generate the finances necessary to ensure their long-term survival. Most are heavily reliant on unpredictable and often short-term sources of funding, typically donations (of both money and goods-in-kind) from churches, members of the public, local shops or schools. Importantly, such donations tend to be rather sporadic, coinciding with events such as Harvest Festival. As a result, while projects may face serious shortfalls at some points in the year, at other times they may operate in surplus – leading to difficulties in storing donated food or clothing, for example.

Yet despite, or more accurately perhaps because of, such apparent 'fragility' soup runs are also remarkably resilient. Because they operate on a shoestring – with 39 per cent of survey projects having an annual budget of less than £500, and 50 per cent less than £1000 (Johnsen et al., 2005b) – financial shortfalls may be counteracted relatively easily. When finances are tight, volunteers simply reach into their own pockets to cover any deficit. Other projects, especially those drawing on the support of wealthier congregations, are able to rely on very generous funding from their churches, many of which continue to operate a traditional tithe system:

> It's all funded completely through the church. At the moment, we've got about 150 people in the church and most of those people are professionals. So we are a very giving church; we do stick to biblical principles about tithing and giving 10 per cent ... so from that point of view we are very privileged, because we do have the funding there to be able to do this without question. I don't think there's ever been a time that we've not been able to fund anything that we've done. And that's ... how it operates with the volunteers that do the food preparation: they basically ... make sandwiches and soup go and buy all the ingredients and they can then submit their receipt to claim the money back, but actually a lot of people don't do that ... we have [one] couple ... I've never known them once claim, and they just see that as their opportunity to give something a little bit more to people who are less fortunate than they are, really. (Caroline, volunteer soup run coordinator, Benington)

As a result of such generosity – a generosity that once again belies the apparent vengefulness of other city publics – many soup runs are in fact somewhat more economically resilient than are other kinds of homeless service (see, for example, Johnsen et al., 2005a, b), because they require so much less in the way of resources to keep operating. Such support stands as testament to the passion and commitment of the organizations and individuals providing soup runs, as well as to the members of the housed public upon whose support they rely.

Conclusions

In chapter 2 we argued that services for homeless people represent part of a wider picture of emerging postsecular spaces in the city, in which new forms of rapprochement between faith-motivated and 'secular' engagement are forming in the shadow of neoliberalism. In some ways it could be argued that the account of outdoor relief in this chapter represents but the latest version of longstanding faith-practices of giving alms to the poor. Yet we would argue that the services examined here are in fact better understood as being inflected with several currents of the *post*secular. Across Britain, people motivated by different forms of faith, and by different forms of secular humanism, have been willing to work together in schemes of food distribution because such schemes provide a mutually acceptable device for putting into practice their desire to care for homeless people. As part of these schemes, homeless people are served regardless of their positionality *vis-à-vis* faith, politics or ethics, such that there is no question here of volunteers only being willing to serve people who are like themselves, or prepared to become more like themselves.

A number of those working on soup runs understand their work as an active protest against contemporary responses (or lack of response) to Britain's homelessness crisis. To their critics, of course, soup runs are the unacceptable face of the voluntary response to this crisis. Staffed by untrained amateurs and 'do-gooders', they are accused of doing little to address the underlying causes of homelessness, and even of helping to sustain 'street lifestyles'. Even to those less critical of their approach, soup runs are often viewed as an irrelevance, offering little more than a sticking plaster when far more radical surgery is needed if the problems of homelessness are to be solved.

Such criticisms are misplaced and ignore the potential of soup runs to serve those who continue to fall between the cracks of more formal provision. Rather than simply sustaining 'street lifestyles', soup runs provide an important 'signposting' service, directing people who wish to take up such services towards day centres and hostels, and offering something to eat at least to those who, for whatever reason, may be unwilling or unable to access those services. Furthermore, though soup run volunteers are the first to admit that they do not hold the solution to homelessness, they also insist on the vital importance of what they do:

> We're really only scratching the surface. Give 'em a bit of food on Friday night and some more on the Saturday, to keep them in this land of the living. If we removed it, some might die ... I don't think we pretend to be doing anything [more] ... a bit of food and drink on a Friday and Saturday night [and] a bit of cheer. (Albert, paid soup run coordinator, Wimpster)

Far from an irrelevance, soup runs keep people alive, providing vulnerable people with an important source of food and other resources (dry clothes and bedding, for example) when few or no other (legal) options are available to them (Evans & Dowler, 1999). As importantly, perhaps, soup runs offer homeless people a 'bit of cheer', providing a means for people to 'go out and demonstrate to guys on the street that there *are* people that care, and that they *are* worth something' (emphasis in original). While so much of the geographical literature on homelessness continues to focus on the recent 'punitive turn' in urban policy (DeVerteuil et al., 2009), soup runs provide a powerful reminder of a quite different current running through the homeless city: the unconditional outpouring of agape and caritas. They are in this sense, perhaps, the purest expression of the voluntary impulse that continues to play such an important role in Britain's homeless services landscape and of what Coles (1997) has called a 'postsecular' ethics; an ethics that holds no expectation of reciprocity and is guided by a sense *for* the other rather than a desire to change the other.

It is, of course, this ethos of open and unconditional acceptance that has bought soup runs into conflict with both central government and other homeless service providers in recent years. It is also one that marks out the contemporary soup run as a remarkably complex space. Like other homeless service spaces, soup runs are simultaneously inclusive and exclusive. While accepting of difference, they also often (inadvertently) exclude others who may be fearful of those using such services. In contrast to other homeless service spaces, their transitory nature, lack of rules, freedom from physical boundaries and visibility to the public all mean that soup runs must also constantly engage with (and adapt to) the multiple, overlapping and often conflicting meanings ascribed to urban space by city authorities, residents, retailers and homeless people themselves, charting a (continually changing) course of least resistance through the city.

Yet if socially, economically and politically fragile, soup runs have also proven themselves to be remarkably resilient. As we go on to demonstrate in subsequent chapters, other homeless service providers have been far less successful in resisting attempts by central government to shape the nature of their service. Soup runs have managed to retain their autonomy, surviving despite (or perhaps because of) the 'malign neglect' (Wolch & Dear, 1993) signalled in the continued absence of statutory funding, and more recent and more aggressive attempts by government to close them down. In the light of such resilience, it seems likely that soup runs will continue to operate in the (marginal spaces of) the city, providing basic but vital sustenance and support to homeless people and others.

Chapter Five

'It's Like You Can Almost Be Normal Again': Refuge and Resource in Britain's Day Centres

Introduction

In this chapter we begin the journey off the streets and into the service spaces in which street homeless people in fact spend so much of their time. Day centres (re)emerged in Britain in the late 1970s and early 1980s as a voluntary response to the limited statutory provision for single homeless people (on community drop-ins and other forms of day services see Conradson, 1999). Though a few of Britain's day centres date back to the Victorian era or even earlier, the vast majority (82 per cent) have come into being since 1980, with almost as many (61 per cent) first opening their doors as recently as 1990 (Johnsen et al., 2005a). Day centres are therefore a much more recent response to the problems of homelessness than soup runs. Like soup runs, however, day centres are almost entirely provided by voluntary sector organizations, with 85 per cent of projects run by churches and other charitable groups (ibid.). In contrast to soup runs, though the vast majority (88 per cent) of day centres continue to rely on the services of volunteers, most also employ at least one manager or paid member of staff (ibid.).

At their most basic, day centres cater for the essential needs of homeless people – providing inexpensive or free food and drinks, advice and information. Over the past decade or so, many have added to these basic services to also provide bathing and laundry facilities, medical care and specialist advice and advocacy – including 'resettlement' programmes aimed at moving people off the streets and into sustainable accommodation of their own (for details of the proportion of projects offering different services, see Johnsen et al., 2005a). Once viewed as a 'Cinderella service' (Waters, 1992), these evolving centres of care have more recently been recognized as an important service and have taken their place alongside 'high support' hostels at the centre of New Labour's programme for tackling street homelessness, acting as the first port of call in a process that aims to move people from the streets, to a day centre, to a hostel, to long-term, sustainable accommodation of their own (Randall & Brown, 2002; CLG, 2006).

The increased emphasis placed on day centres in recent government policy can be understood as part and parcel of a broader drive to move people away from on-street provision to indoor services. Such a drive has been viewed with suspicion by some academics and advocacy groups. Thus, critics have noted that the increasing emphasis on day centres and other indoor services has been coupled with attempts to actively reduce the number of soup runs, for example, and an escalation in the number of arrests of, or use of Anti-Social Behaviour Orders against, those who 'persistently' beg (Johnsen et al., 2005b; Johnsen & Fitzpatrick, 2010). They also point out that if the government's aim really is to provide a more comprehensive package of support to homeless people so as to enable people to make a more permanent exit from the streets, it is odd that the organizations charged with providing that support should still have to struggle so hard for funding (Johnsen et al., 2005a), or that more has not been done to address the continuing shortage of affordable accommodation (Shelter, 2007).

There is, of course, no reason why the government's view of day centres should align with the understandings of homeless advocates or even with those actually providing such services. As a day centre on the south coast of England makes clear in its mission statement, for example: '[This project] rejects the role of containment. "Getting the underclass off the street" may be a side-product of our activities, but the condemnation and discriminatory basis of this approach is not one with which [this project] wishes to be associated' (undated). In the light of so vehement a rejection of this role it is clearly important to try to develop a better understanding of the aims of such organizations and of what exactly it is that day centres provide.

Here we suggest that day centres might reasonably be understood as holding contrary, if not contradictory, positions with regard to neoliberal responses to homelessness. On the one hand, and unlike the soup runs examined in chapter 4, day centres have become incorporated into the *acceptable* face of homeless service provision, assuming an integral role in neogovernmental responses to homelessness in Britain. From a critical perspective, then, day centres are spaces in which government policy is espoused and worked out. Such an interpretation fits well with the revanchist thesis, and would position day centre employees and volunteers as agents of a punitive clearance politics – providing the spaces into which homeless people can be swept.

On the other hand, despite their apparent 'insider' position in the local system of governance for homeless people, day centres can be regarded as key sites of care in the city, providing an opportunity for highly motivated people to become involved in service on behalf of homeless people and presenting a space in which (different) ethics of care are brought into being within a broader rapproachment of the 'secular' and the 'religious' in the contemporary city. Seen in this light, day centres might offer a radical site of resistance to neoliberalism and revanchism, in which self-motivated people get involved in the care of homeless people not as puppets of the state but as practitioners of (varying) ethical and political responses to the failures of the state.

In this chapter we begin the task of examining the spaces, practices and relations of Britain's day centres by charting their history and the quite varied aims and approaches underpinning the work of the different organizations providing such services. From there the chapter moves on to locate the position of day centres in the wider homeless services landscape, before moving indoors to chart the complex dynamics of day centres themselves. Building on the approach taken in chapter 4, where we focused mainly on the experiences of the volunteers engaged on Britain's soup runs, here we attempt to give equal voice to staff and service users alike, and to tease apart some of the differences in the approach to and understandings of their work articulated by volunteer and paid staff. This latter part of the chapter therefore pays particular attention to the rather different relationships between paid staff and service users, and service users and volunteers, evident in day centres. Developing arguments put forward in chapter 4 we suggest that such relationships are best understood as moving around questions of 'boundary maintenance' (Bondi, 2005), and rather different (though complimentary) understandings of a relationship of care.

Britain's Day Centres: History, Development and Ethos

Tracing the history of Britain's day centres, it appears that most began as relatively small-scale endeavours (often developing from a soup run or soup kitchen) set up by members of the public in response to specific and identified local needs – what we earlier called a '*device*' – such as the plight of those sleeping rough. While it is not true of *all* day services, most have religious roots and were, at their outset, almost entirely dependent on donated resources and volunteer labour. From these rather modest beginnings, individual projects tend to have followed one of four main trajectories. Within the first group are those organizations that have remained true to their original aims, seeing provision for the poor and needy as part of their duty as Christians. Today, these projects typically offer only a basic level of service and remain almost entirely dependent on volunteer labour and donated resources. For a number of these, active (but very rarely aggressive) evangelism may comprise an important part of their 'ministry'. Projects developing along the lines of the second trajectory tend to have retained their original religious ethos – this being overtly expressed in the way services are provided – but have 'professionalized', in the sense that the majority of staff are paid and service users are provided with a greater range of facilities and higher levels of support to move into independent living. For a third group, services have 'professionalized' in a similar way but the organization has relinquished its original religious ethos in favour of a more secular approach; actively pursuing statutory grants, for example, even if this means altering the form of service delivery. For these organizations, religious roots tend to remain in palimpsestual form only (for example, in the project title) and no longer act as a driving force defining the nature of service provision. To these three groups (with obvious religious roots) may be added a fourth type of project that has evolved (indirectly) out of the (secular) statutory sector. These projects were most commonly set up by former social workers witnessing first-hand the challenges faced by homeless people (especially those under the age of 25) and frustrated by the plethora of barriers imped-ing their access to services. As a consequence, these highly motivated indi-viduals left the statutory sector and developed their own voluntary or charitable organizations to redress gaps in existing service networks. The resultant projects tend to have been highly 'professionalized' from the outset; employing paid staff, utilizing statutory grants and offering intensive support to service users (Johnsen et al., 2005a).

These different developmental trajectories offer scope for rather different forms of postsecular rapprochement, and can represent quite different eth-ical frameworks for different projects. Though, like soup runs, day centres tend to open their project to all, aiming to provide a safe, warm and wel-coming environment to those excluded from mainstream services (Llewellin & Murdoch, 1996), the style of service delivery – and the ethos underpin-ning it – differs significantly between projects. In an earlier analysis, Waters (1992) drew distinctions between three main approaches evident in the work of British day centres. The first of these, with roots in Christian phi-lanthropy, shares the ethos of *open and non-interventionist acceptance* – or what we earlier recognized as unconditional forms of agape and caritas – practised by Britain's soup runs. The second is better characterized as an ethos of *empowerment*, where service users are provided with access to advice and resources but are free to choose their level of engagement with those services. Service provision in day centres employing the third approach, and favoured by government, is conditional upon the active expression of a desire for *rehabilitation and change*. Inevitably there is scope for these three strands to overlap within the care offered by any one service, but we want to use these different ideal types as a framework for understanding the differ-ent characteristics of day centres, and their varying potential as sites of post-secular response.

According to our survey data, 43 per cent of Britain's day centres empha-size the first of these approaches (Johnsen et al., 2005a), described by one member of staff at a day centre in Wimpster in the following way: 'Support, meals – it's a place where we don't impose any of those things. It's an open access [service] and if you wanna sit there all day on your own saying nothing, nobody's gonna challenge you.' A similar proportion of projects (44 per cent) emphasize instead an ethos of empowerment (ibid.). Such projects tend not to place conditions on receipt of services per se, but encourage service users to take responsibility for various aspects of their lives. The policy of the Help Day Centre regarding payment for meals is a case in point:

> The ethos is centred around encouraging people to be aware that they do have to pay for certain things, and they do have to budget for certain things, and that food is actually an important part of that budgeting. ... Hence we charge a pound per dinner. ... The aim is not to try and force people down roads, but to provide opportunity. ... I can't fix somebody's life, because the life I fix for them might not be one they like, but I can make opportunities happen where possible; I can provide services; I can provide access to services in order for people to make their own path. ... It's empowerment, all down the line. (Manager, Help Day Centre, Benington)

Threatening the diversity of approach that has long been recognized as a strength of the sector (Billis & Glennerster, 1998), day centres have come under increasing pressure from government to adopt the third approach identified by Waters (1992), within which the provision of welfare support is conditional upon an active engagement with those services and the expression by homeless people of the desire to change their lifestyle and behaviour. At the Point Day Centre, for example, though meals and facilities are free, the continued receipt of these services is contingent upon service users meeting staff '*halfway*':

> Rough sleepers are allowed two meal tickets a week in the winter and one in the summer. But saying that, if they're in a care plan and they're getting out of the street life, they wanna give up drugs, they wanna give up alcohol, they wanna make a change in their life, then we'll support them every day. But they have to be seen to be doing something, because I don't advocate keeping someone on the street. I won't give them a meal ticket so they can go and spend their money on drugs and alcohol. So it's about give and take here, you know, like meet me halfway. (Manager, the Point Day Centre, Castlebridge)

In fact, only a very small proportion (13 per cent) of British day centres have (yet) subscribed to such an approach (Johnsen et al., 2005a). Nonetheless, homeless people themselves clearly recognize the different approaches adopted by different organizations. Some strongly reject more active 'rehabilitation', railing against an approach that constructs homeless people as 'children', as 'not yet [properly] socialised' and as incapable of determining the nature of their own lives (Holloway & Valentine, 2000): 'A lot of centres seem to treat them [homeless people] as if they are children. Now hostels do the same, you've probably noticed it yourself' (Alan, 43, former rough sleeper and now squatting, Benington). For others the problem lies with projects that fail to enforce a more 'active engagement' with the support on offer:

> I don't know if you've been to any of the **** [name of major provider] hostels? ... When you go in you tell them everything about yourself: who you are, where you come from, if you have a drink/drug problem, debts, financial problem, if you've lost a job. It's basically to look at exactly how you got there, what issues need addressing. And until you've addressed them you don't leave, and until you've done that assessment you don't leave. And there's none of this, 'Oh, I'll see a key worker when I feel like it.' If you don't see 'em they come and get you. ... It's more proactive. I think there's too much sitting on hands in here ... nothing's done. It's totally up to the individual, and you can't always count on people. (Jo, 37, hostel resident and day centre user, Wimpster)

As a result of these different desires, if the option is available people will often choose one day centre (and one such approach) rather than another. Reflecting the power of an organization's ethos to shape service users' behaviour, however, people will also commonly alter their behaviour so as to avoid transgressing the boundaries of acceptability and 'fit in' with the services that are available, as Phil explains:

> You tend to get a much gentler type of person in there, goes in there, for a start off. That goes without saying straightaway. And also the conversation in there, no one seems to swear in there, you won't hear bad language. ... It's out of respect. There are posters of Christ on the wall. They have free Bibles. I think it's a bit like it's drummed into you as a child. You don't steal from a church, very, very wrong. And that's almost locked into everyone's head from a very young age and it sticks. So when you enter a Christian café you tend to ... moderate your behaviour to fit. ... You alter your behaviour to fit. (Phil, hostel resident and day centre user, Benington)

It is important not to draw too clear a distinction between these different approaches, or to assume that any such differences can easily be mapped on to a distinction between projects with secular and religious underpinnings. For example, the Wesleyan Centre might best be characterized as based upon principles of empowerment. But, as their manager explains, where they feel it appropriate staff may also seek to engage clients in a more active dialogue – challenging them to respond to the opportunities available to them. Even here, however, such a process actually *begins* with acceptance, since only if people feel that they have been accepted for who, and 'where', they are, are they likely to begin this more difficult journey:

> Our fundamental belief is that people need acceptance first, and the experience of many people who come here is that they are quite badly damaged in all kinds of ways, often over a long history, and they are often made to feel

second-class and inferior, and we want to make people first of all feel accepted. As we get to know people – and of course we don't get to know everybody by any means – some people warm to the place and others don't – but as we build relationships with people, then opportunities arise for responding to them. And sometimes that can be about challenging. But the place that we want to start is some kind of trust. (Manager, Wesleyan Day Centre, Benington)

In contrast, just as a number of the secular organizations providing soup runs would seem to have embraced the Christian concepts of unconditional agape and caritas, so some Christian day centres have obviously subsumed these ethical prompts into a wider form of 'muscular Christianity' aimed at the long-term 'rehabilitation' (normalization?) of their clients, and in which 'discipline' plays a key role:

Oh, we're very strict. I remember grabbing these guys by the scruff of the neck and saying, 'Do you want your teeth in line with your toe nails?' [laughter] The guys still talk about it. We are very, very strict, there is no doubt about it. … [But of course] you can be strict in a nice sort of way. I mean … discipline is the most important part of a Christian's life really, and at the end of the day it's not just giving them a cup of tea, you've got to think of their long-term rehabilitation eventually. … If they can't be disciplined in their everyday life there's no way of giving them discipline to change their life. I'm not only just talking about Christian things now, I'm talking about everyday life, giving up drugs. I mean, we've got a lady in there, she used to be a bag lady on the streets and … she lives a *normal* life now, *like everything that we do*. (Manager and founder, St Barnabas Day Centre, Wimpster, emphasis added)

Centre and Margin: Locating Day Centres in the Wider Service Landscape

As we have already argued, day centres can clearly no longer be characterized as the 'Cinderella' of the homelessness service landscape (Waters, 1992). For New Labour especially, day centres have been identified as playing an increasingly important role in attempts to tackle the problems of street homelessness, providing homeless clients with the first step in their move from the streets into sustainable accommodation of their own (ODPM, 1999; CLG, 2006), and providing government with the opportunity to sequestrate the value-added that is vested in existing plant, staff, volunteers and charitable donations so as to offer this service at (considerably) less cost to the public purse than would otherwise be the case. Reflecting this role, a greater proportion of homelessness programme monies has begun to flow their way (Randall & Brown, 2002), and this now provides an increasingly important part of some projects' annual budgets (with 28 per cent of projects reporting that Rough Sleepers Initiative, Homelessness Action

Programme or Supporting People funding provided the mainstay – 75 per cent or more – of their annual funding in 2003; Johnsen et al., 2005a).

Nonetheless, the diversity of approach evident in Britain's day centres means that many of the organizations providing these services remain firmly on the edge of local service networks. Projects that explicitly express their religious orientations especially often feel that they have been marginalized by local authorities that tend to direct their funding to larger (secular) organizations:

> We don't receive funding from the local authority. ... We have tried occasionally ... but they tend to put their money into the ****, which as you probably know is a large voluntary [and secular] organization for the homeless. ... They're well established, they have been well resourced by the local authority for a long time, and they're readily identifiable. And I think the local authority would have some questions about us – I think maybe that's beginning to change a little bit, but there have been questions about funding church-based projects. (Manager, Wesleyan Centre, Benington)

Others are grateful that they have not had to seek local authority funding, with some actively rejecting approaches from the local state, aware that to accept funding would be to place their autonomy, and the more obviously religiously inspired aspects of their work especially, in jeopardy:

> Having had to seek local funding in the past, I find I'm in a very privileged position to not have to do that, and to avoid all the strings attached to being accountable to somebody else for what you're doing, and almost dictating the pace as to what we should be doing. (Manager, Light Day Centre, Benington)

> The Council will give you funding if you will allow one of the Council people to come and be on your committee, and gradually it just squeezes out the Christian side of it, bit by bit. [So] I said, 'No way' ... [because to be honest] God is the only person that can help these people. There's no doubt about it, because there's so much damage done inside their life, they're wanting love. ... I don't think people out there [in other organizations] have got the patience to give what they really need. (Manager, St Barnabas Day Centre, Wimpster)

Though safeguarding their independence, rejecting new sources of statutory funding confronts day centre managers with significant difficulties. Some are clearly adept at playing the 'funding game', obtaining money for areas of their work that fit with the requirements of local authorities or central government but accepting that other, equally important, areas of their work will require other forms of support. But most remain heavily reliant on donations from charitable trusts, members of the housed public and the corporate sector. As a result, many operate on extremely small budgets – 28 per cent on less than £25,000 a year (Johnsen et al., 2005a). In an attempt to make up for regular shortfalls in income most also rely quite heavily on donated goods and services (with 45 per cent relying on donations for at least half of all the food they serve, for example) (ibid.). While such donations are evidence of a broader charitable impulse too often ignored in the academic literature on homelessness (Smith, 1996a; Pleace, 1998; Mitchell, 2003), the unreliable nature of these donations also means that projects are rarely able to operate on anything other than a subsistence basis. Indeed, managers and staff often express their disbelief that they are still operating at all:

> I can't quite believe that we keep going ... we have really severe funding problems ... the next thing we are facing is that unless we can get a big tranche of core funding, either through Supporting People or locally, eventually those charitable sources will run out. ... We're struggling along really. (Manager, Streets Ahead Day Centre, Crossfield)

Because of the very limited budgets with which they have to work, many day centres have to operate in clearly substandard and inappropriate premises. In the early 1990s Waters (1992: 74) concluded that day centre buildings typically dictated services rather than served needs, and were commonly experienced by service users and staff as 'substandard, depressing and institutional'. At the time of our survey very little had changed. Only 9 per cent of Britain's day centres are housed in purpose-built premises, with a little over half (52 per cent) operating out of converted buildings such as warehouses, factories, shops, offices, residential houses, garages and former churches. Seventeen per cent were located in existing church buildings, and 9 per cent in community centres (Johnsen et al., 2005a). The quality of building interiors also remains a problem. When asked to assess the condition of their premises on a Likert scale, for example, only 55 per cent of project managers classified their centre as 'homely' (as opposed to institutional), 42 per cent as 'spacious' (as opposed to cramped) and 27 per cent as 'new' (ibid.; see also Cooper, 1997). Indeed, the chief executive of one project went so far as to say of his premises that:

> [This] is probably the most inappropriate place you could have to bring frightened and vulnerable people. It's cramped, overcrowded, dark, smelly. Dickensian is how I would describe it. The only saving grace is the warmth which comes from the people who work here. (Chief Executive, homelessness charity, near Winton)

Inadequate premises circumscribe the range of facilities an organization can provide, and limit the number of service users that can be catered for. They also run the risk of reinforcing the already low self-esteem of clients. Second-hand fixtures and fittings can too easily convey a sense that those using such premises are second-class citizens; having to clear away tables and chairs at the end of each session reminds service users that the space

Figure 5.1   Day centre

Outside the **** day centre. (Alan, 43)

does not belong to them; and a lack even of suitable spaces in which to hold private meetings with advisors can send the message that neither the issues they need to discuss – nor, by extension, they – really matter.

> There's no confidentiality, as you've seen. ... You're basically, in a way, saying to homeless clients 'Oh, you don't matter, you don't deserve to have private interview facilities. You can't possibly have an issue that you would want to discuss out of earshot of everybody else.' (Manager, the Drop In Day Centre, Sandstown)

To compound matters, and as is typical of other services for homeless people (Dear & Wolch, 1987; Wolch & Dear, 1993), the majority of day centres are located in run-down inner city areas characterized by high levels of crime, prostitution and illegal drug use. While these locations raise issues regarding the safety of staff and service users who must navigate such neighbourhoods to access the service (see chapter 3), they also clearly add to the stigma that many using such services suffer, as people become tainted by what Duncan (1983: 96) has referred to as 'stigma by spatial association' (see also Takahashi et al., 2002). Staff too must negotiate this stigma, and the stigma that is more generally associated with homelessness and homeless people, as the manager of a day centre in Wimpster points out:

I used to have a neighbor that used to come round regular complaining about it [the day centre]. … 'Why don't you spend your time doing other things?' 'There's people with disabled children, disabled people, they didn't ask to be like they are, why can't you help them instead of helping the homeless and drug addicts and what have you?' And, 'That woman', I got labelled, 'That woman' who mixes with the homeless people, you know.

In fact, Britain's day centres find themselves caught in an (apparently) contradictory position. On the one hand, they are increasingly lauded by government as having a major role to play in tackling street homelessness, not least because – as some city managers and police recognize – they render the problems of homelessness less *visible*: 'The police like us here because we to some extent keep people off the streets, especially the drunks. … So we save the police quite a bit of money' (Manager, St Barnabas Day Centre, Wimpster).

On the other hand, especially when located in or near the city centre, they often find themselves subject to vigorous opposition from city authorities (and residents), who equate the problems of homelessness with homeless services – blaming the presence of homeless people on the presence of a day centre. Rather than part of the solution, for city managers keen to promote the image of a successful and prosperous city, day centres can be seen as part of the problem:

I suppose they wanna compete with **** [name of nearby city], they wanna keep that image. So it's about getting them out of **** [name of city] … you know, then it's not seen … I think they'd love for us to shut down 'cos then they wouldn't be here either. … We're just seen as part of the problem it feels sometimes. Again, if we wasn't here, neither would the clients, kind of that mentality. (Ann, paid staff, Care Day Centre, Wimpster)

Spaces of Resource and Refuge

Given this rather ambiguous position, it is worth pointing out again exactly what day centres provide. First and foremost, perhaps, they offer a vital signposting service. Very often, as Becky explains, when you are on the streets, trying to find a place to stay can feel like being on a (rather frightening) wild goose chase – as people try first one hostel, then another and another before (we hope) finding a bed for the night. When there are no hostels, the search for accommodation is even harder, and the role of day centres even more important as they are able to steer people towards (the few) landlords more likely to take homeless tenants:

I learnt a lot of things I didn't wanna know. Spent a lot of time avoiding where I didn't wanna go. It's about going on goose chases really. You know, you go to a hostel hoping they have a place and they don't. (Tanya, 45, ex rough sleeper, Benington)

We was sleeping at ... an outdoor swimming pool. ... And then we come down here, to the day centre. And that's how we got our B&B. ... If it wasn't for these, like I say, I'd still be on the street. 'Cos there's no other help apart from this. (Karalyn, 25, ex rough sleeper, Sandstown)

Day centres are also often the only place homeless people might find something decent to eat, and offer a range of other important material resources:

It [the day centre] supplies the things that actually will help you: some food, something to do ... there's people to advise you, steer you in the areas of housing or medical help ... a place where you can do your washing ... a lot to offer in a very small space. (Tanya, 45 ex rough sleeper, Benington)

Such services are important not only to those on the streets. As Zara, a 19-year-old woman from south-west England, who was staying with a friend at the time, explains: 'I never, ever got money. Only get £82 [from benefits] every two weeks ... I've never got food. The only time I ever have food is when I come in here.' Indeed, as the manager of Benington's Light Day Centre argues, though the Homelessness Action Programme proved relatively successful in moving people off the streets and into hostels and shelters, it was far less successful in finding people accommodation of their own or in supporting the ongoing needs of those who have been rehoused (see also Randall & Brown, 2002). Like soup run coordinators, day centre managers tend therefore to vigorously defend their open door policies, pointing to the importance of the services they provide to the poorly housed as well as homeless people:

I keep saying homeless, but I shouldn't really ... quite a few of the people that come in do have a home, or they have somewhere to live ... because their home's not a home like you or I would know it ... and ... because of the huge government funding, to move people out of hostels; to move people off the street, into accommodation, the big thing [is] them actually arriving there and not having any support. Which is basically what's happening at the moment. They come to centres such as ours, yes, one to have a nice hot meal, maybe, but most importantly, to combat loneliness because they're all stuck in bedsits on their own; to sit and read a newspaper in a pleasant, caring environment, to meet other people, and ... if they need some sort of advice or help as regards some sort of form-filling, or where are they going to move on to next, or whatever. (Manager, Light Day Centre, Benington)

In fact, as this quotation suggests, day centres must be understood as offering far more than these material resources. Most obviously, perhaps, they offer a chance to alleviate the loneliness and social isolation that homeless people and those living in poor housing so often feel. As Tanya explains, when you are on the streets '[getting] more than one syllable is rare ... I have spent a lot of time having conversations with people who just go "Ruh!" like that – "Ruh!"' (on the role of language in homeless people's sense of isolation see also Daly, 1996; Desjarlais, 1996).

For others they offer a vital refuge from the threat of physical assault that is too often experienced by night shelter and hostel residents (May et al., 2006) as well as by those on the streets (Ballintyne, 1999; Newburn & Rock, 2006); or, conversely, from the constant threat of being moved on or arrested by police (on the increased attention turned to homeless people by police, see Fooks & Pantazis, 1999; Johnsen & Fitzpatrick, 2010).

> It's dead heavy [at the shelter]... because of the drugs ... it's all knives and all this and all that, you know what I mean? ... Threatening you with an empty syringe. ... The less time I'm there the better I feel about it like. ... It's bloody safer [here in the day centre] than being there. (John, 44, service user, St Barnabas Day Centre, Benington)

> SARAH: One of the things that's really different about **** to some of the other places I've been in is the fact that it doesn't have day centres, or drop-in centres ... what did you do in the daytime when you were sleeping rough?
> NICOLA: Walk round town.
> SARAH: How did you manage to feed yourself?
> NICOLA: I used to go nicking. Nowt else to do.
> SARAH: Are the public and police quite tolerant of homeless people in ****?
> NICOLA: No, no they're not at all. They tell you to move on and all that.
>   (Nicola, 17, hostel resident, Steeltown)

More generally, but crucially, day centres provide homeless people with a place simply to 'be'. As the American homeless activist Mitch Snyder has argued, 'The question that daily confronts every homeless person is what to do with the day, which seems to stretch out infinitely and inexorably before you' (1982: 110; quoted in Kawash, 1998: 328). With nowhere to go, but also not allowed simply to be still, homeless people must 'always keep walkin' ... Sooner or later you want to sit down. ... But we can't. They keep on us to keep walkin' (Vanderstaay, 1992; 39; quoted in Kawash, 1998: 328).

Day centres thus provide street homeless people with a place of pause in their otherwise endless perambulations around the city. They also provide a place in which they can drop the pretence that is so often an integral part of life on the streets (see, for example, Knowles, 2000; Cooper, 2001). Consider, for example, the apparently mundane problem of keeping oneself clean:

> LUKE: There should be somewhere where you could [go] to get cleaned up though shouldn't there? ... You [have to] go in like Tesco toilets and stuff like that ... walk in like you're going to use the toilet ... [and then] strip wash yourself. ...
> SARAH: Do the staff at Tesco mind, or do they just have no idea?
> MARK: They don't have no idea.
> LUKE: If they had an idea they'd be like ... kick you out. (Martin, 19, and Pat, 28, rough sleepers, Steeltown)

As others have argued (Takahashi 1996; Mitchell, 1997; Kawash, 1998) but Steve puts more plainly, it is the dirt and smell of the homeless body that constitutes such an important element of the stigma that street homeless people face: 'during the day, I think that's the hardest part about being on the street, because ... people look at you and think, "Ooh, that scruffy cunt"' (Steve, 38, hostel resident, Steeltown). Yet if there is no day centre, keeping oneself clean can be a major challenge; especially for women, who may face real problems during menstruation, for example, and for whom 'remaining clean and respectably dressed is a method of self-protection' (Smith, 1999: 121). In light of such difficulties, the ability to take a shower at a day centre takes on considerable significance. As we saw in chapter 3, for example, for Carl the weekly shower is a genuinely transformative experience – 'the best fucking feeling of the week. It's like you can *almost* be normal again' (emphasis added). As Pete explains:

> They've got shower facilities, they've got washing facilities for clothes, they've got feeding facilities. So if you are fucked, and you've got nothing, you're on your arse, you can go in there and at least be human again. Because when ... you live the lifestyles that I have been living most of my life, you might be a human in flesh and blood, but ... you're not a 'human'. (Pete, 32, hostel resident, Winton)

In one sense, then, day centres offer temporary respite from the stigma that confronts homeless people because they offer an opportunity to be 'normal' again – or 'human' as Pete puts it. In another sense, this 'normality' is itself a product of the day centre's position as a space that is tolerant of, and to some degree even welcomes, the expression of difference within a wider 'geography of licence' (Goffman, 1968; Sharp et al., 2000). Rather than 'normal', day centres thus in fact emerge as places of 'unusual norms', where an individual's homeless status, conferred 'other' in most contexts, itself becomes the 'norm' (Parr, 2000). As such, and as Parr (2000) notes of drop-ins for people with mental health problems, bodily appearances, odours and certain behaviours (for example, sleeping under a table) that might be deemed 'odd' or 'inappropriate' elsewhere are accepted without remark, as an extract from our fieldwork diary illustrates:

> The elderly man with a scraggly beard, quite emaciated and dressed in a filthy grey trenchcoat, was seated by himself at the table behind us, eyes half closed and chin on chest, incessantly mumbling to himself as he usually does. At one point the volume of his voice rose dramatically and he began to swear profusely, appearing to be very upset (although nothing inadvertent had happened). One of the other service users seated at my table called out to him 'You're alright Bob' and then re-entered our conversation, seemingly unphased. The old guy immediately calmed down, and resumed mumbling quietly in his usual manner ... I've witnessed this happen on several different

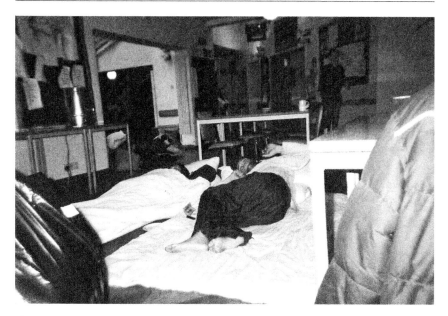

Figure 5.2   Waking up

Chrissie: That's people waking up in the day centre [when it operated as an emergency 'night centre'].

Sarah: Do people have favourite spots where they sleep? What happens if someone new arrives? How do they know where to bed down?

Chrissie: If they pitch it somewhere where someone else usually pitches, they'll get asked 'Oh, do us a favour mate. Move your bedding over please because I normally sleep there.'

Sarah: Are most people pretty cool with that?

Chrissie: Yep. These two are lazy sods. They take ages to get up. 'You don't get any breakfast if you don't hurry up!'

Sarah: That's what the staff say?

Chrissie: [laughs] Well me too! I give them a hand to get people on the move. (Chrissie, 46)

occasions. It appears that his mumbling is quietly accepted by the other service users who only intervene (and then kindly) when he gets genuinely upset by whatever is going on in his head … (Fieldnotes, St Barnabas Day Centre, Wimpster)

Spaces of Refuge or Fear?

It is also important not to romanticize these environments. Day centres clearly offer important spaces of resource and refuge for many homeless people, but it would be a mistake to assume that the 'licence' referred to above extends to all people equally, or that individuals' experiences within such environments are uniformly positive. On the contrary, what for some might constitute a space of refuge can, for others, be perceived instead as a space of some unease and even fear.

Most obviously, perhaps, the open door policy adopted by most day centres means that, like soup runs, they attract a very diverse clientele: younger and older people; men and women; those who have only recently become homeless, and those who may have been on the streets a number of years; people suffering from mental illness; drug users and alcoholics. Add to this mix the fact that very often people using a day centre are angry or depressed or simply overwhelmed by the stress of their circumstances and the atmosphere in such places can, not surprisingly perhaps, be volatile:

> There were 20 to 25ish people inside, most of whom were eating lunch silently, or talking quietly in small groups as they surveyed the situation in the foyer. 'Mad' Rick was however ranting loudly to no one in particular (as usual) and another guy was hurling verbal abuse (replete with expletives) at Simon and Paddy through the foyer window. Rob, one of the other 'regulars', then began to abuse him, insisting loudly that he 'shut the fuck up', ignore Simon and Paddy, and eat his lunch. The staff were clearly on edge and the whole place felt like a bomb about to explode ... (Fieldnotes, St Barnabas Day Centre, Wimpster)

To negotiate such an environment safely people must very quickly develop their 'scanning skills' (Goffman, 1971) – the ability to assess the likely behaviour of others from their appearance and demeanour – and carefully manage the impression they make on others (see also chapter 3):

> SARAH: So the atmosphere in some of these places is obviously quite, ermmm –
> FRANK: [Interrupting] It can be quite tense. Most of the time it's OK ... because everybody knows everybody ... everybody knows everybody's attitudes. ... And then you can tell when there's a new person in there – you know what I mean?
> SARAH: What happens to a new person?
> FRANK: They get sat and they get observed for at least two days – you know what I mean – before anybody will approach them. (Frank, 43, service user, Help Day Centre, Benington)

For the newly homeless especially, 'the first time you come to [a] day centre ... can be a harrowing experience' (Spike, ex rough sleeper, south-west England). Indeed, as Rowe and Wolch (1990) point out, homeless service spaces inevitably expose the newly homeless to what may for them be alien experiences of poverty, crime and substance abuse. As a result, what is a space of licence for those familiar with such scenes may, for others, be a frightening place simply because it is full of homeless people. Indeed, this sense of unease may be experienced by both parties, with those who have been on the streets for some time also sometimes having difficulties in relating to the growing number of housed clients now turning to these services, as Rob explains:

> I don't really go down the day centre [any more]. There's a different class of people down there, they've got flats and their own places to live ... I can't relate to a lot of people down there, we're all from different walks of life. ... It's a funny old world out there, it's really different [now]. (Rob, 47, hostel resident, Benington)

These divisions between the newly and long-term homeless, or between housed and homeless others, are not the only divisions evident in day centres. Far from being a homogeneous 'homeless community', day centre users reflect the same diversity and prejudices evident in wider society, prejudices that follow them into the day centre from the street. One is therefore just as likely to hear sexist, racist or homophobic comments in a day centre as in other informal social settings – such as a bar or a pub (Waters, 1992). In fact, though day centre managers report that a growing proportion of their clients are from British minority ethnic groups, or are asylum seekers or refugees (Brieheim-Crookall et al., 2008), outside of London and a few large cities, Britain's day centres are predominately white spaces. They are also, almost without exception, male-dominated spaces, with project managers estimating that on average 74 per cent of their service users are men (Johnsen et al., 2005a). This imbalance, combined with the volatility of what can at times be an aggressive environment, means that day centres may be particularly intimidating places for women. Indeed, many homeless women will avoid using day centres altogether. Others may use them, but seek to avoid the attention of other service users (thus potentially losing out on the attention of staff) by remaining quietly in the corner or eating and leaving quickly before they are noticed (on the 'shadowy' existence of street homeless women see Wardhaugh, 1999; on contrasting cartographies of women's street homelessness see May et al., 2007):

> Wandered in a few minutes after opening time. ... Things were pretty quiet upon arrival ... but got much rowdier when the regulars arrived. ... Andy: 'Hey Aussie bird – what you doing here?' ... Still, I was glad to have them there as several of the guys I didn't know ... started hassling me. Spotted Carol (19) who, as usual, came in, ate and left again without saying a word to anyone. (Fieldnotes, Wesleyan Day Centre, Benington)

Social relations within day centres are also permeated by very different subcultures of homelessness. As we suggested in chapter 3, crudely speaking, three main subgroups – and their related geographies – can be identified within the broader single homeless population, differentiated by their principal addictions. In street nomenclature these are the 'pissheads', 'alkies' or 'drinkers' (alcoholics); 'smackheads' or 'junkies' (heroin addicts); and 'straightheads' or 'normals' (individuals with no major substance dependencies). Particularly in the current era, where poly-drug use is becoming increasingly prevalent (with addicts often using both heroin and alcohol, for example), these groups are by no means mutually exclusive, with some individuals sitting on the borders of, or falling into overlaps between, more than one group. Nonetheless, when on the streets these groups tend to colonize different parts of the city and do not mix to any significant degree: 'the two don't mix you see, if you're a drinker you're a drinker, if you're an addict, you're an addict, and if you meet each other in the street you're going to kick each other's heads in' (Craig, 24, hostel resident, Winton).

> People are very cliquey, right, very cliquey. You've got the drinkers, you've got the junkies, you've got the dope smokers – you know what I mean – and you've people who don't take nothing. … People who don't take nothing and the dope smokers get on alright. It's the alcoholics and the smackheads and crackheads, like they don't get on with anybody – not even theirselves. (Frank, 43, service user, Help Day Centre, Benington)

In larger cities, where there may be a choice of day services, a particular centre may likewise become the domain of one or other of these groups. As Sean commented, 'you tend to find that [some people] don't use this place … they'd rather use places like the **** [because] it's a bit quieter … different clientele altogether'. But more often, with no alternatives open to them, all three groups are brought together within the same project.

Much of the potential volatility of day centres therefore derives from the fact that these very different groups are brought together in a confined (and often dilapidated) space where differences and pecking orders are accentuated. Bourgois (1995) has argued that people defined and treated as 'undesirables' typically react by creating their own hierarchies. So too homeless day centre users interpret the differences between these groups according to (similar) hierarchies of stigma that they themselves enact (see also Tyler, 1995; Cresswell, 2001). As a consequence, 'pissheads' see themselves as superior to 'smackheads' and vice versa, and 'straightheads' consider themselves more virtuous than either of the other two groups:

> There's such snobbery. An alcoholic is obviously so much better than a junkie, according to the alcoholic … there seems to be a built-in snobbery with the drinkers, that 'We are better than them because we never went that low'. (Frank, 43, service user, Help Day Centre, Benington)

> Now, since this drugs and all like this, there's been this sort of class distinction. 'Our class is better than yours. We are better than you. We don't associate with you.' … They [drug addicts] look down upon the drinker. They are more

upper class than the drinker. ... Okay, at the end of the day, the street drinker, he'll sit down there [begging] and he'll maybe make enough for two or three bottles of cider. His addiction is far less harmful. He can go without a drink for longer than what a guy can go without a fix for. (Alfie, 48, service user, Wesleyan Day Centre, Benington)

Takahashi's (1996) 'continuum of stigma' is helpful here in understanding how such hierarchies are constructed and maintained. In a review of the literature, Takahashi suggests that contemporary representations of homeless people are defined by perceptions regarding their productivity, degree of dangerousness and personal culpability for homeless episodes. The first of these axes is perhaps less relevant to homeless people's own assessments of one another, as it is widely accepted by day centre users that substance dependencies are illnesses that render addicts unable to work, and because fundamental contradictions in the British welfare and emergency accommodation system tend to preclude the participation of homeless hostel residents in the paid workforce in any case (on the latter see Johnsen et al., 2005a; Quilgars et al., 2008). But the second of these axes – perceived degree of dangerousness – is an influential determinant of day centre users' views of one another. Indeed, 'straightheads' often express concerns regarding the behavioural unpredictability and potential violence of 'pissheads'. Similarly, both 'straightheads' and 'pissheads' frequently complain about the threat that the practices of 'smackheads' pose to their own personal safety. Reactivating the same construction of stigma that homeless people more generally face from members of the housed public (where the apparent lack of respect for one's own body and personal hygiene is taken as a sign of a lack of respect for the self and perhaps others), Frank, for example, complains of 'smackheads' that:

They are really dirty people, most of them. ... Some of them are vile, you know what I mean? They've never heard of soap and water and leave their syringes around the day centre. ... They're all scummy to me. I wouldn't trust them as far as I could throw them. (Frank, 43, service user, Help Day Centre, Benington)

Even more important to service users' assessments of one another is the issue of culpability – the third of the axes on Takahashi's (1996) continuum of stigma. Just like members of the housed public, day centre users routinely (even if unconsciously) classify one another according to one of three groups, coined 'unwilling victims', 'lackers' and 'slackers' by Rosenthal (2000). Among the 'unwilling victim' group are those who need to utilize homeless services because of structural forces deemed to be beyond their control (for example, the loss of a job or eviction), thus rendering them 'deserving' in the eyes of fellow service users. Also considered 'deserving' by their peers, 'lackers' are assessed as not 'responsible' for their predicament because of some form of 'incompetence' (most often, mental illness or old age). In contrast, those positioned in the 'slacker' category tend to be deemed 'undeserving' because they are considered to be 'competent' (that is, able to choose an alternative lifestyle) and hence responsible for their homelessness. These categorizations are key influences upon the degree to which the 'unusual norms' exhibited by different people are tolerated within day centres. Service users may, for example, be sympathetic to outbursts such as that articulated by the frail elderly rough sleeper with a mental illness referred to earlier, but tend to be far less tolerant of aggressive behaviour such as that demonstrated by the inebriated street drinkers Simon and Paddy.

Perceptions of deservedness are also strongly shaped by the way in which service users relate to staff, such that individuals who contravene social norms of etiquette (being polite and expressing thanks for the services received) are subject to overt disapproval. As when using a soup run (see chapter 4), service users will in fact 'self-police' when they consider boundaries of acceptability to have been transgressed in a day centre:

> To some extent there's some ownership by people who make up the nucleus of the place. Like they'll say to someone 'look, we don't do that here', or 'don't speak like that to the staff, not here'. (Manager, Wesleyan Day Centre, Benington)

> SIMON: [These places] are run by voluntary staff, so it only takes some person to go in there pissed who is gonna cause a problem. That person is a volunteer, and not being paid to be there; they aren't gonna stand there and have abuse thrown at them. They will shut the place. ... [We] police [it] ourselves. If someone has mucked it up ... for everyone else, we know who has mucked it up. The lad's taken to one side ...
> RON: [interrupting] ... and they'll have him. (Simon, 28, and Ron, 38, hostel residents, Castlebridge)

Finally, and similar again to those using soup runs, assessments of deservedness are made with reference to a person's housing status – with the 'genuinely homeless' (i.e. those sleeping rough) considered more deserving than those in hostels, who in turn are understood as more 'deserving' than those who are housed:

> It's the same at the **** down there, they help the homeless get food and that lot, but there's people what uses this who's got places anyway. Which is wrong ... I can't see the point of them, if they've got a place. ... If I had a place I wouldn't be here. (Shane, early thirties, service user, St Barnabos Day Centre, Wimpster)

Clearly, homeless day centre users share society's intolerance of those they cast as 'undeserving' – partly because of the potential for the undeserving to abuse the goodwill of service providers (and thus threaten the sustainability of the service itself), but also because of the threat such individuals present to their own identities. Just as attempts to exclude homeless people from the public spaces of the city can be read as an attempt to construct a more coherent 'public' in contradistinction to a homeless other (Mitchell, 1997), so within the space of the day centre attempts by homeless people themselves to reinforce the boundaries between the 'deserving' and the 'undeserving' can be read as an attempt to protect (or 'salvage') the self (Snow & Anderson, 1993).

Boundary Maintenance and the Continuity of Care

The atmosphere that pervades day centres depends not only upon the relationships between different service users but also, as is the case on soup runs, and in night shelters and hostels, on relations between service users and staff. Here again, the issue of boundary maintenance (Bondi, 2005) is of paramount importance. For both service users and staff (especially those working under an ethos of empowerment, perhaps) the ideal encounter would appear to be a dialogic one (Conradson, 2003) – that is, one in which staff not only advise but *listen*, responding to the needs of their clients as they are defined by service users themselves.

> I think the most challenging thing is to listen. I think sometimes it's remembering to listen, which can be quite a challenge because I've got quite a big mouth. I think sometimes I get a bit carried away with myself. So that's a big challenge for me, remembering to shut up and listen to what people are saying. (Alison, paid staff, Help Day Centre, Benington)

While this dialogue will (it is hoped) be articulated during formal advice sessions, the relationships on which it is founded depend upon a whole series of more mundane encounters (sharing a game of Scrabble, for example) in which service users and staff interact in ways that step beyond a more formal staff – client relationship:

> [Remembering a favourite day centre] Everybody would be together ... and there would always be a member of staff there, you know. Maybe not every day but every other, they'd have a game of casket or a game of Scrabble or something like that, and we really got on brilliant. (Alfie, 48, service user, Wesleyan Day Centre, Benington)

But such relationships are very difficult to establish and to maintain. Not least, chronic underfunding – and resultant staff shortages – places staff

Figure 5.3   Closed

> This is what is happening at most of the centers, lack of staff. … If one unit closes, that means we're going to get one unit taking two units, where we get the usual lot plus those from the other project. It's three days now on the trot they've been closed. (Alan, 43)

under enormous pressure. Rather than having time to build relationships with service users, staff often struggle simply to get through the day:

> I virtually haven't done anything as far as my job remit is concerned because I'm always having to cover … on top of having to deal with all the stuff you deal with on the floor. … It's like, you do whatever you do to make sure the drop-in opens and that's it. It's just like everything seems to be down to the bottom line of the budget. (Jane, paid staff, Help Day Centre, Benington)

Staff also often struggle to break down more familiar 'professional' boundaries. Very often, for example, far from working towards the dialogic relationship both seek, staff find themselves cast by clients as just another 'authority figure', thus becoming the target for the anger service users often feel towards such figures:

> If they've like gone to the dole [benefits] office and been treated really badly, just as an example – then they come here and sometimes see you as like another authority figure … because you are a worker, even though you're working in a different environment … and that can be quite scary … [because] you know … they're angry. People have crap days, when they go to the dole office they get treated like, you know, they're lower than a normal human

being ... so of course they come here and that anger can still be there ... (Alison, paid staff, Help Day Centre, Benington)

For day centre staff, then, dealing with 'all the stuff' alluded to above by Jane frequently involves listening to disturbing tales of abuse and injustice, handling stressed service users and diffusing potentially volatile situations between service users or between service users and staff. While staff are quick to point to the rewards of their work, it can obviously be very draining. Not least, the constant battle to access assistance for their clients when so little help is available is a source of constant frustration and no little distress:

AMANDA: Every day you have someone ... coming in and saying, well, they basically wanna ... find some kind of accommodation, and at the end of the day there's nowhere that they can go.

SARAH: How does that make you feel?

AMANDA: Terrible ... you want to offer them somewhere to go but you can't. There is nowhere for them to go. You see a homeless woman coming, you know that the women's hostel is fully booked. Where's she gonna go, where's she gonna spend the night? (Amanda, paid staff, Help Day Centre, Benington)

The difficulties of such work have recently increased as a result of the rapid rise in levels of drug use – notably heroin – among Britain's single homeless population (Neale, 2001). Working with addicts can, as Sally relates, be 'heartbreaking, really, really heartbreaking' as you watch 'people fall apart in front of you'. It also makes it far more difficult to build a relationship of trust with that person – partly because 'who' precisely one is attempting to work with will depend in large part on whether that person is under the influence of drugs or alcohol; and partly because it can be so difficult to predict a person's behaviour when they are using some substances (for example, crack cocaine), adding to staff fears about their own safety. As Alison explains, the health and safety procedures associated with working with addicts also reinforce the boundaries between staff and service users in the most obvious, and unsettling, of ways:

ALISON: I find [drugs] quite scary because you can't always judge how people ... if they're really drunk or on high levels of drug ... you're not quite sure how the situation could turn out. Even if you know someone really, really well and they're extremely drunk or they've taken drugs, you can't always predict how that will turn out. And that can be quite scary ...

SARAH: [So] have drugs altered the dynamics in the day centre?

ALISON: I think [they have] to a certain extent. ... For me it's quite, not hard, but sometimes [while] I understand that I work with blood spillages and things like that, I also understand that I'm working with people ... [and] what message am I giving them? ... 'I'm working with you, but I'm too afraid to touch your stuff.' (Alison, paid staff, Help Day Centre, Benington)

Concerned about rising levels of drug use, many of Britain's day centres have responded with modifications to their premises. These include not only the installation of sharps bins (for the safe disposal of used hypodermic needles), but also of ultraviolet lighting in toilets so as to make it more difficult for intravenous drug users to find a vein, for example. Indeed, wider concerns about safety have led many organizations to seek to improve their buildings' security. While most projects use formal reception areas to vet potential service users – with individuals serving bans for previous rule infringements or those obviously inebriated refused entry – many have gone on to install CCTV cameras in entrance ways, or closed off 'nooks and crannies where people can hide away and get up to things that they shouldn't be getting up to' (Stuart, paid staff, Help Day Centre, Benington).

It would be easy to read such developments as evidence of the encroachment of the kind of 'defensive architecture' now commonly used to keep homeless people out of the prime spaces of the city (Davis, 1999) into homeless service spaces themselves. In fact, while managers and staff are wary of giving the impression that service users are being watched (recognizing that for many homeless people the sense of being constantly under surveillance is a very real feature of their lives), these developments are mainly welcomed by service users because they increase their own feelings of security:

> You've definitely always got to consider issues of security and safety. [But] That needs to be done discreetly … because a lot of the time these people do feel as though they are being watched … [that] people are watching them and waiting for them to do something. (Stuart, paid staff, Help Day Centre, Benington)

> This place over the past two years has gone through a total change, a total change … you couldn't move out there for people sitting out there getting pissed, making joints all day – you know what I mean – honestly there was a fight out there every day … as soon as they put a camera outside, that was it, it stopped. … You know, like my mate got iron barred – right – right in the doorway there … then once the CCTV camera went up … it makes me feel a lot safer, 'cos it keeps all the twats out … I know that I can come down here now and be comfortable while I'm here … 'cos they're not here any more. (Frank, 43, service user, Help Day Centre, Benington)

Like the rules imposed at most day centres concerning the use of drink or drugs, or intimidating or violent behaviour, these attempts to secure the premises should therefore be seen not as an attempt to 'contain' or to exclude, but to protect an open ethos by securing the safety and security of all those using a centre – homeless women as well as men, the recently homeless as well as those who have been on the streets some time, staff as well as service users (Cooper et al., 1999).

For service users, at least, much more contentious are the new security features now being installed in some of Britain's day centres in order to protect staff. Alfie offers a

> classic example. We go up to **** a lot, right? Now, when you go into this day centre ... you would never believe it ... you never see a member of staff walking about. It's like all these glass windows ... nobody on the desk, they're all behind these glass windows. Now, if you want a razor and soap and a towel and shampoo to have a shower, you go to one window. If you want advice you go to another window ... we call them Hannibal Lecters, because they're all sat behind the windows there. (Alfie, 48, service user, Wesleyan Day Centre, Benington)

In fact, for Alfie the glass screens of the day centre he describes are understood less as a security feature than as a physical manifestation of the increasing distance between service users and staff that has crept into day centres as a result of growing 'professionalism'. Professionalism is in turn defined less in terms of specialist skills and knowledges than as a process of boundary maintenance, as he goes on to explain:

> Different organizations have got different approaches. Some of these organizations have got this policy, [that] you don't get too involved. I don't mean sexual, I mean involved as in a relationship, a friendship, like an everyday friendship. ... There's only a limited amount of closeness, if you can see what I'm trying to put over. (Alfie, 48, service user, Wesleyan Day Centre, Benington)

Staff too are aware of this (growing?) distance between themselves and service users, if only because they often struggle to maintain it:

> The basic thing I find difficult is my boundaries, because you have to have a certain degree of professionalism. You have to keep a certain stance with – you have to keep, if you like, the worker/user relationship, you can't become too friendly ... [because you will] like some of them more than you do others, it's only natural. ... You have to watch that ... that you don't have favourites ... [but] sometimes I do find problems with that, because I understand their situation so much I just feel like going up to them and saying 'Look, you know', giving them a big hug and saying 'It's okay, it's all right', and I do find problems with that, in that sometimes I feel I want to do more than I can, and say to them 'Hey', tell them more about myself than I really should so that they understand that I really do understand what they're saying to me, and sometimes I find myself biting my lip and I find that a real big problem. (Stuart, paid staff, Help Day Centre, Benington)

Yet if staff sometimes find it difficult to maintain a sense of 'professional distance', their clients seem in fact to want to dissolve this distance. Thus they will often draw a distinction between the services extended to them by

Figure 5.4   Susan

This is Susan [a paid member of staff] from the night centre [a day centre temporarily operating as an emergency shelter]. This is a PR photo we decided. … That's Susan looking busy reading the Homelessness Strategy from the council. She's looking very, very, very intelligent, and thoughtful, isn't she?! Pondering, pondering … I like Susan a lot … [She's a] smashing woman you know. [She] really does enjoy her work. She loves her job. (Chrissie, 46)

professionally trained, paid staff, and the more 'genuine care' offered by project volunteers, for example:

SARAH: Tell me about this day centre and the **** Day Centre. What are the main differences between the two?

ANDY: The **** Day Centre care, they really care. … [Do you know what one of them said once?] …'Now do you want your food? 'Cos it's cooked with love.' Because it's cooked with love, that's what she said. … It's like – how can I put it ... I can't think of the word ... it's genuine. Do you understand? ... It's genuine. They care, they actually care. I mean, they don't get paid, they volunteer to do it ... [and] they do cook their food with love. ... These people [here] get seven-fifty an hour I think it is. It's a big difference isn't it? (Andy, 38, service user, St Barnabas Day Centre, Wimpster)

Managers too recognize that 'it is quite often important to the clients that the people who are helping them are not being paid to do it. ... That matters to them, sometimes quite deeply' (project manager, Benington). Importantly, far from being a source of tension, or the approach of volunteers undermining the professional approach of paid staff, staff and managers tend to see these two approaches as complementary. Thus paid staff defend the notion of 'professional distance' as a useful means of avoiding favouritism, or of projecting their own assessment of a situation on to their clients ('I find myself biting my lip sometimes'). But they also welcome the work of volunteers, recognizing that very often it is the relationships that volunteers build with their clients, as well as the more mundane tasks of cooking and cleaning and serving food that volunteers provide, that give paid staff the (physical and emotional) space to do their work:

> From the volunteers I know ... I'm amazed that they give their time so reliably, so consistently to work here, and invest their energies in working here. And it's them that have a lot of contact with the clients, it's them that actually do the work, so they're an incredibly valuable part of what we do and we actually wouldn't be here without them, literally wouldn't be open without our volunteers. (Annabel, paid staff, Rainbow Project Day Centre, Benington)

Not least, and in contrast to more familiar understandings of volunteer services as necessarily fragile, often transient organizations, managers and staff value the continuity that volunteers bring to their projects, a sense of continuity they cannot always provide but which they recognize as often important to their clients:

> People like me, we find it hard to trust people. We've got a lot of trust issues. Since I've been here three key workers have left. So the trust you build up, then they leave and it's hard. Trust is a lot to us. (Rob, 37, hostel resident, speaking of the transience of hostel staff, Benington)

> Working here for such a long time I have seen so many people come and go, because it's a high pressure job and people move on ... so I've seen quite a lot of staff, and there's been more managers here than there has the years I've worked here. ... So there's always that feeling that they're not ... well, there's never quite a feeling of permanence here anyway. If it wasn't for them [the volunteers] we wouldn't be able to open most days. ... Relief workers and volunteers at the end of the day are the people that really pull the strings together in organizations like this ... if it wasn't for relief and volunteer staff,

these sort of places would really just sink into the ground. (Alison, paid staff, Help Day Centre, Benington).

For many managers and staff in Britain's day centres it is this notion of a continuity of care that distinguishes their approach from the 'outcome-orientated' approach of central government. For some, this distinction is so stark that they would rather struggle with funding and resources than accept the very narrow definitions of a 'successful' outcome that characterize current approaches to tackling street homelessness. Others have sought instead to try to work within this new culture, bidding for money for things that have 'measurable, definable goals' but also ensuring that they 'keep the general support going'. Though below this distinction is one drawn between secular and Christian organizations, the approach being advocated can perhaps be understood as underpinning the work of day centres more widely, and one that is increasingly putting some in conflict with central and local government funding regimes:

> I think the best practice in the secular world is increasingly coming towards where we have been for some time. I don't think, in theory at least, that there is actually much difference between the secular workers and the Christian perspective on this one ... people in the secular world are recognizing the importance of the whole person, but they are operating within an environment that doesn't allow them to function that way. So ... you have to 'specialize' in order to get funding, and partly, you are funded according to performance, achievements and hitting specific targets. And if your target is to get somebody off the street and into a hostel, then that is what you have got to concentrate on doing because if you don't do that bit then you don't get your money. And so there is a tension between what you're actually trying to do, which is to help people, and what you're paid to do, which is to get a body physically from the street and into the hostel even if the hostel experience is a really dire one. So even if two days later they are going to skip it because it doesn't work for a whole number of reasons, you have achieved your target and therefore the money keeps coming. So I think the problem is the system, because the system is set up to reward achievements and the achievements that are being rewarded are not the real achievements that are needed. (Manager, Rainbow Project Day Centre, Benington)

Conclusions

As relatively recent developments in the service landscape, day centres have evolved as a voluntary response to gaps in statutory welfare provision for homeless and other disenfranchised people. They provide what SHiL (1995) refers to as essential 'maintenance' (food, clothing, bathing facilities and primary health care), together with information and advice, and opportunities for social interaction. They are thus vital for both sustaining life and facilitating the transition, for those that want it, from the streets into accommodation of their own. Equally importantly, they provide an environment where homeless people may simply 'be' – providing a space of refuge within an (increasingly) hostile urban environment.

The extent to which such spaces may be positioned in direct opposition to a revanchist logic is, of course, a matter for debate. Though presented here as articulating a space of refuge, day centres might also be read as a tool of containment. Certainly, it is notable, for example, that as the British government has sought ways of reducing levels of street homelessness it has focused its attention (and funding) on those services that immediately take people off the streets, and out of the public eye, rather than on longer-term solutions to homelessness (Fitzpatrick et al., 2000; Shelter, 2007). At the same time, the funding provided to such services remains patently insufficient, giving day centres little chance of actually fulfilling the role they have been prescribed.

Yet, while day centre staff and management also see their primary role as helping people off the streets and into sustainable accommodation of their own, most have rejected the approach to such work championed in recent government initiatives. Thus very few have adopted the ethos of active 'rehabilitation and change' advocated by government, working instead according to an ethos either of non-interventionist acceptance or of empowerment. Most also reject the 'outcome-orientated' approach associated with a 'rehabilitative' ethos and demanded by funding bodies, preferring to try to establish a continuity of care for their clients rather than seeking only to hit specific targets, even if by rejecting such an approach they also make it more difficult to secure the funding they need to continue their work.

Notably, too, far from seeing volunteers as increasingly tangential to, or undermining of, their work, the management and paid staff of Britain's day centres continue to promote the vital role that volunteers play in delivering these services. More specifically, rather than seeking to set the work of volunteers in opposition to a more 'professional' approach, as critics of Britain's soup runs have done, the management and staff of Britain's day centres often point instead to the ways in which the rather different relationships with clients established by paid staff and volunteers complement one another, with the latter playing a key role in helping to establish that continuity of care and the more 'genuine' relationships with homeless people so important to the work that paid staff do.

But we have also been careful not to romanticize such spaces. Though attempting to provide a space of refuge and support, it is clear that day centres remain somewhat ambiguous, and certainly fragile, spaces. Common to most day centres is in fact a discord between the intentions of service providers, who aim to create a therapeutic haven open to all, and the realities of such environments for both staff and service users alike. Most obviously, day centres are themselves often operating in 'survival' mode, struggling with unsustainable funding arrangements and staff shortages. They also cater for people who are very often angry, frightened or depressed, many of whom behave in challenging and unpredictable ways, while also having to support them as best they can in dirty and dilapidated premises. Contributing to the unpredictable dynamics of such environments, the divisions and addictions that structure life on the streets also shape people's experiences of day centres. As a result, what for some operate as 'spaces of license' and refuge are for others more commonly experienced as spaces of continued uncertainty and fear.

More generally, we would see day centres as a significant component in a broader shift towards the postsecular. More so than in the case of soup runs, day centres often bring together staff and volunteers with different kinds of faith-based and non-faith motivation, who are happy to work together in the core task of responding to the needs of homeless people. In one sense, then, day centres provide another 'device' through which an ethical and political response to the problems of homelessness can be practised. They are, however, much more than just a device for the moral selving of staff and volunteers.

While some day centres have chosen to work within a new system of neoliberal governance, they very rarely wholly succumb to its dictates. Others have very clearly chosen to remain outside of that system altogether. Some have become overtly professionalized, even forgoing or at least playing down their original (religious) ethical roots, while others have retained a distinctive faith-identity even while welcoming a range of differently motivated staff and volunteers. The key constant in this quickly evolving landscape is the role of day centres as spaces for the involvement of ethical citizens in the performance of care. It is this that ultimately leads us to suggest that day centres should be understood as offering a (complex and variated) response to, rather than being agents of, revanchism.

Chapter Six

'It's Been a Tough Night, Huh?' Hopelessness (and Hope) in Britain's Homeless Hostels

I'm now getting to a point where I'm sick of it. I'm tired. I want it all to end. Not my life. I want all the 'muck' out of it. I want a nice steady, stay-clean life now, a roof over my head, three meals a day and to be left alone. I find I'm having to fight to get that. Because the ★★★★ [a day centre], God bless them, they're a good organization and I'm thankful that they are there, and it's not their fault. But where they place you, there are people in there who will prey on other people ... you literally walk into a hell hole. So it's not the [day centre's] fault, they're doing a good job. As far as they're concerned they are. They have found you somewhere to live that will feed you and shelter you. What happens in there is down to that hostel ... you can't blame that place [on] the ★★★★, ★★★★ [names of day centres]. You can't blame any of them. Its not where they send you, it's what they [the hostel staff] do when you arrive. It's the staff that run it.

(Chris, 53, former hostel resident, now staying in a warden controlled bed and breakfast hotel, Benington)

Introduction

Much of the work of day centre staff is focused upon trying to secure their clients a place in a hostel. For (most of) the voluntary sector organizations providing hostel accommodation, and for government, hostels themselves are likewise now viewed not as the end but as only part of a longer process; one designed to take people from the streets, usually via a day centre, to a hostel – from where, drawing upon the support of professionally trained staff, a person may finally move forward and into sustainable accommodation of their own (Foord et al., 1998).

Though such aims may be laudable they are far too rarely met. Indeed, Chris's experiences (described above) are indicative of a need to look much more carefully at the role that hostels actually play in such a process and at the experiences of hostel life. Here we attempt to do just that. The chapter begins by locating Britain's hostels in the (somewhat limited) literature on emergency 'shelter' systems. Since a good deal of this literature relates to the United States (Stark, 1994; Veness, 1994; Williams, 1996; Desjarlais, 1997; Takahashi et al., 2002; Brinegar, 2003; Datta, 2005) we contrast developments in the USA (where emergency accommodation tends to be referred to under the rubric of homeless 'shelters') with developments in Britain, where recent years have seen a move away from basic 'night shelter' accommodation to higher support 'hostels'. We offer an overview of these changes, and chart the emergence of 'high support' hostels at the forefront of attempts to tackle Britain's homelessness crisis (Anderson, 1993). In the main body of the chapter we then outline three, contrasting, experiences of hostel life, comparing and contrasting the dynamics evident in Britain's night shelters with two very different kinds of 'high support' hostel. Developing the approach adopted in chapters 4 and 5 we again seek to give voice both to the residents of Britain's night shelters and hostels and to the paid staff and volunteers providing these services. As we show, though Chris's experiences are, unfortunately, by no means unusual, it is also possible to tell a more positive story of hostel life. The chapter thus points to (continued) unevenness in the supply but especially in the quality of the emergency accommodation available to single homeless people in Britain (May et al., 2006), providing a link to chapters 7 and 8, where we focus more fully on the different experiences of homelessness in different 'homeless places'.

Containment or Care? The Changing Contours of the US Shelter System

Early work by geographers on the urban shelter system concentrated on the politics of shelter location (Laws, 1992). Here, scholars sought to explain why it is that homeless shelters and related 'human services' tend to be overrepresented in poorer, run down neighbourhoods rather than spread more evenly across the city (Dear & Wolch, 1994), and explored the stigma that people confront when accessing homeless services (Takahashi, 1998). In the most influential study of the US shelter system, conducted in the mid-1980s, Dear and Wolch (1987) charted the progressive concentration of emergency shelters and related human services in a 'service dependent ghetto'. Noting that the vast majority of such shelters then (as now) were provided by voluntary sector organizations, they suggested that such provision represented a form of 'malign neglect' (Wolch & Dear, 1993) on the part of city managers who seemed content to leave the accommodation and care of homeless people to the voluntary sector, while using the urban planning system to contain homeless services, and thus homeless people, in marginal neighbourhoods and skid row districts.

More recently, of course, it has been argued that a philosophy of malign neglect has given way to a more active approach to the 'management' of marginal groups. Variously framed in terms of the emergence of a 'revanchist' (Smith, 1996a) or 'postjustice' (Mitchell, 2001) urban politics, the suggestion is that the aim of city managers is no longer simply to contain homeless people in the marginal zones of the city, but to banish them from the city altogether, restricting their access to prime public spaces (city parks, railway stations and main thoroughfares) even as the redevelopment and gentrification of skid row districts has seriously depleted the supply of shelters and others forms of accommodation (lodging houses and HMOs) on which homeless people have traditionally relied (Davis, 1990; Hoch, 1991; Metraux, 1999; Amster, 2003; Eick, 2003; Arapoglou, 2004; von Mahs, 2005; Doherty et al., 2008).

As already suggested, we believe accounts of the 'postjustice' city to be overdrawn. Not least, far from declining, the number of shelter beds available to homeless people even in cities like Los Angeles has in fact grown in recent years, with the greatest concentration of beds still found in the downtown/skid row core (DeVertueil, 2006). More importantly, perhaps, neither those who see the primary role of emergency shelters as containing (rather than resolving) the problems of homelessness – that is, as part and parcel of a philosophy of malign neglect – nor those who trace their apparent demise in the 'postjustice city' have stopped to ask what the aims of the organizations providing shelter accommodation might be. Even fewer attempts have been made to examine the politics of shelter life itself, stepping inside these spaces to chart homeless people's own experiences of homeless shelters.

What little work has been done in this regard has mostly been conducted in the United States (Stark, 1994; Veness, 1994; Williams, 1996; Desjarlais, 1997; Takahashi et al., 2002; Brinegar, 2003; Datta, 2005; though see also Warrington, 1997; May et al., 2006), where two very different experiences of shelter life are apparent. At one end of the spectrum of emergency accommodation in the USA are the older style shelters of the popular imagination, catering mostly (though not exclusively) to homeless men and still mainly located in the downtown/skid row core (for a history of such provision see Hopper, 1991). Whether temporary (laid out in church crypts and city armouries) or permanent, such projects tend to provide only the most basic facilities (Matieu, 1993). Even in the giant new 'super shelters' now emerging in cities like Los Angeles, residents still sleep in dormitories and are subject to a myriad of restrictive rules and regulations that would seem to mark out such spaces as more obviously articulating a space of containment and control rather than compassion and care. In short, such projects might best be characterized as operating according to the principles of 'less eligibility' – 'a subtle school of thought which postulates low-grade accommodation in order that there shall be no general desire to "settle down" or "set up home"' (Stewart, 1975: 41–2) – and as doing little more than 'warehousing' homeless people: providing a temporary escape from the streets, but offering little in the way of the kind of support that might enable people to move out of the shelter and into more settled accommodation of their own (Feldman, 2004).

In sharp contrast, a new breed of 'designer shelter' – located in suburban rather than central city locations and catering mainly to homeless women and families (Veness, 1994) – aims to do far more than simply contain the problems of homelessness. Thus residents of 'designer shelters' must usually comply with some form of training and 'rehabilitation' (typically requiring them to attend various 'life skills' classes but also to show evidence of their search for accommodation and employment) designed to move people out of the shelter and (back) into 'mainstream' society (Stark, 1994). Managed through a highly intensive, and sometimes highly intrusive, case management system in which residents work with an assigned welfare officer, or 'key worker', continued residence at the shelter is often contingent upon a person's proven engagement with these programmes (Williams, 1996).

When set against the backdrop of a still dwindling supply of affordable housing, the focus on individual change and 'rehabilitation' characteristic of 'designer shelters' is, for some, evidence of the growing ubiquity of a social services, or 'welfarist', approach to homelessness in the USA, within which it is 'homeless people themselves, rather than poverty, unemployment, or low-income housing shortages [that] are the "problem" to be addressed and corrected by policy makers and service providers' (Williams, 1996: 75; see also Del Casino & Jocoy, 2008). While not wishing 'simply to dismiss [these potentially] compassionate welfare efforts as nothing more than punitive, disciplinary social control measures in disguise', for Feldman too such programmes are evidence of (the re-emergence of) an increasingly common approach to homelessness in the USA, within which homeless people are constructed as 'subjects in the making', capable of re-entering mainstream society only once cured of their pathologies (and actively excluded from that society if unwilling to adopt the cure) (Feldman, 2004: 96).

From Less Eligibility to 'High Support': A Brief History of Hostel Accommodation in Britain

At first sight at least the distinction evident in the USA between more basic shelters operating according to an ethos of 'less eligibility', and a new breed of designer shelter where physical conditions may be better but shelter regimes may remain oppressive, would appear to map quite neatly on to changes to Britain's shelter system over the past 40 years or so, a period that has also seen a move from more basic 'night shelter' accommodation to 'high support' hostels.

In the 1960s and 1970s, for example, emergency accommodation for homeless people in Britain mainly took the form of large, dormitory-style shelters provided by faith-based organizations. Such shelters were characterized by myriad rules and regulations, the absence of meaningful programmes of support and an overreliance on (largely untrained) volunteer staff (Stewart, 1975; Drake et al., 1982; Saunders, 1986). But in the late 1970s, a number of new voluntary sector organizations began to emerge. Taking the lead from campaigning groups such as Shelter and CHAR, for these organizations homelessness came to be understood as a 'housing plus' issue (Foord et al., 1998). That is, though arguing that, ultimately, the problems of homelessness could only be addressed through an increase in the supply of affordable housing, such organizations also recognized that many single homeless people had needs above and beyond mere accommodation. While also seeking to offer an improved shelter experience (with smaller hostels based around single rooms rather than dormitories, for example), these organizations thus began to put in place a package of welfare support for their residents – ranging from help with benefit applications and accommodation searches to drug and alcohol referrals and tenancy support programmes – delivered through a key worker system (Foord et al., 1998). Such developments quickly gained momentum as umbrella organizations began to disseminate examples of 'good practice' based around a housing plus approach: lobbying traditional providers to embark upon a refurbishment of their larger shelters, calling for the use of paid rather than volunteer staff to deliver programmes of support and providing training in these programmes for hostel managers and workers (CHAR, 1985; Van Doorn & Williamson, 2001).

Yet the apparent similarities between these developments and developments in the USA should not be overemphasized. In the first place, the US and British shelter systems serve very different populations. In the USA, the training and 'rehabilitation' programmes now used in 'designer shelters' tend mainly to be aimed at homeless families, including significant numbers of people whose only obvious need (other than secure, well paid employment) is secure and affordable housing (Passaro, 1996; Williams, 1996). By contrast, in Britain homeless families are largely catered for by the local state, which has a statutory responsibility to rehouse them (Pleace et al., 2008). The housing plus approach adopted by a growing number of Britain's voluntary sector organizations has therefore mainly been targeted at single homeless people (both men and women), many of whom do indeed have additional and complex vulnerabilities (most obviously problems relating to drug addiction, but also alcoholism and mental health issues) (Kemp, 1997; Neale, 2001). Furthermore, where residents of 'designer shelters' in the USA may have little choice but to submit to a regime of rehabilitation and change if they wish to remain in the shelter, those turning to Britain's new 'high support' hostels have – up to now – been under no compulsion to engage with such programmes (May et al., 2006).

Nonetheless, coming at a time when Britain's voluntary sector more widely was beginning to 'professionalize' (Harris et al., 2001), the mid-1980s saw the beginning of a significant divergence between the approaches adopted by different homeless service providers. At one end of the spectrum Britain's soup runs continued mainly to be run by volunteers operating according to an ethos of open acceptance. In the middle lay day centres, provided by an increasingly diverse range of organizations, operating according to equally diverse principles, and deploying both paid and volunteer staff. At the other end of this spectrum, hostel providers increasingly moved towards a housing plus approach delivered according to an ethos of empowerment, with paid rather than volunteer staff working intensively with hostel residents to address people's longer-term as well as more immediate needs.

In the light of the growing ubiquity of a housing plus approach in Britain's hostels, it is not surprising that it was the organizations providing such accommodation (rather than those offering soup runs, for example) that emerged as the favoured agents of New Labour's Homelessness Action Programme (DETR, 1999a; Randall & Brown, 2002). Initially at least the HAP appeared to share many of the principles of housing plus; namely, a belief in the necessity of a 'joined-up' approach to tackling homelessness in which those turning to hostel accommodation should be given access to a range of related support services (provided either in-house by professionally trained staff, or via referrals to other service providers), so that they might effect a more sustainable exit from the streets (DETR, 2000). Such an approach certainly appeared to differentiate the HAP from the previous administration's Rough Sleepers Initiative, which, with its emphasis on temporary shelters rather than 'high support' hostels and 'move-on' accommodation, seemed more obviously focused only on getting people off the streets (Fitzpatrick et al., 2000). Encouraged by this apparent shift in emphasis, many of Britain's larger homelessness charities quickly lent their support to the HAP, with some providing significant input to the design of the programme.

In fact, the approach to homelessness adopted by the HAP and subsequently codified in the Supporting People programme differs from a housing plus approach in at least two crucial respects. First, under a housing plus approach the decision as to whether or not to engage with programmes of support remains with hostel residents. In contrast, and echoing the introduction of similar such pressures elsewhere in the welfare system (Peck, 2001b), the HAP introduced an element of compulsion into the system. Thus, while organizations bidding for HAP (and subsequently Supporting People) funding were required to have or to put in place a number of the elements of a housing plus approach (including housing advice and resettlement programs), under the terms of their contract with the RSU/ local authority, organizations were also required to demonstrate the efficacy of these programmes; with strict performance targets measuring the throughput of residents into move-on accommodation, for example (DETR, 1999a, b, 2000). By tying an important element of their funding to the demonstrable success of these programmes of support, hostel managers and staff have thus come under significant pressure to ensure that residents engage with these programmes – moving providers (in theory at least) away from an ethos of empowerment to one of active 'rehabilitation and change' (May et al., 2005). Second, within a housing plus approach, programmes of welfare support are viewed as only one part of a broader package, the other being an increased supply of affordable housing. Under New Labour, increased efforts to ensure that homeless people engage with such pro- grammes have yet to be matched by a concomitant increase in the supply of affordable accommodation (Barker, 2004). As such it is difficult to avoid the conclusion that with the HAP British homelessness policy moved con- siderably closer to the principles underpinning a US approach, within which 'rather than poverty, unemployment, or low-income housing shortages' it is homeless people themselves that are the 'problem' to be 'addressed and cor- rected' through increasingly coercive programs of 'welfare support' (Williams, 1996: 75).

Of course, there is no guarantee that such approaches will be adopted by service providers themselves (May et al., 2005). In the remainder of this chapter we therefore trace the effects of these changes, demonstrating that the situation on the ground is indeed far more complex than this deliber- ately simple narrative – charting a shift from 'less eligibility' to 'housing plus' to a 'welfarist' approach in British homelessness policy – suggests.

Britain's Night Shelters and the Limits to Compassion

Recent surveys of Britain's emergency accommodation (May et al., 2006; Briheim-Crockall et al., 2008) appear to support histories of the sector that chart an increased role for new providers and the growing ubiquity of a hous- ing plus approach (Foord et al., 1998). Certainly, the number of emergency accommodation projects in Britain increased rapidly in the 1970s and 1980s when levels of street homelessness first began to rise, for example, and again in the early 1990s – as voluntary organizations outside of London especially sought to respond to significant shortfalls in emergency accommodation then becoming apparent (table 6.1) (Brown et al., 1996; Ham & Carter, 1996). More significantly, perhaps, while the vast majority (91 per cent) of such projects continue to be managed by voluntary sector organizations, the structure of the sector itself has changed dramatically over the past 40 to 50 years – with a significant increase in the number of organizations active in this

Figure 6.1 Shelter

This is the scene you get from the night shelter before you go through the gates. It's like a prison. They open the gate and everybody stands in the car park. In other words, a confined audience. Some of them are frightened to do it. 'Cos sometimes the police turn up and there's nowhere to go. Left, right, up, down – the only way out is back through that little gate. (Alan, 43)

Table 6.1 Projected number of emergency accommodation projects operating (outside of London), 1945–2001

Date	Number of projects in operation at date and still operating in 2001
1945	19
1969	29
1979	50
1989	91
1997	182
2001	212

field. As our survey of providers revealed, for example, by 2001 there were at least 145 separate organizations (both faith-based and secular) providing emergency accommodation to single homeless people in England, Wales and Scotland, the vast majority overseeing a single project (May et al., 2006).

Reflecting the trend towards professionalization, the vast majority of projects (96 per cent) employ at least one paid member of staff, are heavily dependent upon statutory sources of funding (with three-quarters (77 per cent) relying upon statutory funding for at least 75 per cent of their income, and nine out of ten (91 per cent) for at least 50 per cent of their annual income) and describe themselves as offering either 'medium' (47 per cent) or 'high' (40 per cent) levels of support; providing advice and resettlement programmes, and additional skills training in the latter case, alongside accommodation, food and basic medical care. Finally, the form of accommodation itself has changed. Physically, the typical emergency accommodation project can no longer be captured in the image of a large, institutional shelter. Instead, most projects are either residential conversions (38 per cent) or purpose built units (37 per cent). The majority are based around relatively small hostels (with 20 per cent offering between one and nine beds, and a further 43 per cent between ten and 24) and, in contrast to the early 1990s (when the majority of projects operating outside of London were still unable to offer single room accommodation), 82 per cent of beds are located in single rooms – with only 12 per cent arranged in shared rooms and fewer than 6 per cent laid out in dormitories (May et al., 2006; cf. Randall, 1992).

Yet the impact of these changes should not be overemphasized. Not least, almost a fifth (18 per cent) of the new projects coming on stream in Britain in the 1990s and early 2000s described themselves as still being able to offer only basic 'night shelter' style accommodation. Such projects are far more likely to depend upon the input of volunteers than are 'high support' hostels, are less likely to be in receipt of statutory funding, and still tend to impose the kind of restrictive rules and regulations often thought to be a thing of the past. For example, while fewer than half (47 per cent) of such shelters allow visitors, more than half (56 per cent) still operate an evening curfew, and more than three-quarters (79 per cent) require their residents to exit the shelter during the daytime (May et al., 2006; for an account of similar such conditions in the past see Stewart, 1975).

St James' night shelter, in Benington, is typical of such projects. Founded in 1986, the shelter currently operates out of a converted warehouse. It is staffed entirely by volunteers and wholly dependent upon donations (of both money and gifts in kind) for its continued survival. The shelter itself includes a large kitchen, serving area and dining room, together with a single (mixed sex) dormitory with basic metal 'cots' for 15 men and women. The shelter opens its doors at 9.30 each night (serving a hot meal to residents and others until 10.30 p.m., when the doors are locked), with beds allocated on a first-come, first-served basis. Residents must leave the shelter by 7.30 the following the morning, reapplying for a bed if they need one that evening.

Given this description it would be easy to characterize St James' as operating according to an ethos of 'less eligibility'; with such minimal provision an attempt to sort the 'deserving' from the 'undeserving' (with only those truly in need turning to the service), and to discourage residents from 'settling in' to the shelter rather than seeking alternative accommodation of their own (Stewart, 1975). In fact, nothing could be further from the truth. Not least, when volunteers speak of those they serve, the language employed is not one of distain or reflective of attempts to exert control over residents, but one of 'respect' and of attempts to show respect by offering the best service that they can:

> I got involved 'cos of ****, she's the founder ... I know what it's like to sleep rough ... **** was good to me. ... If she met you on the streets ... she'd get you a cup of tea or sandwich. That means a lot when you're down. I know what it's like to be there, and it's nice to show that we have respect for them [homeless people]. They're humans like the rest of us. (Henry, volunteer, St James' Night Shelter, Benington).

> BILL: When folks come in, it's nice to see places clean and show that we have respect for them.
> CAROL: Yes, that's right, and they're not clients – they're guests. (Bill and Carol, volunteers, St James' Night Shelter, Benington)

Indeed, when conflicts emerge within the volunteer body these conflicts tend to revolve around requests by some volunteers to offer not less but more to residents – requests that must all too often be rejected lest the shelter fall foul of health and safety regulations:

> The last thing we had was about extra beds and putting mattresses down ... that they had done it on other nights. ... And I will say to them, 'Health and Safety will only allow 15 beds' ... that's the Health and Safety for the number of volunteers we had that night. (Volunteer manager, St James' Night Shelter, Benington)

Rather than reflecting a desire to offer only the minimum, the limited facilities on offer at St James' are therefore more obviously a result of basic resource constraints. For example, since first opening its doors in 1986 the shelter has had to move four times before being able to find permanent premises it can afford. Likewise, the inability to allow residents to stay in the shelter in the daytime has less to do with a desire to be deliberately inhospitable than staffing constraints, with volunteers keen to offer additional services (free clothing and footwear, a laundry service or packed lunches, for example) whenever resources, and the supply of volunteers, allows.

But, while volunteers would be keen to improve the physical conditions in the shelter, St James' has also explicitly rejected the kind of additional services associated with a housing plus approach as contradicting its underlying ethos. As its mission statement explains, St James' works according to the principles of 'open acceptance', or what we earlier referred to as service without strings, motivated from a Christian theo-ethics of agape and caritas (Augé, 1998). That is, in common with a number of other such organizations, and with Britain's soup runs, St James' rejects any attempt to change the other, or treat homeless people only as 'subjects in making' (Feldman, 2004), preferring instead to work with who people are now rather than according to what they might become. Likewise, just as some of those using day centres would argue that such a theo-ethics is only (indeed can only be) genuinely articulated by those who have not been paid to provide it, St James' has also deliberately shied away from employing paid staff in favour of a wholly volunteer staff body. As its website puts it:

> Our principle ... is: 'To love a human being is to accept him as he is; if you wait until he is different you are only loving an idea'. This has led [St James'] to operate an 'open door' policy from the start for those who present themselves at the night shelter, with no questions asked and no forms to be filled in. ****'s example of individual caring has also inspired us to be a wholly voluntary organization with no paid staff. (Accessed 9 July 2008)

Like soup runs, the aim of such projects is therefore to extend their services to all without prejudice, and without demanding anything in return. Also like soup runs, however, one result of such an approach is that night shelters often end up taking in a disproportionate number of the most vulnerable or chaotic clients – long-term rough sleepers, people suffering from severe drug or alcohol addictions, or people who have been banned from other services.

> It was a shock, because the night shelter is chaotic, rough sleepers around, people who can't even come into a direct access hostel because they are too chaotic. And so the state of some of these people, physically and mentally, was a real shock to me. But it didn't put me off. (Former volunteer, St James' Night Shelter, Benington)

Further echoing the dynamics found in day centres and on soup runs, as the proportion of such residents grows, others are less likely to approach a shelter at all – fearful of who they might meet there and what might happen in such places. Not surprisingly, perhaps, women especially rarely turn to shelters, frightened both by the violence that frequently flares in them and by the very real risk of sexual assault in mixed dormitories. Indeed, many women remain in situations of domestic abuse rather than run the risks posed by staying in shelters (Tomas & Dittmar, 1995), though men too will sometimes opt to sleep rough rather than face a night in a shelter:

> SARAH: Have you ever used the night shelter?
> MARTIN: No ... I've eaten there, but I've never actually stayed there. ... It's filthy, dirty, ... needles everywhere. I don't want to end up with hepatitis or AIDS ... or lice. (Martin, 43, rough sleeper, Wimpster)

Such environments also pose problems when it comes to recruiting (and retaining) volunteers. As the manager below makes clear, such work is not for everyone, and those who do volunteer will often consider quite carefully where exactly in a project they might work, with many opting for a 'back-stage' role (Goffman, 1971) well away from the chaos of the dining rooms or dormitories (see also Cloke et al., 2007):

> Some people don't like going out front because they find it intimidating. Other people just perhaps aren't confident enough to go out front ... (Volunteer, St Jame's Night Shelter, Benington)

> Yeah. A lot of people that have started as locums, you know, come to the Retreat, don't like it here. Fit in brill over at **** [the 'high support' hostel run by the same organization] where they're more stable but, 'Oh no, I couldn't do that, I couldn't do that, I couldn't –' I mean, a few week ago I had a lad in who self-harmed and, like, slashed up in 'ere and there were blood all over everywhere, and the poor man I were working with. No, he's never been back since [laughter]. (Paid manager, the Retreat Night Shelter, Steeltown)

Crucially, of course, whilst such dynamics might appear at first sight to posi-tion night shelters in a very similar space to soup runs and day centres – with all three seeking to maintain an ethos of open acceptance despite the obvious costs of such an ethos – night shelters in fact occupy a very different position in the gamut of homeless services. Most obviously, the residential nature of a night shelter can pose very real dangers to volunteers and residents alike, as a group of highly vulnerable, often chaotic people are (sometimes literally) locked in a small and dilapidated room for the night with only minimal supervision:

> I went there [the night shelter] last winter. ... Got there quite early. It opens at 9.30. I'd been there since 7 o'clock, so I was the first one there. Right up against the door. By the time all the lads ... I wasn't very well known at all around there ... by the time they had all arrived, I'd been pushed out of my position to the back and they had all got in. It was, 'Move over mate, you ain't known here.' And, 'That's my bed in there.' When you get in, if you manage to get in, you will find an empty bed. You can take any bed. You go to sit on it and you get a big guy come up, 'That's my bed, I slept there last night, get off.' By the time you've stood up every bed is taken. You've got to leave. (Former resident, St James' Night Shelter, Benington)

> You go in there and the staff are really nice. [But] there's a lot of drunkenness, fights, you can't get any sleep. They do offer facilities, but they're very basic. I'm used to having a bath and a shower [in the places] I stay in. In a place like that you can't do it. The water is usually too cold, people in there banging up, drug injections and needles all over the place, I don't like what I've seen, I'm not used to that. (Rob, 47, hostel resident and former resident at St James' Night Shelter, Benington)

For women especially – staff as well as residents – such experiences can be extremely frightening, even more so for those new to shelter life and who may not yet have developed the 'street smarts', or 'scanning skills' (Goffman, 1971), so crucial to negotiating these environments:

> I was approached by a very tall, shy and nervous-looking guy, 30-ish, shortly after the doors opened. He asked if there were any beds spare ... I felt terrible explaining that we didn't have any ... [and] was pleased to see that some of the other service users must have come to some arrangement between them, as he did have a bed by the end of the night. ... It turns out that the guy ... has been banned from other projects for attacking a female staff member. ... So now I wonder if the shy and nervous disposition is a 'cover' enabling him to negotiate the system – or a characteristic of certain mental health problems that I should be wary of in the future. ... Oh to be more knowledgeable about the (often subtle) signs. ... [Finally] as everyone is heading to bed Mr Aggro no. 2 asks **** for sandwiches. She informs him that sorry, it is too late – they were given out earlier. He then asks her to come over closer so that he can talk to her. She declines (and frankly I don't blame her as he'd been leering at me and hyper-ventilating every time I was anywhere near him – seriously creepy ... **** confesses later that she could see his teeth were clenched and was afraid that he was going to hit her ...). He then repeats his demands several decibels louder and with many more expletives. By this point virtually everyone in the dorm is tuned into what's happening and I'm wondering where the heck **** and **** [the volunteer supervisors] are, fearing that things could get out of hand. ... One of the female service users, 20s, gives me a sympathetic smile as she walked past with a pile of blankets: 'It's been a tough night, huh?' I was grateful for her understanding – and sympathetic that she was about to spend the night in the same room as him. (Fieldnotes, St James' Night Shelter, Benington)

The tragedy of Britain's night shelters is therefore that the most vulnerable people, many of whom have very complex needs, often find themselves in the worst possible environment. Though keen to extend a welcome, with very little, if any, training the volunteers staffing such shelters are often ill-equipped to help those they seek to serve – either because they have rejected the value of further such support as contradicting their ethos and approach, or more simply because they lack the basic skills (of conflict resolution, for example) necessary to maintaining both their own and their residents' safety.

Following Fisher and Tronto (1990), for Barnett and Land (2007) the practice of care is made up of four distinct capacities: the capacity to be *attentive* to the needs of others; to take *responsibility* for the needs of others; to provide care *competently*; and to be *responsive* to the ongoing needs of the recipients of care (ibid.: 1067). Drawing on this framework it might be suggested that Britain's night shelters represent the limits to compassion. While the desire of shelter volunteers to care for homeless people cannot be doubted – and is certainly appreciated by homeless people themselves – too often these volunteers are able to articulate only the first two of Barnett and Land's capacities. That is, though certainly attentive to the needs of others, and ready to take responsibility for those needs, such volunteers too often lack the experience and training necessary to care competently, while the ethos of open acceptance around which they work (and which may reject the necessity of training and any attempt to foster change in their clients) leaves them ill equipped to meet the ongoing needs of those they seek to care for.

The Failure of 'Housing Plus'

In the light of the changes to Britain's emergency accommodation sector outlined in the opening parts of this chapter, such experiences should now be the exception rather than the rule and, on the face of it at least, the majority of Britain's hostels offer a quite different environment. Most obviously, perhaps, while still operating on a 'direct access' basis (that is, taking people directly from the streets without a referral from another agency), most have become highly professionalized. Alongside basic food and accommodation, residents are also now offered a wide range of support services, from benefits advice to help in applying for 'move-on' accommodation and referral to more specialist services (mental health projects, or drug or alcohol rehabilitation programmes, for example). Such services are offered either in-house or through the increasingly close working relationships that hostel staff now have with related service providers, the whole package usually being coordinated by a resident's 'key worker' (see May et al., 2006).

Volunteers have by no means been entirely displaced from such spaces and indeed a sizeable minority (46 per cent) of Britain's 'high support' hostels still utilize volunteers in some capacity (May et al., 2006), with some managers stressing that they would in fact:

> collapse without voluntary staff. When I say we need seven paid members of staff, that's actually seven paid members supported by perhaps a team of twenty volunteers. ... If I actually had to start looking at raising the amount of funding that meant that we didn't have to work with any volunteers, we would need to employ a team of fund raisers [just for that]. (Manager, Homeless Support Service, Sandstown)

But their role is becoming much more restricted. Most often, volunteers simply cook or serve food to residents. While such roles remain important – not least because they 'give staff time to become more involved with service users, and give service users a feeling of support from the community, someone else to talk to, and the feeling that somebody cares' (hostel manager, Benington) – managers are also increasingly aware of the difficulties of involving volunteers in such specialized work, with some rejecting the use of volunteers altogether as hazardous for both service users and staff:

We have to be very, very careful. This is a specialized industry, it's hard work and you have to know what you're doing, otherwise you'll put not just yourself but everybody else in danger. ... We've tried it [working with volunteers] in the past, and the ones that we had were disastrous – because they're above any codes of behaviour, they're above any policies and procedures. I can't sack them, I can't reprimand them really, 'cos they'll just say 'Sod it' and go. (Hostel Manager, 'high support' hostel for the under 25s, Sandstown)

This shift to the use of professionally trained, paid staff is part and parcel of a broader shift towards a housing plus approach in Britain's hostels. Though it is also centred upon the provision of a range of additional support services, housing plus should not be confused with the 'welfarist' approach characteristic of US 'designer shelters' (Williams, 1996; Feldman, 2004). Most obviously, though by definition the key worker system that lies at the heart of the housing plus approach remains focused upon the individual and individual change, under housing plus individual change is always linked to broader responses to the problems of homelessness (particularly an increase in the supply of affordable accommodation) and, crucially, remains the choice of the individual concerned. In contrast to the approach taken in many 'designer shelters' (where every resident, irrespective of their needs, must sign up to such programmes if they are to retain their tenancy), British hostel staff are therefore keenly aware that the need for such support

var[ies] a lot from person to person. Some guys aren't interested in our help, and actually don't have many needs anyway other than finding somewhere to live. That is about it. Others [have] complex, multiple needs and are knocking on the door every hour. (Manager, HAP funded 'high support' hostel, Benington)

But a housing plus approach can of course only work if the package of support offered to residents is available. In fact, again and again, hostel managers stress that a continued shortage of affordable housing makes it very difficult to secure 'move-on' accommodation for their residents. Of even greater concern is the critical shortage of 'rehab' beds:

Even though you know you've got a lad who's desperate, desperate to come off the gear, he'll have to wait months for methadone, or the one hospital detox bed in [the city]. (Key worker, 'high support' hostel, Steeltown)

It's really hard to get funding to go into detox or rehab even if you're really committed to do it. The alternative ... the Salvation Army programme ... only [has] beds for men. (Gateway, 'high support' women's hostel, Benington)

Given such shortages, and the increased availability of street drugs, the proportion of hostel residents with an ongoing drugs problem is escalating rapidly (May et al., 2006), making it extremely hard for those who may want to come off drugs to do so, and equally difficult for those who have recently come off to stay clean:

> DEAN: I told my mother, 'I'm with the Salvation Army.' 'Oh, a good Christian organization. You'll be fed and looked after and spiritually motivated', she said.
> SARAH: And is that true of your experience?
> DEAN: No, but I'm now aware of who sells the best 'skunk' [a particularly strong variety of cannabis]. (Dean, 39, resident, HAP funded 'high support' hostel, Benington)

> I've never been anywhere where it's been so drug orientated. All the young ones, everybody there, you know, 99.9 per cent [are using] ... (Don, 52, resident, HAP funded 'high support' hostel, Benington)

> When I came in here I did pick up, I started using heroin again. Going into a hostel, everyone was using, [so] I started using ... the crack and [the] heroin. (Resident, HAP funded 'high support' hostel, Benington)

New directives put in place by some local authorities seem to add to these problems in some areas. For example, in Benington, as too in a number of other cities, HAP funded hostels are supposed to accept only those clients who have come to them via the local authority street outreach team. In reality, as members of such teams confide, hostels often resist these directives (see also May et al., 2005). Nevertheless, the ability of hostel managers to shape their own admissions procedures has been seriously curtailed by such procedures:

> I suppose I come from an era when direct access meant direct access. When I first worked here we very much felt that we were part of the safety net and anyone could walk in off the street ... and get a bed for the night. ... In the last year or two ... with the increasing development of local authority plans and the increasing involvement of the Rough Sleepers Unit ... there is a feeling that to some extent ... we're no longer our own masters, in that we have become subject to the requirements of the city council through the outreach team and the Rough Sleepers Initiative. [Indeed] we now take very few people on a direct-access basis. ... Largely now we're told who we can and cannot admit and referrals to this accommodation have to be filtered through the outreach team. (Senior staff member, HAP funded 'high support' hostel, Benington)

This filtering process is important because of the priority that street outreach teams tend to accord to particular vulnerable groups – notably long-term rough sleepers, many of whom also have significant additional vulnerabilities, ranging from mental health problems to drug or alcohol addictions. The most obvious effect of such schemes is therefore to further increase the proportion of hostel residents with high support needs at a time when the move-on accommodation and additional support available to people remains severely limited, such schemes make it more difficult for those without these needs to access emergency accommodation at all, as Alan explains (for an assessment of the effects of the development of similar priorities in recent US homelessness policy see Del Casino & Jocoy, 2008):

> It's a vicious circle round here. The reason I've found it difficult to get hostel accommodation is because I'm not an alcoholic, I'm not a drug addict, I've no physical or mental disabilities or social disabilities. To the government I'm 'normal'. ... [So] I've gone to the bottom of the list. (Alan, 43, former rough sleeper and now squatting, Benington)

Both voluntary sector advocates of a housing plus approach and central government see 'high support' hostels as the first step on the road to sustainable accommodation. In reality, a shortage of both basic move-on accommodation (the 'housing' element of a housing plus approach) and related support (the 'plus') means that Britain's hostels are silting up. Indeed, in recognition of such problems, more than half (53 per cent) of Britain's 'emergency' hostels now allow residents to stay for a period of up to two years (Briheim-Crockall et al., 2008). Even when it is possible to find people a place to go, as managers make clear, the continued lack of affordable accommodation and of follow-up support means that people very often end up returning to the hostel – part and parcel of a continued 'churning' that sees many homeless people move from the streets, to hostels, to hospital or prison, only to end up back in a hostel again several months later (on 'churning' see also Wolch & DeVerteuil, 2001). Though reinforcing rather than undermining his belief in the need to work intensively with residents and to build relationships with them (if only because he is very likely to see these people again), such churning has left David deeply disillusioned with the current (watered down) housing plus approach:

> It's a very broad issue ... but I've noticed over the last decade that a lot of hostels have changed very little and that the provision that society makes for people who drop through conventional safety nets down to the level of street homelessness doesn't seem to be changing, so ... my feeling ... is that hostels obviously have a use in the current context, but at the same time they are simply a symptom, rather like the tip of an iceberg, of a much broader housing crisis, and homelessness crisis, which doesn't seem to be going away. ... The fact [is] ... I am quite cautious of ticking off 'successful outcomes' because I think that there is a cycle and a lot of people who are rehoused will find themselves in a hostel or similar situation down the line. If you are dealing with people with deep problems, rehousing them isn't going to solve that. You are really working with people full stop. That is what we do, we work with people ... we build a relationship with them. [That way, if] they go off to

prison … [and] come back in six months … at least we have a relationship with them. So when they come in we know who they are, they know who we are and we can pick it up and work for however long they are in the hostel that time. I suppose I have lost a lot of idealism, I have lost [that] result-focused approach, because you end up being too disappointed and too let down, frustrated if you view things like that. (Manager, HAP funded 'high support' hostel, Benington)

The Myth of High Support

That so few people seem able to make a successful exit from Britain's 'high support' hostels might matter less if these hostels provided a better environment for their residents. But continued funding constraints mean that many of Britain's hostels are struggling to provide such an environment. Most obviously, the short-term funding programmes with which projects have to supplement their core funding (from Housing Benefit and Supporting People) are unreliable. They also heighten inequalities between different providers:

> The major difficulty is core funding. There are hundreds of funders out there that [will] say, 'Wonderful new project … of course we'll help to get it off the ground.' [But only] a very minute number who will provide core funding. … [So what you end up with] is reinvent[ing] the same project every three years and just mak[ing] it sound like a new initiative. … It's the art of funding applications. Some people know it, some people don't, and I think you see the differences in which agencies have got money and which ones haven't. (Manager, 'high support' hostel for under 25s, Sandstown)

Though the HAP was intended to provide a major new source of (temporary) funding to Britain's hostels, the flow of HAP monies too remained both relatively restricted and highly uneven geographically (May et al., 2006). Thus, a number of hostel managers complained at the time of a 'postcode lottery' and of difficulties in attracting HAP funding even when confronted by high levels of demand for their services:

> [At the end of the day] we are not London. Money just doesn't just come down here. We are too far away. It's the tourist Mecca of Britain. 'The tourists don't want to see homelessness, sweep it under the carpet' – but they won't give us any money to sweep it with! (Hostel Manager, Winton)

Nor are those organizations that were able to secure HAP, and subsequently Supporting People, funding necessarily much better off. In the light of the resource constraints elsewhere in the system described above, the difficulties in meeting funding targets around move-on accommodation, for example, have left many managers juggling the books – signing up to funding contracts on the basis of targets they know they cannot achieve, in the hope simply of buying themselves more time:

> Either you're going to go for the six months and ... a set of targets ... that you know you're not going to meet, and then justify it afterwards and get yourself six months' breathing space and try and find some funding from somewhere else, or else you can walk away. So I agreed a set of targets that I thought I had no hope of meeting, on the basis of it gave us another six months and time to build and stabilize what we were trying to achieve. (Manager, HAP funded 'high support' hostel, Benington)

Broader tensions in current approaches to tackling street homelessness can also sometimes leave hostel managers in an impossible situation. While charged with the task of making contact with and accommodating rough sleepers, for example, managers sometimes find that the police have got there first, clearing potential clients from the city, and leaving hostels unable to meet their targets:

> I remember one quarter we had an abysmal time on outreach, and one of the main reasons for that was because the police had come in and done a zero-tolerance and driven everybody out, so lots of the work that had been done was gone, you know, and those people moved to other locations within the city or else moved outside of Benington altogether. (Manager, HAP funded 'high support' hostel, Benington)

As a result of the continued difficulties in attracting funding, the majority of Britain's 'high support' hostels therefore supplement the income provided through Housing Benefit and Supporting People with funding from a multitude of other statutory agencies, including local authorities, health authorities, and probation. But a significant proportion of these otherwise highly 'professionalized' projects also continue to rely upon some form of donation. Though few rely to any significant extent upon financial donations, a majority (65 per cent) continue to rely upon gifts-in-kind for at least a proportion (25 per cent) of the food and clothing they provide, while for a significant minority (40 per cent) gifts-in-kind represent a major source of material resource – providing at least 50 per cent of all food served (May et al., 2006).

In the face of this continued financial insecurity it is perhaps not surprising that many hostels struggle to provide a decent environment for their residents. While on paper the physical conditions in Britain's 'high support' hostels have improved significantly over recent years (Foord et al., 1998), when one looks behind the headlines a very different picture emerges. In the first place, whatever the dictates of various 'good practice' guides, the exteriors of many of Britain's hostels remain both obviously institutional, and a clear marker of stigma for those unfortunate enough to have to use

Figure 6.2   Exterior of hostel

> This is the exterior of the **** [name of hostel]. All lovely and tidy! There's needles along there, there's rubbish, there's food, socks, wrappers, dirty towels – just thrown out the window. Because if they've got to wash their stuff they've got to pay. There's no washing facilities. They can go to the toilets and wash it in the sinks there, but where are they supposed to dry it? In their rooms on their radiators? So they just turf it and get new stuff from the day centres, soup runs and that sort of thing. (Alan, 43)

them (figure 6.2). Once inside things rarely improve. Though residents may indeed now mostly enjoy the privacy of their own rooms, for example, such rooms are often anything but 'homely' and can be dangerous (figure 6.3):

> The bedrooms are really small, they haven't even got sockets which I absolutely can't believe, so people end up trying to wire in their TV to the light socket and things like that, which is really bad. (Key worker, HAP funded 'high support' hostel, Benington)

As Alan is quick to point out, such conditions are not necessarily a result (only) of the limitations of the buildings themselves, or the fault of management and staff. Instead,

> it's the people who live here. They crap here, there and everywhere. They don't always use the toilet – they rub it all down the walls. They're puking

Figure 6.3   Hostel room

This is what happens if you get off the street and move into the **** [name of hostel]. A room, six by twelve. You've got a bed, no plugs, no sink, no nothing. You're not even allowed to plug in a radio or anything. You've just got a light, a bed and four walls. You're not allowed to put pictures up. You're not allowed to do anything! If you do put pictures up and damage the paintwork you have to pay for it. Technically you'd be better off going to prison. I mean it's a six by twelve room. You've got to live in that room. (Alan, 43)

everywhere, it's a real shit hole. (Alan, 43, former rough sleeper and now squatting, Benington)

Indeed, as with Britain's day centres, the main concern of many staying in 'high support' hostels is the behaviour of other residents. Like day centres, 'high support' hostels face the problems that emerge when very different people, many of whom have significant support needs, are brought together in a rundown and dilapidated space. While some projects are able to separate these groups (with 'drinkers', 'junkies' and 'straightheads' housed in different parts of the hostel, for example), most are not. As a result, people attempt to carve out their own territory, with different groups colonizing different areas of the hostel, as Dean, who described himself as a 'straighthead', explains:

> Well we tend to sit in the hallway because if you sit in the TV lounge then somebody more often than not has pissed on the seat because they are so gouged out and they will just wet themselves and the whole place smells of urine anyway. ... [So we just] sit and watch the world go by and take the piss and laugh at them. ... We see all the dramas ... watch the kick-offs and the fights starting. You sit there and laugh at it. We know what's happening, we can see something building because they're not very discreet, they're drug addicts. (Dean, 39, resident, HAP funded 'high support' hostel, Benington)

Dean's laughter in the face of such bedlam does not entirely obscure the very real tensions apparent between the different groups he describes. In an increasing number of Britain's hostels these tensions are amplified by tensions between these and other homeless groups; most obviously the growing number of refugees and asylum seekers being housed in Britain's homeless hostels (London Housing Foundation, 2004). Following a familiar narrative, Dean's own complaint against such people is that they appear to have been allowed to 'jump the queue', gaining access to housing and resources denied to more 'legitimate' claimants like himself:

> I shouldn't be here basically. I mean we keep getting queue jumped by some ... refugees. I use that word loosely because if they are refugees they are all well dressed with mobile phones. If I had had my family wiped out I'd be sitting in the corner traumatized. But they're here one day and they're off clubbing the next. If my family were wiped out like they're trying to say, I don't think I'd be celebrating at night clubs. ... A few of them are fine. I mean it's not their fault, it's the government's fault over here for making it so blooming easy for them. ... But it is a bit off-putting when I've worked most of my life, for 24 years, and I'll be here for months and ... five or six weeks later they say [to them] 'You've got a flat'. (Dean, 39, resident, HAP funded 'high support' hostel, Benington)

Others resent having to share hostel space with Schedule 1 offenders (a loose term applied to anyone convicted of an offence against a child), because the presence of such people makes it very difficult for them to remain in contact with their families (for a definition and guidance on Schedule 1 offences see http://www.everychildmatters.gov.uk/socialcare/safeguarding/risktochildren) (figure 6.4).

Thus, though one of the most common complaints from residents is that their time in a hostel leaves them feeling in a state of 'limbo' – feelings that can very quickly lead to depression – in this context at least depression

Figure 6.4   Father's Day card

This is a Father's Day card from my daughter. She's can't come and visit 'cos of Schedule 1 Offenders. They should have a room here where we could go and meet, and draw pictures together and stuff. There's nothing like that here. I love that picture. That's what's stopped me taking heroin. (Rob, 47)

should not be confused with some kind of dampening of emotion. Instead, as we argued in chapter 3, hostel life is for many an emotionally fraught experience, with people reporting the need to constantly and carefully monitor their own and other people's behaviour in order simply to make it safely through the day. Even so, and as in night shelters, the risk of physical violence is an ever present fact of life in many homeless hostels. Both staff and residents must quickly learn who is most prone to violence – a proclivity most often assessed in relation to a person's main addiction. And, while such violence will often have a rhythm (with things settling down around 'pay day'), one of the most stressful aspects of hostel life is that these dynamics are not always predictable. As a result, staff as well as residents must be constantly alert to the threat of attack:

> You get a lad who's had a bag of heroin and he's just gonna lie on his bed and gouch, he's gonna be no problem. You get somebody who's just come in with a bottle of sherry in 'em you don't know how they're gonna react. ... Pay days are usually quiet ... every other Thursday, when they get their personal issues [benefits], that's usually quiet because they've all been out and bought what they've needed to buy. (Hostel manager, Steeltown)

There's always going – I mean, we work around the whole safety aspect of where people sit in a room, if you are, you know – I mean, here for example, if somebody was to come through that door and push me up against – I can't get away. Sometimes I think we dwell too much on that, but there is planning done especially on the ground floor, because if anything's gonna happen it's gonna happen down there. Now, the most vulnerable part probably is where you were sitting today; staff generally don't wanna sit there. (Manager, 'high support' hostel for under 25s, Sandstown)

In the face of such threats, many 'high support' hostels too have begun to pay far more attention to questions of physical security, altering the lay-out of buildings and installing security and related features (CCTV cameras, window bars and fluorescent lighting, for example) to try to reduce the opportunities for violence, theft or drug use. As a member of staff at one hostel commented:

Security is a real issue. People climb in and out of windows, up and down drainpipes, it's dreadful. We put bars on all the windows, so the residents take the windows out of the frame, that's always a constant battle. The building wasn't designed for highly skilled, manipulative drug users. If I was to design something specifically aimed at that group, it would be like a prison. (Key worker, HAP funded 'high support' hostel, Benington)

For many residents too hostels are becoming uncomfortably like prison (figure 6.5), a feeling that begins when they are first 'processed' on arrival:

Do you understand me, Miss? It's sad isn't it? I mean the first thing you see when you come here is this interview room. And look at it. It's a box. ... And then they take a photograph of you. And I don't like photos being taken of me, really. Look at the room, it's a state. You come off the street and you're stuck in here with two members of staff and one of them pulls out a camera and takes a photo for the record. Then they read the contract which says you're entitled to blah blah blah ... (Rob, 47, resident, HAP funded 'high support' hostel, Benington)

Echoing the views of those working in day centres, though some staff clearly welcome the increased attention paid to physical security, others have major reservations as to the dynamics it engenders between residents and staff. Not least, as Paramesh recognizes, a number of residents will have been in prison in the past. Reminding them of this experience is only more likely to further distance them from staff, making it far more difficult to establish the relationships of trust staff are keen to build in an attempt to encourage people to engage with a programme of support:

I think the building, it is a bit of a rabbit warren really, long corridors, lots of little rooms a bit like a prison. And a lot of guys who are obviously in and out of prison

Figure 6.5   Hostel hallway

This is the view of the hallway in **** [name of hostel]. 'Here's your room, get in your cell!' (Alan, 43)

treat this as a bit of an open prison in the sense that ... the way they relate to the staff, calling them Sir and Miss and this kind of thing. It is almost like they feel comfortable. ... If they can polarize things into ... they are the screws ... it kind of makes it a bit easier for them. Whereas if they actually had to start addressing their issues and getting help, [it would] make them quite vulnerable, which some of them aren't ready to do yet. Younger guys are more likely to have that attitude I think sometimes. As they get a bit older and they realize that they have actually got to come to someone for help, then people can begin to work with them some more. (Paramesh, key worker, HAP funded 'high support' hostel, Benington)

Indeed, for staff and residents alike it is this lack of any meaningful communication in many 'high support' hostels that is the most obvious failing of such places. As Colin describes it:

If you have a problem it's no good ... talking to a member of staff. ... They'll listen to you and it's 'Yes, I'll get someone to help you.' And then they [just] vanish upstairs. ... The staff are very hardened towards people because they've been so abused over the years. ... They sit behind their armoured glass with their feet up drinking their tea and you can go and ask them something and they might decide to do something and they might not. [And] it's no good you getting angry. You can't put your fist through armoured glass. Although I've seen people try. (Colin, 53, resident, HAP funded 'high support' hostel, Benington)

While residents often feel abandoned by staff who no longer seem able to provide the care that they need, staff too are aware of the tendency to withdraw (both emotionally and physically) and are very clear as to the reasons for this withdrawal. Though the design of many projects makes contact difficult, and the threat of physical violence is draining, it is the emotional pressure of working in such environments that can lead staff to shut themselves off from those they are supposed to be supporting. As David explains, these pressures are both multiple and overwhelming:

> Sometimes I feel like a probation officer, sometimes like a psychiatrist, sometimes like a nurse, a doctor, a solicitor, a counsellor, a chaplain, a benefits administrator ... we touch on every single thing you can do ... [and] it's very challenging ... sometimes we have to deal with verbal or physical confrontation. ... We have dangerous situations. Occasionally physical restraint situations ... explosions of anger and frustration. So that is very physically challenging. The fact that you might be attacked. ... Then it is very emotionally challenging [working with] people who are ungrateful, people who are constantly criticizing, people who are very unreliable. ... Sometimes I just shut down emotionally and verbally. I just shut them off. Inside I will just be quietly swearing at them. But then I will just think sod you really, I am just not going to deal with you, I will deal with you next week sort of thing. Because I have reached my limit. I have done everything I could and you still want more, so forget it ... physically it's quite demanding, but more it's emotionally demanding because you are dealing with people in and out of prison, in and out of mental hospital, we have had four current or ex residents died in the last two months. So you get the bereavement. ... So emotionally it puts you through a lot. ... It is very stressful, people are off sick ... I suppose you draw on each other. There is a strong team spirit here ... so we share a lot of stuff throughout the day, there are meetings where we do that formally but there is a lot of informal sharing ... (Manager, HAP funded 'high support' hostel, Benington)

Stark (1994) has characterized US designer shelters as a new form of 'total institution'. As David's reference to the work of a psychiatrist, Dean's account of hostel foyers (with its connotations of bedlam) and Rob's comparisons between hostels and prison all suggest, Britain's 'high support' hostels too share many of the characteristics of Goffman's (1961) archetypical institutional formation. As in asylums or prisons, hostel residents 'work', sleep and 'play' in the same space, going about their daily activities always in the company of others and according to the rules of management and staff. As with the asylum or prison there is also

> a basic split between a large managed group ... and a small supervisory staff. [The former] typically live in the institution and have restricted contact with the world outside the walls. The staff often operates on an eight-hour day and is socially integrated into the outside world. Each grouping tends to conceive

of the other in terms of narrow hostile stereotypes. … Social mobility between the two strata is grossly restricted; social distance is typically great and often formally prescribed. Even talk across the boundaries may be conducted in a special tone of voice … (Goffman, 1961: 17–19)

Yet it is important not to stretch the analogy too far. As the previous sections make clear, in other ways Britain's 'high support' hostels lack a number of the features usually ascribed to such formations. Most obviously, perhaps, whatever the desire of government, or of others who advocate an ethos of 'active rehabilitation and change', the various programmes of support now on offer in Britain's 'high support' hostels are very rarely (if ever) forced upon residents. Nor, in truth, is there much evidence that the daily routine is tightly scheduled around the demands of such programmes. Indeed, the feeling among many residents would seem to be that such support is in any case sometimes more apparent than real, such that hostel life may in fact be better characterized by the constant fight to secure access to staff and support.

In the end, it is this disjuncture between the constant monitoring of the asylum and prison, and the lack of such surveillance in Britain's homeless hostels, that warns against a reading of 'high support' hostels as total institutions. Rather than being under surveillance or subject to intrusive personal management regimes (Stark, 1994; Williams, 1996), very often the feeling among residents is that staff actually have very little idea, nor do they want to know, what really goes on in such places. Indeed, with some staff apparently content to leave residents to face the chaos of hostel life alone, when the analogy of prison is raised it becomes clear which some would prefer:

> There's no control … the office is their kingdom and outside the office environment, which is like where we are … there's no control, absolutely no control. (James, 52, resident, HAP funded 'high support' hostel, Benington)

> I preferred prison to this. You get three meals a day, your bedding is there, and at least the staff come around the cells and make sure everything is alright. They found someone here who had been in his room for three days with DVT [diarrhoea and vomiting] before they took him to hospital. This is my first hostel in my life I've been in and never again! This is a nightmare. I hate it. (Rob, 47, resident, HAP funded 'high support' hostel, Benington)

Autonomy, Professionalism … and Kindness

The experiences outlined above are depressingly widespread. But by no means all Britain's 'high support' hostels are as bad as the ones encountered by Dean, Rob, Chris, Colin and James. Describing their arrival at

Gateway, a woman-only hostel in Benington, for example, Julie and Sharon recalled that:

> JULIE: I'd heard about the other places and when somebody said 'Gateway hostel' I thought 'Oh no'. And then [when I got in here] I thought 'this is brilliant'.
> SHARON: I assumed hostels were really horrible, scary and dingy dark places, but this is lovely ...it doesn't seem like a hostel [at all]. (Julie, 20, and Sharon, 23, residents, Gateway 'high support' hostel, Benington)

Opened in the mid-1990s, Gateway has an ethos and design that traces its lineage back to the group homes and open access hostels of the 1970s and 1980s that were inspired by the women's aid movement. As the manager recalls, when the project first opened there were:

> A lot of people [who] felt that [we] wouldn't be able to fill up, wouldn't be able to find 20 homeless women because there weren't 20 homeless women in Benington ... I think in the last 12 months we've turned down 633 requests for accommodation at Gateway. (Manager, Gateway 'high support' hostel, Benington)

That Gateway is able to offer its residents a very different experience to that found in many other 'high support' hostels is obvious; precisely how it achieves this is less so. Certainly the reasons behind it cannot be put down to any essential(ist) difference between men's and women's hostels. Like other projects, Gateway houses a very diverse clientele: from women working in the sex industry and using crack cocaine, to women who have just left a violent relationship and to whom 'street culture' is entirely alien. And, though the hostel may lack the 'hard masculinity' that is part-and-parcel of both life on the streets and life in many mixed sex or all male hostels (Wardhaugh, 1999; Cooper, 2001), it would be naive to think that some homeless women too are not sometimes aggressive or violent (see, for example, May et al., 2007). In fact, four reasons might be suggested as to why Gateway is able to provide a more hospitable and supportive environment than many other hostels: relating to its location, design, the very different relationships between staff and residents evident at Gateway, and the autonomy its management continues to enjoy over the project's admission procedures.

As its manager explains, Gateway was deliberately sited in a suburban location, some distance from the inner-city neighbourhood where much of the city's sex industry, drugs scene and the majority of its homeless services are concentrated. This suburban location therefore means that its residents are some considerable distance from both the day centres and soup runs that provide a focus for the city's street homelessness scene, and the customers and dealers around whom its sex and drugs industries revolve.

Though day centres especially clearly provide an important space of support for many homeless people, and a focus for their own support networks (Hoch, 1991), when seeking to move away from the streets many people recognize they also need to 'move away from the day centre life' in order to distance themselves both from homeless friends (some of whom may, for example, still be using drugs) and from their own homeless identity (Rowe & Wolch, 1990). Understood in these terms, Gateway's location thus provides its residents with a chance to 'get away from everything, have a break and think about what they want to do' in the words of its manager, or to get all the 'muck' out of their lives and simply 'be left alone' as Chris (somewhat wistfully) put it at the start of this chapter. This location also brings into play a certain amount of self-selection among potential residents, as the manager explains:

> Not many women from here would use the day centre and things like that. They're a different group of homeless women, do you see what I mean? The women who use the day centre aren't usually the women who come into Gateway. ... A lot of the women ... at the day centre will have come from that culture of either street homelessness, or street drinking ... whereas, although we do get women like that, we get a lot of women who don't have any connection with that street culture. (Manager, Gateway 'high support' hostel, Benington)

Gateway also differs from other hostels in terms of its design. It is important not to overemphasize these differences, of course. As our fieldnotes make clear, certain aspects of the building's role, and of the relationships played out therein, are still evident both in its fixtures and fittings (which veer on the side of the institutional) and in other, apparently mundane, details such as the notices displayed 'on the cupboard doors in the staff kitchen, reminding people that under no circumstances are staff mugs to be used by residents 'coz of the risk of infectious disease' (Fieldnotes, Gateway hostel). But the hostel has embraced a number of the design concepts recommended by the various good practice guides put out by the sector over the past 20 years or so (see, for example, Garside et al., 1990; Van Doorn & Williamson, 2001). In stark contrast to concerns expressed by both staff and residents over the quality of accommodation and the inappropriate lay-out of many other hostels, Gateway staff are therefore satisfied that the hostel is 'really well designed', offering both a certain level of independence and privacy for residents, and features intended to make both staff and residents feel safer:

> I have no problems with the design at all really. I just think it's really nice. It's got disabled access for people on the ground floor. The kitchen's disabled access. The lounge is disabled access. You've got panic buttons in the bedrooms. Everybody's got a bedsit where they've got their kitchen and their bedroom. They've got facilities for putting their TV up. They've got a shared

bathroom and shower, which is quite nice. I think it's designed really well. (Key worker, Gateway 'high support' hostel, Benington)

More noticeable even than these differences in design are the very different relationships between staff and residents at Gateway. Like most 'high support' hostels, Gateway operates according to the principles of housing plus, offering residents a range of additional support services delivered through a key worker system. But the system in place at Gateway differs from the hostel regimes described earlier in a number of important respects. In the first place, Gateway staff are far more vigilant (and far more consistent) in applying the basic rules of the project (relating to the use of drink or drugs, for example) than are staff in some of the hostels described in the previous section. For Sue, a project worker, such rules are:

> Really, really effective. The eviction process, and the boundaries, and the no drugs and stuff, I find them very effective. Because the women understand that we're very strict on rules, in paying your rent, and visitors staying late, and sneaking visitors in. It's very rare that they sort of break them. Rules are not broken, to my knowledge, very often here, which is unusual. Because I've worked at places like **** [another 'high support' hostel in the city] and they break the rules there every day. You turn around and they've broken the rule. They break the visitor's policy. They break the drugs policy. They break the drinking policy. And you know, that's how it is. But here I find the women that come here, they seem to value the work that we do with them, so they try to stay within the remit. ... Because they actually want to get a place at the end of it. And they actually want to move on and they actually want to get on with their life. So I find that very good. (Key worker, Gateway 'high support' hostel, Benington)

Crucially, the hostel's residents also seem to value these rules. In part this is because they recognize that such rules help to engender a much calmer atmosphere than is apparent in many other hostels (they help 'keep everything good'), and in part because they are not too intrusive ('not so rigid that you have to lie'). But most obviously, perhaps, they abide by these rules because they recognize that they form part of an unwritten contract within which residents who stick to the rules and work with staff (keeping appointments, for example) are in return provided with a tangible package of support:

> There are rules that keep everything good but they are not so rigid that you have to lie. ... And they try to help you as much as they can basically. If you don't talk to them then, well as you were saying, it's like if you don't talk to them then they won't help you. But if you work with them ... they'll give you all the help you need. (Julie, 20, resident, Gateway 'high support' hostel, Benington)

> [We have an] initial interview and ... [a] move-on talk. We also have an ongoing assessment period, like we're constantly sort of trying to get that message through. Basically, work with me. And what we do is – it depends on the issue that the

person's come to us with. If they've come to us with a drug or an alcohol issue we encourage that they sort it out in a way which suits them the best. We encourage them to go to [name of project], or [name of another project], you know, to sort of whatever suits them. We encourage them to seek other specialist advice because we can't do it all. And I like that about Gateway, because we don't just take them and say: 'Right come on, where do you want to live, we want to know where to shove you.' We put support in place. We also do a pre-settlement. We also refer them on to tenancy sustainment so that, you know, after we've like put them into – whether it's high support, medium support, low support, or general needs housing, we also check out with them whether they need ongoing support so we can refer them to another part of ****, which is tenancy sustainment. (Sue, Key worker, Gateway 'high support' hostel, Benington)

Though intensive, the programmes that Sue describes are not compulsory. Instead, residents are encouraged to access any (and only the) support that they need, according to an ethos of empowerment rather than 'active reha-bilitation and change'. As importantly, residents themselves define the nature of the support they think they need, continuing to access that sup-port, if necessary, even after they have been rehoused.

In stark contrast to relations between staff and residents at many other 'high support' hostels, relationships between staff and residents at Gateway also fre-quently move somewhere beyond the more formal relationships of a key worker system. For Julie, for example, one of the most memorable – and most valued – encounters she had with her 'support worker' was when she cut her hair:

Everybody at Gateway is really friendly. You can chat to the staff like they are friends and have a laugh with them as well. ... [Like] the other day my support worker ... cut my hair. I got a free haircut! ... you can be honest with them, even about the naughty stuff. (Julie, 20, resident, Gateway 'high support' hostel, Benington)

It is these kinds of spontaneous acts of kindness that have provided Julie with the confidence – and trust – to work with her support worker, and to talk to her 'even about the naughty stuff'. Staff too are aware that for residents to engage with more formal systems of support (whether around issues relating to drugs and alcohol, or domestic abuse) they must first feel emotionally safe and trust the person they are working with. Such trust is partly engendered through the maintenance of traditional, professional boundaries – around confidentiality, for example. But, as those working in day centres, night shel-ters and on soup runs recognize, it is also clearly dependent upon that diffi-cult to define 'something else' – a sense of engagement with the 'real' person and a genuine expression of care:

The main satisfaction is when you actually meet somebody you have a con-nection with; when you actually have a real contact with them. I think it's quite rare ... [but] it does happen. I've had it with a couple recently, where

I think we could see – it sounds naff – where you see past the roles, you know, where they could see past my role and I could see past their role. Just see each other as people a bit. Obviously, you've got your boundaries and confidentiality and working within that, but yeah I've had that a couple of times yesterday … you're in that professional role, always, but, but where what you're saying is congruent with who you are and how you feel … and I think they know; they can pick up on that genuineness. (Theresa, Key worker, Gateway 'high support' hostel, Benington)

Finally, to provide the space for workers and residents to move beyond these more formal roles, Gateway staff are granted considerable autonomy. That autonomy is replicated in the hostel's admissions procedures. In contrast to the other 'high support' hostels in the city, Gateway never received any HAP funding. As a result, nor did it become subject to the 'Entrenched and Vulnerable' policies put in place by the local authority's street outreach team, with the manager arguing that:

We should not be part of it because it would close too many gaps. We wouldn't be operating as a direct access hostel if we entered into that scheme. We wanted to have the flexibility to be able to take women from the 24/7 Project [a local project working with sex workers] or from wherever they happen to come from. And the city council did accept that that was reasonable, so we didn't become part of that scheme. (Manager, Gateway 'high support' hostel, Benington)

Where the city's other hostels now have little choice over whether or not to accept someone who has been deemed 'Entrenched and Vulnerable' by the local authority street outreach team, and thus exert little control over the proportion of their residents with high support needs, Gateway is still able to determine who it takes in. As a result, though the hostel still accepts a variety of applicants, including women with serious drug or alcohol addictions, the management team tries to ensure a balance of different groups. As the manager explains:

It goes in ebbs and flows really. Sometimes we can have what feels to be a very chaotic group of residents. If we get say very high levels of drug users it can be very, very chaotic … women coming into it will just get consumed by all this chaos and think, they'll just leave, or they'll become part of the chaos. And so it's really important that we try to make sure that there's a balance in that we're not predominantly housing one group above another. … [Because the danger is] you end up not being very productive in what you're trying to do … (Manager, Gateway 'high support' hostel, Benington)

This drive for balance has nothing to do with a desire to make the work of staff easier. Instead, it is driven by a belief that the hostel's programmes are only liable to be effective when residents are ready to engage with them;

something that is by no means always the case among long-term homeless people, or those with serious drug or alcohol addictions. It is also shaped by the recognition that such programmes will only work when the atmosphere in the hostel is such that staff are able to turn their full attention to them, rather than seeking simply to contain the chaos that too often characterizes day-to-day life in other 'high support' hostels.

Conclusions

The very different experiences of Britain's night shelters and hostels given voice here point to the limitations of accounts that offer too sweeping an assessment of the politics of 'shelter life'. It is clear to us, for example, that rather than operating according to the principles of 'less eligibility', as has tended to be assumed in previous studies of such services conducted in the United States (Matieu, 1993; Feldman, 2004), the volunteers struggling to provide accommodation and care in Britain's night shelters are in fact driven by a desire to do the best they can for their 'guests'. Having rejected the kind of support characterizing a housing plus approach as antithetical to the ethos of open acceptance within which they work, however, it is also clear that such shelters currently do little to enable people to make a more permanent exit from the streets.

Yet we would suggest that the real problem with Britain's night shelters has less to do with this failure to embrace a housing plus approach (as government and other homeless providers continue to argue) than with the fact that too often they are the *only* accommodation available to homeless people in a town or city (see chapters 7 and 8), and/or that they often find themselves having to take in people turned away by, or evicted from, other services because they are deemed too 'chaotic'. Consequently, organizations that have rejected a 'high support' approach often find themselves providing accommodation to those most obviously in need of that support. And as the proportion of residents with high support needs escalates, the dynamics in such shelters become more volatile. Compounding these problems, Britain's night shelters have mostly been excluded from the statutory funding that might enable them to address some of these issues (providing some resource for staff training, or the provision of single sex rooms, for example) precisely because they are deemed 'unprofessional'. Rather than articulating the limits to an ethos of open acceptance, Britain's night shelters might therefore be more usefully understood as articulating the limits to a voluntary response when such organizations are denied the financial support they need to properly articulate this ethos, and/or shelter residents are unable to access the support they may need through *other* providers.

Operating according to the principles of housing plus, Britain's 'high support' hostels are equally difficult to situate in the accounts of 'designer shelters' emanating from the USA (Stark, 1994; Veness, 1994; Williams, 1996). Still mostly working to an ethos of empowerment rather than 'active rehabilitation and change', such hostels seek to provide a broad range of support to their residents, but only to those who desire it. Moreover, staff tend to view such support less as the answer to a problem that is understood as lying with the individual (that is, as a 'cure' for individual pathologies), than as part of a broader range of measures (including an increased supply of affordable accommodation) necessary to address the problems of homelessness at a structural level. As the Gateway example indicates, the levels of care and accommodation available to residents in such hostels can be high. And, even if still far from adequate, the increased range of support services put in place through the HAP and associated programmes is enabling organizations like Gateway to begin the process of moving (some) residents through the hostel and into other forms of sustainable accommodation (May et al., 2006).

But it is also clear that too many of Britain's 'high support' hostels fall significantly short of the standards set by organizations like Gateway. Most obviously, a continued lack of affordable housing and related services (most notably, perhaps, drug and alcohol services) means that rather than operating as the first step on a journey to independent accommodation, many of Britain's 'high support' hostels are silting up. Recent restrictions imposed upon some of these hostels' admissions procedures – such as the Entrenched and Vulnerable scheme described above – are further increasing these problems, as staff find themselves trying to work with a growing number of residents with high support needs in a climate of continued funding scarcity that leaves many struggling to provide anything like the quality of accommodation and in-house care that was so keenly anticipated when the sector began to restructure some 20 to 30 years ago. Whatever the strengths of the voluntary response to homelessness, one of its most obvious weaknesses – as with the voluntary welfare response more widely (Fyfe & Milligan, 2003) – is exactly this unevenness in both the supply and quality of accommodation and care offered by different service organizations (May et al., 2006). It is to questions of unevenness, and the ramifications of this unevenness for people becoming homeless in different places, that we turn in the remaining chapters.

Chapter Seven

Big City Blues: Uneven Geographies of Provision in the Homeless City

Introduction: Uneven Landscapes of Provision

Thus far we have presented a picture of the relatively extensive, and complex, networks of service provision for single homeless people in Britain. Although much academic attention, and certainly the bulk of popular imagination, has tended to focus principally on homelessness and services for homeless people in the capital city of London, it is clear that networks of non-statutory provision have sprung up in a wide range of places, including in many quite small towns and in rural settings. These hostels, day centres and soup runs represent *both* a local response to the plight of homeless people, *and* an opportunity for local people (and the organizations they develop or join up with) to be involved in 'doing something' about the problems of homelessness.

Such networks will be shaped at least to some extent by the availability and targeting of statutory funding, and some non-statutory organizations will accordingly become involved in an increasing professionalization of their services, with improved physical infrastructure and extended support services. Both within these 'insider' organizations and in the 'outsider' services that plough a furrow beyond joined-up local governance there is a performativity of care that reflects local and individual expressions of ethos and responsible citizenship. These expressions are a fundamental response to homelessness in Britain.

But there is also marked geographical unevenness in the distribution and quality of such services. Although this unevenness has been exacerbated by recent policy initiatives that have injected funding into particular places and particular kinds of services, thus producing something of a postcode lottery in the distribution of state-funded service, this is not the only reason why service provision remains uneven. In this chapter we begin the task of first mapping, and then attempting to explain, this unevenness. Here we focus

Table 7.1   Top and bottom ten towns and cities in England, Wales and Scotland according to provision of direct access bed spaces in 2002

Top 10		Bottom 10	
Place	Direct access beds per 1000 popn	Place	Direct access beds per 1000 pop
Darwen	1.6	Luton	0.02
Coventry	1.27	Rotherham	0.03
Great Yarmouth	1.24	Huddersfield	0.03
Louth	1.17	Glasgow	0.03
Sittingbourne	1.09	Bridgend	0.03
Wigston	0.94	St Helens	0.04
Stourbridge	0.90	Southend on Sea	0.04
Nottingham	0.86	Poole	0.04
Perth	0.83	Northampton	0.04
Blackpool	0.83	Andover	0.04

on these questions in relation to Britain's towns and cities. In chapter 8 we turn to an examination of homeless service provision and consumption in Britain's rural areas.

Of course, our research provided a snapshot of the uneven geographies of service provision for homeless people in the early 2000s, and we would emphasize again at this point that there will have been significant local changes since then. Nevertheless, the snapshot poses interesting questions about the reasons behind this unevenness. As part of this research, for example, we produced survey data sets that charted the provision of direct hostel bedspaces in different places in 2001/2. Table 7.1 gives an example of one indicator of such unevenness, showing the ten 'top' and 'bottom' centres of provision according to the number of emergency hostel beds per 1000 population at the time. Such unevenness raises questions of spatial equity, with people in one place apparently more able to access services than people in another. However, it should be emphasized that the survey revealed little significant variation in levels of *occupancy* in night shelters and hostels in different places. Instead, results showed the sector as a whole to be struggling to meet demand, with occupancy levels averaging 92 per cent and more than half of all organizations responding to the accommodation survey reporting 100 per cent occupancy (May et al., 2006).

What, then, lies behind this variegated pattern of services? Our attempts to correlate service provision with variations in potential 'need' (assessed via a series of surrogate measures relating to levels of deprivation, the structure of local housing markets and the number of rough sleepers) proved fruitless.

We have concluded that the uneven landscape of service provision for homeless people cannot be explained simply in terms of an unevenness of need. Instead, we want to suggest that locally distinctive service infrastructures can be understood in terms of three localized *layers* of circumstances.

The first layer is *historical.* We suspect that the history of the presence or absence of caring institutions will in some ways both shape a local recognition of the needs of particular groups of people and inflect a local culture of care. Of course we recognize that in some cases local institutions of care can provoke localist prejudice and a reactionary NIMBYism that marks out those needing care as transgressors of boundaries of local orthodoxy, and therefore as targets for attempts to purify local space (see Sibley, 1995; Cloke et al., 2000b). However, we want to argue that there may also be more positive historical layers at work here. It seems, for example, that patterns of service provision for homeless people in particular places can be shaped by the local antecedence of large institutions dealing with homelessness, such as the longstanding presence of 'spikes' (workhouses), or Salvation Army or Church Army hostels. The historical presence of these institutions can shape local cultures of response to homelessness (see Corbin, 1999), both by legitimizing the issue of homelessness locally and by helping to generate further responses to a problem that is alive in public culture and discourse in the locality. It is also clear that the presence of particular services in particular places can be explained by particular local people responding to specific local circumstances. Here, we would point to the activities of charismatic local individuals who, perhaps responding to the locally legitimated public discourse, work to start up services that are shaped by particular local configurations of ethical dynamics (Bryson, 2001). Given their reliance on public donations and volunteer labour, we would also point to the likelihood that the abundance of local services might reflect local or regional variations in economic health (see also De Vita, 1997).

The second layer is *political.* In the light of these localized historical cultures of caring and service provision, local authorities have responded very differently to issues of servicing and policing homeless people within their jurisdiction. In the case studies presented in this chapter, for example, Benington City Council's long-term and highly coordinated response to what is accepted as an important local problem of homelessness contrasts with Steeltown Borough Council's persistent refusal until quite recently to act on the issue of street homelessness, with the council preferring instead to 'export' homeless people to a nearby city. Unevenness also arises because of the distribution mechanisms of RSI/HAP funding (see chapters 2 and 6), which means that some places receive very significant resources that both fund and shape service provision, while others remain dependent on more localized resources. Even where central government funding is provided, further unevenness results between funded services (often hostels) and other services (such as night shelters), which become marginalized and 'othered' financially and strategically.

The third layer is *organizational*. Different places are associated with quite different organizational trends that impact upon service provision (see Cloke et al., 2005). One factor here is the longstanding presence (or corresponding absence) of one of the big non-statutory service providers, such as the Salvation Army or the YMCA. Another factor is the degree to which small local initiatives have sprung up in particular places. Commonly, what started out in the 1970s and 1980s as small charismatic efforts have grown into larger professionalized outfits. This is not always the case, however, and elsewhere starter organizations have split, leading to the development of smaller offshoots based on a particular ethos or attitude to funding (see Cloke et al., 2005). A more recent trend is for large-scale national level organizations to subsume smaller ones, leading to economies of scale and national-level training regimes, but sometimes to reduced local responsiveness. All of these organizational dynamics are important in the development of particular localized responses to homelessness. It is also significant that local media are liable to give greater coverage to homelessness issues when provided with stories by active local service agencies (Archard, 1979; May, 2003b).

But these differentiated patterns of service development and provision do not tell the whole story. We also want to argue that the emergence of local circumstances of homelessness and service provision relies on particular interconnections between service *provision* and service *consumption*, resulting in culturally significant local '*scenes*' of homelessness. Our research with service providers and homeless people has interrogated how this interaction between provision and consumption leads to very different place-distinctions. Even where places have the 'same' level of services, they may have a very different 'feel', which is both experienced by homeless people and made more material in the complex cartographies and tactical spaces that they generate in the city or town concerned. The importance of these scenes lies both in the particular experiences of being homeless in a particular place, and in the characterization of that place in the tacit knowledges and urban myths of wider communities of homeless people. For example, although the majority of service users in most places are local, homeless people do migrate (Cloke et al., 2002). While the complexity of their movements, and reasons for moving, cannot be reduced to the simple 'lure' of 'service magnets', or the search for housing and employment (May, 2000a, 2003a), our research did trace a variety of such movements that interconnected with particular homelessness scenes. These included: young people, often drug-dependent, seeking out key nodal locations where drugs are thought to be readily available and inexpensive and where there are perceived high levels of emergency services – in other words, 'good' places to be homeless in; people of all ages seeking out places that represent to them the countercultural 'edge' (often linked with practices and places associated with New Age phenomena);

people of all ages seeking out short-term employment; people of all ages – but often younger people – 'commuting' to and from larger centres to sell the *Big Issue*, to beg or even to engage in survivalist crime in places where they will not be recognized; and older people travelling on ancient route ways following the location of friaries and former spikes (though this is waning).

Different places figure differently in terms of the confluence of these mobility networks. Accordingly, in our research we identified a range of different kinds of homeless places, including: places that export homelessness elsewhere because of the lack of in situ services; places that serve their immediate local area, are not on significant mobility routes and are not recognized by homeless people as magnets for homeless people; regional magnets serving as places of intervening opportunity; and national magnets where mobility routes, emergency services and drug availability are perceived to come together. We need to emphasize here not only that places can combine different functions (for example, a city can be both a regional and a national magnet as well as serving its local population), but also that the 'status' of places changes; for example, with shifting regimes of policing/ regulation, or as people realize that services have become saturated. These tactical mobilities by homeless people both shape and are shaped by the cultural 'scenes' of homelessness experienced in particular places, and thereby contribute strongly to an understanding of the uneven geographies of emergency service provision and consumption in Britain.

In order to explore further these issues of unevenness of service provision and differentiated homelessness scenes, the remainder of this chapter presents a detailed account of two case studies – the cities of Benington and Steeltown – through which we explore how and why different cities emerge as distinctive homeless places. The evidence presented was researched in 2002–3, and we recognize that there will have been significant changes in both places since that time, not least with the growth of more rigid policing of on-street homelessness in many places, undergirded by the use of Anti-Social Behaviour Orders to clear homeless people from the streets (Johnsen & Fitzpatrick, 2010). However, the two cases were selected at the time on the prima facie evidence that, despite having roughly similar population sizes, Benington (with a population of 381,618 in 2001) had an extensive network of emergency services for homeless people while Steeltown (population 286,865) had very few such services. Indeed, Benington had no fewer than five emergency hostels for single homeless people, between them providing 211 'direct access' beds (or 0.55 beds per 1000 population). These were complemented by four day centres, a soup kitchen and at least one soup run provided every night of the week. Steeltown, in contrast, had only one 13-bed direct access night shelter (The Retreat) (0.04 beds per 1000 population) and a Sunday morning breakfast service. There were no day centres for homeless people over the age of 25, and the city's only soup run had been discontinued a few years previously.

Given the suggestion of strong servicing and underservicing respectively we undertook intensive interviews (with local authority coordinators, service managers, staff and volunteers, as well as with homeless service users themselves) and periods of participant observation in a range of service environments in each city, in an attempt to render more complex, and problematic, the apparently simple suggestion that Benington and Steeltown might be regarded as 'good' or 'bad' places in which to be homeless because of the levels of provision to be found there. What follows is therefore less of a comparison of 'high' versus 'low' provision geographically, and more of an appreciation of how the complicated coming-together of political, institutional, social and cultural factors in particular settings can produce distinctive, but fluid, 'homeless places'.

Different Histories of Provision

The landscape of services for homeless people in Benington is both extensive and varied (table 7.2), and represents in comparative terms a high level of services for a city of its size. Services are largely congregated in the Westhill area of the city, not far from the city centre, and share this space with other significantly marginalized activities, notably drug dealing and solicitation for prostitution. These co-presences reflect to some extent the availability of inexpensive land and buildings in a part of the city that has largely escaped gentrification and commercialization, and the cumulative impact of marginalized people and activities in the neighbourhood, which, together, reinforce the marginality of the area and render it a space of fear for many of the city's residents (homeless as well as housed – see chapter 3). Homelessness, drug addiction and prostitution are interconnected socially as well as spatially – many homeless people use drugs, and some may be involved in prostitution – and the co-proximity of these activities is seen by service providers as an impediment to rehabilitation. As one hostel manager

Table 7.2   Benington's emergency services for single homeless people in 2003

Direct access hostels and night shelter (219 beds)	5
Temporary winter night shelter (45 beds, open seasonally)	1
Day centres (daily)	4
Soup kitchen (nightly, fixed site)	1
Soup run (nightly)	1
Multi-agency advice centre	1
Population (in 2001)	381,618

told us, the hostels are 'handy for all the services you *don't* want them [the residents] to be going to'.

Services for homeless people have been a feature in Benington for more than a century, and significant service providers have a long history of involvement in the city. The Salvation Army originally ran two hostels in the city, before opening their current purpose-built hostel in the mid-1970s. Another of the current hostel buildings has been operating as a hostel for homeless people since 1904, first as a municipal lodging house run by the local authority, then as a Salvation Army hostel and more recently operated by the North Benington Housing Association in its local identity as the Benington Churches Housing Association. Yet another of the current hostels was established in the early 1900s and eventually became part of another large (national) social housing group in the 1980s. The Benington Cyrenians have also been active service providers in this area. Established in 1969, the organization initially ran two 'homes' for homeless people, establishing ancillary soup run and soup kitchen services in the early 1970s. Originally staffed entirely by volunteers, the organization quickly became professionalized and opened Britain's first ever purpose-built day centre in 1986. A splinter group from the original volunteers set up their own independent organization in the mid-1980s, establishing a night shelter in 1986 and setting up a soup run trust in 1987. Benington Cyrenians continued to expand their activities, opening a specialized women-only hostel (Gateway) in 1995, and following financial crises in the late 1990s the organization became linked with another large social provider made up of a coalition of 13 housing, social economy and care organizations working throughout Britain.

Local churches have also actively participated in providing services for homeless people. The Wesleyan Centre opened in 1988; an interdenominational group began in 1984 and is currently responsible for another of the day centres; the Salvation Army corps in Westhill established the Light drop-in service in the late 1980s as part of broader community outreach work; members of local Christian churches have set up the 24/7 Project to support female sex workers; and several other churches have also been involved in a series of soup run projects. Other services have come and gone, notably two direct access hostels funded by the Rough Sleepers Unit in the 1990s. However, service provision in Benington has remained significant, drawing on strong historical roots and undergoing notable expansion in the 1980s, when the scale and problems of homelessness became increasingly visible.

By contrast, emergency services for homeless people in Steeltown are a much more recent phenomenon, with no services being offered until the late 1980s. Since then service provision has expanded and professionalized, but remains very different in scale and extent from the service landscape in Benington (table 7.3). Steeltown's direct access night shelter (the Retreat, operated by the local Pathway group) is located in an industrial area adjacent

Table 7.3   Steeltown's emergency services for single homeless people in 2003

Night shelter (13 beds)	1
Soup kitchen	1
Drop-in centre	1
Advice centre	1
Population (in 2001)	286,865

to the city centre – an area labelled by one staff member as 'Pathway Island' – while other services are part of a broader hub of voluntary activities sited in an area that also forms the red light district. As in Benington, services for homeless people are subject to spatial as well as social marginalization.

Local press coverage and organizational mission statements from homelessness agencies indicate that problems of homelessness in Steeltown only became visible towards the end of the 1980s. At that time, a local United Reformed Church began to provide a Sunday morning breakfast service offering food, clothing and bathing facilities to homeless people. Around the same time a group drawn from local churches founded a Christmas breakfast project, drawing funding from Crisis at Christmas. In the early 1990s a splinter group began a project to provide accommodation for homeless people. The group included secular people with experience in the voluntary sector who began to pressure the city council about the visible problem of homelessness in Steeltown. A member of the management committee told us: 'When we started there were quite a few rough sleepers about. You could wander around the market and there'd be people laying out in the market stalls at night, especially the older people with alcohol problems.' Failing initially to attract council support, the group established Christmas 'sleep stations' in any building they could borrow for a winter. The services, run by volunteers, served around 20 people every night.

The organization quickly formalized itself as the Pathway Group (the name signifying a continuing Christian ethos) and set up a 13-bed direct access night shelter in a burnt out building leased at a low rent from the city council. The campaigning that led to the establishment of the night shelter demonstrates how local and national media, national pressure groups and local councils and organizations can all contribute to the formalization of a local response to service needs. The local campaign in Steeltown received a heightened public profile after a local rough sleeper was found dead in a bus shelter. This publicity contributed to the council's decision to release the building, and at the same time the national organization Crisis offered professional and financial assistance, spurred on by national media coverage of the stabbing to death of a volunteer in a homeless hostel in Oxford. The Pathway night shelter was established along professional, business-orientated lines but the project was difficult to sustain until new links were forged with a regional housing association, securing funding for a new high support referral-only (rather than 'direct access', or emergency) hostel. The original night shelter was closed, but reopened eight months later because many local service users were failing to cope with the demanding rehabilitation regime of the new hostel, and rough sleeping continued to be a problem for local and non-local homeless people alike. Spin-off projects from the Pathway group include an advice centre and a (referral-only) 'Assertive Outreach Project', so called specifically in an attempt to secure central government funding. A drop-in centre for homeless people under the age of 25 open one afternoon per week has also recently been established by Steeltown Housing for Young People.

Accounting for Different Service Developments

In Benington the involvement of significant service providers – for example the Salvation Army, the Cyrenians and housing trusts/associations – has ensured a long history of provision that will have been shaped by some form of recognition of the needs of local homeless people, and in all probability will have helped to shape public perceptions of the homelessness 'problem' in the city. The long-term co-presence of homeless people and emergency homelessness service has produced a groundswell of understanding that Benington has grown to be a centre for homelessness. By contrast, Steeltown has only recently been recognized as a place where services for homeless people are required, although what precisely has shaped this lack of historical response is unclear. Local agency representatives concur that the need for such services has only recently been evident, suggesting that prior to the Thatcher era Steeltown had been a relatively stable community that 'looked after its own'. It is also possible that people experiencing homelessness in Steeltown over this period would have accessed services in nearby cities. Homelessness in Steeltown only became more visible with the onset of mass unemployment, the emergence of new employment regimes and consequent changes to family, household and community dynamics:

> You'd got a fairly stable immigrant population that had either come to work in the railways or in the steelyards, and some people in the pits, but communities remained stable, and that changed as a result of the miners' strike and the steel strike. These hard industries went, the employment pattern was changed, there were more women entering part-time employment, there was fairly mass unemployment in this area. … The nuclear family units, and some of the big extended family units in some villages, all that started to disappear with the demise of the heavy industries and the changes in employment patterns, and people coming and going, families breaking up. (Representative, Volunteer Bureau, Steeltown)

These historical and organizational layers of difference interconnect with more directly political concerns in the two cities. In general, the restructuring of the local state during the 1980s involved the increasing introduction of the market, moves towards the enabling of citizen involvement, a transition to neocorporatist state arrangements and a broader harmonization with more general societal shifts towards post-Fordism (Cochrane, 1990; Rhodes, 1992; Goodwin et al., 1993). Clearly, however, different segments of the local state, especially local councils, emerged from this restructuring with different priorities towards issues such as homelessness – not least because of the different kinds of institutional histories outlined above. So whereas council records in Benington show an active involvement with the issue of homelessness in the city throughout the post-war period (a clear awareness in these records of services provided for homeless people in the city suggests that the presence of service provision made it difficult for the local authority to ignore the issue even if it wished to do so), several of our interviewees from agencies in Steeltown (including those currently managing local authority housing services) alluded to the fact that Steeltown's local authority had historically refused to recognize homelessness as a genuine local issue. Instead, until the 1990s homelessness services were seen as 'Cinderella services' (Representative, Steeltown Borough Council) that were overshadowed by a focus on the area's huge stock of general needs housing – a focus that was dogged by allegations of corruption and mismanagement. Only when new management was introduced into the local authority was the practice of 'sweeping homelessness under the carpet' discontinued, and greater priority given to encouraging support services for homeless people. Inevitably, the local politics of homelessness policy produces different forms of blame culture in such circumstances. Our interviews in the Steeltown context revealed claims that the initiatives introduced by the Pathway Group had effectively 'created' a demand for homelessness services in the city by attracting homeless people who would otherwise not be there. The counterclaim from those managing these services is that the opening of the night shelter simply rendered *existing* needs more visible (cf. May, 2003a).

These local state politics interconnect with the 'enabling' trajectory adopted by the central state. Although considerable levels of financial initiative have been on offer from the centre over recent years, Steeltown's service providers have benefited little from central government funding, partly due to the history of non-recognition of homelessness as a local issue, partly because of the lack of an established infrastructure of existing service providers and partly because of what the representative of a local homeless charity described as the county's position within the 'postcode lottery' (referring to perceived inequalities in the nationwide distribution of such funding). By contrast service delivery in Benington benefited from considerable funding from both the Rough Sleepers Initiative and Homelessness Action Programme, though it is also clear that the receipt of such funding has fundamentally altered the nature of services and their delivery in the city. This somewhat double-edged funding opportunity – the availability of resources but with significant strings attached – has been welcomed by some service providers as a fundamental underpinning of continuing service provision in the city:

> Without it [RSI/HAP funding] we'd be knee-deep in problems … without them we wouldn't have had the services that we've got now. The local authority, coupled with the RSU, have been enormously effective in developing strategies, getting people around the table that haven't ever met before, and developing a huge range of services for rough sleepers. (Manager, local authority street outreach team, Benington)

The very different evolution of emergency services for homeless people in Benington and Steeltown can also be explained, at least in part, by the local strategies that have been developed alongside these very different organizational and funding infrastructures. In Steeltown, the strategic development of services has been driven locally by the local authority in concert with the Pathway Group. The virtual absence of central government funding may have restricted the scale of investment, but it has also permitted local agencies unrestricted strategic opportunities such as the continuing formal provision of night shelter services and the ability to operate access regimes to emergency accommodation that are not directly tied into central dictates on reducing rough sleeping. In Benington, the importance of RSI and HAP funding has resulted in a strategy that is driven by a central government agenda of reducing the numbers of people sleeping rough:

> The main aim has been decided by the government, and the government have funded the scheme and … most of the services. So they have dictated the aim and the aim has been primarily to reduce the number of rough sleepers. (Representative, homelessness team, Benington City Council).

Within this context, however, local decision-makers have introduced their own extreme measures to prioritize hostel spaces for those deemed to be in greatest need via a Priority Access Scheme implemented in 2000. The scheme is justified by its proponents as follows:

> If we are in a situation where we're all competing for limited resources, it seems fair that people who are deemed to be most vulnerable are given the first shout at what vacancies there are. (Representative, the AC (Advice Centre), Benington)

> [T]he only way to do it was to give priority to bookings in hostels to people that we recognize as being entrenched and vulnerable – they were on our rough sleepers list and they were known to be rough sleepers – rather than to people turning up at the AC and saying they were homeless that night. (Representative, homelessness team, Benington City Council)

In fact, the practical implications of the Priority Access Scheme are that referrals to hostels come from the local authority's street outreach team's 'Entrenched and Vulnerable' ('E&V') list, and to get on to that list individuals must have been seen to be sleeping rough for a minimum of two weeks, and/ or be deemed 'especially vulnerable'; for example, because of serious physical illness or disability. They must also have a 'local connection' (a concept taken from the then Department of Environment, Transport and Regions Guidance Notes on statutory homelessness, which insist a person must either have been employed in a place or resident in that place for six months prior to their application for assistance, in order to be accepted as statutorily homeless) (for a critical reading of local connection schemes see May, 2003a). The scheme thus clearly works in favour of local people and against homeless people who may have just got off the bus from another place.

The result of the E&V Scheme has therefore been to transform a core part of the ethos of many of Benington's 'direct access' hostels. Hostels that had previously operated a policy of direct access can no longer do so, and some managers display considerable reluctance to embrace this change, partly because of concern over the type of (assumedly chaotic) people they will be housing, partly because of anxiety (unfounded) over potential loss of existing funding from the (then) Housing Corporation's supported housing management grants, and partly because the referral scheme has removed their power to turn away service users that they have previously banned. Nonetheless, most hostels now abide by the scheme, although one (Gateway women's hostel) insists on maintaining its direct access protocol because homeless women are less likely to sleep rough and therefore are unlikely to make it on to the E&V list (see chapter 6). With this caveat, the chances of a single homeless person with no drug or alcohol addiction getting a hostel bed in Benington are minimal, because hostels have become silted up with those who have been assessed as in priority need. The very significant network of emergency services for homeless people in the city, therefore, may in practice have less impact than assumed on key categories of homeless people who find themselves ineligible to access them (see also chapter 6).

Overall, our research suggests that local authorities respond very differently to issues of servicing homeless people within their jurisdiction. In our case studies, Benington City Council's long-term and highly coordinated response to what has become accepted as an important local problem of homelessness contrasts with Steeltown Borough Council's persistent refusal until quite recently to act on the issue of street homelessness. Unevenness also arises because of the distinctive mechanisms for RSI and HAP funding, with Benington receiving very significant resources that both fund and shape provision, but Steeltown having to depend on more localized resources. These conclusions interconnect with historical/organizational layers of difference, and pose questions about the precise relationship between expressed need and service provision. Accordingly we now turn to a comparative analysis of service users in the two cities.

Different Service Users

Lest it be imagined that Benington's highly developed service infrastructure merely reflects significantly greater numbers of homeless people in the city, the 2001–2 local authority housing statistics show that 3223 people presented themselves as homeless in Benington, compared to 3303 in Steeltown. Even allowing for the limitations of these statistics as proxy measures for the scale of single homelessness, it is clear that the expression of need in both places is not dissimilar. Significantly, however, 1444 (45 per cent) people were accepted as statutorily homeless because in 'priority need' in Benington, while only 187 (5.7 per cent) were so accepted in Steeltown. Such variation suggests very different cultures of homelessness and responses to homelessness in the two places.

Our interviews reveal a number of similarities among the single homeless population in Benington and Steeltown. In both places this population has become significantly younger, with 76 per cent of all night shelter users in Steeltown during 2001–2 being under the age of 35, and a similar picture emerging in Benington:

> If you look back to ten years ago, when we were working with the hostels and we had cold weather shelters … it was a lot of middle-aged alcohol-damaged men … but as drug use has increased and become more chaotic we've seen a gradual reduction in the age-group … [and] a lot more younger people. The majority of the clients are [aged] 25–40. I would say 80 per cent are white males [aged] 25–40. (Representative, homelessness team, Benington City Council)

Changes to housing benefit for under-25s have made it increasingly difficult for this age group especially to afford accommodation, particularly in a high cost housing sector such as that in Benington, while there is also evidence of a wider problem of the price of bed and breakfast (B&B) placements being too high for people on under-25s housing benefit.

Another similarity between single homeless people in Benington and Steeltown is the prevalence of drug dependency. As we have shown in earlier chapters, our service-provider and service-user interviewees consistently categorized the single homeless population into 'smackheads' (drug dependents), 'pissheads' (alcohol dependents) and 'straightheads' (no dependencies), although there are complicated overlaps between these groupings. As the average age of single homeless people has decreased, so the type of dependency has changed, from the older street drinker towards the younger user of heroin and/or crack cocaine. Both cities have developed reputations as sources for inexpensive, easily accessible heroin, and hostel and night shelter staff attest to a significant recent increase in the use of crack cocaine especially. This changing composition of the service user group presents significant challenges for hostel managers in Benington, where services were not set up to cater for the needs of the 'smackhead' population. By contrast, Steeltown's more recently established services were initiated with the support needs of drug-dependent people firmly in mind. Interestingly, the 'straighthead' group of homeless people features strongly among the hostel and day centre population in Benington, but not in Steeltown – where the more plentiful availability of public and private sector housing seems to result in people without support needs being able to more easily bypass the emergency service network altogether by, for example, persuading private landlords to accept benefit recipients as tenants.

One significant difference between service users in the two places concerns the local connections of homeless people, with Steeltown's overwhelming localism contrasting sharply with Benington's increasingly sizeable non-local segment of the homeless population. Staff of the Pathway Group told us that 95 per cent of service users are local to Steeltown or surrounding towns, and that Steeltown does not appear to be on any established 'circuit' of homelessness by which homeless people are attracted from further afield. Neither is Steeltown recognized as a centre for homelessness or homeless services, with Leeds, Sheffield or even Manchester presenting more attractive places for mobile homeless people not wishing to travel to Birmingham or London. Benington, by contrast, has a greater and increasing proportion of 'incomers'; the Benington City Council Homelessness Strategy reports that the number of callers presenting at the AC from outside Benington has risen from 13 per cent in 1995–6 to 21 per cent in 2000–1. Benington, therefore, can be seen to be operating as a national magnet for homeless people, due to a range of factors: its place in the regional network, attracting demand from neighbouring areas of low provision; its national reputation as a perceived centre of service availability; the assumed availability of affordable drugs; perceived opportunities for begging; and its place on wider and more random circuits of migration. Indeed, the city is evidently a key node on migratory circuits used by homeless people:

> It is evident to us that there is a migratory route ... Benington, being the largest urban conurbation in an immensely large rural area suffering its own deprivation, ... Plus there's also the well-trodden festival route – it was interesting to note with no Glastonbury [music festival] last summer we didn't have any stragglers sticking in Benington, which has happened in the past. (Manager, local authority street outreach team, Benington)

Thus it would seem that in-migrant homeless people are attracted to the nodal opportunities of Benington, especially the perceived high level of services and particularly emergency accommodation and drug treatment services. Interestingly, this reputation may slowly be changing given that access to services is increasingly being limited both because they are working at capacity and because of the introduction of the local connection rule. Nevertheless, Benington's reputation as a 'city of refuge' is clearly influential in the attraction of non-local homeless people: 'Benington is a bit of a Mecca for homeless people I think … people have heard that Benington is a good place to come if you are homeless, if you want to be rehoused. So people have flocked in. (Paid staff member, hostel, Benington). This reputation is enhanced by knowledge among homeless people of the local investment of RSI and HAP funding, which is readily incorporated into the communicated and tacit knowledges about different homeless places. As John, a 52-year-old hostel resident in Benington, explains:

> You get to know a lot, living the sort of life I do. You get to know a lot talking to the lads wherever you are … I know what's there, where and what to expect and where to go and all that just by talking to the lads. … You know where's what and where to get digs and what the drop-ins are before you get there. It's like code in'it. (John, 52, hostel resident, Benington)

Benington's reputation is therefore as a good place for services for homeless people, although some recently first-time homeless people inevitably take time to learn 'the code'.

Another attractive feature of Benington is the perceived availability of cheap drugs:

> It's because it's [Benington is] a drug shopping centre. The police will admit it, drugs are rife in Benington and it's cheap – the drugs are cheaper in Benington than they are in London … people come here from all over because they've got a habit and it's cheaper here. (Hostel manager, Benington)

> People come into Benington because there's more heroin available and it's cheaper in Benington than in most other places in the country. (Hostel manager, Benington)

The implication here is that homeless people make rational choices about where to move to in order to find a good place to be homeless, to buy drugs and so on, and we are convinced that – given the tacit and displayed knowledges indicated by many of our homeless interviewees – many such choices are made in respect of Benington. However, there is also evidence that other homeless people just seem to 'end up there'. Phil, for example, describes how his arrival in Benington was something of an 'accident':

> I was hitching a lift. I thought first of all I was going to go to Swindon and this guy pulled over and picked me up and he was going to Benington. So I stayed for the ride and went to Benington. … It wasn't planned. It was just ad hoc. It was just a case of pointing your finger at the map and go, and it just happened to be Benington. (Phil, 53, day centre user, Benington)

These different forms of place magnetism have implications for the local authority's attempts to get the message out to homeless people that they should not come to Benington because the facilities are now so over-stretched. Even if the message is made to sound convincing, and becomes integrated into urban storytelling among homeless populations, it may not be heard by those whose arrival is more circumstantial than rational (see also May, 2003a).

Other, more institutionalized, sources of homelessness have also exerted localized impacts on the homeless populations in Benington and Steeltown. For example, Steeltown's proximity to a number of prisons has meant that the night shelter has served many people who were recently discharged and had nowhere else to go. A similar impact is experienced in Benington from nearby prisons and drug and alcohol rehabilitation centres. Perhaps even more importantly, services in both cities are now having to provide for an increasing volume of asylum seekers (for a review of homelessness among British minority ethnic groups, refugees and asylum seekers in Britain, see McNaughton-Nicholls & Quilgars, 2009). In Benington, homeless asylum seekers have added significantly to the pressure on direct access bed spaces:

> I know that three hostels have approximately between a third and a quarter of their beds taken up by either asylum seekers or refugees ... when they're given leave to stay, or their refugee status, they are then turfed out of their accommodation that's been arranged for them through the council and then through NASS [National Asylum Support Service] and they're given a few days to find something else. ... That's why they end up with us. (Local authority street outreach team worker, Benington)

These new segments of the homeless population alter the dynamics of hostel life significantly: the asylum seekers in Benington (most of whom are Somalian) stick together socially and often offer a strong negative reaction when encountering the unfamiliar culture of illicit drug use. In turn local hostel residents display resentment over issues of 'queue jumping' (see chapter 6). There are fewer asylum seekers in Steeltown's hostels, largely because the less pressured housing market makes it easier to place people into permanent housing. One impact, however, is a shortage of bedsits and bed and breakfast accommodation available for referral from the local authority, as landlords prefer to contract their accommodation to NASS than to let to what are perceived as more chaotic and less remunerative single homeless tenants.

Thus, while there are some significant similarities between the single homeless populations in Benington and Steeltown, reflecting ubiquitous prompts to homelessness and the increasing relevance of drug addiction in the lives of many homeless people, the interaction between homeless people, emergency services and housing markets in the two places results in rather different sets of issues and experiences for both service providers and service users.

Different Experiences of Consuming Services

Many of the principal contrasts between homelessness in different places will only emerge in detailed understandings of what it is like to live a homeless life in a particular town or city. An integral part of assessing the unevenness of provision and consumption of services for homeless people is therefore to consider both inter-city and intra-city differences in the experiences of homeless people when using emergency services. The varying regimes of care presented by service providers represent key nodal points in the mobility of homeless people in and through the city, and different mixes of people and contexts contribute significantly to the overall character of particular homeless places. In Benington, for example, we have already traced the expectation among homeless people of a service-rich environment. However, it soon becomes clear to many potential service users that different emergency services provide varying levels of support, and are underpinned by differential ethos and regimes of care. Some of the principal inter-service differences are outlined below in an account by two local authority outreach workers:

> STEVE: In a way it's very good because the hostels are set up in different kinds of ways, you know, like 'Hostel A' has a reputation for being a much more stable, sort of controlled, environment, and for some people that's very good because they want – that's really what they're looking for.
>
> GRANT: 'Hostel B', for example, has always had the reputation of being quite open and relaxed, there's 24-hour access, you can just come and go as you please 24 hours a day, which suits some people's lifestyle ... 'Hostel C' is a different kind of regime for want of a better word. It's still kind of set in a very old style of hostel management, in that it's very regimented, really.
>
> STEVE: Yeah, for example they don't have any sharps bins in the hostel, and that client group would consider they're very strict about evicting people for suspicion of drug use, and so on. You're not supposed to drink inside 'Hostel C', are you?
>
> GRANT: Yeah, and they still don't allow people to even have alcohol in their room in 'Hostel C', whereas 'Hostel A' more recently, and 'Hostel B' in 1993, allowed you to drink alcohol in your room.

Our interviews suggest that service users are well aware of these kinds of differences and commonly relate particular hostels to key regimes and practices even if, as becomes clear below in the rather different characterization of 'Hostel C' as 'smack and crack city', their understandings of these regimes do not always accord with the understandings of workers (see also chapter 6). Thus 'Hostel B' is viewed as tolerant of drug dependency ...

> I've been an addict for 15 years and I always used to smoke it, but as soon as I moved into the hostel, everyone was banging up [injecting] in there and no one

smoked it, and within a couple of months I was actually banging it up, IV-ing it ... there was needles all over the place. (Ron, 35, hostel resident, Benington)

... while 'Hostel C' is described as 'crack and smack city' ...

That's a nightmare – you know what I mean – because it's crack and smack city. Everybody in there under the age of 30 is on drugs – everybody – know what I mean? People that go in there completely and utterly straight leave there three months later with a raving smack habit – there's that much of it in there. (Frank, 43, day centre user, Benington)

Similar variations occur between different day centres. For example, the secular focus of some day centres is on empowering individuals by providing them with the knowledge and resources needed to make a positive change in their lives. Service users pay a nominal fee, and are 'registered' by name as they enter the building. By contrast 'Day Centre B', below, accentuates free facilities and unchallenged identities:

We try to create an atmosphere of a home, if you like, in the best sense. So it's completely open access, just as you did you walk straight in off the street; you can just come in, nobody's going to challenge you, ask who you are, take your name, address, anything else, and the ethos is about just welcoming people, making them feel at home in any way, and trying to provide the kind of services that you would get in a home. (Manager, 'Day Centre B', Benington)

Given these differences, and taking note of the fact that some homeless people use all of the day centre services available, in general the different day centres cater for different 'types' of clientele (see also chapter 5).

On the surface, then, Benington's extensive network of emergency services seems to offer homeless people some choice between different spaces of daytime and nighttime care. Equally, if a user is banned from using one particular service, they can – in theory at least – access other services. However, a range of other factors serve to complicate this apparent environment of choice, and to restrict the options available to individual homeless people.

Most obviously, perhaps, the relative dearth of move-on accommodation results in hostels 'silting up', and produces long waiting lists for hostel spaces. Hostel vacancies in Benington usually arise because of evictions rather than because people have moved on to other supported accommodation, with evictions exacerbating the 'revolving door' syndrome by which individual homeless people live in cycles of hostel living and sleeping rough (on the 'churning' of the homeless population see Wolch & DeVerteuil, 2001). Key demographic groups also experience serious accommodation shortages. For example, there is very little provision for men under the age of 18 in Benington, and places for women are severely restricted. The women-only hostel, for example, turned down 633 requests for accommodation in the year to April 2002, representing a 'massive problem' for service coordinators. The biggest barrier to accommodation is, however, 'normality'. That is, people with lesser levels of vulnerability are leap-frogged on waiting lists by those who are considered to be more 'entrenched' and/or 'vulnerable', usually because of health-related problems due to drug dependency and/or mental illness. We interviewed many individuals, including Anthony and Alan, who are exasperated by the way in which their 'normality' acts as a barrier to hostel access:

> The first thing I did was went down to the Housing Benefit Office and asked them what they could do, what places were about and stuff. Unless you are the person who goes out robbing cars or sticking a needle in your arm they really can't sort you out, can't help you … because you are not a high priority. (Anthony, 26, hostel resident, Benington)

> The reason I found it difficult to get hostel accommodation was because I'm not an alcoholic, I'm not a drug addict, I've got no physical or mental disabilities or social disabilities, so to the government I'm normal. (Alan, 43, hostel resident, Benington)

For a variety of reasons, then, and despite the significant array of emergency services in the city, levels of rough sleeping in Benington remain high, as evidenced by the fact that the overwhelming majority of our homeless interviewees were either sleeping rough at the time we spoke with them or had done so in the recent past.

The consumption of emergency services in Steeltown is different in a number of important respects. The local housing market is such that local authority housing for single people can be accessed without delay – as long as the person concerned is able to cope with living in dilapidated high-rise tenements, many of which are dominated by squatters living the hardened heroin-dependent lifestyle that so many homeless people are attempting to leave behind:

> If you wanted a council house today, I could give you the keys to a council house, but I couldn't guarantee you'd be there in three weeks' time, or I wouldn't guarantee that you'd want it. (Representative, Housing Department, Steeltown Borough Council)

> You could find them accommodation today but whether that will be suitable for their needs and in the long term, you know. It's getting them a place but whether they're gonna be back again in, let's say the Retreat [night shelter] in a month's time because that accommodation was totally unsuitable. (Paid staff member, Pathway hostel, Steeltown)

Accordingly, many single homeless people in Steeltown simply do not approach the local authority for housing because they know that they will only be offered hard-to-let properties. Local rough sleeping statistics are low, but they mask very significant informal forms of homelessness, especially squatting and casual or short-term rough sleeping. So while local authority representatives recognize only limited 'casual' rough sleeping, non-statutory service providers point to a more extensive problem:

> They [the local authority] just don't acknowledge them I think, I think that's the top and bottom of it ... the fact that people say that there isn't any rough sleeping's just a nonsense really. I mean, just the physical amount of blankets that we will hand out on a night, you know, people wouldn't – I mean, yes, people would come for them if they were in squats, but people are rough sleeping, we know they are. (Representative, Pathway, Steeltown)

The picture painted in the quote above is supported by accounts of rough sleeping by local homeless people themselves, which emphasize the 'hiddenness' of their practices.

> There are quite a few places in Steeltown where I've slept rough. I've slept behind the ... prison, under the bridge. I've slept in the bus station toilet. I've slept behind Tesco's, behind KwikSave, quite a few places. (Sally, 21, hostel resident, Steeltown)

> MARTIN: There's flats in Steeltown ... high rise and at the bottom is this chute. You go to the top, put rubbish in and it goes down to the bottom into the bins, and we just go behind there ... we snuggle up and get warm, basically, get our head down there ...
> PAT: They get cleaned every day. Yeah, the cleaners come to the flats with dirt cloths.
> MARTIN: If it were dirty I wouldn't sleep there. If you go behind back of bins anyway it's alright, put the bins in front and basically for shelter and the shutter down so far, that's it.
> PAT: It's warm, dry, shelter. It's better than being outside under a bush, you know what I mean, freezing and that. (Martin, 19, and Pat, 28, rough sleepers, Steeltown)

Although the local authority claims that they can *always* find a bed for single homeless people somewhere, and that there is no need for them to sleep rough, the night shelter in Steeltown runs at full capacity and regularly has to turn people away. On such occasions, local appreciation of the housing 'scene' in Steeltown often means that single homeless people will bypass the local authority system because what they are likely to be offered is so 'grim'. Another member of Pathway staff, Ann, told us that the local authority will usually refer homeless people to a bed and breakfast hotel, the nature of which is wholly unattractive:

> ANN: There's one in particular that is really grim ... everyone sort of raises their eyebrows when they mention it. There's people who say, 'Well, why

don't you try and get into there?' and they just say like, 'No way'. Some people would sooner sleep rough than access some of the B&Bs.

SARAH: Is that because of the other people using the B&Bs, or the actual physical infrastructure of the place itself, or what?

ANN: Both really. There's one – I mean, the one in particular where they usually refer sort of our client group to is worse than the night shelter. There's a hell of lot of drug use going off, a lot of bullying. There's not really much services provided there for them either, you know, it's basically just a bed. If they want food they've gotta pay extra, they've got no facilities, they can't get access to a kitchen or anything like that, and, you know, there's however many to a room. (Paid staff member, Pathway, Steeltown)

As a result, hidden rough sleeping and squatting are common tactics deployed by single homeless people in Steeltown. The high levels of squatting are due, at least in part, to the availability of derelict or disused buildings in the town, and ironically such buildings are often found in the very estates in which the local authority will attempt to place statutory homeless households. Our homeless interviewees regarded these buildings as 'dangerous' environments, far inferior to the night shelter. With Steeltown's limited roster of services operating at capacity, those who are turned away or banned are left with few alternatives but to sleep rough or squat, and it is clear that Steeltown's distinctive housing market has presented particular infrastructures that have shaped, both positively and negatively, the opportunities for such activities.

However, it is in the consumption of daytime services that the sharpest contrast emerges between Benington and Steeltown. In Benington the established network of daytime services provides single homeless people with material resources, advice and information, and opportunities for social interaction and recreation. Except on a Saturday, there is always a service open offering free or inexpensive food, and the lives of many homeless people are highly structured by the opening times of the services on their 'food route'. Homeless people in Benington also regularly negotiate the prime public spaces of the city, journeying to places where they can 'earn' or 'hang out' (see chapter 3). However, their visibility is contextualized by a supportive service environment from which day-to-day necessities can be obtained. By contrast, with the exception of the Sunday morning breakfast service, there are no formal daytime services providing shelter, food, clothing and information for homeless people over the age of 25 in Steeltown. Rough sleepers and night shelter residents (who are required to vacate the premises between 8.30 a.m. and 9.30 p.m.) will therefore often have no specific service space to occupy within the city.

This lack of daytime services has significant implications for the daily lives of single homeless people in Steeltown. In line with the findings of

Wardhaugh (2000), the lack of food services means that many homeless people either go hungry or steal food:

SARAH: What did you do in the daytime when you were sleeping rough?
NICOLA: Walk round town.
SARAH: Yeah? How did you manage to feed yourself and things, 'cos there's no –
NICOLA: I used to go nicking. Nowt else to do. (Nicola, hostel resident, Steeltown)

The lack of day centres also means that homeless people in Steeltown have great difficulty conducting basic tasks such as personal ablutions and laundry. In turn, their sometimes scruffy appearance attracts unwanted attention from the police. Toilet facilities in the centre of the city have been 'protected' against use by homeless people (see Davis, 1990; Ruddick, 1996; Mitchell, 1997), through the use of security guards or attendants, the restriction of entry by charging or using tokens, and by extensive CCTV coverage. Even in the public library there is a sign on the door declaring that 'toilet facilities are for legitimate library users only!' (cf Lees, 1997).

In the absence of formal services, then, homeless people in Steeltown spend their days negotiating temporary access to the functions afforded by a variety of public spaces. Tracey, a 20-year-old night shelter resident, describes how she spends much of the day walking the streets, trying to find places to keep warm:

In the day basically all I do is just sit in train stations, anywhere just to keep warm. If I've got any money I'll sit in a café for an hour ... and then we just wander around the streets. ... There's not much else to do. If you haven't really got nowhere to go during the day, then there's nowt else for you to do. (Tracey, 20, night shelter resident, Steeltown)

She goes on to describe how it can be a bit 'hit and miss' as to whether or not her presence in such spaces (e.g. bus station waiting rooms) is tolerated:

Some days you get away with sitting in them, other days they tell you to move on ... it just depends on how many times you go in the same place. If they keep seeing you then they're gonna know you're not waiting for a bus, so they won't let you stay. (Tracey, 20, night shelter resident, Steeltown)

For those homeless people actively involved in the drug scene, much of their day is spent accessing money and 'gear' to support their habit – very much part of the 'work' involved in being homeless (Rowe & Wolch, 1990). Indeed, the various activities of generating cash, obtaining drugs and then using them appear to be so time-consuming that little time is left for accessing services and facilities. Although most such accounts were inevitably discussed off the record, one homeless man agreed to be quoted: 'My life, really is – I get up from here and I'm basically, I'm in town all day and seeing how much money I can earn, shoplifting all day. ... Out there, walking around town, sneaking in shops ... and getting stuff, selling it' (Wayne, 24, night shelter resident, Steeltown).

The conditions in which these different daytime homeless lives occur are strongly influenced by changing regimes of regulation. Both cities have spaces that are rendered inaccessible to anyone looking remotely 'deviant'. Benington's downtown shopping centre has its own dedicated police team funded by local retailers, and homeless people are actively excluded – a process supposedly legitimated by the provision of collection boxes in retail stores taking donations for local homeless charities (for an account of the failures of 'diverted giving' schemes see Dean & Melrose, 1999). Steeltown's shopping centre is similarly policed by its own security staff, and homeless people who beg must avoid being identified in central city CCTV coverage if they are to avoid attracting the attention of the police. Moreover, despite such tactics on the part of homeless people, the lack of an underlying infrastructure of daytime emergency services in Steeltown clearly renders homeless people there somewhat more prone to the strictures of regulation than in Benington, where service spaces are available during the day.

Different Homeless Scenes

Of course, this account of our research in Benington and Steeltown does scant justice to the complexities of providing and consuming emergency services for homeless people. Even so, there is enough evidence here to suggest that generic assessments of places as being 'good' or 'bad' places to be homeless that move around only a consideration of the services for homeless people available in such places require very careful scrutiny. The 'homeless scenes' we encountered in Benington and Steeltown have been shaped by a local confluence of a number of factors, including: public and organizational recognition of the problems of homelessness and the need for a response; the historical development of services and service networks; and the congregation of particular groups of homeless people. These particular local confluences in turn help to shape the differential experiences of being homeless in a city. Although the existence of specific night and daytime service nodes provides key spaces of care around which homeless lives tend to gravitate, different living experiences are also shaped socially and spatially by other local factors, not least the configuration of local housing markets, the changing nature of regulation and policing of public spaces, the potential for street earning opportunities, and the cultural atmosphere of the city in response to homelessness.

Homeless people themselves also develop their own discursive narratives around these localized convergences of service and living environments, such that Benington and Steeltown have developed very different homeless 'scenes'. These narratives are in turn associated with particular practices, as discursive traits shape action-choices in particular locations. Moreover, there is evidence not only that such scenes are painted differently by different types of homeless people – for example, reflecting different gendered and age identities, as well as the subcultural and the intra-group distinctions between 'smackheads', 'pissheads' and 'straightheads' illustrated above – but also that the discourses of homeless scenes vary over time, reflecting the changing confluences of circumstances in the particular places concerned.

For example, the initial impression of Benington's homelessness scene is that it represents a 'good' place to be homeless. Discursive narratives of the scene emphasize the perceived extent and quality of the emergency service infrastructure:

Hostel-wise, Benington is one of the best, it's got to be the best. (Jack, 45, hostel resident who has travelled extensively throughout Britain)

[Benington is] probably one of the best places to be homeless if you're gonna be homeless, because they've got what you need here basically. (Ralph, 35, day centre user, Benington)

You don't go hungry in Benington. There's always somewhere to go, somewhere to eat. That's nice to have. (Ray, 35, hostel resident, Benington)

Other perceived characteristics of Benington's scene emphasize the generosity of local public reaction:

[Benington] has still got a wide range of people, so you get people that are willing to give you a chance, and that won't just diss you off, really. And they'll help you. They'll buy you food. They're generally more helpful. (Kate, 24, rough sleeper, Benington)

In contrast, initial narratives of Steeltown's homelessness scene appear less well developed, perhaps because homeless people there, being more localized, tend to have less comparative experience to draw upon in these narratives. Where comparisons are made, Steeltown's scene is represented with some ambivalence, often reflecting the partial nature of local services. For example, Sam, a 26-year-old night shelter resident in Steeltown, compares the city's homelessness scene with that in Crossfield, where he has also been homeless, and where there are day centre facilities but no direct access accommodation (see chapter 8). He concludes:

If you could combine the two and have the day facilities of Crossfield and this [the night shelter in Steeltown] then it would be perfect, but ... there's nothing worse then sleeping rough, is there? I'd rather be sleeping at nighttime than not safe at nighttime and [having] somewhere to go in the day. (Sam, 26, night shelter resident, Steeltown)

However, our interviewees also identified a number of changing factors that serve to destabilize these initial narratives and suggest that a person's growing experience of a particular homelessness scene often renders narratives of that scene more complex and dynamic. For example, once a homeless person is 'settled' in a city and becomes familiar with its scene, it may become evident to them that its quality as a homeless place is determined less by the existence of services than by *access to* those services. Hence, while many people appear to assume before they arrive that a city such as Benington will offer them access to a wide range of services, they find that gaining access to these services is, in reality, often much more difficult than they anticipated:

SARAH: You just thought that because Benington was bigger that you …
DON: That I would have more opportunity and stuff, yet but it is not, the more bigger the city the more homeless people you've got, that is what I found really.
SARAH: More competition for the services that are there?
DON: Yes. (Don, 26, hostel resident, Benington)

Indeed, Benington's reputation as a 'good place' to be homeless has declined in recent years, not simply because of a reduction in the availability of bed spaces, which have gradually silted up, but also because public sympathies towards homeless people appear to be waning. Many interviewees claimed that the public has been 'desensitized' to homelessness, because of the visibility, scale and longevity of rough sleeping and begging in the city, and because media portrayals of issues supposedly associated with homelessness (begging, drug use, crime and so on) and increasingly strong regulatory responses have hardened negative attitudes: '[Public perceptions have] become extremely hardened. It used to be at one time, if someone were out begging a lot of people would stop, some out of interest and some out of kindness and compassion' (Chris, 53, day centre user, Benington). This suggestion of compassion fatigue is reinforced by Alfie, a self-identified retired 'old man of the road' who is now housed but still uses local day centres:

ALFIE: Benington in the late eighties early nineties was considered a goldmine town –
SARAH: For homeless people?
ALFIE: Yeah. People who have begged around the country, they say 'Oh, here's a goldmine'.
SARAH: Why is that? Why do they have that impression?
ALFIE: Because here they were making money. Christ, I'm being totally honest now, I've sat on that bridge before now and on a poor Saturday you

take £80, that's a piss-poor Saturday ... because there's money in Benington, there's wealth in Benington. ... Benington was always noted as not one of the best, it was *the* best. Like, okay, these guys travel the country, professional beggars and that, they could come to Benington and make a fortune, and I mean make a fortune ...

SARAH: Is that the case now?

ALFIE: No I can assure you it's not, because of this heroin, and because of – there's a new breed on the streets now. In my days it was the street drinkers and the, sort of, wayfarers, people that just travelled about. There was no addiction about. Okay you may get a few, say, hippie types who smoke a bit, right. Apart from that there wasn't this heroin thing. This heroin business has a lot to answer for. People can see this happening quite openly. They are not, like – if you're a member of the public, truthfully, would you give a pound or two pound to a beggar, knowing that it was going to go into a drug dealer's pocket? I'm very sorry but I wouldn't. I wouldn't, no way on this earth. So, everything has gone harder, right, the money just isn't there. ... Benington has a reputation for being quite nasty, it's a very hard, very nasty city, very cold, you know. I don't mean cold in temperature, I mean cold in sort of like not warm-hearted. ... They don't give a lot of money here now. They used to, right, they used to. (Alfie, 48, day centre user, Benington)

By contrast, the increasing prominence and influence of the Pathway organization in Steeltown appears to be having a positive impact on the public enculturation of the homelessness scene in the city:

Generally speaking, the only mention of homelessness in the press these days comes through Pathway, and if there is any discussion on homelessness, because we're the homelessness organization in the area, the press tend to approach us. We've got a pretty good relationship with the local press, and the local radio ... and they tend to approach us. If there's a problem related to homelessness that sort of becomes apparent they'll approach us and say, 'Well, what is this problem and what's being done about it?' rather than just going straight out and saying, 'homelessness down to heroin addiction all over Steeltown' or whatever. (Representative, Pathway management committee, Steeltown)

Here, there is a suggestion that Pathway has secured the role of a 'primary definer' of the homelessness scene, such that it is able to shape local media coverage (on media constructions of homelessness see May, 2003b). Our interviewees also implied that the lesser scale of visible homelessness and positive portrayals of homeless people in the local media meant that the policing of homeless people (especially those who beg) is undertaken in a more tolerant fashion in Steeltown than in other comparable places.

JAN: I think it's [Steeltown is] quite parochial. I think people know who they are. I think those beggars have been there for months if not years, so I think that's probably it ... they become quite tolerant of it.

SARAH: So they just become part of the landscape?

JAN: Yeah, I think so. ... People just get to know them. They do become somebody that you can go and have a chat to ... so therefore they become part of the Steeltown family, and are accepted, I think. (Representative, Pathway, Steeltown)

GRAHAM: I think the police'll come and talk to 'em and – but it's been a very sort of – it seems to have been quite a low key thing, because street begging's not been a big problem.

BARBARA: I think if they're quiet and they're not causing a nuisance I think the police are probably quite tolerant of them. (Representatives, Steeltown Borough Council)

This sense that people who beg in Steeltown are becoming part of the local urban fabric and are concomitantly being accepted as local characters reflects the arguments of Dean (1999) and Fitzpatrick and Kennedy (2001) about the importance of the localized cultural image of begging. There is a strong contrast here with the campaigning of Benington's local newspaper to rid the city of the invasion of beggars from elsewhere – in its 'Beggar Off' campaign.

Narratives of the homelessness scene in a particular city, then, appear to be wrapped around the imaginative and material traits of physical service infrastructure, public generosity, the politics of clearance and regulation, and the interconnections with other scenes, notably that associated with drugs. The relative weighting of these factors in the determination of how good/bad a place is to be homeless will vary from person to person. Alfie talks here of his role in advising other homeless people about the scenes in other places:

I can tell them exactly what's there, this is in the old box. ... So you get these youngsters now, like it's a classic, and they say to me 'Alfie, where's the best place to go?' 'Well, tell me what you mean by the best place, I don't know what you mean by "best"?' I said 'Oh you mean resource-wise. Right. Well, what is it you're looking for, because what would appeal to you wouldn't appeal to me and vice versa.' (Alfie, 48, day centre user, Benington)

In this way, although most homeless interviewees thought Benington was good because of the range of services, for 19-year-old local Zara, it had 'got to be the worst' place because she wanted to stay with her boyfriend. None of the hostels can take couples, they'd been kicked out of a B&B for reasons she did not understand and they'd had no fortune getting anywhere with council housing because they were not high priority:

Benington's got to be the worst place for homeless people. ... It's just ... you got nowhere ... there's nowhere ... like the council an' that, they don't care about it ... they just chuck you on the streets ... they don't care about it ... they ain't hardly got anywhere where people could stay an' that if they're homeless. (Zara, 19, day centre user, Benington)

It is these kinds of complexities that militate against oversimplified and highly politicized assumptions correlating high levels of service provision with a place being a 'good place to be homeless'. Clearly in the current policy climate, a possible response to a local homelessness scene that is thought to be a 'good' place to be homeless might be to consider withdrawing services (or support for services) on the grounds that such reductions will deter the in-migration of non-local homeless people (and see May, 2003a). Any such understanding provides an inaccurate and grossly oversimplified assessment of the connections between emergency service provision, the lives of single homeless people, and the complex and dynamic nature of homeless scenes in British cities.

Conclusions

Understanding the uneven provision and consumption of emergency services for homeless people is in many ways a complex and locally specific task. Although generalizations can be made about the city as a site in which homelessness is produced, and in which services for homeless people develop, different cities exhibit different socio-economic and institutional histories, which condition both the occurrence of homelessness and service responses to homelessness (see also DeVerteuil et al., 2009). In this chapter we have outlined a series of different historical, organizational and political layers of explanation by which locally distinctive service infrastructures may be understood. However, our research emphasizes that the emergence of significant local circumstances may also be traced in the interpenetration of service networks, different mixes of service users and place-specific experiences of being homeless – including factors such as the ability to earn money begging on the streets, the availability of affordable drugs, and the room for manoeuvre within local regimes of regulation. Although a set of common practices associated with homelessness will occur regardless of location, these practices take local shape as homeless people negotiate infrastructure and translate practices into specific place practices. Thus broad general rules are negotiated for local specificity, and result in both local discourses of homelessness and locally distinctive practices of homelessness, which may be spatial, social and cultural (and almost certainly a mix of the three). These specificities of discourse and practice give rise to culturally significant local homelessness 'scenes'.

Our research with service providers and homeless people has interrogated how these interactions between provision and consumption lead to place distinctions, and suggests that even where places offer seemingly similar levels of services they may have a very different 'feel'; a feel that is both experienced by homeless people and made material in the complex cartographies and tactical spaces that they generate in the city concerned. Thus in the cases of Benington and Steeltown, very different institutional histories and political grasp of homelessness issues have led to rather different service landscapes, which are made yet more complex by tacit knowledge among homeless people about the conditions of access to, and quality of, particular services. However, the homelessness scenes in Benington and Steeltown are also co-constructed by the culture of their street life – the begging opportunities, the ease of scoring drugs, the hassles of regulation and policing, the degree of necessity and choice built into day-to-day journeys through the city. Benington's initial reputation as a place of refuge, a goldmine of generosity and helpful regulation, for example, seems to be changing as the scene has come to reflect a harder, nastier compassion fatigue and aggression against non-locals on the streets, and a service infrastructure geared to the expectations of RSI and HAP funding rather than any attempt to be widely accessible. Steeltown's early disregard for homelessness meant that the local scene was slow to get started, but current evidence suggests that the deficiency of day services, and the harsh regulation of public buildings, may be accompanied by other regimes of kindness in which homeless people can be accepted as part of the local 'family'.

Uneven geographies of homelessness, then, reflect more than simply different numbers of homeless people and of the services that have been established to respond to their needs. Unevenness also needs to be understood as a collective culture of place, people, organizations, facilities and experiences, that co-constitutes the *feel* of a place for a homeless person. Recognition of different homeless 'scenes' helps us to understand why a particular place might be a 'good' or 'bad' place to be homeless. Recognition of *changing* homeless scenes begins to open out broader issues in understanding how and why people respond to homelessness in their cities. This chapter suggests that urban cultures of generosity wax and wane; apparent public compassion fatigue and deliberate policies of tougher policing of on-street homelessness, for example, suggest a declining culture of generosity in cities such as Benington. As increasing numbers of homeless people are respectively brought 'in from the cold' (DETR, 2000) and driven off the streets, the collective consciousness of the need for care and generosity can be interpreted as declining.

The fear must be that the increased attention to homelessness and generosity to homeless people in Steeltown over recent years might yet follow a similar trajectory. Yet our research does not reveal local scenes of homelessness that are dominated by cultures of revanchism or postjustice, and to explain homeless cities simply in these terms is to ignore and disempower both the ability of homeless people as tactical authors of at least some of their own life experiences, and the extraordinary acts of generosity and care being exercised by the staff, volunteers and charitable donors who ensure a network of non-statutory services in the homeless city. Far from being simple handmaidens of the state, incorporated into revanchist regimes, such people perform care in a way that inflects many British cities with continuing subcultures of generosity and resistance that contradict the culture of revanchism and reinstate ordinary ethics of justice in the everyday lives of homeless people. That the distribution and effectiveness of these non-statutory services is uneven in presence and effectiveness may yet be a prompt to continue to diffuse best practice to ill-served places, giving local people a stronger sense that they too can 'do something about' homelessness in their locality.

Chapter Eight

On the Margins of the Homeless City: Caring for Homeless People in Rural Areas

Introduction

The 'big city' focus of chapter 7 contrasts markedly with the focus of this chapter, where the emphasis is on the provision of services for homeless people in rural areas. The inclusion of a chapter dealing with rural homelessness may appear unusual in a book on the homeless city, but we do so for three sets of reasons. First, we want to explore how geographies of care for homeless people are organized in what might be perceived to be rather difficult terrains of service, where clients and volunteers are sparsely distributed and where service provision can be hampered by diseconomies of scale. Alternatively, these difficult and small-scale conditions can produce rather different regimes and spaces of care, which provide an interesting contrast with city-based facilities. Second, there are complex interconnections between homelessness in rural and urban areas. The commonly assumed connection is that people who become homeless in rural areas will often migrate to larger towns or cities where the service infrastructure is more advanced and accommodating. However, the complex mobilities of homeless people can also be found in reverse – that is, urban-to-rural movement, in particular in rural areas where there is a strong focus on tourism. Here, either because of the termination of temporary employment in the tourist sector, or simply because some rural and/or coastal places can sometimes be perceived as 'better' places than cities to be homeless in, there can sometimes be a significant in-migration of urban people who are homeless or who are vulnerable to becoming homeless. Third, there seems to be a clear scalar factor in the provision of services in different sized towns or cities. Those towns serving rural hinterlands are often (but not always – see below) the first point in the urban hierarchy where homelessness becomes visible, and where fixed-point services are developed in response to this visibility. It is therefore especially interesting to explore how key, highly motivated individuals in these kinds of places have been instrumental in starting up a formal response to the needs of particular kinds of homeless people.

This rationale notwithstanding, however, until relatively recently at least, homelessness was popularly perceived to be an urban phenomenon of little relevance to the countryside or to rural communities. In rural areas, the issue of homelessness has been conflated with wider and more apparent questions of housing need, and so the presence of, or need for, services to meet the needs of homeless people in these areas has been deemed irrelevant in discussions of both rurality and homelessness. Over the past decade, however, research in England (Cloke et al., 2002) and internationally (Cloke & Milbourne, 2006) has begun to uncover some of the problems and dynamics of rural homelessness, focusing on the experiences and mobilities of individuals who connect with rural space and society in different ways. In this chapter we explore some rather different articulations of the rural homelessness that is unfolding in Britain today, and in particular we emphasize two significant dynamics which together shape the experiences of homeless people in different rural environments. First, rural places are characterized by particular local qualities that affect both the circumstances of homelessness and the provision of services in response to those circumstances. Second, the contemporary governance of homelessness unfolds unevenly in different rural areas, producing distinct local service environments with varying degrees of 'insider' and 'outsider' status in relation to 'joined-up' responses to homelessness more generally.

We approach these issues through an analysis of four case studies of services for homeless people in different rural areas. In the first, a friary house just outside Castlebridge in southern England, we describe a small-scale service, hidden away in the depths of the countryside, meeting the needs of a declining and rather forgotten group of 'wayfarers'. Run by an 'outsider' agency that operates almost entirely beyond local authority influence and without government funding, this service represents a seemingly anachronistic island of care in an otherwise purified sea of rurality. Formal homelessness services in the county are centralized in major urban centres, and the friary house also serves as a place of last resort for those homeless people who are excluded from that formal system. The second example is set in Winton, south-west England, regarded by homeless people as a 'therapeutic place'. The setting here is one where 'outsiders', including small groups of homeless people, seem welcome (or at least familiar) and so an 'insider' organization has been able to develop a particular ethos of care within systems of local authority coordination and central government funding. By contrast, the third case study relates how a Nightstop scheme in Crossfield, central England, represents a culturally cohesive coming together of volunteers and what are perceived as 'deserving' homeless young people to produce an emergency scheme for overnight accommodation that 'fits' with the socio-cultural dynamics of the place. The non-statutory service agency concerned works closely alongside statutory providers to establish a localized response for some homeless youngsters, while other more dysfunctional cases are dealt with by sending them to a nearby city, thus avoiding their potentially transgressive presence in the rural town. Finally, our fourth case study concerns what might be described as a postindustrial rural resort setting (Sandstown, in northern England), where the local authority has been preoccupied with maintaining place-image in order to offer therapy for tourists, to the extent that problems of homelessness were denied for a long period and coordinated responses to homelessness have been slow getting off the ground. Local opinion seems strongly opposed to the presence of homeless people, who are strongly policed as part of a local strategy to purifiy the space of the town. Services for homeless people have arisen through the efforts of the voluntary sector, and the result is some considerable unevenness in provision. Local 'deserving' needs can be met via a purpose-built foyer, but for others referral to a local bed and breakfast establishment is the best they can hope for. These four case studies offer considerable insight into the localized dynamics of place and service provision in different rural settings. Before delving into these localized examples, however, it is important to frame our analysis in terms of both the dynamics of rural homelessness and the ways in which the changing governance of homelessness impacts on rural areas.

Rural Homelessness

It is now widely argued (see Cloke et al., 2000b) that homelessness and rurality have become discursively non-coupled such that homelessness in rural areas has been rendered invisible, or at least significantly underemphasized, compared with the more obvious associations of homeless people and the city. The reasons behind this non-coupling are complex, but three broad explanations can be advanced. First, rural morphologies tend to hide homelessness: there are few obvious places of concentration and consequent visibility. Such morphologies tend to be reinforced by the tactics of homeless people themselves, and there is evidence that people experiencing the stigma of homelessness in a rural setting will either leave that place seeking housing or shelter elsewhere (Wright & Vermond, 1990; Button, 1992) or choose to make themselves 'invisible' by forms of mobility and rough sleeping incognito that are aided by morphologies of rural landscapes and agricultural buildings. Second, non-coupling occurs because of a series of socio-cultural barriers that exist within the practices, thoughts and discourses of rural residents themselves, which lead them to deny that homelessness can exist in their idealized rural setting (Cloke et al., 2002). Third, standard conceptualizations of rurality (as space) and homelessness (as social problem) have also served to drive these two constructs apart. Thus homelessness becomes 'out of place' (Cresswell, 1996) in rural settings, representing a transgression of socio-spatial expectations and resulting in a purification of rural space (Sibley, 1995) in which the rejection of difference is embedded in the social system. Again, homeless people may be forced to deploy tactics of invisibility in order not to challenge their excluded position from the purified social-spatial boundaries that currently place tight culturally constructed constraints on the in-placeness of homelessness in rural areas.

For these reasons rural homelessness has only been raised as a significant issue during the past 15 years or so, with all previous and much current emphasis being placed on problems of social housing instead (Rogers, 1976; Larkin, 1979; Milbourne, 1998, 2005), and with virtually no recognition that some of the people facing housing problems are in fact experiencing forms of homelessness (Milbourne & Cloke, 2006). Early explorations of rural homelessness (Newton, 1991; Lambert et al., 1992) used official homelessness statistics to suggest that, despite recognized undercounting in rural settings, significant evidence existed of homelessness in rural areas. Subsequent studies (Cloke et al., 2001a; Streich et al., 2004) confirmed that by the early to mid-2000s rural homelessness comprised around a fifth (18 per cent) of total homelessness in England, with levels of 'statutory' homelessness rising faster in rural areas than in England's cities (Woods, 2005).

Ethnographic research into people's experiences of homelessness in rural areas (Cloke et al., 2000b, c, 2003b; Robinson & Reeve, 2002; Robinson, 2003, 2006) has begun to provide detailed life histories of the complex journeys and pauses that constitute rural homelessness. For example, Cloke et al. (2003b) emphasize the different kinds of mobilities engaged in by homeless people in a rural context. The stereotypical expectation is that homeless people will move away from villages and small towns and migrate to larger urban settlements, which are recognized as somehow approved and appropriate spaces for meeting their needs. However, other mobilities have also been encountered. Short-distance, short-stay moves *within* rural areas, ranging from sofa-surfing to a willingness to put up with what would normatively be regarded as 'unfit' housing, are a key component of rural homelessness and a key expression of the desire of some rural homeless people to 'stay local'. Homeless people also move *into* rural areas, associating them variously as sites of leisure, work, escape or traveller 'honeypots' (see Lowe & Shaw, 1993; Halfacree, 1996; Hetherington, 2000). Equally, some homeless people move *through* rural areas, living out transient life-styles of routes or circuits that fold their existence in and out of rural settings, relying on rough sleeping and/or knowledge of the different forms of localized 'shelter'. Indeed, it has been further suggested that homeless people in rural areas are made 'legible' (Scott, 1998) via a series of moral codings that classify them as local/non-local, settled/passing through and visible/invisible. As Cloke and Milbourne (2006: 26) suggest,

'The local/settled/invisible gains more acceptance, but rarely achieves the sort of contact with state bureaucracies that allows enumeration and therefore legibility. The non-local/passing through/visible is least likely to be accepted by these localized bureaucracies as having priority need, leading once again to a situation in which homeless people displaying these characteristics "don't count"' (see also Cloke et al., 2001c).

Thus far, these accounts of rural homelessness have made little attempt to connect the experiences of homeless people with the emergency service infrastructure or its governance. In part, the stereotypical assumption that homeless people have to move away from rural areas to gain access to services rules out any expectation that homeless services will exist in rural areas. In part, those services that are recognizable in smaller urban places – the hostels, shelters and day centres where congregational homelessness becomes visible – tend to be incorporated automatically in 'urban' discourse. Nevertheless, two sources of research evidence suggest that emergency responses to homelessness do occur in rural settings. First, life history and autobiographical evidence indicates rural 'stopping off points' for homeless people. For example, Donohue's (1996) *In the Open: Diary of a Homeless Alcoholic* describes sojourns in US rural towns such as Henderson, where he received significant care and kindness. Donohue evaluates Henderson as resource rich – a good place to be homeless in, at least for a while, where his unfamiliarity and out-of-placeness engenders generosity rather than marginalization from residents. Second, there is evidence that emergency facilities for homeless people in provincial towns such as Taunton, Somerset (Cloke et al., 2000c) can serve their surrounding hinterland, and might therefore be included in *rural* discourses in terms of a 'social spatialization' (Shields, 1991), by which rural practices give meaning to the seemingly urban spaces concerned.

Governing Homelessness

The problems of homelessness, and the development of appropriate responses to these problems, have been widely regarded as a powerful barometer through which to evaluate the dynamics of contemporary neoliberal society (DeVerteuil, 2003). As we described in chapter 2, while the post-war years saw little direct intervention by statutory government agencies to deal with the needs of single homeless people in Britain (Pleace & Quilgars, 2003; May et al., 2006), the 1960s and 1970s might best be understood as decades of 'malign neglect' (Wolch & Dear, 1993), as successive governments were content to allow a range of voluntary sector organizations to take responsibility for providing for the single homeless (Saunders, 1986; Hutson & Liddiard, 1994; Foord et al., 1998; Fitzpatrick et al., 2000). However, during the 1970s and 1980s new voluntary organizations emerged to help raise the standards of non-statutory provision (Foord et al., 1998; Harris et al., 2001), with the result that by the 1990s such provision was becoming unevenly professionalized (Harris et al., 2001).

The election of the New Labour government in 1997 ushered in a new 'postwelfare' regime (Dean, 1999), as continuing concerns about the level of street homelessness and the ability of the emergency service network to cope with the demands placed upon it led to a series of new initiatives and an underlying shift in the governance of homelessness (Brown et al., 1996; Ham and Carter, 1996). Weak regulatory structures and the relative autonomy of non-statutory providers were transformed through the development of tighter regulatory controls designed to induce the self-regulation of non-statutory welfare services and service users alike. As a result, new and complex relations emerged between central and local government and different non-statutory 'partners', prompting recognition both of the importance of governmentality at the 'extremities' as well as the core of such relations (Gilbert, 2003) and of the limits of governmentality – with the only partial and fragmented penetration of social policy in different organizational and geographical spaces understood as articulating the inability of social policy to reach the social and spatial margins of society (Clarke & Newman, 1997; Larner, 2000; May et al., 2005).

For the purposes of this chapter, we want to highlight three interconnecting aspects of the complex and fragmented relations associated with governmentality and homelessness. First, non-statutory service providers have tended to gravitate towards being either 'insider' or 'outsider' services. As we have argued elsewhere (May et al., 2005), the involvement of both central government (through RSI and HAP funding regimes) and local government (through taking the lead in developing local homelessness strategies) may mean that local non-statutory service providers come under considerable pressure to conform to statutory requirements in order to secure ongoing funding. Thus hostels, for example, can become enmeshed in schemes that prioritize those homeless people with a 'local connection' and who are regarded as 'entrenched and vulnerable' by local authorities. But such 'insider' organizations contrast with others working outside of such partnerships – typically voluntary-run night shelters, day centres and soup runs (see Johnsen et al., 2005a, b), which bear the brunt of local criticism regarding the quality of their service, and which are consequently 'encouraged' to reorientate their efforts into more 'productive' provision that does not support street homelessness (Moore, 2002).

Second, a 'revanchist' urban politics (Smith, 1996a), with its emphasis on securing urban spaces for the middles classes, can be contrasted with evidence of the 'spaces of care' that have emerged in the interstices of a 'revanchist city' to provide comfort and care to the excluded, including homeless people (Conradson, 1999, 2003; Parr, 2000, 2003; Cooper, 2001). These spaces of care represent complex spaces of inclusion and exclusion that not only facilitate the expression of care of and the distribution of resources to homeless people, but also make room for an articulation of difference that is less well expressed in more tightly regulated public spaces (Waters, 1992; Johnsen et al., 2005a). However, and as we showed in chapters 4, 5 and 6, the different ethics of care evident in such spaces do not easily map on to the 'insider/outsider' status of organizations. Instead, though the increasing professionalism of insider services can be viewed in terms of raising the quality of service in some ways, the charitable ethos of those outsider services that are least penetrated by the new governmentalities of social policy may also bring into being important, if quite different, modes of care (Cloke et al., 2005, 2006).

Third, the fragmented governance of homelessness has produced considerable geographical unevenness in the provision of services for homeless people. Although, for example, the 2002 Homelessness Act requires *all* local authorities to formulate comprehensive multi-agency responses to homelessness within their jurisdiction, it is clear that the 'home spaces' (Peck & Tickell, 2002) of such governance – for example, some large urban centres – attracted considerable funding through initiatives such as the Rough Sleepers Initiative and the Homelessness Action Programme, while other towns and cities, and other types of geographical space, 'hardly seem[ed] to register in the minds of those allocating central government funds for the alleviation of street homelessness – despite compelling evidence of significant problems of street homelessness' (May et al., 2005: 705). In this chapter we direct attention to the ways in which these three aspects of the contemporary governance of homelessness play out in what are assumed to be the geographical extremities of social policy in Britain.

The friary and the wayfarers

The first case study involves a friary located in an isolated setting just outside Castlebridge in southern England. The friary was established in 1921 by a Franciscan brother who became motivated to 'rehabilitate' the increasing numbers of unemployed men (or 'wayfarers') roaming the roads at the time. A separate house was used to give shelter and sustenance to these men at a time when workhouses (or 'spikes') were being closed down (Humphreys, 1999). This house continued to be used in this way until 2003, with a succession of ordained and lay Franciscans ministering to wandering homeless men for more than eight decades. At the time of our research (2003) the friary house had ten beds, and was administered by a lay resident (Saul) and overseen by one of the brothers (Mervyn). It was funded by charitable giving both from the wider Franciscan community and by donations from other guests at the friary. As such, this particular project had a complex multifaceted character, though the Christian ethos of the friary house clearly separated it from other more mainstream services. As Saul told us:

> We are mainly a religious place; this is a spiritual place, a house of prayer. Our first way of looking at them [homeless people] is as people of God, not a number on the road. As they are coming into a place of prayer, we should expect to treat them a bit different from what a statutory body would. I believe there is really room for places like this. (Saul, lay resident, The Friary, Castlebridge)

The emphasis, then, was on meeting the material and spiritual needs of individuals, and although the rules of the friary house restricted visitors to one weeknight or one weekend every six weeks (so as to provide for a range of different people and to discourage dependency on the service), these rules were implemented flexibly in response to particular circumstances.

In these terms the friary house can be characterized as an 'outsider' organization (see May et al., 2005), run on a shoestring and neither receiving government funding nor seeking formal coordination with joined-up local authority policies to keep people off the streets. In fact, in the wider area services for homeless people are only provided in central places, and there is evidence of a number of agencies wishing to purify rural space both through formal policing and by more subtle cultural construction. In this context the friary can be seen to have escaped significant formal involvement with the professionalism and governed regulation associated with multi-agency strategies, and in so doing the service was considered by other local service providers as 'out of the loop' and unprofessional. Indeed, any such professionalism was clearly differentiated from the work of the house, as Brother Mervyn relates:

> Every now and again the council organizes something. I went to a day conference, with sort of PowerPoint talks; all about the many ways to get funding from the Supporting People thing. It was all beyond me! It was all a bit back-slapping; a nice junket day-off. But … it hasn't made any difference to the way we work. (Brother Mervyn, The Friary, Castlebridge)

Hence, the 'way we work' remained geared to the traditional task of ministering to 'wayfarers', understood as old-fashioned gentlemen of the road and spiritually contextualized because 'Christ himself was a person of the road, a wayfarer' (Saul) (on wayfarers see Bahr, 1970; Rossi, 1989; Blau, 1992). Over the years the friary had become interconnected with distinct forms of homeless mobilities *through* rural areas, in this case being part of a 'south coast run' – a journey from Cornwall to London interspersed by convents, churches, shelters and other 'outsider' services for those older homeless people whose mobile lifestyle consists of 'getting in' somewhere for the winter, and travelling along the 'run' at other times of the year. Saul described to us how sleeping rough (under a hedge, in a bus shelter, in a shop doorway) was interspersed with more formal services offering beds for the night, and how walking, hitch-hiking and jumping trains without paying all formed part of the mobility of the 'run' for a group that were described as skilful and 'wily' travellers.

Though we interviewed several residents at the friary house, in this context one of the interviewees (Bill) best illuminates the character of the contemporary wayfarer. Bill differentiates wayfarers like himself from other homeless people of different generations on the grounds of cleanliness, work ethic and culpability (to compare with similar, if older, distinctions between 'hobos', 'tramps' and 'bums' see Anderson, 1993; Cresswell, 2001). Whereas a tramp is viewed as 'dirty and won't clean himself', according to Bill wayfarers keep themselves clean. To do so they have traditionally used public ablution facilities such as at railway stations, but as these have progressively been closed, less formal means have been employed: 'You can go in a stream and wash yourself. I've stripped off in broad daylight and just washed myself and got myself clean and got dressed and then walked, carried on' (Bill, resident, The Friary, Castlebridge). Bill also defines his own wayfarer-type in terms of an insistence on working his way around the country:

> We could go up to people, like the nuns, we could go up to the nunneries and knock on the door – 'Any work to be done today, madam?' – and she will say, 'yes, go round the back, I'll give you a sandwich and a flask of tea'. And you go round and you do chimney sweeping, brushing up leaves. ... And she says 'where are you moving on to?' And you say 'well we don't know just yet'. And she says 'well there's a shed there if you wanna kip down'. And that's how you did it. (Bill, resident, The Friary, Castlebridge)

Such principles are contrasted by Bill with what he sees as the something-for-nothing expectations of other, particularly younger and substance-dependent, homeless people, which he argues can be discerned by charitable people in the countryside: 'If somebody else went up and knocked on the door and say, the person is on drugs or drink, they would know the difference, because you can tell it, you can read it' (Bill, resident, The Friary, Castlebridge). Part of this tell-able, read-able differentiation is the belief that wayfarers have been *made* homeless whereas other groups have made *themselves* homeless. Speaking of younger homeless people, Bill argues: 'They've made themselves homeless, but the wayfarers didn't make themselves homeless. We were made homeless by government schemes or whatever' (Bill, resident, The Friary, Castlebridge).

These differentiations are significant in the context of the friary house. Bill and other wayfarers recognize the countryside as their territory. Although acknowledging that many homeless people are spreading out from the cities into smaller rural towns, perhaps to escape from the harsh, drugs-orientated urban scene (Bill calls them 'country louts'), he maintains that deeper rural areas, which require walking through, remain the habitus of wayfarers, and therefore that facilities such as the friary house, which are located in the deep countryside (requiring an 11 mile walk from the nearest main public transport), suit wayfarers' needs. The deep countryside therefore remains relatively safe and therapeutic, in contrast to the towns, which he sees as increasingly risky in terms of aggravation both from local youths and from other homeless people, and where services are less and less suited to his needs.

It is important to emphasize here that walking in the deep countryside is not viewed in any way as romantic by wayfarers like Bill. Though he talks about walking through the country as a way of 'putting yourself at peace with the world', rather than peace of mind in a comforting sense he talks also of 'learning to blank everything out' as you walk, indicating that walking serves as a response to his feeling of exclusion rather than as a celebration of nomadism (see also May, 2000a). Indeed, Bill's life is a story of going from being in local authority care as a child, to being in prison, to being homeless. He thus sees himself as doubly excluded – his homelessness a result of social exclusion, and his current position on the edges of the homeless population a result of the contemporary governance of homelessness, which has little to offer him. Certainly, conventional hostels and shelters are increasingly designed to meet the needs of other kinds of homeless people, such that the friary house, and others like it, represented one of the few remaining spaces geared towards the needs of people like him.

Yet both the shrinking numbers of wayfarers, and the changing nature of homelessness more generally, have meant that facilities like the friary house are subject to changing demands and circumstances. Even these avowedly 'outsider' services are becoming implicated in the mainstreaming of how homelessness is encountered in rural areas. Both the geographical and institutional spaces of rural care are being significantly infiltrated by 'urban-style' homelessness and different kinds of socially excluded people. Brother Mervyn, for example, recognized a reduction in the flow of wayfarers at the friary house – 'I certainly think that our numbers have dropped in comparison with the mid-eighties. Less pass through here.' As a result, serving the older generation of wayfarers, who were often content to make their own way to the friary house, had gradually been replaced with serving other groups of homeless people:

MERVYN: Two years ago I went with the names of 280 people who had been here the year before, and we found that the average age was in the 50s.
SAUL: If you look at the average age now, though, look how young it is.
(Brother Mervyn, and Saul, lay resident, The Friary, Castlebridge)

These shifting demographics reflect in part a shifting role for the friary house. Although not wishing to become more professionalized or wrapped up in the governance of service coordination, Mervyn and Saul recognized that their ministry was inevitably being impacted by changes to service provision elsewhere, and by the need to liaise with other service providers:

> We liaise with all the housing agencies, with the council, with the hospital, with the mental health people, with all the people doing similar work to us, with privately run and council-run hostels in "" and "" [names of nearby market towns], with night shelters in "", Rough Sleepers Initiative in "" [names of larger cities somewhat further afield], Salvation Army hostels ... (Saul, lay resident, The Friary, Castlebridge)

With nomination rights to hostels increasingly being claimed by statutory agencies, there is a tendency for on-the-edge services such as the friary house to be used to house homeless people with nowhere else to go, especially those whose support needs or behaviours make them 'difficult to deal with'. As Saul suggested, 'we often get social services ringing us on a Friday saying "I've got a person here I cannot get in anywhere".' It is not incidental that such referrals are greatly more cost effective for the local authority than finding bed and breakfast accommodation for the people concerned.

Over recent years the friary house has therefore become increasingly used to catering for younger homeless people, often suffering from addiction or mental illness, who have nowhere else to go either because of the lack of other facilities, or because they have been banned from those facilities. This change has led to friction between wayfarers and other homeless people, and between service users and the religious and 'dry' ethos of the friary house. Interviews with younger homeless users of the house reveal that the character of the service, and its ethos, are both well known and acceptable to potential clients, and indeed that the friary house forms part of the advice given to homeless people by both homeless colleagues and other agencies:

> Someone said, go to the friary, it's good, but don't take the piss or get pissed up there. If you take the piss in this kind of place, someone will go 'I love you, but fuck off' and does it in a way which is proper. (Nick, 38, resident, The Friary, Castlebridge)

> They don't have to tell you the rules. There is an expectation obviously, because of the place it is ... you respect the fact that they have chosen this way of life. They do treat you like an equal, which you don't get very often do you? (Ray, 24, resident, The Friary, Castlebridge)

Nevertheless, very inebriated users *were* turned away; even an end-of-the-line service will have its patience exhausted in such circumstances, and to be turned away from the friary house would often necessitate a recognition that it was time to move on to a new area altogether. As Saul sometimes related to people leaving the house, 'you might have to face the fact that you have drained this place [meaning this rural area] and you're too well known, and you're not going to get back in the system here'. From being a stopping-off point for traditional wayfarers, then, the friary house began to become a stopping-off point for homeless people with nowhere else to go in an area whose statutory and charitable capacity they had exhausted. This in turn changed the nature of the service, and in December 2003 the friary house in fact closed its facilities for homeless people: partly because of declining demand from wayfarers, and partly because it could not adequately cope with the support needs of its new clientele, many of whom had mental health and/or substance misuse problems requiring specialist service provision that was beyond the scope of the organization.

The hostel and the transients

Our second example of a rural service for homeless people is a large but anonymous house in a market town ('Winton', population 3500) in southwest England. Since the mid-1980s a local charitable organization – St Austen's – has been developing a response to homelessness in and around a city in the south of the region. Beginning in the basement of a church, it has increased its scope through the purchase of additional properties for conversion to five- or six-bed hostels, each with a manager on site during working hours, and through the employment of outreach workers. Each project is supported by a local group of 'friends', and in the case of Winton the recognition of a suitable hostel property, and much of the necessary funding, came from locally galvanized support that reflected the perception articulated by a St Austen's outreach worker that there are anything 'up to 20 to 30 people out there somewhere', sleeping rough in the surrounding countryside. Although the ethos of St Austen's centres on principles of Christian acceptance, and the involvement of many of the friends is faith-motivated (Cloke et al., 2005, 2006), each of the hostels takes on a local character, in part associated with its location, and in part with the (often secular) approach of the manager concerned.

Winton's history as a small rural centre was interrupted by expansion through London overspill in the 1980s, a change that extended the housing base but increased pressure on local labour markets. As importantly, Winton has a specific and enduring history of care, as a manager of the hostel (Jim) told us:

> Winton has had a psychiatric hospital for over 200 years, and there's been some form of hostel, from a leper colony upwards, for over a thousand years. So it's got a historical culture of people with a lot of mental illness perhaps spending a long time in hospital, and then wanting to resettle in the town they've become used to. (Jim, hostel manager, St Austen's hostel, Winton)

This history demonstrates a place that has become used to the presence of needy others in its midst, and more concretely has meant that many 'local' users of the hostel have experienced mental illness and are going through a period of personal rehabilitation prior to living on their own (see Philo et al., 2003).

Although the criteria for release of funds under the HAP are thought to work strongly against this kind of area, the St Austen's organization has over the years become increasingly professionalized. Jim explains:

> Over the years, the needs of people who are homeless, and the numbers of them, and the way that you would define homelessness in a more professional way, has meant that we've had to formalize the work we're doing. (Jim, hostel manager, St Austen's hostel, Winton)

The new governance of homeless services impacts on the work of St Austen's in two ways. First, and ironically, the HAP has added to the workload of hostel staff and associated outreach workers because the assertive approach taken by HAP-funded street outreach teams in nearby urban areas has served to displace some people to sleep rough in the surrounding small towns and villages. Second, the old 'open access' ethos has been replaced by strong coordination with local authorities for whom St Austen's is the only provider in the area. Although core funding remains reliant on charitable giving, the general manager (Simon) indicated not only that RSU and local authority funding has been acquired for new outreach projects, but that the organizational structure has been 'radically overhauled', with the management committee now consisting of a wide range of multiskill professionals. With the onset of Supporting People legislation (see May et al., 2005) the organization is again having to react to changing circumstances, as Jim concedes: 'Not necessarily that we have to change very much at all, but the way we seem to be thinking about it has got to change' (Jim, hostel manager, St Austen's hostel, Winton).

The wider area served by St Austen's consists of 80,000 people scattered over 400 square miles, with the largest town having a population of only 12,000 people. Such rural localities are ill-served by headcounts of street homelessness – much homelessness is sufficiently hidden to resist such counts – and present considerable difficulties for service providers, not least in terms of actual costs incurred by mobile outreach services, which far exceed the standardized cost assumptions inherent in central government funding programmes. As Jim admits, 'It's almost impossible to say how many [homeless people] there are at any one time. What we can say is that on any given day we're probably working with 120 different people' (Jim, hostel manager, St Austen's hostel, Winton).

Managers do, however, recognize a distinction between largely hidden forms of local homelessness and more transient homeless people whose problems come to light at times of crisis. As Jim suggests:

> There's a lot of what they call 'homeless at home' ... people who are in a crisis are often supported by people in their own families. There's an awful culture of 'sofa surfing' amongst friends ... month-in, month-out [that]

never really gets flagged up with social services. ... There is also a large number of people who ... like the transient lifestyle, but do get into crisis every now an' again through substance misuse or mental health or just a physical problem. Then they ... start getting flagged up. (Jim, hostel manager, St Austen's hostel, Winton)

Interestingly, there is little evidence of prejudice against non-local homeless people here in terms of who is granted access to the hostels. Indeed, there is a recognizably seasonal division between service users:

Over the Christmas period up to spring, the vast majority of people who come to us have a local connection. They've either lived here a while, used to live here, were from here, have family here. In the summer there's a huge transient influence. (Jim, hostel manager, St Austen's hostel, Winton)

Our interviews, undertaken in the summer months, reveal that the Winton hostel is serving a range of transient men who have endured some particular crisis of homelessness. Harry is 45 years old, originally from Manchester and had been living in the hostel for four and a half months. A drug addiction led him into homelessness and he then found his way through a range of different urban hostels:

When I left Manchester, I went down to Plymouth, Plymouth to Bristol, Bristol to Weston-super-Mare, to Taunton, back to Knutsford in Cheshire – things didn't work out there, smack city – back from there to Taunton, and then here. Well I went to the office in "*** and I was in a night shelter [in Cambourne] for twelve nights. (Harry, 45, hostel resident, Winton)

Harry's transience was mobilized by hitchhiking up and down motorways and seeing where he finished up. Eventually he decided that a move to the rural south-west would get him out of the heroin scene: 'So the only way to try to sort it out was to get out of it, and that's what I did. But I went to Newlyn, which was a big mistake – there's more drugs in Newlyn than ...' So he ended up in Winton, in a space of care sufficiently intimate yet visible that he had maintained a regime of self-detox for at least two months.

Des's journey to Winton was less complex. A 49-year-old homeless man with a self-confessed 'severe drinking habit', he had lost his job in Oldham some eight weeks previously, and with no local family connections to rely on had decided to head to the south-west: 'I'd always heard about the surfing and all, and I've always fancied doing it, so I thought I'd give it a go, so I was in Newquay for about two weeks' (Des, 49, hostel resident, Winton). Des's search for accommodation led him to a referral process that resulted in access to the Winton hostel, which he regarded as 'like a stepping-stone from, I suppose you could call it, off the street, to here, to finding your own place'. The hostel prohibits the drinking of alcohol, and Des has acceded to this rule, reporting that 'I've not had a drink since I've come here'. Although it would be unwise to suggest overly romanticized connections between rurality and addiction therapy, living in 'quiet' Winton seems to have contributed to decisions made by both Harry and Des to address their respective addictions, and points to a therapeutic role for rural-based facilities of care (Gesler, 1992).

Another resident of the Winton hostel service was Keith, a 32-year-old born in London with a history of living on the streets and in squats, and latterly of journeying around as a 'traveller'. Although 'traveller' can represent heterogeneous attitudes, practices and lifestyles (see Lowe & Shaw, 1993; Halfacree, 1996; Hetherington, 2000), Keith regards the core of travelling to be a journey of transience towards the new: 'I suppose a traveller is someone that wakes up in the morning and thinks, right, what new place am I going to today? And that is my attitude every morning' (Keith, 32, hostel resident, Winton). Keith describes his history as one in which 'I've never been homeless, but I've always been homeless'. For several years he followed well-worn routes around Kent, Worcestershire and Wales, working in agricultural settings associated with hops, apples, daffodils and Christmas trees, living in the back of cars, caravans and vans and at one stage owning his own coach. Reflecting on this experience, he differentiates strongly between 'the real traveller people' who 'keep the cogs of society greased' because of their willingness to work, and 'parasitic homeless families' who appear to adopt the traveller lifestyle but are regarded by Keith as 'spoiling what we have'. As with the wayfarers of Castlebridge, then, there is a claim to authenticity here, in contrast with the perceived culpabilities of other homeless people. Keith's sojourn in Winton (he had only been there for six days) came as a result of a decision to try a different form of lifestyle:

> I've seen a lot in my life, and I've just had enough. It's time to ... take a back seat, slow down, do something I haven't done before, and see what being straight does, and live in a house, live in ... the concrete jungle. (Keith, hostel resident, Winton)

Such decisions are rarely straightforward, and Keith's transition to a 'straight' life living 'in the concrete jungle' is taking place over a number of years and still involves dreams of buying a coach and travelling around Europe. However, he told us of a number of factors in his current situation that he found helpful to the process. For example, he enjoys the 'Cornish attitude', which he finds suitably laid back – 'they let you do what you want, they let you be you'. He values the solitude of a rural area that is recuperative from the negative attributes of cities, which he has experienced but wants to move away from. And he appreciates the values expressed through the hostel, its management and its organization. The latter seems most obviously related to the local management style – the manager has lived a traveller lifestyle in the past and Keith responds well to the resultant environment: 'This is definitely one of the better organizations ... it is run road rules, traveller style. It's run by an ex-traveller, it's not textbook' (Keith, 32, hostel resident, Winton). There is a strong sense here that Keith feels understood and accepted in a way that he finds atypical of some other service settings he has experienced. Part of this acceptance reflects how the ethical positionings of the organization are performatively brought into being (see Conradson, 2003) in the everyday life of the hostel through the style and experience of its manager:

> I like this, because there's a lot of love here ... it's not done for the wrong reasons, it comes from the heart here, you know, it's not done from the pocket, or for the pocket ... as other places are. This is done from the heart ... it's just done because it can be done. (Keith, 32, hostel resident, Winton)

Keith's experience suggests that the Winton hostel has been able to maintain some form of independent charitable ethos despite pressures to professionalize, and that the capability for a small intimate facility in a 'quiet' place to be run with rules, and heart, but without the pressures of Christian or secular proselytizing, represents good practice of postsecular care (see chapter 2) in a rural location. St Austen's represents an insider organization that has nevertheless been able to maintain its own ethos and management style, which has proved particularly effective for these kinds of residents, especially given a setting that is perceived as therapeutic by those residents.

Nightstops for homeless teenagers

Our third example draws on research undertaken in a small market town (Crossfield) in central England. Crossfield has a population of just over 40,000 and acts as a service centre for surrounding rural areas. As with many other such rural centres, homeless people have historically failed to find a place in the popular imaginary of the town, and it was only in the late 1980s and early 1990s that two non-statutory service providers – Streets Ahead and the Lighthouse – were established to cater for the needs of homeless people from the town and its surrounding areas. Typically, the numbers of street homeless people in Crossfield have been relatively low, thereby not reaching the critical mass of public visibility required to engage a local popular perception of homelessness in the area. Moreover, until recently, local homeless people have been diverted to a nearby city, where there has been a longstanding provision of hostel and shelter services for homeless people. Indeed, the local authority has funded service-providers in the city to cater for the needs of people from within its jurisdiction, thereby cementing a historical service dependency on the neighbouring city and obviating the need to provide local emergency services.

The need for localized services began to be recognized in the late 1980s with the formation of Streets Ahead, first as an inter-agency group operating out of a youth centre, and then as a registered charity which from 1994 has provided both advice and outreach services. Similarly, the Lighthouse drop-in centre was established in 1994 by the Crossfield District Housing Coalition, a charity formed by local people with concerns about homelessness. One of the main drivers of third sector provision of services for homeless people was the plight of a particular client group of 16–18-year-olds who were caught in a benefit-trap if forced to leave home, but who were often fearful of having to migrate to the city to make use of the services there. As one of the founders of Streets Ahead told us:

> It was identified that there was nowhere as an emergency placement for young people who needed somewhere overnight. I became aware of that as a manager of social services in Crossfield, because a lot of young people would come in and say 'I've been chucked out of home', normally at five o clock at night. ... They'd be too old to consider for foster care ... so we would offer them train fares to [nearby city] to go to a night shelter there. (Elizabeth, Co-founder and management committee member, Streets Ahead, Crossfield)

These concerns suggest two important local factors that often motivate service provision for homeless people in rural towns. First, it was a member of the public-sector service professions that in the course of her statutory responsibilities recognized a service need for homeless people that could only be provided by starting up a charitable organization to deal with that need. Second, in the absence of significant and visible 'on-street' homelessness, it was those teenagers who were too young to be considered for statutory benefits that triggered the response.

Initially, Streets Ahead established short-term projects such as a Crisis Winterwatch day scheme, and a Christmastime night shelter, but the lack of in situ emergency accommodation, and the continuing problem of having to send homeless young people off to the facilities in the neighbouring city, led to the search for a form of more reliable yet local accommodation provision. Again, there is wider evidence (see Cloke et al., 2002) that homeless people in rural areas will often be reluctant to migrate to the emergency facilities in the 'big city', and so the conundrum for local third sector organizations is to find a form of emergency support that is affordable (Streets Ahead, for example, receives less than 25 per cent of its funding from statutory sources) and does not require a significant critical mass of users to make it functional. The answer for Streets Ahead, having heard about the Nightstop schemes that had been established in Nottingham and Leicester, was to investigate the possibilities of the Nightstop model. Having done so they 'decided to adopt that [the Nightstop model], to at least give some options for young people who needed something' (Elizabeth, co-founder and committee member, Streets Ahead).

Nightstop effectively establishes a group of trained volunteers in a locality who are willing to offer their own homes as a place of short-term refuge for young people who experience an emergency form of homelessness. Referrals are made through the host organization (in this case Streets Ahead) to ensure that people requiring specialist support (for example, in the case of illness or addiction) can be channelled elsewhere where such support can be provided. The idea, ideally suited to the needs of teenagers, is to provide an early intervention in the life of a homeless person, providing a 'normal' (as opposed to an institutionalized) response to a sudden bout of homelessness by welcoming them into a Nightstop home to receive short-term care before moving on into supported foyer or rented accommodation in the town. Previous attempts by social services to provide 'supported lodgings' (likewise in private residences but with longer stays) in the town had proved a struggle, and so the success of Nightstop is to match homeless young people with willing volunteers in such a way as to sustain rather than burn out the volunteering spirit of local people. Volunteers are therefore only asked to accommodate people for a few nights at most, and can register their availability at particular times and not others, thus allowing them to opt in and out of the scheme as their circumstances dictate. The evidence from Crossfield is that such volunteers exist, and are the key to the success of the Nightstop scheme. As one of the managers of Streets Ahead told us:

> I'm humbled by Nightstop hosts, I truly am. … They're brilliant, totally brilliant … a lot of them don't even claim their expenses … they come along for training for free and I have to say we've run it since May 1999 and we've still got a load [of the original hosts] with us; they take people at the drop of a hat. (Sheila, Co-manager, Streets Ahead, Crossfield)

Interestingly, the source of these volunteers is significantly linked to an active Christian presence in the town: 'We've got quite good links with local churches and we've always recruited through local churches, so a lot of people [who volunteer] are people that go to church or know of people that go to church' (Sheila, Co-Manager, Streets Ahead, Crossfield).

In our interviews with three Nightstop hosts, each explained how their faith was a motivating factor in their decision to volunteer. Mary attributes her participation thus: 'I think part of it is being a Christian and a churchgoer; it's not just [about] going to church, it's helping people in the community.' Debbie told us about how a Streets Ahead project worker toured different local groups to talk about Nightstop, 'and she actually came to one of our church services and talked about it … and we responded to her plea for volunteers'. And Fay explained: 'I've been a Christian for nearly four years now … and there's a flow I hope, but not an overpowering flow, that they know that somebody *does* care.' These examples point to a wider trend both of faith-based involvement in local practices of volunteering with homeless people (see Cloke et al., 2005, 2007) and of collaborations between faith-motivated people and others in localized forms of the kinds of postsecular rapprochement detailed in chapter 2. They also highlight the importance of individuals, as well as agencies, in the understanding of how service and care are performed in local circumstances.

Indeed, there is a complex mix of organizational ethics and training, and individual ethics and performativity, at work here. As we argued in chapter 4, the organizational spaces of emergency care for homeless people can be expected to be constructed at least partially from the ways in which organizational ethics are variously represented in, or transformed by, the ways in which volunteers bring their particular ordinary ethics to bear in their work. Yet although this offers an understanding of how such ordinary ethics influence why volunteers present themselves in such spaces, and what they are aiming to achieve through that presence, there can be no automatic assumption that the resultant space of care will be imbued by particular ethical characteristics. Indeed, it is clear that organizational spaces of care are performatively brought into being, not simply in terms of performing to impress, or performing routines, but also in acting out care unreflexively and through improvisation during eruptions of non-routine events and practices (Conradson, 2003; McCormack, 2003).

Take, for example, the ways in which a Nightstop host – Fay – describes the ways she tries to make her new guests feel 'at home'. Despite the fact that interviews are in many ways an inappropriate medium through which to record and understand these kinds of performativities, her account points to the significance of *performing* spaces of care:

> They always come with a [Streets Ahead] member, and they're introduced, and I try and break the ice straight away by saying 'I'll put the kettle on, what do you want?' and 'while that's on shall we go round the house' ... so when we go round the house I sort of make jokes and laugh with them – try and make them feel at home, and by the time you've got down again – because it's a three-storey house – the person who brought them has usually got on with making the tea and ... they go off and then I find they relax. 'Cos I just say 'Do you wanna bath? Do you wanna have something to eat first? Tell me your plans' – and then they open up and they're very shy in the beginning but it doesn't take them long. And I say 'If you wanna put your feet up, put your feet up' and I tell them the rules about smoking. I'm a non-smoker ... but I say 'the veranda's free and if you really must smoke in the bedrooms, fine but can you sit near the window ...?' Once they know that you're not going to be hard on them, they relax. And we laugh about the shower, the fact that they have to press the button down and put the knob on, and unless you do that it's too hot or cold, and we laugh about that. (Fay, Nightstop host, Streets Ahead, Crossfield)

Fay's routines and improvisations performatively bring her home into being as a space of care. The tour of the house not only affords one-to-one conversation with the homeless guest (the organization 'official' is immediately sidelined) but also acts out the house as a place of opportunity. Rules are conveyed, but the conversational emphasis is on what can be done, and what the young person wants. Fay intersperses the performance with humour and fun. She is self-deprecating and seeks out ways for her guest to relax. Later she describes her act as treating the guest just like she would treat pals of her son. There is the caring mother here, but without the fussiness that can sometimes arise between mother and children. Fay weaves an acceptance and an ethic of (in her case Christian) care through the experience. As a result she offers her guest 'home-space', if only for the brief stopover, and she empowers her guest to treat the experience as something more than just a bed for the night. It is unsurprising that Fay keeps in contact with many of her previous 'guests' as a result of this kind of relational performance. And, although some of her actions may reflect the organizational training given to Nightstop hosts, Fay brings particular performative capacities and affects to her caring.

These kinds of caring conditions can in many ways be seen to match the key needs of many of Streets Ahead's clients, many of whom are younger teenagers who have been 'chucked out' of the family home for a variety of reasons. A co-manager of Streets Ahead, Sheila told us that 'the people that we seem to work with very roughly fall into two client bands'. First she described the predominant caseload group as '16–17-year-olds who need a bit of a parenting role and who respond extremely well to our housing support service'. These are young people who fall foul of family dysfunctionality, often because of alienation and/or aggression from a new stepparent, and find themselves forced to live independently without access to benefits. Nightstop is a crucial first step in a joined-up process that works towards a set of restorative goals that include access to supported accommodation, and (re)integration with opportunities for education, training and employment. The second client type according to Sheila is the more problematic 'young people that won't engage at all, so they … don't want support thank you very much'. These young people are more likely to become 'intentionally homeless', and although Streets Ahead tries to assist, the usual modus operandi is to send them to emergency accommodation services in the nearby city in the first instance.

Nightstop in Crossfield, then, seems to be culturally in keeping with its setting. It relies on the active presence of a sustainable group of highly motivated volunteers drawn principally from social networks associated with churches in the area. Such volunteering seems to go well beyond the idea of 'moral selving' (Allahyari, 2000) in that any desire for a simply positive moral identity-coding would seem to be achievable without the potential fears and challenges of welcoming a young vulnerable stranger into your own home, and dealing with the emotional charge of a short-term caring relationship. It also relies on the sifting of potential service-users to ensure that anyone with illness, addiction or behavioural issues is directed to the more specialist scrvices in the city where such needs can be better dealt with. The relationship is, then, one of pseudo-familial and community relations that fit well within the rural culture and setting in which charitable self-help within the community for needy local people outweighs any sense of homeless young people being out of place in the cultural and material spaces of the town. As Nightstop host Fay suggests: 'The first time you do it you think "Oh gosh, what have I let myself in for?" But when they first come … they're just like your own kids really – very vulnerable – you can't help but want to help them and get involved' (Fay, Nightstop host, Streets Ahead, Crossfield). Fay's reaction confirms the Nightstop identity as attempting, as far as possible, to provide a 'normal' experience for the homeless young person in a regularized home setting rather than an institutional one. The purified space (see Cloke et al., 2002) of the rural place is not transgressed by this identity, which renders Nightstop 'in keeping' with the cultural ethos of its surroundings. This is not to suggest that the accommodating culture of the place stretches to all forms of service provision for homeless people, of course. A plan in the town to convert a redundant housing association property for elderly people into accommodation for young vulnerable mothers, for example, received vehement opposition from local people, ostensibly on planning grounds, but interpreted by local service managers as an expression of the out-of-placeness of supposedly 'undeserving' homeless people in the same community in which Nightstop is accepted. This strongly suggests that rural responses to homelessness cannot be universalized, but will be required to take full account of localized place-imaginaries and often unspoken orthodoxies of what is, and what is not, 'in-place'.

The advice centres and young homeless people

Our fourth illustration involves Sandstown, a sizeable town (population 106,000) serving an extensive rural hinterland in northern England. The manager of one significant non-statutory agency in the town provides context about the attitudes towards homelessness therein:

> It's a seaside resort, it's a holiday town, it's a tourist attraction, and the vast majority of people in positions of power spend most of their energies in promoting that aspect of the town. They certainly don't want people's problems in the town, and if we have them they don't want them to be seen, because it ruins the nice clean holiday town image … the way that statutory agencies work [is] … reminiscent of the ways statutory bodies worked in the 1960s. (Claire, Manager, day centre, Sandstown)

Interviews with statutory and non-statutory service providers paint the picture of an entrepreneurial town where the provision of emergency services for homeless people is discouraged as being detrimental to the image of a prosperous seaside resort, and where the context of a local authority seemingly out of touch with the modern welfare consensus has resulted in fragmented forms of charity and philanthropy struggling to produce local spaces of welfare. Accounts of the postindustrial city (see Adams, 1986; Hubbard & Hall, 1998; Marshall, 2001) tend to trace how such places reflect the push towards a postindustrial and entrepreneurial logic and how, in an urban context, these changes are accompanied by similar shifts in welfare provision to a more entrepreneurial, managerialist (post) welfare model. But in Sandstown the promotion of place image and touristic entrepreneurship has not (yet) been matched by a parallel transformation of welfare systems, which have until very recently remained rooted in traditional models of local state power. Officers of the local authority, for example, acknowledge their restricted ability to house single homeless people: 'If a single person went on our register and they'd got very high needs, perhaps no fixed abode, moving around friends, got very high points ... it may be a long time before we can help them' (David, Housing Officer, Sandstown Borough Council). They also operate on the understanding that 'counts have reflected very small numbers, if any, rough sleepers' (David) and that the vast majority of their applicants are 'homeless but not necessarily roofless, and it may well be very short term, temporary, for a few nights until they can sort something else out' (Len, Housing Officer, Sandstown Borough Council). Accordingly, recent national homelessness programmes have not impacted tangibly on the town largely because for the local authority to apply for funding would be to admit to the existence of a homelessness 'problem', which might in turn contradict the logic and images of tourist entrepreneurism.

Instead, services for homeless people in Sandstown have grown through particular individual and organizational initiatives. Largely inspired by the vision and work of one woman, Linda, who had dealt with the consequences of youth homelessness while working in the local Youth Enquiry Service, a video was made to graphically portray the existence and conditions of homelessness in the town. The local inter-agency Housing Forum then put together a steering committee (where again Linda was a formative influence) to seek charitable funding, and a grant from Comic Relief led to the establishment of Safe in the early 1990s. Starting off as a drop-in and advice centre for young people aged 16–25, this non-statutory organization began to expand its activities into what it perceived as gaps in the service infrastructure for young homeless people. Linda persuaded the Foyer Federation to establish a small foyer in the town, which was subsequently taken over by a local housing association with plans to extend the foyer project in two further stages. Safe retains a significant involvement in the management of the initial foyer, and has more recently secured a range of funding to make a small number of flats available to young homeless people in the town.

The ethos of Safe is principally one of professional service. Linda told us: 'I have very very strict policies, procedures, codes of behaviour and standards that I expect every single member of staff in this organization to meet. I want a quality service and I want it to be the best' (Linda, Manager, Safe foyer, Sandstown). Accordingly, Safe uses trained paid staff rather than volunteers, and prizes its local organizational presence even to the extent of active participation in town centre management and regeneration, thereby charting a sensitive political pathway between service provision and alignment with the postindustrial push towards image-based town centre renewal. Safe effectively deals with a client group (16–25 years old) that the local authority is unable to help. Indeed, speaking of the organization's relationship with the local authority, Linda told us: 'certainly they're quite glad we're here – we take a lot of responsibility off them'. Here, then, is a local non-statutory organization that assumes considerable localized power due to the absence of local authority led initiative in the homelessness sector, although there is evidence that this role is fraught with potential tensions, not least with the local authority itself.

In 1997, a further initiative emerged from the local Housing Forum reflecting the lack of service response for homeless people over the age of 25 in Sandstown. The initial idea was to establish a Winterwatch scheme using funding from the national homelessness charity Crisis, in conjunction with establishing a new local accommodation facility for homeless people to be run by the national organization Emmaus. However, these plans were foiled by extremely strong local opposition to the setting up of an Emmaus centre in the area, as a result of which a new charity – Sandstown Homeless Project (SHP) – was formed in 1998 to coordinate short-term emergency accommodation (usually in bed and breakfast establishments) for rough sleepers under the Winterwatch scheme, and to provide drop-in and advice facilities for homeless people over 25. Initially the initiative appears to have been hampered by unclear objectives stemming from the fragmented interests of different members of the management committee, many of whom were faith-motivated. More recently, a paid manager has been employed to bring greater professional standards to the work of the organization. SHP now receives funding from a range of charitable giving, as well as from the local authority and from Crisis. However, the organization works out of unsuitable building space, and needs to rely on volunteers to carry out its work. Moreover, the absence of direct access hostel accommodation in the town means that SHP have to rely on the goodwill of local private sector landlords. Claire, who manages the service, told us: '90 per cent of our clients live in bed and breakfast and guest house provision. In Sandstown we have people that have lived in bed and breakfast for 20 years' (Claire, Manager, SHP, Sandstown). This situation is highly vulnerable to any phasing out of the use of government funding to pay for bed and breakfast accommodation for homeless people – settings that are widely acknowledged as both expensive and unsuitable for vulnerable groups (Quilgars et al., 2008).

Homelessness in and around Sandstown predominantly affects local people or those with local connections – the lack of emergency accommodation and analogous services for rough sleepers means that the town is not attractive to in-migrant homeless people. The local advice centres therefore serve local young people, including a significant proportion of young women. Heidi, for example, is a 17-year-old local woman who left home at 16 because of irreconcilable differences with her parents. She was helped by Safe to gain access to the foyer for six months, after which she was able to return to live with her parents while she waited to be allocated one of Safe's local flats. Her experience of the foyer was difficult, reflecting the visibility and stigma of homelessness for a local person in a small town: 'When I moved in there, I lost all my friends because they thought I was taking drugs, that I was injecting, because of the image that it's got ...' (Heidi, 17, former foyer resident, now living with her parents, Sandstown). Heidi also found the foyer's rules too restrictive, and that financially the payments for rent and services in the foyer left her unable to afford any luxuries. However, her continuing use of Safe's drop-in led her to undertake further education training and part-time employment.

A similar story emerges from Corinne, another 17-year-old woman who was living in the foyer. After suffering domestic violence in her home in Scotland she moved to Sandstown at the age of 15 to live with her sister. When the relationship broke down, she was put in contact with Safe, having been told by the local authority that they were unable to help. After a temporary stay in bed and breakfast accommodation, Corinne was accepted into the foyer. Her positive reaction to the care she received there is evident:

> Well actually it was quite good. ... You get the support; there's your action plans and they check to make sure that everything's okay. They got me into training and I started Life Skills training programme. ... They do work placements to get you into another job ... (Corinne, 17, former foyer resident now living in private rented accommodation, Sandstown)

Corinne maintains her contact with the drop-in service:

> I usually come in every day after training, 'cos you get your meals as well ... come in to see if everyone else is here. There's always activities ... there's barbecues and trips out to the beach, and golf, and things like that so we come in every day. (Corinne, 17, former foyer resident now living in private rented accommodation, Sandstown)

For Heidi and Corinne, Safe offers a wide-ranging set of responses to the homeless experience of young people unable to depend on family support. However, Safe also offers support for young women whose homelessness is complicated by addiction. Wanda is a 22-year-old woman, born in Sandstown and 'on drugs since I was 13'. She ended up rough sleeping at the age of 16, after falling out with her family and succumbing to chaotic drug addiction:

> I was always in trouble with the police, and I just couldn't get on with my mum, and carried on taking drugs, and it just got stronger – drugs like amphetamines and heroin – and I just ended up being on the streets through it all. (Wanda, 22, former foyer resident, now in local authority accommodation, Sandstown)

Wanda was allocated a place in the foyer, but transgression of the rules caused by her drug-fuelled lifestyle led to her being evicted, at which point she was rough sleeping and engaging in 'survivalist crimes' (Carlen, 1996), which led ultimately to periods of imprisonment. During her last spell in prison she underwent a nine-day detox, and on her release Safe brokered a return to her parental home while waiting for local authority accommodation, which has become possible as she has been placed on a priority list due to contracting hepatitis through her drug use. Wanda's stay highlights the precarious nature of Sandstown's emergency accommodation provision. If a person falls foul of the regulations under which the foyer is operated, there were few options other than a return home to prevent a return to living on the streets prior to housing allocation.

People over the age of 25 and experiencing homelessness will often have had a longer history of service needs. Karen, aged 26 and born in Sandstown, was helped by SHP into local bed and breakfast accommodation. Her history of being in local authority care, violent relationships, mental health problems and drug addiction is all too familiar among homeless people, as is her pattern of mobility: first to Leeds and then to London, seeking out places where emergency facilities were available. Karen returned to her home town thinking that 'it's quite easy to get a place if you've got money to get a bond'. However, she and her partner slept rough in Sandstown for two weeks before getting in contact with SHP:

> We was sleeping at, it's called The Spa, and it used to be an outdoor swimming pool, where the chalets are, I used to sleep in them. And then we came down here to the day centre and that's how we got our B&B. ... If it wasn't for these [SHP] I'd still be on the street 'cos there's no other help apart from this. (Karen, 26, private rented flat, Sandstown)

Like Safe, SHP is playing a crucial role in supporting local homeless people in Sandstown. Even with her health problems, Karen has been told to expect to wait at least six months before local authority accommodation becomes available. Indeed, with very little local authority housing to access, the role of organizations like SHP and Safe is crucial in helping young women like Karen and Wanda secure accommodation, as Linda from Safe explains: 'If you were in Middlesbrough and you went to the local authority and asked for a council house you'd have the keys by this afternoon' (Linda, Manager, Safe Foyer, Sandstown).

In this example, then, 'insider' organizations have forged a local response to homelessness despite a difficult environment in terms of local authority resources, strategy and involvement. Although there are signs of change in this context, the conflicts between promoting the place virtues of a seaside resort and accessing all available resources to deal with the needs of home-less people remain highly politicized. As a result, the therapeutic landscape of Sandstown for tourists is in opposition to the potential provision of thera-peutic places of care for homeless people. The needs of 'deserving' cases are being met thanks to strong interventions from the non-statutory sector, but for others the only supportive infrastructure is the local network of bed and breakfast hotels, which can be inaccessible during the summer, and at best represent unregulated and potentially problematic spaces of supposed care.

Conclusions

How do these rural service providers and users interconnect with contem-porary governmentalities and mobilities of homelessness? By choosing to include small-scale, rural-based or rural-serving homeless places in our research we beg questions of the geographical unevenness and marginality experienced in the frostbitten extremities of the hand of welfare policy. Each area is disadvantaged by rough sleeper count mechanisms from claiming an unambiguous problem of rough sleeping, yet each displays clear evidence of the existence of homelessness. Although care should be exercised in gener-alizing from these few case studies, we suggest that rural place characteris-tics and linkages, though differing from place to place, certainly influence particular co-constitutions of problems and responses to homelessness. Aside from minor references to rural areas as potential workplaces (in agri-culture and fishing), three strands of rural characteristics serve as especially significant to homelessness in the case studies presented here.

The first strand conforms to an orthodox understanding of rurality as a close-knit community that looks after its own, but defends its space against outsiders or transgressors (Cloke et al., 2000b). The case study of Crossfield and its surrounding area seems to suggest the evolution of a response to homelessness that affirms, and is affirmed by, these cultural characteristics. Young, vulnerable and 'deserving' homeless people are given temporary refuge in the homes of ethically motivated local people. Locals care for locals, although others – perceived as less deserving – are shunted off into the nearby city where support services for their types of needs are apparently more suit-able and – not just by-the-by perhaps – out of sight of the rural setting. The second strand suggests that rurality offers a place of escape and of potential therapy. For example, in references to escaping the drug scenes of big cities, or even notorious smaller towns, interviewees relate the potential of dealing with addiction in smaller, quieter places, where individuals can be known but not rejected, and where drug use or alcoholism may be more intensely visible and therefore controlled. This is not to overromanticize a rurality that is clearly not immune to the everyday presence of addictive substances (Hyde, 1997), but it may be to indicate some therapeutic potential in rural places (Philo et al., 2003). The third strand is one that associates rurality with leisure, although here the perceptions of a laid-back surfi-culture in the south-west, where homeless people felt able to articulate their individuality and difference, contrasts strongly with the equally touristic but distinctly less accommodating vibes in the seaside town of Sandstown, where purification of place and resistance to homeless services have been evident. Rurality is also significant in terms of its place in wider linkages of transience. It offers the natural habitus of the 'deep' countryside for wayfarers fluidly travelling their 'routes', and it contains key cultural and even spiritual waymarkers for new age travellers in their search for the new and the natural.

These characteristics of rurality reflect ways in which some countryside locations are characterized by 'care-at-home', while others exert an attraction to in-migrant homeless people, or people who become homeless subsequent to their in-migration. For people who become homeless in their own locality, rurality presents the potential security of a known 'home area' – a place where initial reliance on friends can lead on to contacts with local advisors and, potentially, to local resettlement. Where no such local advice services and move-on accommodation exist, out-migration to larger, service-rich, places becomes far more likely. Rurality also offers a sense of a secure place to come back to: somewhere it is possible to be helped with the necessary bond for taking on a new flat, for example, once the out-migration option has been explored and found wanting.

The particularities of rural places are matched by distinctive historical, political and organizational circumstances at the local level, which have been influential in the specificities of service provision emerging in these places. So, the friary house, for example, represented more than 80 years of local provision for homeless men, and its existence and position in the contemporary landscape of provision is specific to that historical record of service. Similarly, the recent service initiative in Winton appears to benefit from a historic presence of other (psychiatric) forms of service provision in the town, a presence that has brought an enduring familiarity with the proximity of needy 'others'. In Sandstown, by contrast, there is an apparent absence of service history, which could be interpreted as a history of denial or spatial purification in order to protect the town's tourist image from being compromised by otherness.

Politically, it can be argued that the case studies all represent 'outsider' status services, but there are important differences here within a range of places where the reach of central government funding and regulation appears limited or absent. For example, there are contrasting local government initiatives at work here, ranging from a seeming absence of modern welfare consensus in Sandstown, with the result that the development of Safe has effectively taken over some of the responsibilities of the local authority, to the more interventionist local authority regimes in south-west and central England, where local organizations are being drawn into varying degrees of joined-up local strategies. Organizational circumstances are influenced significantly by individual innovation – witness the role of particular individuals in setting up services in Crossfield, Sandstown and the friary – which appears formative in any explanation of why services are developed in some places, but not others. However, the characteristics of those services are at least partly formed by the ethos of the individuals and organizations concerned, with the faith-based ethos of the friary house and the Crossfield Nightstop volunteers contrasting with the ethos of professionalism spoken about at Safe. Interestingly, it appears that the influence of ethos can change over time, with the faith-beginnings of organizations such as St Austen's appearing to be subject to transforming discourses of professionalism.

These place and organizational characteristics combine to contextualize the development of particular spaces of care in these marginal rural locations. Other factors are also important – the state of the built infrastructure in SHP, for example, appears to hinder the comfort-capacity of the service and thereby seems likely to influence the social relations of care concerned (see also chapter 5). However, it is clear that distinct spaces of care are performatively being brought into being through, for example, the faith and family influences of Nightstop volunteers, the faith-ethos, acceptance and dignity of the brothers at the friary house, the high-energy professionalism and involvement of managers at Safe, and the traveller-savvy atmosphere achieved by the particular experience of a manager at St Austen's in Winton. In each of these cases, symbiotic relations are being achieved with the particular groups of homeless people concerned. Thus the brothers and lay Franciscans achieved a time-deepened affinity with, and 'heart' for, the dwindling band of wayfarers, and had to adjust to their new role as receivers of homeless people excluded from other institutions and with nowhere else to go. The original vision of acceptance remained, but it was being increasingly morphed into the contemporary circumstances of last resort at the end of the line of exclusion. Ultimately, the organization was simply unable to meet the specialist needs of those who were landing on its doorstep, and the closure of the friary house suggests that its role as a space of acceptance was overrun by the nature and magnitude of the needs of its new users.

The appointment of an ex-traveller as manager of the Winton hostel chimes with providing the necessary grasp of the needs of transient non-local service users. Rules are upheld in the hostel, but a place of potential acceptance and rehabilitation is created in an atmosphere of increasing service professionalism. Homeless young people are 'taken in' by Nightstop volunteers in Crossfield, and made to feel cared for and 'at home'. Young homeless people find their needs met in a highly personalized yet professional advice centre that is able to offer some real hope of move-on accommodation in Sandstown, due to efforts to collaborate with resource-rich insider organizations such as the Foyer Federation.

Of these examples, it is easy to see how the Winton, Crossfield and Sandstown services could benefit from increased central resources so as to bring an influx of capacity to the places concerned. The efficacy of any such inclusiveness, however, would depend on the accompanying regulatory regime, which could involve, for example, a redirection of focus away from the high service dependants in Crossfield, the non-locals in Winton and those young people in Sandstown who might not meet criteria for access to statutory services. Moreover, the social acceptability of local services could be disrupted if the scale of operations changed through such resource input. The potential for local opposition to obvious incursions of homeless culture should not be underestimated.

The friary house was perhaps the service least compatible with new governmentalities of welfare (Ling, 2000). Yet it, too, represented a valuable space of care, and it might be argued that similar kinds of services should remain part of the cartography of rural homelessness services because of the importance of a caring role that is immune from regulatory odium. Such service spaces will, however, find it difficult to survive if they are merely used as dumping grounds for the most needy and troublesome of homeless people who become excluded from the 'insider' service environment, yet require the kind of specialist support that is only available from insider organizations (see also chapter 6).

The contemporary governance of the service providers and clients associated with rural homelessness is, then, currently highly fragmented and partial in terms of the reach of welfare policy into rural localities. There are certainly signs that existing non-statutory service providers are being drawn into elements of statutory control over their service delivery, and that the availability of small-scale finance, and wider expectations about the professionalism required for high-standard service delivery, represent incremental changes to the technologies of welfare delivery in places such as Sandstown and Winton. However, these signs can be overstated, and until centrally funded initiatives specifically reflect the needs of homeless people in rural areas, rather than consistently underestimating those needs, responses to rural homelessness will remain patchy and sporadic. Nevertheless, even within this context of neglect (see Evans, 1999; Robinson, 2003) it is important to recognize at least two forms of emergent spaces of care in rural settings. Both those professionalized and professionalizing organizations (such as seen in Sandstown and Winton), which might be regarded as working towards a more 'insider' role, and the seemingly old-fashioned 'outsider' charities (illustrated by the friary house, which has not in fact survived) will be continuing to offer care to particular needy groups in the foreseeable future. Although the former might profitably be drawn further into the coordination and funding of contemporary governance, accepting the necessity of concomitant changes in the regulatory environment, we suggest that there will always be a place for specialist spaces of acceptance such as the latter, operating largely outside the reach of such governance, where those excluded from formal services can still receive care.

Chapter Nine

Conclusions

So much of the contemporary literature on homelessness is prefigured by accounts of societal revenge, or postjustice, that one might be forgiven for questioning whether anyone out there cares about the plight of homeless people. If homelessness serves as a litmus test of how society deals with its most disadvantaged members, then revanchist accounts of how homeless people are swept up and expunged from the public spaces of the city present a damning indictment of how the politics of welfare has become detached from any ethics of compassion. In this book we have presented a rather different perspective on homelessness, emphasizing the relationships of care that are brought into being in Britain's night shelters and hostels, day centres and soup runs. Instead of viewing such spaces as the designated cells into which swept-up lives are herded – and therefore as part and parcel of the punitive regimes of postwelfare – we have characterized the serving of homeless people as a key marker of a second current of postsecular compassion running counter, and sometimes in explicit resistance to, the vicissitudes of neoliberal urban governance. Here we want to draw out some wider arguments about urban revanchism, neoliberal governance, the role of voluntary sector welfare organizations in providing for the needs of homeless people, and the place of volunteering in the postsecular city in the hope of both drawing things together and opening things up to continued discussion and debate on the politics of the homeless city.

Urban Revanchism, Neoliberal Governance and the Voluntary Attitude

As we emphasized at the beginning of this book, the winds of revanchism have by no means left Britain untouched. The past decade in particular has seen a growing number of attempts, emanating both from public–private partnerships (for example, Business Improvement Districts) and more directly from the state (for example, Designated Public Places Orders) to 'reclaim' the streets of Britain's towns and cities for 'respectable' and 'mainstream' consumers. There is therefore little doubt that Britain's street homeless population now inhabit a more hostile urban environment than in the recent past, and that particular groups (for example, those engaged in begging or street drinking) often bear the brunt of this hostility. Furthermore, it would appear that this environment has become rather more antagonistic in the period since the research on which this book is based was conducted (Johnsen & Fitzpatrick, 2007, 2010). Most obviously, as part and parcel of its 'Respect Agenda', the New Labour government has clamped down very hard over the past few years on what it has described as a 'problematic street culture': rendering begging a recordable offence, and providing the local state with the necessary apparatus (in the form of Anti-Social Behaviour Orders) to banish particularly 'problematic' street homeless people from the prime spaces of the city altogether.

While these kinds of developments – and the role that the local state in particular now plays in helping to secure the conditions for economic growth – have received considerable attention, scholars of homelessness have had far less to say about other ways in which the state has sought to manage problems of street homelessness. Yet, in the British context at least, the state's primary role in such processes is less obviously related to these more explicit attempts to 'manage the streets, than to attempts to manage the welfare response to homelessness – by exerting greater control over the voluntary sector organizations that provide the mainstay of emergency services to street homeless people. Both the motivations behind, and the effects of, British government policy in this field have been remarkably ambiguous.

On the one hand, the aim of government is quite clearly to deliver 'clean streets', through a reduction in levels of rough sleeping but also in the number of (voluntary sector) organizations whose activities are held to help 'sustain a street lifestyle' (ODPM, 1999: 4). Thus, in the case of the ongoing No One Left Out initiative, for example, the target is to reduce levels of rough sleeping in London to zero by 2012, a policy presumably designed, at least in part, to help secure a more attractive streetscape in time for the London Olympics. The Games would also seem to have been a factor in the recent (unsuccessful) attempt by London Councils (the body representing London's thirty-two local authorities) to stop soup kitchens (but not commercial organizations engaged in promotional activities) from distributing free food and drinks on London's streets (Evans, 2007). On the other hand, the rash of new initiatives introduced by New Labour over the past decade or so (ranging from the Homelessness Action Programme to Local Homelessness Strategies, Supporting People and No One Left Out) have released a significant amount of new public money to the voluntary sector organizations providing emergency services to single homeless people, and sought to improve the quality of these services.

Even here, however, and as we have shown, the effects of such policies have been mixed. While a very significant number of organizations and areas of service delivery (most notably, soup runs) have remained 'outside the loop' of government funding and regulation altogether, the 'insider' organizations working within the system also often articulate an ambiguous response to these initiatives. Most obviously, though benefiting from increased funding and (in theory at least) able to access a greater array of specialist services for their clients, this has often been at the cost of a challenge to the ethos and practices of the organizations involved. Hence, providers have found themselves under increasing pressure to 'manage' (i.e. ration) their admissions procedures so that they are catering only to the most vulnerable people on the streets, for example; to adopt an ethos of 'active rehabilitation and change' so as to more effectively manage the 'progress' of their clients from their service to independent accommodation; and to demonstrate the success of any such programmes through a plethora of 'performance indicators'. As a result of such changes some organizations clearly feel that they have lost the flexibility that is necessary to respond to the varying needs of different services users, and the continuity of care that was once a hallmark of their approach. At the same time, real improvements to the quality of the accommodation and care such organizations are able to provide have been much slower to materialize than many anticipated. Hence, the residents of some 'high support' hostels still sometimes recount often quite horrific experiences of the conditions in central government funded facilities, and managers and staff talk of the difficulties they face in providing meaningful care for their clients.

Indeed, while we do not deny the very real benefits that these programmes have brought to some service providers and service users, it is clear that the managers and front-line staff of Britain's voluntary sector welfare organizations often remain cynical of recent government initiatives in this area, and suspicious of the motivations behind them. For example, while apparently underpinned by the 'housing plus' approach that many such organizations subscribe to, the continued failure of government to provide the move-on accommodation and related support that this approach demands left many hostel managers and staff with a somewhat different view as to the real intentions of the HAP:

> I don't think that it [the HAP] was motivated by compassion or even well founded research. I think that was purely political. ... The public at large don't like seeing people on the streets. It is bad for tourism, it is bad for people's sense that we are a wonderful, progressive society. And the government wants to reduce that visible problem. (Manager, HAP funded 'high support' hostel, Benington)

Moreover, even if they recognize that such programmes have changed the way they must work – sometimes for better – hostel staff are also extremely suspicious of recent claims as to the apparent 'success' of these programmes, and of the technologies (Larner & Walters, 2000) used to determine that success:

> I think people just knew it [the rough sleeper count] was a fix, everybody. People were either angry or sarcastic or just laughed and just derided it. Nobody took it [the street count on which their work is assessed] as anything other than just a bodged statistic … I know that this [resettlement] unit is affected by that count. … And the way I understood it was that if the figure had fallen sufficiently then future funding would be secured. So at the same time as everyone thought the figure was a joke, no one was going to criticize it too much because it was actually probably good news for their funding. So it was a bit of a tricky one. (Resettlement worker, HAP funded 'high support' hostel, Benington)

There is very real cause for concern here. First, through the HAP, and more recently through Supporting People and No One Left Out, central government has sought to exert greater control over both the supply and the nature of the emergency services available to single homeless people in Britain, imposing new governmental techniques designed to shape the 'conduct of conduct' of the voluntary sector organizations providing those services. While voluntary sector organizations themselves may be aware of these attempts, and reject both the premise on which they are based and the technologies through which they are enforced, these technologies leave very little room for dissent. Even if recognizing that the targets relating to a reduction in rough sleeping may be meaningless, for example, front-line staff often have very little option but to abide by such targets if their organization is to survive. One quite clear effect of these techniques is therefore to undermine a fundamental role of the voluntary sector: namely, to act as an advocate of homeless people and, where necessary, a critic of government.

Yet, we should also be wary of according too much power to such technologies (see May et al., 2005; cf. Ling, 2000). Many of Britain's voluntary sector welfare organizations have found ways to operate in the interstices of government policy. Hence, even while seeking to provide local authorities and central government with the figures necessary to secure the next round of funding, for example, both day centre and hostel staff often continue to work to quite different criteria: operating according to an ethos of empowerment rather than active rehabilitation and change, and seeking to maintain the continuity of care that is so important to their clients, rather than simply moving people through the system in order to hit an arbitrary set of targets.

Indeed, just as recent government initiatives have not (yet) taken complete control of the voluntary sector organizations providing front-line accommodation and care to homeless people – turning such organizations into another arm of some kind of 'shadow state' (Wolch, 1990) – we would also argue that some of the most effective responses to the needs of homeless people are emerging in organizations that operate largely beyond the reach of government. In the current context, for example, we might compare the experiences of staff and residents in Benington's HAP funded hostels to the experiences of those living and working in Gateway; point to the flexibility and 'savvy' of the manager of St Austen's hostel in Winton, who is able to work so effectively with fellow 'travellers'; or emphasize the more modest, but highly effective, interventions made by Nightstop hosts in Crossfields.

More generally, it is clear that this new system of governance has not yet entirely destroyed what earlier we struggled to define, but what we might now perhaps refer to as a *voluntary attitude*; that 'certain something' in the approach of volunteers and paid staff that would seem to be so effective when working with homeless people, and that homeless people themselves recognize as a 'genuine' attempt to care. Such an attitude may at first appear similar to an ethos of 'open acceptance'. But it is better understood as sitting alongside, or providing part of, that ethos rather than being reducible to it. Indeed, though we would suggest that such an attitude cannot find expression in an ethos of 'active rehabilitation and change' (since any such forcible attempt to provide 'support' is, quite understandably, very likely to be interpreted by welfare recipients as anything but 'caring'), it may form part of an ethos of empowerment. Furthermore, and as homeless people recognize, while this attitude may well be most obviously articulated by volunteers themselves, it is often apparent in the approach of paid staff too – in the mundane act of sharing a game a Scrabble recounted by Alfie in chapter 5, for example, or in the spontaneous acts of kindness that opened up a space for dialogue between Julie and her key worker at Gateway in chapter 6.

As we hope will by now be clear, we are not promoting such an attitude as the solution to homelessness. As we argue below, these solutions lie, in part at least, in deeper structural changes. Nor are we suggesting that it offers the best way to structure all of the services (soup runs, day centres and hostels) that continue to play such a vital role in responding to the more immediate needs of homeless people. Instead, we are suggesting that such an attitude provides an always necessary, if not always sufficient, part of that response. Or, put another way, while a voluntary attitude may sometimes need to sit alongside other approaches (approaches usually subsumed under the notion of 'professionalism'), it must always form part of that approach.

Let us offer just three, rather obvious, examples. This voluntary attitude is clearly vital to the work of volunteers on Britain's soup runs. As we argued in chapter 4, such volunteers provide a remarkably important service. In the case of soup runs, the voluntary attitude might therefore be deemed both necessary and sufficient. It also clearly underpins the work of managers and volunteers in Britain's night shelters, where it is currently much less successful in meeting the needs of very vulnerable people (necessary but not sufficient). Finally, it is also apparent in the otherwise much more 'professional' approach taken by paid staff in many day centres and some 'high support' hostels, where staff recognize its importance in helping them to establish the relationships of trust that are so vital to the successful take-up by more vulnerable clients of the support on offer (spaces in which neither a 'voluntary' nor a 'professional' attitude is sufficient on its own, but when combined prove remarkably effective).

Rather than setting 'professional' and 'voluntary' attitudes in opposition to each other, as both government and other critics of the voluntary effort have tended to do, we therefore advocate an approach that recognizes the ways in which they may complement each other. To be truly effective, however, this complementary relationship must be extended out across the emergency service landscape as a whole. That is, such a landscape must have room for those organizations in which a voluntary attitude provides the basis for their work, and those organizations in which it sits alongside a 'professional' approach. Such a move in turn requires not only an increased recognition of, and respect for, the values of a voluntary *attitude*, but also a more accommodating relationship between the voluntary *sector* and the state.

Given the apparent success of projects like Gateway, we would suggest that it is no coincidence that it is often the organizations that have remained beyond the control of the state that are able to offer the highest levels of accommodation and care to homeless people. In the case of hostels, for example, the greater autonomy enjoyed by such projects has allowed them to continue to control their own admissions procedures – enabling them to work with a more manageable mix of residents. But such autonomy has a price. As we have shown, when unable to access projects like Gateway, many of Britain's most vulnerable people end up either in another 'high support' hostel (the result of being found 'Entrenched and Vulnerable' by an outreach team, perhaps) or in a night shelter, neither of which is likely to be able to offer the care that they need. The most obvious solution to such problems would therefore seem to be to try to better match the needs of different homeless people with different service providers. Within this more varied service landscape, there should be room for both soup runs and organizations like St James' night shelter (providing free food and shelter to those whose only obvious need is emergency accommodation) and more obviously 'professional' organizations, employing trained staff able to offer high levels of support to those who wish to access it.

Within such a system the role of the state becomes one of gatekeeper – seeking not (as now) to determine the approach a project must take with its clients, but matching different service users to the most appropriate service provider. Such an approach will only work, of course, if the other services from which some homeless people need to draw support (whether drug and alcohol treatment programmes or tenancy sustainment) are available, and the affordable housing all such people need is provided. It will also only work if this more varied provision is available locally, such that homeless people have real choice as to what kind of service they turn to.

There is a plea here, then, for both an increase in emergency service provision for single homeless people, and for greater equity in the relative distribution of those services – a distribution that must take account of the more complex dynamics shaping service production and consumption in different 'homeless places' outlined in chapters 7 and 8. And yet, such a plea may seem premature. Most obviously, to its critics (though clearly not to government) the voluntary sector apparently provides little more than a sticking plaster that covers up the symptoms of homelessness while leaving the root causes untreated. According to such arguments, far from promoting the case for the voluntary sector, the voluntary effort should be rejected because it does little more than legitimate the continued failure of government to address these structural issues. It is to this question we now turn.

The Role of Emergency Services for Homeless People

It is clear that the problems of street homelessness represent only a very small part of a much larger and ongoing homelessness crisis. In Britain, for example, the numbers of people sleeping rough or staying in emergency hostels and night shelters are dwarfed by the tens of thousands of families accepted as 'statutorily homeless' by local authorities each year, who in turn represent only a tiny proportion of the hundreds of thousands of people who make up Britain's 'hidden homeless' population (Crisis, 2004).

It is also clear that this much deeper and broader problem can only be addressed by beginning to address the nature of Britain's housing and labour markets. As long as levels of unemployment remain high (and the number of people trapped in low paying, insecure work even higher; Wills et al., 2009b) and the British housing market continues to be characterized by high prices in the owner occupation and private rental markets, and by an undersupply of affordable housing (Barker, 2004), the number of people at risk of homelessness will also remain high. Indeed, research has shown that, far from forming a separate subgroup, many of Britain's night shelter and hostel residents form part of a much larger 'episodically homeless' population made up of people who experience numerous, if short-lived, episodes of homelessness throughout their lives – interspersed by periods of low wage work or unemployment and time spent moving within the bottom end of the British private rental market (May, 2000a).

Of course, a significant proportion of single homeless people also have other vulnerabilities – for example, drug or alcohol addictions – and are from backgrounds (of family violence, for example) that render them much more likely to experience homelessness than others. But both these vulnerabilities and these backgrounds might also be more properly understood as themselves multidimensional and structural in origin: relating to a complex amalgam of (intergenerational) family poverty, overcrowding and poor education, for example (Fitzpatrick, 2000; Fitzpatrick et al., 2009).

The problems of homelessness, then, are clearly related both to much deeper problems with Britain's employment and housing markets, and to a systematic failure of other arms of the British welfare (and penal) system (for a sophisticated reading of the relationships between 'structural' and 'individual' causes of homelessness see Fitzpatrick, 2005). It is no coincidence, for example, that those leaving institutional 'care' and prison are still overrepresented in a single homeless population that also now includes both recent migrants from the A8 Accession Counties who are ineligible for welfare benefits, and refugee and asylum seekers (Hill, 2006; Homeless Link, 2006, McNaughton-Nicholls & Quilgars, 2009).

If such is the case, then it is clearly unrealistic to expect voluntary welfare organizations to fully meet the needs of homeless people *and* to address the deeper problems that underlie Britain's homelessness crisis. Indeed, for some, the voluntary response to homelessness runs the risk of legitimating both the government's failure to address these deeper problems (because public attention is being focused only on the most immediate needs of street homeless people, rather than on the needs of a much larger homeless population and on the causes of homelessness) and more sinister attempts by the state to render the problems of homelessness less visible and to deliver 'clean streets' (Mitchell, 2003; Del Casino & Jocoy, 2008).

Such criticisms are based upon a misunderstanding of what voluntary organizations are trying to achieve, and run the risk of a politics of abandonment. The whole basis of a 'housing plus' approach is the recognition that many single homeless people have complex needs above and beyond their (immediate) need for shelter. Such needs include addressing their addictions, accessing health care, securing employment and help with sustaining independent accommodation. Such problems undoubtedly have structural 'roots', but they also require a more immediate response. While changes to the structure of Britain's labour market may start to alleviate problems of poverty that contribute to problems of drug addiction, for example, a person using heroin or crack cocaine also needs more immediate help in addressing their addiction. The problem with Britain's hostels, according to hostel managers, is therefore not that hostels themselves do not have a valuable role to play as a first point of contact in accessing related services (for example, drug treatment or mental health provision), but that under the current regime such services are all too rare – leaving hostels as:

> Dumping ground for prisons, mental hospitals, general hospitals, the police, probation officers. The RSU strategy [is that] hostels are just places where you can put people who are a problem basically. ... That is why hostels can be so

chaotic because they have a very broadly defined role. They will take anyone ... (Manager, HAP funded 'high support' hostel, Benington)

Problems of homelessness must therefore be tackled at two levels simultaneously, with responses aimed at addressing both the underlying causes of homelessness and the more immediate needs of homeless people – for sustenance, shelter and support. Voluntary sector workers themselves are in no doubt as to the need for this twofold response, or where their own activities fit within it, as Albert reminded us in chapter 4 when talking of his work on a local soup run, for example:

> We're really only scratching the surface. Give 'em a bit of food on Friday night and some more on the Saturday, to keep them in this land of the living. If we removed it, some might die. ... I don't think we pretend to be doing anything [more] ... a bit of food and drink on a Friday and Saturday night [and] a bit of cheer. (Albert, paid soup run coordinator, Wimpster)

As Albert makes plain, while the root causes of single homelessness must of course be addressed, and the utility of preventative approaches properly explored (Pawson, 2007), we must also respond to homeless people's more immediate needs – because, if these needs are not met, people might die. The people currently meeting those needs in Britain are mainly doing so through the auspices of voluntary organizations. In the absence of an effective statutory response to problems of single homelessness, to abandon the voluntary response is, quite simply, to abandon homeless people.

Ethical Citizenship and the Postsecular City

Beyond helping to meet the more immediate, material, needs of homeless people, Britain's voluntary sector organizations currently fulfil a second, equally important though less widely recognized role; that is, providing members of the housed public with an opportunity to 'do something' for 'the homeless'. As we have shown, the changing landscape of Britain's voluntary sector, in which mainstream service provision increasingly involves highly professionalized corporatist organizations, will often mean that there are less and less opportunities for volunteers to participate in meeting these needs. However, alongside these corporatist organizations there remain myriad smaller and more traditional organizations whose services continue to rely on the resources of volunteers. These more traditional organizations tend to be poorly resourced, and outside of the formal joined-up governance of homelessness enabled by state organization and funding. Indeed, the services provided by traditional organizations – usually involving the meeting of basic needs for food and a place to sleep – are those that have increasingly been stigmatized for keeping homeless people 'on the street'. It is interesting, then, that it is these marginalized and 'outsider' organizations that are the principal sources of opportunity for volunteers wishing to do something to help meet the needs of homeless people, and that the parts of the voluntary sector that have been embraced by the state as part of its Third Way discourse are becoming more and more closed off to individuals whose propensity to volunteer seems in fact to mimic the state's valorization of volunteering as civic duty and good citizenship. Interestingly too, whereas staff and management of marginalized services often have a clear understanding of their disadvantageous place in the homeless service sector, there is little evidence that volunteers have knowledge of, or reflect upon, their marginalized status; suggesting, perhaps, little appreciation that the volunteer experience could potentially be easier, and certainly more professionalized, in less marginalized service settings.

Of course, volunteers are often branded as little more than self-righteous do-gooders – such that providing the opportunity to volunteer may be perceived as offering rather less to homeless people than it does to volunteers themselves, providing such people with just another opportunity for moral selving (Allahyari, 2000). In fact, our research suggests that the motivation of volunteers is far more complex than these stereotypes convey, and that volunteering usually involves elements of both giving and receiving. There is certainly evidence from our interviews with volunteers that they derive benefit from their volunteering, which provides companionship, camaraderie, sociability, and a boost for self-esteem, and, for some, forms part of a process of personal rehabilitation. It is also clear that volunteering can become unreflexively habitual, and that its focus can shift away from the needs of homeless people per se, becoming instead a matter of loyalty to fellow volunteers and/or to the organization concerned. Certainly volunteers will often hold ambivalent views about homeless people, acknowledging their status as both victim and culpable individual. However, our research also suggests that these self-serving motivations are almost always intertwined with some form of identification with the plight of homeless people, and that the participation of volunteers reflects that identification; not in terms of guilt, but in terms of giving something of themselves to others. Motivation, then, is didactically worked out as volunteers bring themselves into contact with homeless others.

More generally, we would argue that volunteering can best be interpreted as a way of bringing ordinary ethics into extraordinary circumstances. By ordinary ethics we refer to the complex everyday caring and relations with others that are widespread through society. Accordingly, volunteering is not reducible to faith or political belief (although such factors can be important), but should be seen as a connection between ordinary ethics and an organized space of care, whereby individuals who variously identify with the needs of particular others respond to particular devices (most often, an existing organization) that enable volunteer involvement. Despite the current political culture, which seeks to promote volunteering as an integral part of what citizenship should entail, people volunteer because they want to, not because of any sense of obligation or civic duty. That is, volunteering reflects a form of ethical rather than political citizenship. We also suggest that volunteers will be reflexive in choosing particularly suitable devices for volunteering (seeking to niche themselves in particular organizations and particular front/back roles), though this is not to say that collective volunteering is unimportant, most obviously because these reflexive choices will often be influenced by wider social networks – very often, but not always, churches.

Recent years have therefore seen an important shift in the nature of volunteering, towards a more reflexive process of deploying ordinary ethics into spaces of care and compassion. In many places, it has been the homelessness sector that has been most obviously implicated in this process. Homeless people are somehow able to catch the attention of ordinary ethics, to signify what is wrong and to prompt a response. The voluntary sector organizations that exist to serve homeless people provide a ready-made device into which this desire for ethical citizenship can be poured.

Indeed, we would argue that in providing this opportunity to volunteer, Britain's voluntary organizations are providing at least two quite crucial things beyond the more immediate help that they afford homeless people. First, and as Albert reminded us, volunteering provides an opportunity for ordinary people to show that they care – or to spread 'a little cheer', to use his words. Such demonstrations of care are of crucial importance not for what they offer volunteers, but for what they offer homeless people: the reaffirmation of a shared humanity, and a sense of hope in an often hostile world. Second, if we are indeed to address the underlying causes of homelessness we need to build a sense of political engagement and a sense that change is possible. Such has in fact long been the role of some of Britain's larger homelessness charities who in the 1970s, 1980s and 1990s repeatedly challenged the direction of British housing and homelessness policy. But as the larger 'insider' organizations that now make up a growing part of Britain's homeless services landscape become more professionalized, and more reliant on state funding, their advocacy role has declined. Instead, it may therefore be volunteers themselves, perhaps acting through the auspices of the plethora of smaller, 'outsider' organizations that continue to dot this landscape, that offer the best platform around which to build a politics of protest and to remind others of the possibility of change.

Put another way, then, voluntary organizations offer a device through which both to serve homeless people and to help to foster a broader politics of hope that stands in stark contrast to the politics of revenge or abandonment that alledgedly characterizes the revanchist, or postjustice, city. In Britain at least this politics is currently unfolding as part and parcel of a broader realignment of the secular and the religious. Indeed, while the past ten to fifteen years has clearly seen a more significant public role for faith-motivated action in Britain's cities, this is nowhere more evident than in the provision of services for homeless people. Thus our research into the ethical basis of the voluntary organizations providing these services indicates the significant involvement of faith-based organizations in this field, and of the importance of a faith-derived ethics as a driving force for action in this arena.

At the same time, our understanding of organizational ethos in this context calls into question any neat ethical distinction between faith-based and secular ethics of generosity and service. Service provision for homeless people in Britain involves Christian organizations functioning in a secular humanist world, and often engaging in partnership projects involving Christian and non-Christian organizations and individuals. Equally, secular organizations seem often to implicitly draw on ethical principles that are equivalent to those that provide the foundation for faith-based service organizations. This complexity of ethos is compounded by variations within different categories of organizations in terms of professionalism, rule-regimes and the expectations of self-responsibility on behalf of clients, with the principal fault-line of organizational ethos reflecting divisive moralities in terms of the expectations imposed on service users. While some organizations unashamedly desire some kind of conversion of the homeless other, elevating spiritual needs alongside more commonly recognized physical and emotional needs, others expect homeless people to raise their own levels of self-responsibility – reflecting an ethos of care only in return for deliverable changes in lifestyle and attitude. Yet other organizations espouse something closer to postsecular charity, eschewing both evangelism and any expectation of change in the self of homeless people.

How then, have services for homeless people contributed to a wider opening out of opportunities for postsecular rapprochement? We would argue that there are several circumstances at work here. Perhaps most obviously, faith-based organizations such as the Salvation Army have been drawn into governmental practices of tendering out services as part of a wider 'joined-up' response to local homelessness. Here, the incorporation of FBOs into the formal practices of governance will be seen by many as evidence that the work of these organizations should be interpreted in terms of the neoliberal objectives of that governance. Indeed, in some circles, 'incorporation' has become an implicit and explicit criticism, suggesting that FBOs have reneged on their ethical basis in order to take the government's shilling. That such a critique is wide of the mark can be suggested from two bodies of evidence. First, FBOs continually emphasize that the 'value-added' from their involvement is not simply an ability to use their plant, volunteers and fund-raising capacity to provide pseudo-state services at lower economic cost. Instead, they seek to add value by pursuing a more holistic approach to service, including a capacity to deal with spiritual as well as material issues. Second, FBO involvement in services for homeless people is relationally inscribed, meaning that the character of care provided is performatively brought into being by individuals for whom faith is a motivating force. In this way, various performances of faith fall into place among secular programmes designed to serve and support homeless people. Such involvement is far from problem-free, with many potential conflicts between secular decision-makers and faith-motivated service providers, but nevertheless, the pivotal place of FBOs in responding to homelessness represents a considerable blurring of secular and spiritual spaces in the city.

Postsecular rapprochement also occurs *within* many organizations providing services for homeless people. Put simply, not all people working within FBOs are faith-motivated, and many seemingly secular organizations will attract staff and volunteers who are motivated by faith. For example, the night shelter in Benington is run by a Christian trust, espousing Christian principles, but it draws volunteers from a range of secular networks, including the local university and Rotary Clubs in the city. This kind of organization will therefore have people working side by side who do not necessarily share the same spiritual or ideological motivation, but who are willing to work together on the issue in hand. This trend has been noticed elsewhere (see Wills et al., 2009a) in the context of how different faith and secular groups seem willing to put on hold those parts of their moral or spiritual ethos that might be divisive, so that they can collaborate on a particular issue of mutual interest. Postsecularism, therefore, should not be regarded as some kind of new totalizing set of ethics, but rather as a series of comings-together around particular issues of ethical compatibility.

There is also evidence that postsecular rapprochement is being fuelled by a willingness on the part of some FBOs to engage in particular forms of service relationships with their clients. The accusation of proselytizing has often been aimed at faith-based organizations that are involved in social service. However, this connotation of seeking to use practices of service provision to convert service users to some alien religion seems to misrepresent the priorities and modus operandi of Christians involved in serving homeless people. Not only is there a significant ethos present in many FBOs of 'service without strings' – or what Coles (1997) terms postsecular caritas – but the accusation of proselytizing oversimplifies the practice of evangelism at work in other FBOs, much of which eschews any form of 'preachiness' or enforced involvement in religious rituals in favour of working relationally to serve both material and spiritual needs. That there are many forms of 'evangelistic' involvement that do not push religion on to clients seems to have escaped the attention of those who are eager to accuse FBOs of proselytizing, and much more needs to be known about the ways in which relational friendship and incarnational service come together in these arenas.

We are arguing here, then, that there are interesting and potentially significant changes to the social geography of the city resulting from emergent postsecular rapprochements of different kinds. The provision of services for homeless people is one of the key features in this new urban landscape, bringing faith-motivated and secular people together within organizations and spaces devoted to the ideas of care and compassion for the socially excluded. Indeed, both the material, embodied, presence of homeless people in the city, and the spectre of homelessness more generally, appear to have the power to prompt outbreaks of postsecular activity that is as yet lacking in other areas of potential service. Such developments are easily ignored within frameworks emphasizing the punitive nature of governance and social responses to homelessness. But in our view they mark an important conceptual pathway that pays more, and much needed, attention to the construction and peopling of spaces of homelessness in which homeless people experience compassion and care as well as punitive control.

References

Adams, C. (1986). Homelessness in the post-industrial city: views from London and Philadelphia. *Urban Affairs Quarterly*, 21(4): 527–49.

Alcock, P. & Craig, G. (eds) (2001). *International Social Policy: Welfare Regimes in the Developed World*. Basingstoke: Palgrave Macmillan.

Allahyari, R. (2000). *Visions of Charity: Volunteer Workers and Moral Community*. Berkeley: University of California Press.

Amin, A. & Thrift, N. (2002). *Cities: Re-imagining the Urban*. Cambridge: Polity Press.

Amster, R. (2003). Patterns of exclusion: sanitizing space, criminalizing homelessness. *Social Justice*, 30: 195–221.

Anderson, B. (2000). *Doing the Dirty Work: The Global Politics of Domestic Labour*. London: Zed Books.

Anderson, I. (1993). Housing policy and street homelessness in Britain. *Housing Studies*, 8(1): 17–28.

Anderson, N. (1923). *The Hobo: The Sociology of the Homeless Man*. Chicago: University of Chicago Press.

Anonymous (2001). Rough treatment. Letters to the Editor, *Guardian*, 8 August.

Arapoglou, V.P. (2004). The governance of homelessness in the European South: spatial and institutional contexts of philanthropy in Athens. *Urban Studies*, 41: 621–39.

Archard, P. (1979). *Vagrancy, Alcoholism and Social Control*. Basingstoke: Macmillan.

Augé, M. (1998). *A Sense for the Other*, trans. A Jacobs. Stanford, CA: Stanford University Press.

Badiou, A. (2001). *Ethics*. London: Verso.

Bahr, H. (1970). *The Disaffiliated Man: Essays and Bibliography on Skid Row, Vagrancy and Outsiders*. Toronto: University of Toronto Press.

Baker, C. (2007). *The Hybrid Church in the City*. Aldershot: Ashgate.

Baker, C. & Skinner, H. (2006). *Faith in Action: The Dynamic Connection between Spiritual Capital and Religious Capital*. Manchester: William Temple Foundation.

Ballintyne, S. (1999). *Unsafe Streets: Street Homelessness and Crime*. London: IPPR.

Barker, K. (2004). *Review of Housing Supply*. Norwich: HMSO.

Barnett, C., Cloke, P., Clarke, N. & Malpass, A. (2005). Consuming ethics: articulating the subjects and spaces of ethical consumption. *Antipode*, 37: 23–46.

Barnett, C. & Land, D. (2007). Geographies of generosity: beyond the 'moral turn'. *Geoforum*, 38: 1065–75.

Bartley, J. (2006). *Faith and Politics after Christendom: The Church as a Movement for Anarchy*. Milton Keynes: Paternoster.

Bauman, Z. (1993). *Postmodern Ethics*. Oxford: Blackwell.

Beaumont, J. (2008). Faith action on urban social issues. *Urban Studies*, 45: 2019–34.

Beaumont, J. & Dias, C. (2008). Faith-based organizations and urban social justice in the Netherlands. *Tijdschrift voor Economishe en Sociale Geografie*, 99: 382–92.

Beckford, J. (2003). *Social Theory and Religion*. Cambridge: Cambridge University Press.

Bell, D. & Valentine, G. (eds) (1997). *Consuming Geographies*. London: Routledge.

Bennett, J. (2001). *The Enchantment of Modern Life: Attachments, Crossings and Ethics*. Princeton NJ: Princeton University Press.

Beresford, P. (1979). The public presentation of vagrancy. In T. Cook (ed.), *Vagrancy: Some New Perspectives* (pp. 141–66). London: Academic Press.

Berger, P., Davie, G. & Fokas, E. (2008). *Religious America, Secular Europe? A Theme and Variations*. Aldershot: Ashgate.

Bevir, M. & Rhodes, R. (2003). Searching for civil society: changing patterns of governance in Britain. *Public Administration*, 81: 41–62.

Billis, D. & Glennerster, H. (1998). Human services and the voluntary sector: towards a theory of comparative advantage. *Journal of Social Policy*, 27(1): 79–98.

Blau, J. (1992). *The Visible Poor: Homelessness in the United States*. New York: Oxford University Press.

Blomley, N. (1994). *Law, Space and the Geographies of Power*. New York: Guilford Press.

Blomley, N. & Klodawsky, F. (2007a). Rights, Space and Homelessness 1. Session convened at the annual conference of the Association of American Geographers, San Francisco, April.

Blomley, N. & Klodawsky, F. (2007b). Rights, Space and Homelessness 2. Session convened at the annual conference of the Association of American Geographers, San Francisco, April.

Blomley, N. & Klodawsky, F. (2007c). Rights, Space and Homelessness 3. Session convened at the annual conference of the Association of American Geographers, San Francisco, April.

Blond, P. (1998). Introduction: theology before philosophy. In P. Blond (ed.), *Postsecular Philosophy: Between Philosophy and Theology* (pp. 1–66). London: Routledge.

Bloom, L. & Kilgore, D. (2003). The volunteer citizen after welfare reform in the United States: an ethnographic study of volunteerism in action. *Voluntas*, 14: 431–54.

Bondi, L. (2005). Making connections and thinking though emotions: between geography and psychotherapy. *Transactions of the Institute of British Geographers*, 30(4): 433–48.

Borden, I. (2001). *Skateboarding, Space and the City: Architecture and the Body*. Oxford: Berg.

Bourgois, P. (1995). *In Search of Respect: Selling Crack in El Barrio*. Cambridge: Cambridge University Press.

Brenner, N. & Theodore, N. (2002). Cities and geographies of 'actually existing neoliberalism'. *Antipode*, 34(3): 349–97.

Briheim-Crockall, L., Evans, A., Iles, D. & Watson, P. (2008). *Survey of Needs and Provision: Services for Homeless Single People and Couples in England*. London: Homeless Link and Resource Information Service.

Brinegar, S. (2003). The social construction of homeless shelters in the Phoenix area. *Urban Geography*, 24(1): 61–74.

Brown, S., Casey, L., Dunbar., Firth, L., Grant, C., Randall, G., Turner, A., Williamson, D. & Warner, D. (1996). *Evaluations of the Extent of Rough Sleeping Outside Central London*. London: Shelter.

Brownhill, S. & Sharp, C. (1992). London's housing crisis. In P. Thornley (ed.), *The Crisis of London*. London: Routledge.

Bryson, J. (2001). Services and internationalisation. *Service Industries Journal*, 21: 227–40.

Buckingham, H. (2009). Competition and contracts in the voluntary sector: exploring the implications for homeless service providers in Southampton. *Policy and Politics*, 37(2): 235–54.

Butler, J. (1990). *Gender Trouble: Feminism and the Subversion of Identity*. London: Routledge.

Butler, J. (1993). *Bodies that Matter: On the Discursive Limits of 'Sex'*. London: Routledge.

Butler, J. (1997). *Excitable Speech*. London: Routledge.

Button, E. (1992). *Rural Housing for Youth*. London: Centrepoint.

Caputo, J. (2001). *On Religion*. London: Routledge.

Caputo, J. (2006). *The Weakness of God: A Theology of the Event*. Bloomington: Indiana University Press.

Carey, G., Braunack-Mayor, A. & Barraket, J. (2009). Spaces of care in the third sector: understanding the effects of professionalisation. *Health: An Interdisciplinary Journal of Health, Illness and Medicine*, 13(6): 629–46.

Carlen, P. (1996). *Jigsaw: A Political Criminology of Youth Homelessness*. London: Routledge.

CHAR (1985). *Replacing Night Shelters*. London: CHAR.

Clarke, J. & Newman, J. (1997). *The Managerial State*. London: Sage.

Clary, E. (1996). Volunteers' motivation: findings from a national survey. *Nonprofits and Voluntary Sector Quarterly*, 25: 485–505.

Cloke, P. (1995). Rural poverty and the welfare state: a discursive transformation in Britain and the USA. *Environment and Planning A*, 27(6):1001–16.

Cloke, P. (2002). Deliver us from evil? Prospects for living ethically and acting politically in human geography. *Progress in Human Geography*, 26: 587–604.

Cloke, P. (2009). Geography and invisible powers: philosophy, social action and prophetic potential. In C. Brace et al. (eds), *Emerging Geographies of Belief*. Chicago: University of Chicago Press.

Cloke, P. (forthcoming). Theo-ethics and faith praxis in the postsecular city. In J. Beaumont & A. Molendujk (eds), *Exploring the Postsecular: The Religious, the Political and the Urban*. Amsterdam: Brill.

Cloke, P., Barnett, C., Clarke, N. & Malpass, A. (2009). Faith in ethical consumption. In L. Thomas (ed.), *Consumerism and Sustainability*. Basingstoke: Palgrave Macmillan.

Cloke, P., Cooke, P., Cursons, J., Milbourne, P. & Widdowfield, R. (2000a). Ethics, reflexivity and research: encounters with homeless people. *Ethics Place and Environment*, 3: 133–54.

Cloke, P., Johnsen, S. & May, J. (2003a). What the f**k's the point of that? The cultural geographies of homelessness. Paper presented to the Cultural Geographies at the Coalface: Discussions on Applied Cultural Geography session of the RGS-IBG Annual Conference, London, 5 September.

Cloke, P., Johnsen., S. & May, J. (2005). Exploring ethos? Discourses of charity in the provision of emergency services for homeless people. *Environment and Planning A*, 37(3): 385–402.

Cloke, P., Johnsen, S. & May, J. (2007). Ethical citizenship? Volunteers and the ethics of providing services for homeless people. *Geoforum*, 38: 1089–101.

Cloke, P., May, J. & Johnsen, S. (2008). Performativity and affect in the homeless city. *Environment and Planning: Society and Space*, 26(2): 241–63.

Cloke, P. & Milbourne, P. (2006). Knowing homelessness in rural England. In P. Milbourne & P. Cloke, P. (eds), *International Perspectives on Rural Homelessness* (pp. 121–37). London: Routledge.

Cloke, P., Milbourne, P. & Widdowfield, R. (2000b). Homelessness and rurality: 'Out of place' in purified space? *Environment and Planning D: Society and Space*, 18(6): 715–35.

Cloke, P., Milbourne, P. & Widdowfield, R. (2000c). Partnership and policy networks in rural local governance: homelessness in Taunton. *Public Administration*, 78: 111–34.

Cloke, P., Milbourne, P. & Widdowfield, R. (2001a). Making the homeless count? Enumerating rough sleepers and the distortion of homelessness. *Policy and Politics*, 29: 259–77.

Cloke, P., Milbourne, P. & Widdowfield, R. (2001b). The geographies of homelessness in rural England. *Regional Studies*, 35: 23–37.

Cloke, P., Milbourne, P. & Widdowfield, R. (2001c). Interconnecting housing, homelessness and rurality. *Journal of Rural Studies*, 17: 99–111.

Cloke, P., Milbourne, P. & Widdowfield, R. (2002). *Rural Homelessness: Issues, Experiences and Policy Responses*. Bristol: Policy Press.

Cloke, P., Milbourne, P. & Widdowfield, R. (2003b). The complex mobilities of homeless people in rural England. *Geoforum*, 34: 21–35.

Cochrane, A. (1990). The changing state of local government in the UK: restructuring for the 1990s. Unpublished paper, Urban Politics Group, Political Studies Association, London, July.

Cochrane, A. (1994). Restructuring the local welfare state. In R. Burrows & B. Loader (eds), *Towards a Post-Fordist Welfare State?* (pp. 117–35). London: Routledge.

Coleman, R. (2004). Images from a neoliberal city: the state, surveillance and social control. *Criminology*, 12: 21–42.

Coles, R. (1997). *Rethinking Generosity: Critical Theory and the Politics of Caritas*. Ithaca, NY: Cornell University Press.

Collins, D. & Blomley, N. (2003). Private needs and public space: Politics, poverty, and anti-panhandling by-laws in Canadian cities. In Law Commission of Canada (ed.), *New Perspectives on the Public–Private Divide* (pp. 40–68). Vancouver: University of British Colombia.

Communities and Local Government (2006). *Places of Change: Tackling Homelessness through the Hostels Capital Investment Programme*. London: CLG.

Communities and Local Government (2008a). *No One Left Out – Communities Ending Rough Sleeping*. London: CLG.

Communities and Local Government (2008b). *Changing Supporting People funding in England: Results from a Pilot Exercise*. London: CLG.

Connolly, W. (1999). Suffering, justice and the politics of becoming? In D. Campbell & M. Shapiro (eds), *Moral Spaces: Rethinking Ethics and World Politics*. Minneapolis: University of Minnesota Press.

Conradson, D. (1999). Voluntary welfare spaces in the city. Unpublished PhD thesis, School of Geographical Sciences, University of Bristol.

Conradson, D. (2003). Spaces of care in the city: the place of a community drop-in centre. *Social and Cultural Geography*, 4: 507–25.

Cooper, A. (1997). *All in a Day's Work: A Guide to Good Practice in Day Centres Working with Homeless People*. London: CHAR.

Cooper, A., Evans, N. & Sutton, P. (1999). *Better by Design: A Practical Guide to Day Centre Design*. London: National Homeless Alliance.

Cooper, R. (2001). The intersection of space and homelessness in central Auckland. Unpublished MA thesis, Department of Geography, University of Auckland.

Corbin, W. (1999). The impact of the American dream on Evangelical ethics. *Cross Currents*, 55(3): http://www.crosscurrents.org.

Crang, M. (2000). Relics, places and unwritten geographies in the work of Michel de Certeau (1925–86). In M. Crang & N. Thrift (eds), *Thinking Space* (pp. 136–53). London: Routledge.

Crang, M. (2001). Rhythms of the city: temporalised space and motion. In J. May & N. Thrift (eds), *TimeSpace: Geographies of Temporality* (pp. 187–207). London: Routledge.

Cresswell, T. (1996). *In Place/Out of Place: Geography, Identity and Transgression*. Minneapolis: University of Minnesota Press.

Cresswell, T. (2001). *The Tramp in America*. London: Reaktion Books.

Crisis (2004). *Hidden Homelessness: Britain's Invisible City*. London: Crisis.

Daily Express (1994). Tell them to beggar off for the good of everyone, 5 November.

Daily Mail (1994). Get tough on beggars, says Major, 28 May.

Daily Mail (1998). Be a buddy to the homeless, says Blair, 7 June.

Daily Telegraph (1990a). Homeless are scandal, 20 March.

Daily Telegraph (1990b). Judge attacks Minister over homelessness, 29 March.

Daily Telegraph (1998). Blair urges public to be 'buddies' to homeless, 7 June.

Daly, G. (1996). *Homeless: Policies, Strategies and Lives on the Streets*. London: Routledge.

Dangschat, J. (1997). Local political reactions on the surplus population of Hamburg. Paper presented at Homelessness and Urban Restructuring: The Americanization of the European City? The Contradictory Geography of Socio-spatial Injustices in Global(izing) Cities, John F. Kennedy Institute, University of Berlin, October.

Datta, A. (2005). 'Homed' in Arizona: the architecture of emergency shelters. *Urban Geography*, 26(6): 536–57.

Davie, G. (2007). *The Sociology of Religion*. London: Sage.

Davis, M. (1990). *City of Quartz*. London: Vintage.

Davis, M. (1999). *Ecology of Fear: Los Angeles and the Imagination of Disaster*. London: Vintage.

Davis-Smith, J. (1995). The voluntary tradition: philanthropy and self-help in Britain 1500–1945. In J.D. Smith, C. Rochester & R. Hedley (eds), *An Introduction to the Voluntary Sector* (pp. 9–39). London: Routledge.

Deacon, A. (2000). Learning from the US? The influence of American ideas upon 'New Labour' thinking on welfare reform. *Policy and Politics*, 28(1): 5–18.

Dean, H. (ed.) (1999). *Begging Questions: Streel-level Economic Activity and Social Policy Failure*. Bristol: Policy Press.

Dean, H. & Melrose, M. (1999). Easy pickings or hard profession? In H. Dean (ed.), *Begging Questions: Street-level Economic Activity and Social Policy Failure* (pp. 83–100). Bristol: Policy Press.

Dear, M. & Wolch, J. (1987). *Landscapes of Despair: from Deinstitutionalization to Homelessness*. Princeton, NJ: Princeton University Press.

Dear, M. & Wolch, J. (1994). The service hub concept in human planning services. *Progress in Planning*, 42: 173–271.

de Certeau, M. (1984). *The Practice of Everyday Life*, trans. S Rendell). Los Angeles: University of California Press.

Del Casino, V.J. & Jocoy, C.L. (2008). Neoliberal subjectivities, the 'new' homelessness and struggles over spaces of/in the city. *Antipode*, 40(2): 192–9.

Department of Environment, Transport and Regions (1999a). *More than 250 Projects to be Funded to Tackle Homelessness Outside London*. London: Department of Environment, Transport and Regions, press release 5 February.

Department of Environment, Transport and Regions (1999b). *Homelessness Action Programme: Projects which Will Continue to Receive Funding 1999/2000*. London: Department of Environment, Transport and Regions, press release 5 February.

Department of Environment, Transport and Regions (2000). *Coming in from the Cold: Delivering the Strategy*. London: HMSO.

Derrida, J. (1996). *The Gift of Death: Religion and Postmodernism*. Chicago: Chicago University Press.

Desjarlais, R. (1996). The office of reason: on the politics of language and agency in a shelter for the 'homeless mentally ill'. *American Ethnologist*, 23(4): 880–900.

Desjarlais, R. (1997). *Shelter Blues: Sanity and Selfhood among the Homeless*. Philadelphia: University of Pennsylvania Press.

Deutsche, R. (1990). Architecture of the evicted. *Strategies*, 3: 159–84.

DeVerteuil, G. (2003). Homeless mobility, institutional settings, and the new poverty management. *Environment and Planning A*, 35(2): 361–79.

DeVerteuil, G. (2006). The local state and homeless shelters: beyond revanchism? *Cities*, 23(2): 109–20.

DeVertueil, G., May, J. & von Mahs, J. (2009). Complexity not collapse: recasting the geographies of homelessness in a 'punitive' age. *Progress in Human Geography*, 33(5): 646–66.

De Vita, C. (1997). *Viewing Nonprofits Across the States*. Washington, DC: Center on Nonprofit and Philanthropy, The Urban Institute.

de Vries, H. (2006). Introduction: before, around and beyond the theologico-political. In H. de Vries & L. Sullivan (eds), *Political Theologies: Public Religions in a Postsecular World* (pp. 1–88). New York: Fordham University Press.

Dewsbury, J.D. (2000). Performativity and the event: enacting a philosophy of difference. *Environment and Planning D: Society and Space*, 18: 473–96.

Dewsbury, J.D. & Cloke, P. (2009). Spiritual landscapes: existence, performance and immanence. *Social and Cultural Geographies*.

Dinham, A., Furbey, R. & Lowndes, V. (eds) (2009). *Faith in the Public Realm: Controversies, Policies and Practices*. Bristol: Policy Press.

Doel, M. (1994). Deconstruction on the move: from libidinal economy to liminal materialism. *Environment and Planning A*, 26: 1041–59.

Doherty, J., Busch-Geertsema, V., Karpuskiene, V., Korhonen, J., O'Sullivan, E., Sahlin, I., Tosi, A., Petrillo, A. & Wygnanska, J. (2008). Homelessness and exclusion: regulating public space in European cities. *Surveillance and Society*, 5: 290–314.

Donohue, T. (1996). *In the Open: Diary of a Homeless Alcoholic*. Chicago: University of Chicago Press.

Drake, M., O'Brien, M. & Biebuyck, T. (1982). *Single and Homeless*. London: HMSO.

Driver, F. (1993). *Power and Pauperism: The Workhouse System 1834–1884*. Cambridge: Cambridge University Press.

Duncan, J. (1983). Men without property: the tramp's classification and use of urban space. In R.W. Lake (ed.), *Readings in Urban Analysis: Perspectives on Urban Form and Structure* (pp. 86–102). New Brunswick, NJ: Centre for Urban Policy Research.

Duneier, M. (1999). *Sidewalk*. New York: Farrar, Straus and Giroux.

Eckstein, S. (2001). Community as gift-giving: collectivistic roots of volunteerism. *American Sociological Review*, 66: 829–51.

Eick, V. (2003). New strategies of policing the poor: Berlin's neoliberal security system. *Policing and Society*, 13: 365–79.

Erikson, K. (1996). *Wayward Puritans: A Study in the Sociology of Deviance*. New York: Wiley.

Evans, A. (1999). *They Think I Don't Exist. The Hidden Nature of Rural Homelessness*. London: Crisis.

Evans, L. (2007). Housing justice welcomes London Council's decision to drop soup run ban. http://www.housingjustice.org.uk/hj/newsreleases/2007/nr20071116.htm (accessed 27 January 2008).

Evans, N.S. & Dowler, E.A. (1999). Food, health and eating among single homeless and marginalized people in London. *Journal of Human Nutrition and Dietetics*, 12: 179–99.

Fairclough, N. (2002). *New Labour, New Language?* London: Routledge.

Farnell, R., Furbey, R., Hills, S., Macy, M. & Smith, G. (2003). *'Faith' in Urban Regeneration*. Bristol: Policy Press.

Feldman, L.C. (2004). *Citizens without Shelter: Homelessness, Democracy, and Political Exclusion*. Ithaca, NY: Cornell University Press.

Fisher, B. & Tronto, J. (1990). Towards a feminist theory of care. In E. Abel and M. Nelson (eds), *Circles of Care*. Albany: State University of New York Press.

Fitzpatrick, S. (2000). *Young Homeless People*. London: Routledge.

Fitzpatrick, S. (2005). Explaining homelessness: a critical realist perspective. *Housing, Theory and Society*, 22(1): 1–17.

Fitzpatrick, S. & Jones, O. (2005). Pursuing social justice or social cohesion: coercion in street homelessness policies in England. *Journal of Social Policy*, 34: 389–406.

Fitzpatrick, S., Kemp, P. & Klinker, S. (2000). *Single Homelessness: An Overview of Research in Britain*. Bristol: Policy Press.

Fitzpatrick, S. & Kennedy, C. (2001). The links between begging and rough sleeping: a question of legitimacy? *Housing Studies*, 16: 549–68.

Fitzpatrick, S., Quilgars, D. & Pleace, N. (eds) (2009). *Homelessness in the UK: Problems and Solutions*. Coventry: Chartered Institute of Housing.

Fitzpatrick, S. & Stephens, M. (2007). *An International Review of Homelessness and Social Housing Policy*. London: CLG.

Fooks, G. & Pantazis, C. (1999). The criminalisation of homelessness, begging and street living. In P. Kennett & A. Marsh (eds), *Homelessness: Exploring the New Terrain*. Bristol: Policy Press.

Foord, M., Palmer, J. & Simpson, D. (1998). *Bricks without Mortar: 30 Years of Single Homelessness*. London: Crisis.

Forrest, R. & Murie, A. (1988). *Selling the Welfare State*. London: Routledge.

Foucault, M. (1979). *Discipline and Punish*. New York: Vintage Books.

Foucault, M. (1991). Governmentality. In G. Burchell, C. Gordon & P. Miller (eds), *The Foucault Effect: Studies in Govermentality* (pp. 87–104). Hemel Hempstead: Harvester Wheatsheaf.

Frankena, W. (1987). Beneficence/benevolence. In E. Frankel, F. Paul, J. Miller, J. Paul & J. Ahrens (eds), *Beneficence, Philanthropy and the Public Good* (pp. 1–20). Oxford: Blackwell.

Frost, M. (2006). *Exiles: Living Missionally in a Post-Christian Culture*. Peabody, MA: Hendrickson Publishers.

Fyfe, N. (2005). Making space for 'neo-communitarianism': the third sector, state and civil society in the UK. In N. Laurie & L. Bondi (eds), *Working the Spaces of Neoliberalism* (pp. 143–63). Oxford: Blackwell, Oxford.

Fyfe, N. & Milligan, C. (2003). Out of the shadows: exploring contemporary geographies of voluntarism. *Progress in Human Geography*, 27: 397–413.

Garside, P.L., Grimshaw, R.W. & Ward, F.J. (1990). *No Place Like Home: The Hostels Experience*. London: HMSO.

Gesler, W. (1992). Therapeutic landscapes: medical issues in the light of the new cultural geography. *Social Science and Medicine*, 34: 735–46.

Giddens, A. (1998). *The Third Way: The Renewal of Social Democracy*. Cambridge: Polity Press.

Gilbert, T. (2003). Exploring the dynmaics of power: a Foucauldian analysis of care planning in learning disabilties services. *Nursing Inquiry*, 10(1): 37–46.

Goffman, E (1959). *The Presentation of the Self in Everyday Life*. New York: Doubleday.

Goffman, E. (1961). *Asylums: Essays on the Social Situation of Mental Patients and Other Inmates*. Harmondsworth: Penguin.

Goffman, E. (1968). *Stigma: Notes on the Management of Spoiled Identity*. Harmondsworth: Penguin.

Goffman, E. (1971). *Relations in Public: Microstudies of the Public Order*. New York: Basic Books.

Goodwin, M., Duncan, S. & Halford, S. (1993). Regulation theory, the local state, and the transition of urban politics. *Environment and Planning D: Society and Space*, 11(1): 67–88.

Goodwin, M. & Painter, J. (1996). Local governance, the crises of Fordism and the changing geographies of regulation. *Transactions, Institute of British Geographers*, 21: 635–48.

Graham, S. & Marvin, S. (2001). *Splintering Urbanism: Networked Infrastructures, Technological Mobilities, and the Urban Condition*. New York: Routledge.

Gregson, N. & Rose, G. (2000). Taking Butler elsewhere: performativities spatialities and subjectivities. *Environment and Planning D: Society and Space*, 18(4): 433–52.

Guardian (1990). 15 million pounds to get homeless off the streets: charities condemn cosmetic plan, 23 June.

Guardian (1994). 'Offensive' Major beggars belief, 28 May.

Gutierrez, G. (1988). *A Theology of Liberation*. Maryknoll: Orbis.

Habermas, J. (2002). *Religion and Rationality: Essays on Reason, God and Modernity*. Cambridge, MA: MIT Press.

Halfacree, K. (1996). Out of place in the country: travellers and the rural idyll. *Antipode*, 28: 42–72.

Ham, J. & Carter, M. (1996). *Steps from the Street: A Report on Direct Access Hostel Provision*. London: CHAR.

Harris, M., Rochester, C. & Halfpenny, P. (2001). Voluntary organisations and social policy: twenty years of change. In M. Harris & C. Rochester (eds), *Voluntary Organisations and Social Policy in Britain* (pp. 1–21). London: Palgrave.

Harrison, M. (1996). *Emergency Hostels: Direct Access Accommodation in London*. London: Single Homeless in London and Resource Information Service.

Heddy, J. (1990). *Housing for Young People: A Survey of the Situation in Selected European Community Countries*. Paris: Union des Foyers des Jeunes Travailleurs.

Hedges, C. (2006). *American Fascists*. New York: Free Press.

Herbert, S. & Brown, E. (2006). Conceptions of space and crime in the punitive neoliberal city. *Antipode*, 38: 755–77.

Herriot, P. (2008). *Religious Fundamentalism*. New York: Routledge.

Hetherington, K. (2000). *New Age Travellers: Vanloads of Uproarious Humanity*. London: Cassell.

Higate, P. (2000a). Ex-servicemen on the road: travel and homelessness. *Sociological Review*, 48: 331–48.

Higate, P. (2000b). Tough bodies and rough sleeping: embodying homelessness amongst ex-servicemen. *Housing, Theory and Society*, 17: 97–108.

Hill, A. (2006). Homeless Poles too ashamed to leave UK. http://www.guardian.co.uk/society/2006/sep/10/homelessness.asylum (accessed 3 July 2009).

Himmelfarb, G. (1991). *Poverty and Compassion: The Moral Imagination of the Late Victorians*. New York: Vintage Books.

Hoch, C. (1991). The spatial organization of the urban homeless: a case study of Chicago. *Urban Geography*, 12: 137–54.

Hoggett, P. (1994). The modernization of the UK welfare state. In R. Burrows & B. Loader (eds), *Towards a Post-Fordist Welfare State?* (pp. 38–48). London: Routledge.

Holloway, S.L. & Valentine, G. (2000). Children's geographies and the new social studies of childhood. In S.L. Holloway & G. Valentine (eds), *Children's Geographies: Playing, Living, Learning* (pp. 1–28). London: Routledge.

Home Office (1998). *Getting It Right Together: Compact on Relations between Government and the Voluntary and Community Sector in England*. London: Home Office, Cm. 4100.

Homeless Link (2006). *A8 Nationals in London Homelessness Services*. London: Homeless Link and the Housing Corporation.

Hopper, K. (1991). A poor apart: the distancing of homeless men in New York's history. *Social Research*, 58(1): 107–32.

Howley, K. (2001). Envision television: charting the cultural geography of homelessness. *Ecumene*, 8: 345–50.

Hubbard, P. (2004). Revenge and injustice in the neoliberal city: uncovering masculinist agendas. *Antipode*, 36(4): 665–86.

Hubbard, P. & Hall, T. (1998). The entrepreneurial city and the 'new urban politics'. In T. Hall & P. Hubbard (eds), *The Entrepreneurial City: Geography, Politics and Representation* (pp. 1–30). Chichester: Wiley.

Huber, E. & Stephens, J. (2001). *Development and Crisis of the Welfare State: Parties and Policies in Global Markets*. Chicago: Chicago Univerity Press.

Humphreys, R. (1999). *No Fixed Abode: A History of Responses to the Roofless and the Rootless in Britain*. London: Macmillan.

Hutson, S. & Liddiard, M. (1994). *Youth Homelessness: The Construction of a Social Issue*. London: Macmillan.

Hutter, R. (1997). *Suffering Divine Things: Theology as Church Practice*. Grand Rapids, MN: Eerdmans.

Hyde, E. (1997). Drug use and rurality. Unpublished PhD thesis, School of Geographical Sciences, University of Bristol.

Independent (1992). Charter for homeless attacks vagrancy laws, 4 April.

Johnsen, S. (2010). Using social geography. In V.J. Del Casino, M. Thomas, P. Cloke & R. Panelli (eds), *A Companion to Social Geography*. Oxford: Wiley-Blackwell.

Johnsen, S., Cloke, P. & May, J. (2005a). Day centres for homeless people: spaces of care or fear? *Social and Cultural Geography*, 6(6): 787–811.

Johnsen, S., Cloke, P. & May, J. (2005b). Transitory spaces of care: serving homeless people on the street. *Health and Place*, 11(4): 323–36.

Johnsen, S. & Fitzpatrick, S. (2007). *The Impact of Enforcement on Street Users in England*. Bristol: Policy Press.

Johnsen, S. & Fitzpatrick, S. (2010). Revanchist sanitization or coercive care? The use of enforcement to combat begging, street drinking and rough sleeping in England. *Urban Studies*, 47(10).

Johnsen, S. with Fitzpatrick, S. (2009). *The Role of Faith Based Organizations in the Provision of Services for Homeless People: Summary of Key Findings*. York: Centre for Housing Policy, University of York.

Johnsen, S., May, J. & Cloke, P. (2008). Imag(in)ing homeless places: using autophotography to (re)examine the geographies of homelessness. *Area*, 40(2): 194–207.

Jones, A. & Johnsen, S. (2009). Street homelessness. In S. Fitzpatrick, D. Quilgars & N. Pleace (eds), *Homelessness in the UK: Problems and Solutions* (pp. 38–52). London: Chartered Institute of Housing.

Jordan, B. (1999). Begging: the global context and international comparisons. In H. Dean (ed.), *Begging Questions: Street-level Economic Activity and Social Policy Failure* (pp. 43–62). Bristol: Policy Press.

Katz, C. (2004). *Growing Up Global: Economic Restructuring and Children's Everyday Lives*. Minneapolis: University of Minnesota Press.

Kawash, S. (1998). The homeless body. *Public Culture*, 10(2): 319–39.

Kearns, R (1993). Place and health: towards a reformed medical geography. *The Professional Geographer*, 45: 139–47.

Kemp, P. (1997). The social characteristics of single homeless people in Britain. In R. Burrows, N. Pleace & D. Quilgars (eds), *Homelessness and Social Policy* (pp. 69–87). London: Routledge.

Kendall, J. (2000). The mainstreaming of the third sector into public policy in England in the late 1990s: whys and wherefores. *Policy and Politics*, 28(4): 541–62.

Knowles, C. (2000). Burger King, Dunkin Donuts and community mental health care. *Health and Place*, 6: 213–24.

Lambert, C., Jeffers, S., Burton, P. & Bramley, G (1992). *Homelessness in Rural Areas*. Salisbury: Rural Development Commission.

Larkin, A. (1979). Rural housing and housing needs. In J. Shaw (ed.), *Rural Deprivation and Planning* (pp. 71–80). Norwich: GeoBooks.

Larner, W. (2000). Neoliberalism: policy, ideology, governmentality. *Studies in Political Economy*, 63: 5–25.

Larner, W. (2003). Neoliberalism? *Environment and Planning D: Society and Space*, 21: 509–12.

Larner, W. & Craig, D. (2005). After neoliberalism? Community activism and local partnerships in Aotearoa New Zealand. In N. Laurie and L. Bondi (eds), *Working the Spaces of Neoliberalism* (pp. 9–31). Oxford: Blackwell.

Larner, W. & Walters, W. (2000). Privatisation, governance and identity: the United Kingdom and New Zealand compared. *Policy and Politics*, 28(3): 361–77.

Laurenson, P. & Collins, D. (2006). Towards inclusion: local government, public space and homelessness in New Zealand. *New Zealand Geographer*, 62(3): 185–95.

Laurenson, P. & Collins, D. (2007). Beyond punitive regulation? New Zealand local government's responses to homelessness. *Antipode*, 39: 649–67.

Laws, G. (1992). Emergency shelter networks in an urban area: serving the homeless in Metropolitan Toronto. *Urban Geography*, 13: 99–126.

Leeds Simon Community (2001). *Statement on the Value of Soup Runs*. Leeds: Leeds Simon Community.

Lees, L. (1997). Ageographia, heterotopia and Vancouver's new public library. *Environment and Planning D: Society and Space*, 15: 321–47.

Lees, L. (1998). Urban renaissance and the street: spaces of control and contestation. In N. Fyfe (ed.), *Images of the Street: Planning, Identity and Control in Public Space* (pp. 236–53). London: Routledge.

Leigh, L. (1979). Vagrancy and the criminal law. In T. Cook (ed.), *Vagrancy: Some New Perspectives* (pp. 95–118). London: Academic Press.

Levinas, E. (1994). *Outside the Subject*, trans. M. Smith. Stanford, CA: Stanford University Press.

Levinas, E. (1998). *Entre Nous: On Thinking-of-the-Other*, trans. M. Smith & B. Harshaw. New York: Columbia University Press.

Levitas, R. (2007). *The Inclusive Society: Social Exclusion and New Labour*. Basingstoke: Macmillan.

Ling, T. (2000). Unpacking partnership: the case of health care. In D. Clarke, S. Gewirtz & E. McLaughlin (eds), *New Managerialism, New Welfare?* (pp. 82–101). London: Sage.

Link, B., Schwartz, S., Moore, R., Phelan, J., Struening, E., Stueve, A. & Colten, M. (1995). Public knowledge, attitudes and beliefs about homeless people: evidence for compassion fatigue? *American Journal of Community Psychology*, 23: 533–55.

Llewellin, S. & Murdoch, A. (1996). *Saving the Day: The Importance of Day Centres for Homeless People*. London: National Day Centres Project, CHAR.

Lofland, L. (1973). *A World of Strangers: Order and Action in Urban Public Space*. New York: Free Press.

London Housing Foundation (2004). *Survey of Homelessness Sector Services Provided to Asylum Seekers and Refugee Clients: Executive Summary*. London: London Housing Foundation and Broadway.

Loughlin, J. (2004). The 'transformation' of governance: new directions in social policy. *Australian Journal of Politics and History*, 50(1): 8–22.

Lowe, R. & Shaw, W. (1993). *Travellers: Voices of the New Age Nomads*. London: Fourth Estate.

Lowe, S. (1997). Homelessness and the law. In R. Burrows, N. Pleace & D. Quilgars (eds), *Homelessness and Social Policy* (pp. 19–34). London: Routledge.

Lowndes, V. & Chapman, R. (2005). *Faith, Hope and Clarity: Developing a Model of Faith Group Involvement in Civil Renewal*. Leicester: Civil Renewal Research Programme Report, De Montfort University.

McCormack, D. (2003). An event of geographical ethics in spaces of affect. *Transactions, Institute of British Geographers*, 28: 488–507.

MacLeod, G. (2002). From urban entrepreneurialism to a 'revanchist city'? On the spatial injustices of Glasgow's renaissance. *Antipode*, 34(3): 602–24.

McNaughton-Nicholls, C. & Quilgars, D. (2009). Homeless amongst minority ethnic groups. In S. Fitzpatrick, D. Quilgars & N. Pleace (eds), *Homelessness in the UK: Problems and Solutions* (pp. 73–88). Coventry: Chartered Institute of Housing.

Maile, S. & Hoggett, P. (2001). Best value and the politics of pragmatism. *Policy and Politics*, 29(4): 509–16.

Mair, A. (1986). The homeless and the post-industrial city. *Political Geography Quarterly*, 5: 351–68.

Malpass, P. (1985). Beyond the 'Costa del Dole'. *Youth and Policy*, 14: 12–15.

Marr, M. (1997). Maintaining autonomy: the plight of the American skid row and Japanese yoseba. *Journal of Social Distress and the Homeless*, 6(3): 229–50.

Marshall, R. (2001). *Waterfronts in Post-Industrial Cities*. Oxford: Spon.

Matieu, A. (1993). The medicalisation of homelessness and the theatre of repression. *Medical Anthropology Quarterly*, 7(2): 170–84.

Matustik, M. (2008). *Radical Evil and the Scarcity of Hope: Postsecular Meditations*. Bloomington: Indiana University Press.

May, J. (2000a). Housing histories and homeless careers: a biographical approach. *Housing Studies*, 15(4): 613–38.

May, J. (2000b). Of nomads and vagrants: single homelessness and narratives of home as place. *Environment and Planning D: Society and Space*, 18(6): 737–59.

May, J. (2003a). Local connection criteria: evidence from Brighton and Hove. *Housing Studies*, 18: 29–46.

May, J. (2003b). The view from the streets: geographies of homelessness in the British newspaper press. In A. Blunt, P. Grufudd, J. May, M. Ogborn & D. Pinder (eds), *Practising Cultural Geography* (pp. 23–38). London: Arnold.

May, J. (2009). Homelessness. In R. Kitchin & N. Thrift (eds), *International Encyclopaedia of Human Geography*. London: Elsevier.

May, J., Cloke, P. & Johnsen, S. (2006). Shelter at the margins: New Labour and the changing state of emergency accommodation for single homeless people in Britain. *Policy and Politics*, 34(4): 711–30.

May, J., Johnsen, S. & Cloke, P. (2005). Re-phasing neo-liberalism: New Labour and Britain's crisis of street homelessness. *Antipode*, 37(4): 703–30.

May, J., Johnsen, S. & Cloke, P. (2007). Alternative cartographies of homelessness: rendering visible British women's experiences of 'visible' homelessness. *Gender, Place and Culture*, 14(2): 121–40.

Meijs, L. & Hoogstad, E. (2001). New ways of managing volunteers: combining membership management with programme management. *Voluntary Action*, 3: 41–61.

Metraux, S. (1999). Waiting for the wrecking ball: skid row in postindustrial Philadelphia. *Journal of Urban History*, 25(5): 690–715.

Milbank, J. (2005). Materialism and transcendence. In C. Davis, J. Milbank & S. Žižek (eds), *Theology and the Political: New Debates* (pp. 393–426). Durham, NC: Duke University Press.

Milbank, J. (2006). *Theology and Social Theory*. Oxford: Blackwell.

Milbourne, P. (1998). Local responses to central state social housing restructuring in rural areas. *Journal of Rural Studies*, 14: 167–84.

Milbourne, P. (2005). Rural housing and homelessness. In P. Cloke, T. Marsden & P. Mooney (eds), *Handbook of Rural Studies* (pp. 79–96). London: Sage.

Milbourne, P. and Cloke, P. (2006). Rural homelessness in the UK: a national overview. In P. Cloke & P. Milbourne (eds), *International Perspectives on Rural Homelessness* (pp. 79–96). London: Routledge.

Milligan, C. and Conradson, D. (2006). *Landscapes of Voluntarism: New Spaces of Health, Welfare and Governance*. Bristol: Policy Press.

Mitchell, D. (1997). The annihilation of space by law: the roots and implications of anti-homeless laws in the United States. *Antipode*, 29: 303–36.

Mitchell, D. (1998a). Anti-homeless laws and public space I: begging and the First Amendment. *Urban Geography*, 19: 6–11.

Mitchell, D. (1998b). Anti-homeless laws and public space II: further constitutional issues. *Urban Geography*, 19: 98–104.

Mitchell, D. (2001). Postmodern geographical praxis? The postmodern impulse and the war against homeless people in the 'post-justice' city. In C. Minca (ed.), *Postmodern Geography: Theory and Praxis* (pp. 57–92). Oxford: Blackwell.

Mitchell, D. (2003). *The Right to the City: Social Justice and the Fight for Public Space*. London: Guilford Press.

Mitchell, D. (2005). The SUV model of citizenship, floating bubbles, buffer zones, and the rise of the 'purely atomic' individual. *Political Geography*, 24(1): 77–100.

Mohen, J. (1999). *A United Kingdom? Economic, Social and Political Geographies*. London: Arnold.

Moore, K. (2002). Soup of the day. *Connect*, 9: 17–18.

Morrison, J. (2000). The government-voluntary sector compacts: governance, governmentality, and civil society. *Journal of Law and Society*, 27(1): 98–132.

Nash, C. (2000). Performativity in practice: some recent work in cultural geography. *Progress in Human Geography*, 24(4): 653–64.

Neale, J. (1997). Homelessness and theory reconsidered. *Housing Studies*, 12: 47–71.

Neale, J. (2001). Homelessness among drug users: a double jeopardy explored. *International Journal of Drug Policy*, 12: 353–69.

Newburn, T. & Rock, P. (2006). *Living in Fear: Violence and Victimization in the Lives of Single Homeless People*. London: Crisis.

Newman, J. (2000). Beyond the New Public Management? Modernizing public services. In D. Clarke, S. Gewirtz and E. McLaughlin (eds), *New Managerialism, New Welfare?* (pp. 45–61). London: Sage.

Newman, J. (2002). The New Public Management, modernization and organizational change: disruptions, disjunctures and dilemmas. In K. McLaughlin & S. Osborne (eds), *New Public Management: Current Trends and Future Prospects* (pp. 77–92). London: Routledge.

Newton, J. (1991). *All in One Place: The British Housing Story 1971–91*. London: CHAR.

Nylund, M. (2001). Mixed motives of young Nordic volunteers. In H. Helve & C. Wallace (eds), *Youth Citizenship and Empowerment* (pp. 99–109). Aldershot: Ashgate.

Oakley, M. (2005). Reclaiming faith. In A. Walker (ed.), *Spirituality in the City* (pp. 1–14). London: SPCK.

Observer (1994). Major chases votes with new attack on beggars. 29 May.

Office of the Deputy Prime Minister (1999). *Coming in from the Cold: The Government's Strategy on Rough Sleeping*. London: Office of the Deputy Prime Minister.

Office of the Deputy Prime Minister (2003). Policy briefing: The Homelessness Act. http://www.homelessact.org.uk.

Parr, H. (2000). Interpreting the 'hidden social geographies' of mental health: ethnographies of inclusion and exclusion in semi-institutional places. *Health and Place*, 6: 225–37.

Parr, H. (2003). Medical geography: care and caring. *Progress in Human Geography*, 27: 212–21.

Passaro, J. (1996). *The Unequal Homeless: Men on the Street, Women in Their Place*. New York: Routledge.

Pawson, H. (2007). Local authority homelessness prevention in England: empowering consumers or denying rights? *Housing Studies*, 22: 867–84.

Peck, J. (2001a). Neo-liberalizing states: thin policies/hard edges. *Progress in Human Geography*, 25: 445–55.

Peck, J. (2001b). *Workfare States*. New York: Guilford.

Peck, J. & Tickell, N. (2002). Neoliberalising space. *Antipode*, 34: 380–404.

Phillips, R. (2000). Performativity in practice: some recent work in cultural geography. *Progress in Human Geography*, 24: 653–64.

Philo, C. & Parr, H. (2000). Institutional geographies: introductory remarks. *Geoforum*, 31(4): 513–21.

Philo, C., Parr, H. & Burns, N. (2003). Rural madness: a geographical reading and critique of the mental health literature. *Journal of Rural Studies*, 19: 259–81.

Pile, S. & Thrift, N. (eds) (1995). *Mapping the Subject: Geographies of Cultural Transformation*. London: Routledge.

Piven, F.F. & Cloward, R. (1993). *Regulating the Poor: The Functions of Public Welfare*. New York: Vintage Books.

Pleace, N. (1998). Single homelessness as social exclusion: the unique and the extreme. *Social Policy and Administration*, 32: 46–59.

Pleace, N., Burrows, R. & Quilgars, D. (1997). Homelessness in contemporary Britain: conceptualisation and measurement. In R. Burrows, N. Pleace & D. Quilgars (eds), *Homelessness and Social Policy* (pp. 1–19). London: Routledge.

Pleace, N., Fitzpatrick, S., Johnsen, S., Quilgars, D. & Sanderson, D. (2008). *Statutory Homelessness in England: The Experience of Families and 16–17 Year Olds*. London: Department of Communities and Local Government.

Pleace, N. & Quilgars, D. (2003). Led rather than leading? Research on homelessness in Britain. *Journal of Community and Applied Social Psychology*, 13: 187–96.

Popke, E.J. (2003). Poststructuralist ethics: subjectivity, responsibility and the space of community. *Progress in Human Geography*, 27: 298–316.

Pound, J. (1971). *Poverty and Vagrancy in Tudor England*. London: Macmillan.

Proctor, J. & Smith, D. (eds) (1999). *Geography and Ethics: Journeys in a Moral Terrain*. London: Routledge.

Quilgars, D., Johnsen, S. & Pleace, N. (2008). *Youth Homelessness in the UK: A Decade of Progress?* York: Joseph Rowntree Foundation.

Raco, M. (2005). Sustainable development, rolled-out neoliberalism and sustainable communities. *Antipode*, 37: 324–47.

Raco, M. & Imrie, R. (2000). Governmentality and rights and responsibilities in urban policy. *Environment and Planning A*, 32: 2187–204.

Rahimian, A., Wolch, J. & Keogel, P. (1992). A model of homeless migration: homeless men in Skid Row, Los Angeles. *Environment and Planning A*, 24: 1317–36.

Randall, G. (1992). *Counted Out: An Investigation into the Extent of Single Homelessness outside London*. London: Crisis and CHAR.

Randall, G. & Brown, S. (1993). *The Rough Sleepers Initiative: An Evaluation*. London: HMSO.

Randall, G. & Brown, S. (1996). *From Street to Home: An Evaluation of Phase 2 of the Rough Sleepers Initiative*. London: HMSO.

Randall, G. & Brown, S. (2002). *Helping Rough Sleepers off the Streets: A Report to the Homelessness Directorate*. London: Office of the Deputy Prime Minister.

Rhodes, R. (1992). Changing intergovernmental relations. In P. Cloke (ed.), *Policy and Change in Thatcher's Britain* (pp. 55–76). Oxford: Pergamon.

Rhodes, R.A.W. (1997). *Understanding Governance: Policy Networks, Governance, Reflexivity and Accountability*. Buckingham: Open University Press.

Richards, D. & Smith, M.J. (2002). *Governance and Public Policy in the United Kingdom*. Oxford: Oxford University Press.

Robinson, D. (2003). *Hidden Homelessness in Rural England: Homeless People Staying with Family and Friends*. Research Note CRN74. London: Countryside Agency.

Robinson, D. (2006). The hidden and neglected experiences of homelessness in rural England. In P. Cloke & P. Milbourne (eds), *International Perspectives of Rural Homelessness* (pp. 97–120). Routledge, London.

Robinson, D. & Reeve, K. (2002). *Homelessness and Rough Sleeping in North Lincolnshire*. Sheffield: CRESR, Sheffield Hallam University.

Robinson, P. (ed.) (1989). *Unemployment and Local Labour Markets*. Aldershot: Avebury.

Rogers, A. (1976). Rural housing. In G. Cherry (ed.), *Rural Planning Problems* (pp. 85–124). London: Hill.

Rose, G. (1997). Situated knowledges: positionality, reflexivities and other tactics. *Progress in Human Geography*, 21: 305–20.

Rose, N. (1996). The death of the social. *Economy and Society*, 25: 327–56.

Rose, N. & Miller, P. (1992). Political power beyond the state: problematics of government. *British Journal of Sociology*, 43: 173–205.

Rosenthal, R. (2000). Imaging homelessness and homeless people: visions and strategies within the movement(s). *Journal of Homelessness and Social Distress*, 9: 111–26.

Rossi, P. (1989). *Down and Out in America: The Origins of Homelessness.* Chicago: Chicago University Press.

Rowe, S. & Wolch, J. (1990). Social networks in time and space: homeless women in Skid Row, Los Angeles. *Annals of the Association of American Geographers,* 80: 184–205.

Ruddick, S. (1990). Heterotopias of the homeless: strategies and tactics of place-making in Los Angeles. *Strategies,* 3, 184–210.

Ruddick, S. (1996). *Young and Homeless in Hollywood.* New York: Routledge.

Sack, R. (1997). *Homo Geograhicus: A Framework for Action, Awareness and Moral Concern.* Baltimore: Johns Hopkins University Press.

Salvation Army (2008). *A Home for All? Homelessness Challenges for Labour's Third Term.* London: Salvation Army.

Saunders, B. (1986). *Homeless Young People in Britain: The Contribution of the Voluntary Sector.* London: Bedford Square Press.

Scott, D., Alcock, P., Russell, L. & Macmillan, R. (2000). *Moving Pictures: Realities of Voluntary Action.* Bristol: Policy Press.

Scott, J. (1998). *Seeing Like a State.* New Haven, CT: Yale University Press.

Scott, P., Baker, C. & Graham, E. (eds) (2009). *Remoralising Britain: Social, Ethical and Theological Perspectives on New Labour.* London: Continuum.

Shapps, G. (2007). *Roughly Sleeping: How a Black Hole in the Street Count Leads to a Systematic Underestimate of the Number of People Sleeping on the Streets.* http://www.shapps.com/reports/Roughly%20Sleeping.pdf.

Sharp, J.P., Routledge, P., Philo, C. & Paddison, R. (2000). (eds) *Entanglements of Power: Geographies of Domination/Resistance.* London: Routledge.

Shelter (2002). Research interview with authors, February.

Shelter (2007). *Shelter's Response to the CLG Green Paper – Home for the Future: More Affordable, More Sustainable.* London: Shelter.

Shields, R. (1991). *Places on the Margin: Alternative Geographies of Modernity.* London: Routledge.

SHiL (1995). *Time to Move On: A Review of Policies and Provision for Single Homeless People in London.* London: Single Homeless in London.

Sibley, D. (1995). *Geographies of Exclusion.* London: Routledge.

Slater, T. (2004). North American gentrification? Revanchist and emancipatory perspectives explored. *Environment and Planning A,* 36(7): 1191–213.

Smith, D. (2000). *Moral Geographies: Ethics in a World of Difference.* Edinburgh: Edinburgh University Press.

Smith, J. (1999). Gender and homelessness. In S. Hutson & D. Clapham (eds), *Homelessness: Public Policies and Private Troubles* (pp. 108–32). London: Cassell.

Smith, N. (1992). New city, new frontier: the Lower East Side as Wild West. In M. Sorkin (ed.), *Variations on a Theme Park: The New American City and the End of Public Space* (pp. 61–93). New York: Hill and Wang.

Smith, N. (1993). Homeless/global: scaling places. In J. Bird, B. Curtis, T. Putnam, G. Roberson & L. Tickner (eds), *Mapping the Futures: Local Cultures, Global Change* (pp. 87–119). London: Routledge.

Smith, N. (1996a). *The New Urban Frontier: Gentrification and the Revanchist City.* London: Routledge.

Smith, N. (1996b). Social justice and the new American urbanism: the revanchist city. In A. Merrifield & E. Swyngedouw (eds), *The Urbanization of Injustice* (pp. 117–36). London: Lawrence and Wishart.

Smith, N. (1998). Giuliani time: the revanchist 1990s. *Social Texts*, 57(18): 1–20.

Smith, N. (2001). Global social cleansing: postliberal revanchism and the export of zero tolerance. *Social Justice*, 28(3): 68–74.

Snow, D.A. & Anderson, L. (1993). *Down on Their Luck: A Study of Homeless Street People*. Berkeley: University of California Press.

Social Exclusion Task Force (2007). *Reaching Out: Think Family. Analysis and Themes from the Families at Risk Review*. London: Cabinet Office.

Social Exclusion Unit (1998). *Rough Sleeping: Report by Social Exclusion Unit*. London: HMSO.

Sorkin, M. (ed.) (1992). *Variations on a Theme Park: The New American City and the End of Public Space*. New York: Hill and Wang.

Sparke, M. (2008). Political geographies of globalization (3): resistance. *Progress in Human Geography*, 32(1): 1–18.

Spradley, J. (1970). *You Owe Yourself a Drunk: An Ethnography of Urban Nomads*. Boston: Little and Brown.

Stallybrass, P. & White, A. (1986). *The Politics and Poetics of Transgression*. London: Routledge.

Stark, L. (1994). The shelter as 'total institution'. *American Behavioural Scientist*, 37(4): 553–62.

Steinfels, P. (2001). Holy waters: plunging into the sea of faith-based initiatives. In E. Dionne Jr & M.S. Chen (eds), *Sacred Places: Civic Purposes*. Washington, DC: Brookings Institution Press.

Stewart, J. (1975). *Of No Fixed Abode: Vagrancy and the Welfare State*. Manchester: Manchester University Press.

Streich, L., Havell, C. & Spafford, J. (2004). *Preventing Homelessness in the Countryside: What Works?* Cheltenham: Countryside Agency.

Swanson, K. (2007). Revanchist urbanism heads south: the regulation of indigenous beggars and street vendors in Ecuador. *Antipode*, 39: 708–28.

Swyngedouw, E. & Kaika, M. (2003). 'Glocal' urban modernities: exploring the cracks in the mirror. *City*, 7(1): 5–21.

Swyngedouw, E. & Kaika, M. (2005). The making of 'glocal' urban modernities: exploring the cracks in the mirror. *Art-e-Fact*, 4: http:/aertefact.mi2.hr.

Takahashi, L. (1996). A decade of understanding homelessness in the USA: from characterization to representation. *Progress in Human Geography*, 20: 291–310.

Takahashi, L. (1998). *Homelessness, AIDS, and Stigmatization: The NIMBY Syndrome in the United States at the End of the Twentieth Century*. Oxford: Clarendon Press.

Takahashi, L., McElroy, J. & Rowe, S. (2002). The socio-spatial stigmatization of homeless women with children. *Urban Geography*, 23(4): 3102–22.

Taylor, C. (2007). *A Secular Age*. Cambridge, MA: Harvard University Press.

Thrift, N. (1996). *Spatial Formations*. London: Sage.

Thrift, N. (1999). Steps to an ecology of place. In D. Massey, J. Allen & P. Sarre (eds), *Human Geography Today* (pp. 295–322). Cambridge: Polity Press.

Thrift, N. (2000). Afterwords. *Environment and Planning D: Society and Space*, 18: 213–35.

Thrift, N. (2004). Summoning life. In P. Cloke, P. Crang & M. Goodwin (eds), *Envisioning Human Geographies* (pp. 81–103). London: Arnold.

Thrift, N. & Dewsbury, J.D. (2000). Dead geographies and how to make them live. *Environment and Planning D: Society and Space*, 18: 411–32.

Tomas, A. & Dittmar, H. (1995). The experience of homeless women: an exploration of housing histories and the meaning of home. *Housing Studies*, 10(4): 493–517.

Tosi, A. (2007). Homelessness and control of public space – criminalizing the poor? *European Journal of Homelessness*, 1: 224–35.

Tyler, A. (1995). *Street Drugs*. London: Hodder and Stoughton.

Van Doorn, A. & Williamson, D. (2001). *Emergency Accommodation for Homeless People: Good Practice Companion*. London: Homeless Link.

Van Til, J. (1988). *Mapping the Third Sector: Voluntarism in a Changing Social Economy*. New York: The Foundation Center.

Vasquez, M. & Marquardt, M.F. (2003). *Globalising the Sacred: Religion across the Americas*. New Brunswick, NJ: Rutgers University Press.

Vattimo, G. (1999). *Belief*, trans. L. D'santo and D. Webb. Cambridge: Polity Press.

Veness, A.R. (1993). Neither homed nor homeless: contested definitions and the personal worlds of the poor. *Political Geography*, 12: 319–40.

Veness, I. (1994). Designer shelters as models and makers of home: new responses to homelessness in urban America. *Urban Geography*, 15(2): 150–67.

Von Mahs, J. (2005). The sociospatial exclusion of single homeless people in Berlin and Los Angeles. *American Behavioral Scientist*, 48: 928–60.

Wagner, D (1993). *Checkerboard Square: Culture and Resistance in a Homeless Community*. Boulder, CO: Westview Press.

Wallace, S. (1965). *Skid Row as a Way of Life*. Totawa, NJ: Bedminster Press.

Wallis, J. (2001). Eyes on the prize. In E. Dionne Jr & M.S. Chen (eds), *Sacred Places: Civic Purposes*. Washington, DC: Brookings Institution Press.

Wardhaugh, J. (1999). The unaccommodated woman: home, homelessness and identity. *The Sociological Review*, 47: 91–109.

Wardhaugh, J. (2000). *Sub City: Young People, Homelessness and Crime*. Aldershot: Ashgate.

Warrington, M. (1996). Welfare pluralism or shadow state? *Environment and Planning A*, 27: 1341–60.

Warrington, M. (1997). Sheltering the single homeless: some issues for the voluntary sector. Unpublished paper, Department of Geography, University of Cambridge.

Waters, J. (1992). *Community or Ghetto? An Analysis of Day Centres for Single Homeless People*. London: CHAR.

Whatmore, S. (2002). *Hybrid Geographies*. London: Sage.

Williams, J.C. (1996). Geography of the homeless shelter: staff surveillance and resident resistance. *Urban Anthropology*, 25(1): 75–113.

Wills, J., Datta, K., Evans, Y., Herbert, J., May, J. & McIlwaine, C. (2009a). Religion at work: the role of faith-based organizations in the London living wage campaign. *Cambridge Journal of Regions, Economy and Society*, 2(3): 443–61.

Wills, J., Datta, K., Evans, Y., Herbert, J., May, J. & McIlwaine, C. (2009b). *Global Cities at Work: New Migrant Divisions of Labour*. London: Pluto Press.

Winchester, H. & Costello, L. (1995). Living on the street: social organisation and gender relations of Australian street kids. *Environment and Planning D: Society and Space*, 13: 329–48.

Wiseman, J. (1979). *Stations of the Lost: The Treatment of Skid Row Alcoholics*. Chicago: University of Chicago Press.

Wolch, J. (1990). *The Shadow State: Government and the Voluntary Sector*. New York: The Foundation Center.

Wolch, J. & Dear, M. (1993). *Malign Neglect: Homeless in an American City*. San Fancisco: Jesse-Bars.

Wolch, J. & DeVerteuil, G. (2001). Landscapes of the new poverty management. In J. May & N. Thrift (eds), *TimeSpace: Geographies of Temporality* (pp. 149–67). London: Routledge.

Wolch, J., Rahimien, A. & Koegel, P. (1993). Daily and periodic mobility patterns of the urban homeless. *Professional Geographer*, 45: 159–68.

Wolch, J. & Rowe, S. (1992). On the streets: mobility paths of the urban homeless. *City and Society*, 6: 115–40.

Woods, M. (2005). *Rural Geography: Processes, Responses and Experiences in Rural Restructuring*. London: Sage.

Wright, T. & Vermond A (1990). Small dignities: local resistances, dominant strategies of authority and homelessness. Paper presented to the Annual Meeting of the American Sociological Association, Washington DC.

Yeung, A. (2004). The Octagon model of volunteer motivation: results of a phenomenological analysis. *Voluntas*, 15: 21–46.

Žižek, S. (2000). *The Fragile Absolute*. London: Verso.

Žižek, S. (2001). *On Belief*. London: Routledge.

Zukin, S. (1991). *Landscapes of Power: From Detroit to Disney World*. Berkeley: University of California Press.

Index

Note: page numbers in **bold** refer to tables; an '*n*' after a page number refers to a note on that page.

Printed in Great Britain
by Amazon